The Chosen We

SUNY series, Critical Race Studies in Education

Derrick R. Brooms, editor

The Chosen We

*Black Women's Empowerment
in Higher Education*

RACHELLE WINKLE-WAGNER

Foreword by

DIANA SLAUGHTER KOTZIN

Cover Credit: *Disagreement* by Theola Jane Goosby

Theola Jane Goosby is an artist who combines various mediums, including pastel, acrylic, oil, and pigment pen. Her work integrates unique imagery of the human form into dreamlike contexts and shows the diversity of relationships between friends, lovers, and family. Some of these pieces represent the struggles of relationships as well as the joy of these experiences. Her work has spanned over 30 years. She was born in Victoria, Texas, in 1949; raised in Houston; and lived in Austin for more than 30 years. She is currently based in Georgetown, Texas.

Published by State University of New York Press, Albany

For information, contact State University of New York Press, Albany, NY
www.sunypress.edu

Library of Congress Cataloging-in-Publication Data

Name: Winkle-Wagner, Rachelle, author.
Title: The chosen we : Black women's empowerment in higher education / Rachelle Winkle-Wagner.
Description: Albany, NY : State University of New York Press, [2023] | Includes bibliographical references.
Identifiers: LCCN 2023009055 | ISBN 9781438495422 (hardcover : alk. paper) | ISBN 9781438495446 (ebook) | ISBN 9781438495439 (pbk. : alk. paper)
Subjects: LCSH: African American women—Education (Higher) | African American women college students—Social conditions. | African American college graduates—Interviews. | African American women—Interviews. | Universities and colleges—United States—Sociological aspects.
Classification: LCC LC2781 .W567 2023 | DDC 378.1/982996073—dc23/eng/20230718
LC record available at https://lccn.loc.gov/2023009055

*To all the Black women who engaged this project of
collective empowerment—thank you for choosing each other
and showing us all how to honor a collective vision of liberation.
To all our daughters, those born as such and not,
and to my own Eleanor and Abigail,
may you find and create a Chosen We
that can elevate others in that way
that the women show us here.*

Contents

Part I
Black Women's Self-Determination in
Education from Here to Eternity

Part II
From Individualism to Transformative Community
at Predominantly White Institutions (PWIs)

Introduction to the Foreword Author, Dr. Diana Slaughter Kotzin

Dr. Rachelle Winkle-Wagner

I worked on this book for over a decade, and so I am delighted to finally complete this project which was initiated soon after my first book in 2009. I met Dr. Diana Slaughter Kotzin at the University of Pennsylvania when I was on a one-year visiting assistant professor and deciding what to do as I worked on turning my dissertation into a book focused on *Race, Gender, and Identity among Black Women in College*. Then Dr. Diana Slaughter-Defoe, and the inaugural Constance E. Clayton Professor in Urban Education, Diana invited me for breakfast at the faculty club in the Inn at Penn. We talked about her college experiences at the University of Chicago, about her return there for a 40-year alumni event where she alone became ill (sort of like a food poisoning). Speaking candidly, she said at the time she wondered if she had become ill from prior experiences such that being enmeshed in that sociocultural environment perhaps brought back negative memories. Thus, Diana encouraged my research in this project beginning way back in 2006, suggesting that I interview college alumni.

I lost contact with Diana for a long time while I conducted, analyzed, and interpreted the obtained interviews. But it seemed very important to reconnect with her as the book came to fruition because the entire project would have never happened had it not been for her conversation with me that first year after my PhD program. I invited her to write the Foreword to my book because, in the end, her early advice, empathy and wisdom helped me to initiate, focus, and sustain this entire project over many years when others were unsupportive, and even unkind. And I am deeply grateful to Diana for modeling to me what it means to be scholar who elevates and creates pathways for others.

Foreword

DIANA SLAUGHTER KOTZIN

Life expectancy, specifically how long an organism is projected to live after birth until death, is determined by rates of infant mortality, and by advances in medicine and access to high-quality health care. Poverty and racism both conspire to reduce life expectancy in African Americans and they have done so for decades. Accordingly, the cultural worldview of African American women differs from that of White women, especially regarding the role of education in their lives, and their anticipated responsibilities for the welfare of their families of procreation.

Nearly 50 years ago, I published an essay review in what is now the *American Journal of Education* of sociologist Joyce Ladner's new book: *Tomorrow's Tomorrow: The Black Woman* (Slaughter, 1972). At that time, I reported the rate of infant mortality to be significantly higher for Black than White women and, also, that "maternal mortality is still four times as high for Black women as for White women. Black women constituted 42 percent of all maternal deaths in 1967, although they were estimated to be only 7–8 percent of all American females.[1] . . . Recent social statistics on the education, occupation, and income status of Black and White women are also dissimilar. In 1969, 12.3 percent of White women ages 25–34 had four years of college or more, in comparison with 5.6 percent of Black women" (Slaughter, 1972, pp. 301–302). Comparable high school graduation percentages were 77 percent for White women, ages 25–29, and 52 percent for Black women. Since over 50 percent of Black women were employed in domestic or service positions, their median incomes placed 60 percent of families headed by Black women below the poverty line, while those headed by White women placed only 30 percent below the poverty line. Importantly, however, I also reported that in the 1960s, the full-time work of educated Black women served to balance and equate the respective earnings of Black and White two-parent households since, in those days, White women either did not work outside the home or, if they did, tended to work part-time rather than full-time.

Given advances in public health care and medical technology during the twentieth century in the United States, not surprisingly between 1900 and 2000 our nation experienced notable changes in life expectancy among all gender/racial groups identified as Black/White, Female/Male (Stanley, 2022). Among Black women born in 1900, for example, 11 percent of that birth cohort were expected to be alive at age 65, and 5 percent at age 85; for those born between 1930 and 1950, 6 percent would reach age 85, but for those born between 1980 and 2000, 17–18 percent would reach age 65, and 6–7 percent of the same cohort were projected to reach age 85. The figures at birth represent a 121 percent increase in projected life expectancy between 1900 and 2000 for Black women. In contrast, the comparable figure at birth for Black men was 106 percent; comparable figures for White men were 60 percent, and for White women: 63 percent.

Clearly, the life expectancies of Black Americans significantly improved in the twentieth century, over 100 percent at birth for both genders. However, only Black women achieved a life expectancy rate at birth on par with White Americans. By 1980, at birth Black and White females, as well as White males, shared a life expectancy of over 70 years. I believe the resiliency shown by Black women in this example, of what is undoubtedly a collective accomplishment, is an important focus of this volume. Specifically, how did Black women empower themselves (i.e., become the *Chosen We*?) to achieve this and similar accomplishments, and what was the role of higher education in the process?

Using Black feminist theory to buttress her argument, Winkle-Wagner's analyses of the oral histories of 105 college-educated Black women suggest answers. The women's collective, but barely conscious, ability to create shared communities of relational identities, in addition to cognitive self-identities, provided the essential psychological context for their personal survival and somewhat remarkable achievements in a historically cruel, unforgiving, and oppressive American sociocultural environment.

Several chapters of *The Chosen We* detail the oral histories of Black women who graduated from college between 1954 and 2014. Some chapters focus on the impact of "PWIs" (Predominantly White [Educational]

Institutions) on the identity development of Black girls and women. A variety of support systems, formal and informal, contributed favorably to the women interviewed, but all brought in some aspect of Black culture. I read the chapters with great interest. A native Chicagoan, my own undergraduate and graduate education through my doctoral degree was obtained at the University of Chicago, a PWI, between 1958 to 1968 in human development and clinical psychology.

After reading the chapters, I reflected and realized that I had similarly buffered myself in those college years by pledging Delta Sigma Theta Sorority, then and now a predominantly Black sorority, in my second year of college and by resolving to also attend graduate school in the city of my birth where extended family and other African American friends lived. In fact, I never applied for graduate studies to any other university, although four years earlier I had applied, and been accepted, to two other colleges, one in Chicago, Illinois, and the other in in Palo Alto, California. During all the subsequent years, I was blessed. Unlike many participants in PWIs in the *Chosen We* study I experienced no significant health challenges of any kind.

My first major health challenge arose when I was preparing to retire at age 70 from the Graduate School of Education at the University of Pennsylvania in 2010–2011. I was diagnosed with Stage 1 breast cancer, following a routine mammogram. Living in Philadelphia for nearly 13 years after experiencing the better air and water quality of Chicago and Evanston possibly adversely affected my health (Villarosa, 2020). Blessed by the medical miracles performed at the University of Pennsylvania Hospital, I became a breast cancer survivor. At this age, I experience only the virtually unavoidable diseases linked to an aging body. Here is where my personal story ends. But who knows? Perhaps my excellent health all those years is correlated with working and living in my hometown during most of the early, formative, and therefore most stressful, years of my career, 1970–1997; but perhaps not, since correlation does not equal causation. My young parents (ages 17 and 20), for instance, could have just passed on good genes.

Alternately, perhaps I gradually developed beneficial coping strategies in the PWI environments I experienced for over 50 years (1958–2011). For example, during my first college year, I lived in the all-White female dormitory and experienced considerable social isolation, but in my sophomore year I chose to live at home with my great-grandmother, though I believe I thought then that I would have greater flexibility in socializing and dating the fellows I met while pledging (1959–1960) my sorority by living at home in my protected Black neighborhood. Later, I returned comfortably to the University of Chicago campus in my third and fourth college years.

I do know that connecting intellectually with developments in the vibrant civil rights movement during my graduate school years energized and heightened my own personal self-awareness as a Black woman. The larger sociocultural context buttressed me in ways that my informal and formal group affiliations never could have, and that Black and White people I met at the University of Chicago, a PWI, strongly contributed positively to my own identity development as a Black woman.

There is one final consideration: mental health. I believe it entirely possible that for over 50 years, I did not permit myself to be physically ill for any protracted period of time, no matter the losses, anxieties, or depressive episodes potentially experienced, and that it was not until I was preparing to retire that I literally let myself *live a little* . . . that is, I let myself be physically ill, and finally attended to the long-delayed needs of my body, my mind, and my soul.

Whatever the truth of my life story, I am honored to have been invited to introduce the readers of this important volume to the oral histories of other college-educated Black women in my generation and beyond. The telling of these stories, particularly in reference to the women's perceived impact of their college environments on their self-concepts and identity development, is long overdue.

DIANA SLAUGHTER KOTZIN, PHD, has been Constance E. Clayton Professor Emerita in Urban Education of the University of Pennsylvania since July 2011. Her research and teaching interests included school culture, primary education, and home–school relations facilitating academic achievement. Before joining Penn's Graduate School of Education (1998), Diana taught at Northwestern University's School of Education and Social Policy (1977–1997) and served on the faculties of the Department of Psychiatry at Howard University (1967–1968), the Child Study Center at Yale University (1968–1970), and Human Development and Education at the University of Chicago (1970–1977). Diana obtained a BA (1962), MA (1964), and PhD (1968) from the Committee on Human Development, University of Chicago, where she specialized in developmental and clinical psychology. In 1969 Diana's dissertation received the first Distinguished Research Award from Pi Lambda Theta (National Honor and Professional Association) for the most outstanding doctoral thesis completed by a woman in reference to education. Her research on early intervention and maternal and child development led to appointment in 1979–1981 as a public member of the National Advisory Board on Child Abuse and Neglect, US Department of Health and Human Services. In 1981–1987 she was an elected member of the Governing Council of the Society for Research in Child Development and served between 1987 and 1991 as appointed member of the Committee on Child Development Research and Public Policy, National Research Council, Commission on Behavioral and Social Sciences and Education, National Academy of Sciences. Elected Fellow of Divisions 45, 37, 1, and 7 in the American Psychological Association, in 1993–1994 she received an award from the Association for Distinguished Contribution to Research in Public Policy. In 2007, the University of Chicago awarded her its Lifetime Professional Achievement Citation. In 2012 she was elected to the National Academy of Education, and in 2022 she was elected to the American Academy of Arts and Sciences.

Acknowledgments

As the title of this book suggests, this research project and the resulting book were in many ways a collective project that spanned a dozen years of people who showed me what it means to share freedom and liberation. The depth of my gratitude and the way in which I was changed by the generosity and community shared with me by not only those women who participated in the oral histories but also my gatekeepers, advisors, and champions of the project leave me in a state of awe. The project—from the beginning to the end of this book—are to me a sign that even during dark times, there is light in the world for us to find in our community with one another. And I am infinitely grateful to the participants for showing me that.

The idea for the project came from an esteemed scholar in psychology, Diana Slaughter Kotzin (formerly Slaughter-Defoe), the Inaugural Constance E. Clayton Professor in Urban Education (now emerita) at the University of Pennsylvania (Penn). My first thanks must also go to her here. Dr. Kotzin was among only a very small handful of Black students who graduated from the University of Chicago in the 1960s, where she then also earned a PhD in human development and clinical psychology. A professor at Northwestern University for 20 years, she later spent 13 years in the Graduate School of Education at the University of Pennsylvania before retiring. At the time, she was a fully promoted professor at the University of Pennsylvania and she mentored me while I was in a one-year visiting professor position at Penn. During one of our breakfasts together, she was asking about the book I was writing at the time, a conversion of my dissertation ethnography about Black women students in a predominantly White university. She interrupted me midsentence and proclaimed, "Rachelle—you should now really be interviewing people like me who graduated from college during a time when institutions were just starting to include Black students!" We ultimately laid out the path for this project in that conversation. A few days later, I asked her if she wanted to collaborate on the project. She was nearing the end of her career and had the good sense to decline a project that she likely understood might take a decade or more to complete. I did remain in touch with Dr. Kotzin over the dozen years of the project, although admittedly, there were times when my own uncertainty about how I would finish it kept me away for months at a time. When I finished data collection, I spent a lovely day with her and her husband in Chicago, telling her all the many details of the findings and how I would lay out this book. At that point, I also asked her to write the foreword for the book and we outlined that too. While of course *all* errors and missteps are my own, she was the initial gatekeeper on the project, and she and her story remained in my mind the entire time. I also count her as a crucial advisor for me on this work throughout the process. And often, in the times when the project was difficult, it was Diana Slaughter Kotzin who I imagined in my mind as a reason to keep going.

To my five other gatekeepers on the project—also friends and collaborators—there would be none of this without you. Carla Morelon—you were the first gatekeeper for me in New Orleans after I spent years trying to make contacts in my own cities (Lincoln and Omaha, Nebraska) with very slow progress. You showed me what it meant to open doors, both in allowing me to stay in your home during my data collection process and in opening up your community to me. Bridget Kelly, Tangela Blakely Reavis, Courtney Luedke, and Carmen McCallum are the gatekeepers who made it possible to include Atlanta, Chicago, Detroit, and New Orleans in this project. I endeavored to publish as much as I could with the gatekeepers before the book would be published in an attempt to pay forward their importance to the project (see appendix C for a reading list). I am deeply indebted to you all for your wisdom, for giving fresh air to the project, for the interviews that gatekeepers collected, and for our continued collaborations. Stay tuned for another book from this enormous set of oral histories.

I spent my sabbatical year at the Institute for Research in the Humanities at the University of Wisconsin–Madison as a race, ethnicity, and indigeneity fellow. I am grateful to have been able to build community with humanities scholars, and to have been accepted as a type of historian and racial theorist there too. My work is so much better for having been in that community.

There were multiple doctoral students who talked with me about this book over the years, and some of these scholars, who were students at the time, also published with me on other parts of the data or conducted early rounds of data analysis with me. Some of these scholars also aided me in the "not fun" parts of writing such as reference work and copyediting. Thank you for your brilliance: Tangela Blakely Reavis, Jamila Lee-Johnson, Brittany Ota-Malloy, Jacquie Forbes, Shelby Rogers, Ashley Gaskew, Paris Wicker, Janella Benson, Khadejah Ray, Imani Barnes, and LaShawn Faith Washington.

To those who read various drafts of various iterations of the project, thank you. While of course all errors are mine here, I know this work is so much better for your thoughtful comments and for the time you spent. Thank you to Xueli Wang who read the entire manuscript, Mike Wagner who read multiple versions of the proposal and the entire manuscript, and to those who read various versions of chapters along the way: Dorian McCoy, Christy Clark-Pujara, Linn Posey-Maddox, Clif Conrad, Lesley Bartlett, Thandi Sulè, Dina Maramba, Milagros Castillo-Montoya, Bridget Turner Kelly, Courtney Luedke, Sue Robinson, Cherene Sherrard-Johnson, Jamila Lee-Johnson, Tangela Blakely Reavis, Deborah Faye Carter, Angela Locks, and Carmen McCallum. I had multiple conversations about ideas with Clif Conrad when I was writing the proposal for the book, and I am very thankful for his collegiality and for his commitment to inquiry and ideas. Thank you to Bridget Goosby for dozens of conversations on these findings about community and what they mean for Black women—and for collaborating with me, picking up exactly where this book leaves off, to consider how campus spaces relate to health outcomes for Black women.

Thank you to my write-on-site writing group at the University of Wisconsin–Madison for listening to me talk about this book for so many years, for carving out space to share space to do our writing, and for generally supporting me and my scholarly work. You make the life of a scholar far less lonely—and much more joyful. Thanks specially to writing group members over the years: Linn Posey-Maddox, Christy Clark-Pujara, Erica Turner, Cherene Sherrard-Johnson, Bianca Baldridge, Ain Grooms, Keisha Lindsey, and AJ Welton.

To my virtual writing group, The Resistance Collective, I am so grateful for our shared accountability, our laughter, and our writing time together every week. Thanks so much for your brilliance, advice, and for your collaboration: Deborah Faye Carter, Angela M. Locks, Carmen McCallum, Thandi Sulè, and Dina Maramba.

Thanks to State University of New York Press and specifically to my acquisitions editor Rebecca Colesworthy and the Critical Race Studies in Education series editor Derrick Brooms. You are actively seeking to make visible the lives, stories, and knowledge of Black women, who have often been erased and made invisible. Thank you for *seeing* this work, for elevating these stories, and for asking all the right questions at the right time to make this book better. I am immensely grateful that *The Chosen We* found a home with SUNY Press—the book is better for it. Thanks also to the anonymous peer reviewers who offered such thoughtful ideas as I finished the manuscript. And thanks for others who have helped so much along the way, such as Cecelia Cancellaro, a copy editor who asked important questions on an earlier version of this book (helping me realize I might have written two books instead of one). Thanks to my professional transcriptionist Brie Williams, who transcribed nearly all the oral histories initially.

To my parents, thanks for the conversations, childcare, and support you have given this work. Thanks also to my sister, Brenda Winkle, and my niece, Mya Wilber.

Finally, to the team I most enjoy calling my own, Team Waggle, thank you. All sacrifices that were made for this book were made by them specifically. My daughters, Eleanor Winkle-Wagner and Abigail Winkle-Wagner, do not remember a time when I was not working on this book. And they have actively been "Team Book" since they could speak. They have also learned from the wise women in this book that their liberation is tied to others, and I see it in who they are every single day. And to Mike Wagner, my most brilliant, kind, and unequivocally equity-minded partner, thank you for the hundreds of conversations you have had with me about this work, the listening for hours, the reading of all of the bad drafts, and the handling of all other things during the many instances where I needed to pull back on homelife to travel, to think, to write, and to finish writing this book. You said, "Yes, go do it!" every single time without fail. And I felt chosen every time. Thank you for who you are and for our life.

Part I

Black Women's Self-Determination in Education from Here to Eternity

When you educate a girl, you educate a family, a community, a country. If we care about climate change, if we care about poverty, if we care about maternal child health, then we have to care about education.

—Michelle Obama, quoted in Lolly Bowean,
"Michelle Obama's Goal"

It was a sunny fall afternoon when I nervously knocked on the beautifully kept door of Rita Mae's home in New Orleans, Louisiana. One of my friends had paved the way for me to connect with her. I knew that my friend, who became a "gatekeeper" on this project (appendix C for a reading list), had told Rita Mae that I was White and that I had well over 15 years of experience working with Black[1] women.[2] Since Rita Mae was one of the first Black[3] women above the age of 50 with whom I had met for this book, I was anxious about whether I could build the trust necessary for her to share her story with me. The shaky sense of balancing on the edge of the cliff between building trust between a Black woman and a White woman who have never met, and the cavernous, disturbing possibility that I could cause more racial harm, would become very familiar to me in the decade that I spent working on this book (appendix A). Eventually, I would put that edginess on like a sweater and use it for what it was: potential—that explicitly revealed both my vulnerability as a White woman who has spent her career working with Black women and a hope for change in how we might see one another. On that first day with Rita Mae, my obligations to the people whose experiences I share in this book nearly overwhelmed me.

I embarked on the process of writing this book because after I completed my first book, *The Unchosen Me: Race, Gender, and Identity among Black Women in College* (Winkle-Wagner, 2009a), I realized that there was more to the story than I initially thought. Through a critical ethnographic analysis of Black women's college experiences at a predominantly White institution (PWI), *The Unchosen Me* asserted that Black women navigated impositions in their identities from multiple actors on campus (peers, faculty, administrators). While many of the students in *The Unchosen Me* were successful—they graduated from college—the identity impositions took significant tolls on the women's satisfaction with their experiences and, in some cases, led them to leave the institution or to leave college altogether.

The critique of *The Unchosen Me* was in the deterministic overtones implied by identity impositions, as if there were impositions that ultimately Black women could not fully resist on a predominantly White campus (Chambers, 2010; Dàvila, 2012; Hernandez, 2010). As Will Tyson (2010) stated in his review, "Winkle-Wagner does not describe how these women took ownership of their lives to adapt to the pressures placed on the self. . . . I wanted to see more about how these women actively define their own identity and take charge of how they are perceived by others on campus" (p. 1036). I had already begun to reanalyze the data because I had realized that the book lacked much evidence of resistance and agency from Black women, when some reactions to the book confirmed my thoughts. While there was little evidence of resistance within the data, I inquired whether it might be due to both the way the questions were asked and the relative youth of the women in that study.

The Chosen We contemplates Black women's agency, resistance, and self-identification in and beyond higher education settings. These themes are especially evident in the oral histories of older women who had been given the gift of time to reflect on their college experiences. Through oral histories of Black women who graduated from college between 1954 and 2014, I assert that *Chosen We* communities are one of the major ways that Black women have resisted impositions on who they should be in and beyond college. *Chosen We* communities were sometimes informal relationships, such as friendship groups, families, or communities-of-origin, the neighborhoods and communities one might consider a home or hometown. *Chosen We* communities were also formal student organizations such as Black student unions, Black sororities, or academic organizations (e.g., Black sociologists, Black accountants, etc.). Sometimes, as was the case with historically Black colleges and universities (HBCUs), entire campuses were framed as *Chosen We* communities—a community that generally affirmed and supported at least a student's racial/ethnic identities in a meaningful way. By definition, *Chosen We* communities are rooted in relationships and identities that one has the freedom and agency to *choose*, and therefore to opt to leave behind if and when those communities are no longer sustainable or healthy.

"I Learned about People, and I Learned about My Degree": Rita Mae's Story

When Rita Mae greeted me at the door, I was struck by her gracefulness. Her beautiful home had a lovely mauve and teal color palette that was woven throughout every room. Even her carefully chosen casual Saturday attire alluded to her elegance. She matched from head to toe in colors that complemented her home. The grand piano in the hallway struck me right away and I confided to Rita Mae that I had been an undergraduate piano performance major but had stopped playing in recent years, a fact I shared with few people. She told me the piano was her husband's and had been the root of his work as a classical musician. This provided us a space to connect with one another as we talked about our favorite piano pieces and about how difficult it is to have a career in music. As we drank tea, I learned that Rita Mae had attended predominantly White colleges and universities, in northeastern, midwestern, and southwestern states. My anxiousness melted away as I realized the project had never been and would never be about me; it was about the minute-by-minute possibility of building trust to allow peoples' lives to emerge.

Rita Mae grew up in the South during the 1950s, at a time when schools were just starting to be forced to integrate racially, although admittedly many schools never really did integrate. Her primary and secondary schooling experience was in a neighborhood public school that was entirely Black. Her teachers and administrators had all earned at least a master's degree. The assumption was that all students in her high school would attend college. In that segregated Black high school, the students were taught that they could be anything. She recounted:

There were 405 of us that graduated when I graduated, and five years later I think there were about 300 who had bachelor's degrees, and when we did our thirtieth high school reunion, we did a little survey and we had PhDs, EdDs, MDs, law degrees, you name it. So those were the expectations that people had. You couldn't teach in my high school unless you had at least a master's degree. The principals had EdDs from Columbia University, Teachers College. That was one of the schools that allowed Black people [to attend], after they earned a bachelor's and a master's degree at a HBCU in the South. There were not a lot of PhDs or EdD programs in the South that had allowed people to get a doctorate. So, each summer, these people would go to Columbia, and they had places where they could stay and they may take one or two or three classes and it may have taken them 10 years but, they got their doctorate.

During the days of segregated education, Rita Mae's high school was a good example of education that was created by and for Black people (Walker, 1996, 2000), a *Chosen We* amid a White supremacist and racist society (Kendi, 2016; Leonardo, 2013). Rita Mae attended segregated Black schools in the South that were likely underresourced, which was common when racial separation in education was legal in the United States (Walker, 1996, 2000, 2001).

Yet her teachers and administrators were highly educated, having earned bachelor's degrees from historically Black colleges and universities (HBCUs) in the South during a time when higher education was also highly segregated (Smith, 2016; Walker, 2001). After having earned bachelor's degrees, Rita Mae's administrators and teachers often attended a highly prestigious Ivy League university, Columbia University, for their graduate-level degrees. While most higher education institutions were segregated during the 1950s and 1960s, some institutions, particularly Ivy League institutions like Columbia University, became well-known pathways to advanced degrees for African American people (Smith, 2016).

Rita Mae recounted her family's participation in one of the major Black migration patterns (Wilkerson, 2011) from southern states to the northern states and cities on the West Coast that occurred from the time of Enslavement (before 1865) to the time of Reconstruction (1865–present). More than six million African American people left racial hostility to try to create more positive lives. Rita Mae explained, "Most people had friends and relatives in Alabama so New York, Harlem, was one of the places that people left my city to go to." Referencing Black migration from southern states like Alabama to northern states like New York (Wilkerson, 2011), Rita Mae in her youth knew the pathway through higher education for Black people well. People would first attend an HBCU in the South, then migrate to northern states and stay with the generations of other Black people who had preceded them while earning a terminal degree from one of the precious few doctoral-granting institutions that admitted African American people at that time.

Racial segregation is a moral, economic, and social scar in the history of the United States that came directly out of the unconscionable and unforgivable enslavement of Black people. While school integration was meant to provide better resources and opportunities for Black people, it is important to note that many of its effects were quite negative due to the *way* that it was implemented (Walker, 1996, 2001). Black schools with Black teachers and administrators were teaching Black children in empowering, self-determined ways. Integration abandoned all of this for White teachers and administrators, who implemented White Eurocentric curriculums and pedagogies (Anderson, 1988; Walker, 1996, 2000, 2001; Watkins, 2001). It is not surprising, given the "White architects of Black education" as Watkins (2001) called them, that Black children left schools where their innate brilliance and possibility were honored, and entered schools in which they were seen and treated as deficient, inferior, and problematic. Rita Mae is a part of this history; she was on the cusp of this change. She had been educated in an all-Black school where her endless potential was assumed. It is not that integration was an obviously negative project. However, integration's deliberate abandonment of empowering Black classrooms and schools was yet another example of racial reform efforts that may have never been intended to heal the racial inequality that founded the United States. Through the story of Rita Mae, and others like her, this book takes up the history of Black excellence and explores how it was collectively promoted across generations, with and without the support of White teachers, administrators, and educational systems.

After attending high school in Alabama, Rita Mae opted to leave the South to attend college at the University of New Haven in Connecticut. She also took courses at Connecticut State University. She had family in the Northeast with whom she could live. She graduated with a social sciences degree from New Haven in the 1960s. She earned a master's degree at Michigan State University in a similar field in the 1980s. Rita

Mae got married in her 30s and had children. Her graduate-level degree piqued her interest in more education, and she moved to Arizona where she earned a doctoral degree in a social sciences discipline in the 1990s at Northern Arizona University.

Rita Mae's first year at the private, predominantly White, University of New Haven, which was founded as a branch of Yale University in the 1920s, ushered in a lot of new experiences and contacts with new people:

> I think I learned about people and about my degree. It was an engineering college, an offshoot of Yale. It was predominately male, very few females, and they had a strong Business Department and a strong Social Science Department. I was a commuter student; I lived with my aunt, and she lived in a predominantly Italian community. The predominant students there [at UNH] were Italian, Irish, and Jewish. A lot of Jewish kids came from New York. I remember being in a predominantly White environment and among a lot of males; my passion for sociology came about.

Rita Mae used the new experience—being around mostly Irish, Italian, and Jewish students in college—a type of sociological study of her own. She drew upon the history of Whiteness in the United States where many groups, even those with fair complexions, were not considered "White" for a long time. In recent years, most people would simply refer to all these student populations as White. But at the time when Rita Mae was in college, Irish, Italian, and Jewish people were not necessarily considered White in the United States (Yancy, 2003). These groups, particularly Italian and Irish populations, eventually became "White" and were included as such in the census and other demographics (Lieberson, 1980; Yancy, 2003, 2016). When they initially came to this country, however, they were often "othered" and they were not given many of the economic and social privileges attached to Whiteness (Lieberson, 1980; Yancy, 2016). Jewish populations were also often not completely accepted as "White" in the United States (Brodkin, 1998; Goldstein, 2006). While Jewish people are not typically considered a visible minority group, meaning that they are not phenotypically (skin tone) different from many European American groups, during the 1960s, there were still remnants of anti-Semitism from World War II and the Holocaust, during which millions of Jewish people were brutally murdered in the name of ethnic cleansing (Brodkin, 1998; Goldstein, 2006).

Rita Mae continued: "I had a Chinese professor and there was a chapter in my sociology class, there was a chapter on a 'Negro' family, and he skipped the chapter. He didn't do the chapter and I went to him, and I said, 'Well why, why aren't we having, why aren't we going to do this chapter?' He said, 'Because you're the only Negro in the class.'" Rita Mae's professor, who was Asian American, decided that the chapter about the Black family would not be useful or important to study because there was only one Black student in the class. Rita Mae used the word "Negro" because that is likely the word that was used to describe the Black family in her textbook at the time, even though the term has been associated with the oppression and derogation of Black people (Smith, 1992). The United States Census Bureau continued to use the term "Negro" until 2013 (Brown, 2013). Rita Mae elaborated on what happened next:

> For each class you'd have to write a paper and so what did I write my paper on? The "Negro" family. I took all of the sociology courses that were taught there. I learned a lot. Everything I wrote about was some aspect of Black sociology, of the Black family. I got to know all the Black sociologists and had a really good time learning about them. At that point I had probably gone through college and had never known what a Black sociologist was or whether or not there were any at all.

Rita Mae refused to accept the invisibility of Blackness that her professors imposed on her. She took every opportunity to elevate Black families and Black scholars, choosing to build Black intellectual thought up around her, even in a predominantly White space. This was all learning she did on her own in addition to what she was learning in her coursework—she supplemented the Eurocentric learning with Black sociologists and her own interest in Black families.

There were very few Black students on campus at the University of New Haven. Rita Mae lived with her aunt. On campus, Rita Mae found that she mostly became friends with Jewish students: "I knew about prejudice, but I really probably didn't know the word racism until later on. I thought as a group, probably the students who were the friendliest were the Jewish students. So, I got the chance to visit them in New York, and most of their parents were merchants, owned factories and different things." Rita Mae remarked that many of the Jewish friends she made in college became lifelong contacts for her. They still travel back to meet up for reunions.

After finishing her undergraduate degree, Rita Mae pursued graduate education. She started her master's degree at Southern Connecticut State University and eventually transferred to Michigan State University because by that time she was married, and her husband was pursuing his own PhD in Michigan. She began her doctoral degree at the University of Tennessee, but because she had children by then and her husband's career had taken off, it was more difficult for her to finish. She ended up waiting until she moved to Northern Arizona University a few years later to complete the degree.

During her doctoral program, Rita Mae took on a leadership role to build a stronger community of Black women around her than she initially encountered when she entered the program. She explained, "The one thing that I did when I was at Northern Arizona University is I had an African American Woman's support group because African American women were the minority women there. The majority of women were Native Americans at the school, Native Americans, Hispanics, White." Black women felt isolated at Northern Arizona because there were not many Black students at the institution. Rita Mae noticed this isolation and decided to build a *Chosen We* community for younger Black women on campus. Realizing that a similar community would have helped her own sense of belonging in education, Rita Mae decided to create community for subsequent generations of Black women. She recalled:

> I met with them on a Sunday afternoon, and we talked about different things. Finding peace with yourself, getting a good education, and these men [the athletes] probably may not be lasting relationships even if you got to them, based upon their kind of lifestyle of an athlete. And then making sure they master their subjects and took care of themselves. "You don't have to be married by the time you're 21." I used myself as an example. I didn't get married until I was 31. I didn't think bad about myself. It allowed me to do a lot of things, meet a lot of people, have a lot of experiences, understand a lot of things, think for myself and so forth. I led that.

Rita Mae saw her role in her doctoral program as a leader who could help build community for younger Black women on campus. She used her own life experiences as examples that younger women could follow. By focusing on the community she built, she also reinforced her own self-esteem and sense of self. Throughout this book, and consistent with Rita Mae's oral history, is the story of the continuous renewal of Black women creating communities of greatness or identifying those that already existed. Often these spaces were initiated before integration and have been created in obvious and subtle ways on college campuses ever since. As the oral histories in this book emphasize, being part of *Chosen We* communities was a transformative experience for the women in this book, and one that has a great deal to teach us about not only Black women but racial history, redemption, and hope in the United States as well.

Chapter 1

The Collective History of Black Women's Ways of Knowing

We are African women, and we know, in our blood's telling the tenderness with which our foremothers held each other. It is that connection which we are seeking. We have stories of Black women who healed each other's wounds, raised each other's children, fought each other's battles, tilled each other's earth and eased each other's passages into life and into death. We know the possibilities of support and connection for which we all yearn, and about which we dream so often.

—Audre Lorde, *Sister Outsider*

An underappreciated story of the 2020 presidential election and the current sociopolitical time in the United States is the role that Black sororities, historically Black colleges and universities (HBCUs), and community played in the election of the first Black and Asian American woman vice president, Kamala Harris (Harris, 2019). Black women like Stacey Abrams in the state of Georgia were credited with helping to elect both Biden-Harris and the first Black senator in the state of Georgia (Reverend Raphael Gamaliel Warnock, who is also an HBCU graduate) (Rutledge, 2021). The real story is that Black women have been building community to empower each other, and the nation, for generations (Jones, 2009; Waxman, 2021). Much of this community initiates on college campuses—both HBCUs and predominantly White institutions. The untold story of Black women's communities in and beyond college is revealed in this book as Black women identify the ways in which they chose each other, themselves, and the betterment of the world around them. The story revealed here is about the *Chosen We.*

In a country that was not created by or for their success, Black women have demonstrated stunning resilience, agency, and power (Jones, 2009; Moraga & Anzaldúa, 2015; Patton & Haynes, 2018; White, 1999a, 1999b). They have done so despite attempted erasure and silencing from racist and sexist social structures and people. Black women have achieved, led, and persisted, primarily without the support of those around them (Collins, 2002/2009; Jones, 2009; Solomon, 1985). A reasonable question to ask is how they have done so. As Audre Lorde (2012) captured so well, it was often because they "held each other" and knew "the possibilities of support and connection for which we all yearn" (p. 152). *The Chosen We* demonstrates that maintaining connection and community among themselves has been the primary way that Black women have persevered and thrived in and beyond higher education for the past 60 years.

While community with one another was a path toward success for many Black women, it was often fostered amid unimaginable structural, institutional, and social oppression. It is within what well-known Black feminist theorist bell hooks (2000) referred to as a "white supremacist, capitalist patriarchy" (p. 118) that Black women have uplifted each other and prospered. As hooks (2000, pp. 118–119) asserted: "The social hierarchy in white supremacist, capitalist patriarchy is one in which theoretically men are the powerful, women the powerless; adults the powerful, children the powerless; white people the powerful, black people and other non-white people the powerless. In a given situation, whichever party is powerful is likely to use coercive authority to maintain that power if it is challenged or threatened." Some, including hooks (2000), might add that the White supremacist, capitalist patriarchy is also heteronormative, as those who are heterosexual are put in positions of power over those who identify as gay, lesbian, bisexual, transgender, or queer (Ingraham, 1994; Smith, 2010). It is within the scenery and resultant scripting of the White supremacist, capitalist patriarchy that Black women have accomplished and thrived. They did this despite living in the midst of a society that was created to exclude them through neglect, erasure, and subjugation to men and White people.

The oral histories in *The Chosen We* are stories of hope, perseverance, accomplishment, and power. What makes these oral histories even more remarkable is that Black women have faced unyielding discrimination and arduous hurdles since the founding of the United States (Fredrickson, 2015; Hull et al., 1982; Moraga & Anzaldúa, 2015). Black women were enslaved, involuntarily forced to work without pay for generations even after enslavement was illegal, fought their way to freedom primarily on their own, earned their right to vote, and continued to fight for their own civil liberties (Blackmon, 2009; Davis, 1983; Franklin, 1969; Jones, 2009; Kendi, 2016).

While these formidable challenges were designed to keep them from ever fully participating in society, Black women have pursued upwardly mobile aspirations such as earning college degrees and building noteworthy careers. Black women were the unsung heroes of the civil rights movement, planning the marches and upholding their families and communities (Collier-Thomas & Franklin, 2000, 2001; Robnett, 2000). They were central, though largely unnamed, in the struggle for women's liberation: as Black women began to claim their freedom, they also challenged the patriarchal ideas that kept White women dependent on men (Giddings, 1996/1984; White, 1999b). Black women also initiated the more contemporary Black Lives Matter movement, shedding light on police brutality, mass incarceration (Alexander, 2012), and contemporary injustices faced by Black people (Taylor, 2016). In the arts, Black women's voices, poetry, writing, and ideas have been adapted, if not sometimes co-opted, to create our nation's artistic artifacts (Davis, 1983; Giddings, 1996/1984). Even in higher education, a bastion of liberty and social mobility, Black women have had to fight their way onto campuses, into classrooms, and to earn their degrees (Commodore et al., 2018; Patton & Croom, 2017; Winkle-Wagner, 2015). Black women were set up to bear enormous despair, sorrow, and loss in the United States. They were not set up to survive well in this country, let alone to thrive.

Education has been a significant factor in fostering Black women's success, and yet a full understanding of how Black women have navigated education, particularly at the higher levels (e.g., undergraduate, graduate, or professional school) is often ignored or erased by many scholars (but see Evans, 2008; Giddings, 1996/1984; Hull et al., 1982). Black women's scholarship and, relatedly, their lives in and out of college, are often neglected within the academy and in the US more generally, even when they are "hidden in plain sight" (Patton & Haynes, 2021). As I demonstrate in this book, it is not that Black women have not been writing about and finding some consensus on ways to be successful in and beyond college. Rather, it is that those who center Black women—many of whom are Black women themselves—have too often been systematically silenced or ignored.

Throughout the book, I ask: How have Black women survived and thrived in higher education amid formidable challenges? I ask this knowing from my previous work and from relationships with Black women that Black women had the answer to this question all along. My goal here is not to pretend that the question is necessarily new to Black women—they have been finding ways to survive and thrive for generations. Rather, I pose this question to begin the effort to make more visible what Black women have known all along: that their success and survival were bound to one another. *The Chosen We* answers this question, offering critical oral histories (appendix A) that unapologetically center Black women. These are stories of individual and collective empowerment that are tied to Black women's community with one another and with other Black people. The Black women interviewed for this book developed their *We* while also maintaining a strong sense of individuality (their *Me*). The ability to assert both their individual and group identities was the key to their success.

The Chosen We shows that despite the insurmountable difficulties placed in their paths, many Black women have not only survived but flourished, primarily without acknowledgment (Davis, 1983; Hull et al., 1982; Jones, 2009; Jones & Shorter-Gooden, 2004; White, 1999a, 199b). Black women have been the lifeblood of the generational, racial uplift through higher education, highlighting how the actions of one generation of a particular racial group can influence the progress of others in that group over many years (Giddings, 1996/1984; Hull et al., 1982; Jones, 2009; Jones & Shorter-Gooden, 2003; White, 1999b). Yet comprehensive stories about Black women's triumphs in and through higher education are largely untold (Jones, 2009; White, 1999b; Winkle-Wagner, 2015). Black women's *silenced* accomplishments as the creators of uplift for Black people means that there is little understanding of how, amid tremendous racism, sexism, and classism, they lifted themselves and their generations up into serving as leaders in their communities and in the nation (Davis, 1983; Giddings, 1996/1984).

While their full stories often remain untold, particularly in many mainstream academic publications, Black women are held up as an exemplar in education (Commodore et al., 2018; Patton & Croom, 2017; Winkle-Wagner, 2015). Black women have been enrolling in college at higher rates than other groups since the 1940s (Giddings, 1996/1984; Patton & Croom, 2017). As a result, scholars have framed Black women as "Superwomen" (Harris-Lacewell, 2001; Thomas et al., 2004; Woods-Giscombé, 2010) or as "magical" (e.g., the social media hashtag #Blackgirlmagic) (Porter & Byrd, 2021). These frames do not attend to the complexity of Black women's lives (e.g., Jones, 2009), nor do they offer insight into *how*

Black women created success in a country that was set up for them to fail. In many ways, these tropes work to make invisible the realities of Black women's challenges *and* solutions for their own lives. Aside from a few noteworthy exceptions (e.g., Giddings, 1996/1984; Hull et al., 1984; Jones & Shorter-Gooden, 2003; Patton & Croom, 2017; White, 1999b), there is a limited understanding of Black women's lives. Too often, Black women's "lives are narrowed down" (Winkle-Wagner, 2015), meaning their generational collective wisdom is ignored. Black women's complex stories need to be shared so Black women entering college have a map for success (Patton & Byrd, 2021); higher educational institutions can work toward better inclusion of students of color, and they and other communities of color can be fully included in society.

The Chosen We elevates the experiences and oral histories of accomplished, college-educated Black women who earned success despite experiencing reprehensible racist and sexist barriers. In so doing, the book provides a new approach to social science research where the lives and histories of participants are advanced, and all of the participants are treated as partners rather than passive objects of study. To that end, sometimes the women in this book wrote their own histories or cowrote them with me (appendix A for notes on methodology; appendix B for participants quoted in the book). Sometimes they used pseudonyms and sometimes they named themselves; the choice was theirs. The chapters are organized thematically, presenting narrative oral histories from individual women who exemplified themes as a way to demonstrate the ways in which Black women's lives intersected and were similar to one another, even across time and geographic differences (see appendix B for participants quoted in the book; appendix C for a reading list of other publications from the project).

The oral histories in this book demonstrate that college was the tipping point—the place and time for Black women to seize their individual and collective liberation. Importantly, the Black women whose lives are revealed in this book have manifested the wisdom that many other groups in the United States have failed to grasp: their liberation, and the liberation of others, *intersects*.

The Oral Histories and Structure of *The Chosen We*

This book chronicles the college experiences of 105 Black women alumnae who were successful in that they graduated from college and, in most cases, went on to become leaders in their professional fields and in their communities. For over a decade, my research team and I interviewed these women in five different metropolitan areas (see appendix A for a detailed methodology): Atlanta, Georgia; Chicago, Illinois; Detroit, Michigan; Lincoln/Omaha, Nebraska; and New Orleans, Louisiana. The women all graduated from college with at least a bachelor's degree over a 60-year time period, between 1954 and 2014. Of the 105 women, 36 graduated from historically Black colleges or universities (HBCUs) for their undergraduate degrees and 69 attended predominantly White institutions (PWIs). Nearly half of the alumnae (44 women) were the first in their families to attend college. Some women came from poverty, some came from solidly middle-class families, and others came from great wealth. As a testament to their accomplishments, over half of the alumnae (66 women) also earned some type of advanced degree such as a master's degree. Of those who earned advanced degrees, 30 of the alumnae earned a terminal degree such as a PhD, JD, or MD. Over the 12 years that I traveled around the United States interviewing these alumnae, I continued to interact with many of these women for years after our initial meeting, and many of them had a hand in crafting their own stories for this book.

The Chosen We blends oral history, empirical social science, and social theory to offer compilations of Black women's college experiences in and through college. I reveal recurring comparisons of Black women's experiences over time to demonstrate that Black women have struggled and endured alone, but they have empowered and persevered together. The book also uncovers the importance of the type of institutions that students attend for higher education, comparing Black women's experiences not only by region and era, but also by whether they attended a predominantly White institution or a historically Black college or university.

The major contribution of the book is that it highlights how Black alumnae used educational settings to activate empowering individual (*Me*) and community (*We*) identities. This finding spanned across the 60-year time frame of college graduation and across geographic regions. The type of institution that the women attended determined how they navigated their community (*We*) and individual (*Me*) identities.

Black women identified predominantly White institutions as more individualistic and therefore identified and maintained collectivist spaces (e.g., organizations, friendships, physical spaces like a campus union) to create *Chosen We* communities. The alumnae of historically Black colleges and universities described their institutions as more attuned toward promoting community notions of identity, a type of *Chosen We*. Out of this community, the women identified ways to find empowering notions of individuality out of that collectivist space.

The women carried these lessons with them throughout their lives and careers, helping other Black women along the way. These findings contradict most other studies on Black women's success that are focused only on how individuals were successful in college (Patton & Haynes, 2021; Winkle-Wagner, 2015). Additionally, while other research, even my own, suggests that college success can be detrimental to Black women's sense of self (Winkle-Wagner, 2009a), *The Chosen We* illustrates ways in which Black women have resisted, persevered, and thrived in higher education settings—together.

The Chosen We includes contributions that engage in:

1. Elevating Black women's stories of hope to understand how they collectively gained access to and persevered through higher education across multiple decades and multiple geographic spaces in the United States amid enormous barriers and challenges.

2. Revealing how individual and group identities can work together in order to explore how Black women have identified individual identities (*Me*) and collective identities (*We*), as a way to empower themselves and others even within oppression, discrimination, and stereotypes.

3. Understanding the role of higher education institutions, both predominantly White and historically Black college and universities, in shaping Black women's experiences in and beyond college.

4. Providing an example of how to conduct social science research where research participants, particularly those who have been historically marginalized, can work as partners in the crafting of the stories about them.

First, by demonstrating that individual and collectivist identities can be wedded together in ways that offer empowerment not just during college but across Black women's lifetimes, the critical oral histories in this book reframe how identity should be studied and understood. Rather than a polarity between the study of cognitions and what is happening in one's mind (the primary focus of psychological notions of identity) over what is happening to a person as they interact in society (the primary focus of sociological notions of identity) (Hogg et al., 1995; Stryker & Burke, 2000), the Black women's stories in this book suggest that people can identify, activate, and use both individual and collectivist notions of identity simultaneously as a way to empower themselves and others. These findings also have implications for theories of identity (e.g., Hernández, 2016; Mead, 1934; Winkle-Wagner, 2009a). The blending of the *Me* (individual) and the *We* (community) aspects of identity suggests that future research on identity should work to ensure people are understood both in terms of their own cognitive processing of their identities and relative to their social interactions of collectivist identity. The joining of the *Me* and *We* also indicate a need for higher education faculty and administrators to foster the success of students in ways that honor both the collectivist and individual identities.

Second, the book is at once a historical analysis of how race and gender have been experienced by Black women in a White supremacist, patriarchal society alongside a contemporary analysis of how far the country has come in creating inclusion across race and gender lines. Through the various generational cohorts of women in the study, which I considered in 10-year time periods (i.e., 1960s, 1970s, 1980s, 1990s, 2000s), it is evident how society has and has not changed. This allows for a clearer explication of what remains to be done to create better and fuller liberty and inclusion of Black women and other Communities of Color in the United States. At times, it is startling how similar the more recent college graduates' experiences were to Black women who graduated as many as 50 years earlier. In other ways, in large part because of the labor of prior generations, Black women alumnae from the 1990s and 2000s seemed to have access to more professional possibilities, as well as opportunities for who they could become as individuals and community members.

Third, the comparison between PWIs and HBCUs that I emphasize within this book allows for a more nuanced analysis of how these very different institutional types can ultimately create some of the same outcomes in their students—highly accomplished leaders. In comparing the two institutional types, I outline lessons that both might be able to take from each other. I also report evidence of the various geographic experiences (e.g., Daché-Gerbino, 2018; Daché, 2022) among Black women who attended colleges in the Midwest, North, South, West, and East. For instance, Black women who attended PWIs in the South often described very overt forms of racial hostility, even in more recent years (e.g., being called racial epithets, crosses being burned on campuses, etc.) while women in the northern and eastern states still experienced racism but it was often more subtle (e.g., exclusion from group work in classrooms, experiencing racial stereotypes from peers, etc.). HBCUs are primarily only in southern states. All the women who attended HBCUs felt a sense of "family" or "home" on campus, but they often experienced racism off campus. This allows for a larger discussion about ways that geographic regions, and the institutions within those regions, have dealt differently with racial inclusion (see also Daché-Gerbino, 2018; Daché, 2022; Daché et al., 2022).

Finally, as one of the single largest analyses of oral histories of Black women's college experiences across the country and over time, the book allows for a richer portrait of how Black women have thrived amid tremendous barriers. While I do not attempt to generalize the findings of this book to other populations, there are many transferrable lessons that can be garnered to the inclusion and support of other populations of students of color in education. Black women's oral histories of how they navigated racist and sexist systems, including those represented by higher education institutions, are crucially important in not only understanding how to make educational spaces more inclusive but also how to rethink larger social systems and policies. To that end, Black feminist epistemology is embedded throughout this book.

Elevating a Critical Black Feminist Way of Knowing

Brittany Cooper (2017) claimed, "Black women are serious thinkers, and it is our scholarly duty to take them seriously" (p. 152). Black women and their thinking have long been left out of mainstream social spaces, academic spaces, and philosophical thought (Davis, 1971; Moses, 1989; Zinn, 1989). Additionally, Black women are often left out of discussions about race and about gender (Cooper, 2017; Cottom, 2018; Guy-Sheftall, 1995). It is no wonder then that while Black women writers, often with little recognition or acknowledgment, made inferences to a collective notion of identity, and that they were given little credit for that too (Giddings, 1996/1984; Guy-Sheftall, 1995). As a White scholar, my goal here is to honor and elevate these ideas, without naming them as my own, because they are intimately connected to the oral histories I am writing here.

In *The Chosen We*, I am emphasizing a critical Black feminist episte-mology (Collins, 2000/2009) that highlights experience, social structures, and practice as a way of knowing. Epistemology, how one comes to know what one knows, is at the heart of all research and thinking.[1] I start with epistemology as a way to deliberately identify how this way of thinking might differ from other ways that Black women's experiences have been researched.[2] Black feminist epistemology influenced my approach to theory[3] and ultimately the construction of the theoretical concept of the *Chosen We*, which is specified in chapter 2. Thus, I consider how critical theory,[4] which is centered on justice, equality, and attempts to uncover and remedy social oppression, might move beyond a set of suppositions toward a way of knowing about the world.[5]

I highlight Patricia Hill Collins's (2000/2009) call for a Black feminist epistemology to demonstrate how critical theories that center a blended race, class, and gender analysis can be a way of knowing (epistemology). In my larger work, I contemplate how Collins's (2000/2009) arguments might relate to other critical theorists such as Jürgen Habermas (1984, 1987)[6] and particularly Habermas's moral ideas that theory cannot only critique but also must stimulate social change. I blend other critical theories and Black feminist theory, in part, because of my own positioning as a White woman. While I *learn* from Black feminist thinkers throughout this book and the oral histories often invoke or connect with Black feminist thought, as a White woman I stop short of considering myself a Black feminist thinker (and it is worth saying that more than once).

Rooted in generations of thinking, Collins (2000/2009) called for a Black women's epistemology (Crotty, 1998) that centered Black women's lived experiences. As a prelude to the ways that the women in my own study described their experiences, Black women's epistemology honors knowing that comes from the physical body, the emotional self (Lorde, 2012), and the mind. Collins (1989) aimed to create a way of knowing that would counter the Eurocentric, masculine ways of knowing in mainstream social science research. The entire project of Black women's epistemology connects to the way one can engage collective and individual experience simultaneously.

Collins (1986, 2000/2009) emphasized the following themes in a Black feminist epistemology (pp. 279–290): experience as a criterion of meaning; dialogue to assess knowledge claims; an ethic of caring for others; an ethic of personal responsibility; and Black women as agents of knowledge. Each of these ideas are centered in this book.

Experience as a criterion of meaning: Black women scholars have long used their own lived experience alongside empirical evidence that they collect to push back on dominant ways of thinking and knowing (e.g., Brown, 1989; Jordan, 1981, 1985, 2015/1992; Ladner, 1986; Lee, 1996; Lorde, 2012; Mitchell & Lewter, 1986). Individual and collective experiences of Black women would become part and parcel to knowledge production and dissemination. Knowledge is created from experience. A more collective notion of Black women's experience, the *We*, as I am referring to it, would likely drive knowledge in this case.

Collins's description of knowledge as linked to experience is a clear critique of ways of knowing that render experience as less important than so-called expert researchers' ideas of the "other." As Collins (1989) described it, often traditional research practices, which are often White and male, have imposed distance between researchers and participants, as if those being studied were objects, omitted emotions, and pushed away from noticing ethics and values. A Black feminist approach requires that participants are humanized, emotions are centered, and that ethics and values are elevated as part of the research process. Many traditional research approaches "narrow down" Black women's lives in ways that make their real, lived experiences invisible or less meaningful (Winkle-Wagner, 2015). In creating a Black feminist epistemology, Collins (1986, 1989, 2000/2009) created a new language, new knowledge form, and a new way of being and thinking in the world that centered "Black women's standpoints."

Centering experience made an inherent claim to the intersection of identities and oppressions. The idea that experience is intersectional was initiated in writing as far back as the 1800s with Sojourner Truth, who wrote her famous essay "Ain't I a Woman?" in 1851 (Guy-Sheftall, 1995). Truth pointed out at this early date her concerns that Black women would be left to fight for their own freedoms as women and as Black people, implying that Black men and White women would not fight for Black women's justice. Anna Julia Cooper (1988/1892) added in her book that Black women are "confronted by both a woman question and a race problem and are as yet an unknown or an unacknowledged factor in both" (p. 45). She summarized, "Only the Black women can say, when and where I enter . . . then and there the whole Negro race enters with me" (Cooper, 1988/1892, p. 31). Cooper asserted that Black women are often the leaders in the fight for freedom of women and Black people. Her argument was that Black women must center themselves in the fight for their own freedom, and that they were inextricably linked to all humanity and all efforts toward justice. Cooper was laying the foundation for what would later be called "intersectionality" (Crenshaw, 1991) or the idea that identities, oppression, and histories are overlapping.

Other scholars have also identified the importance of describing, studying, and highlighting the interlocking systems of oppression that Black women experience (Davis, 1971; Jordan, 2015/1992). Deborah K. King (1988) described the "multiple jeopardy" experienced by Black women where their racial classification, sex, class, and other identities all have been institutionally exploited in the United States. Theorists of intersectionality, an offshoot of Black feminist thinking, particularly focused on the notion of intersecting and overlapping identities and oppressions (Cho et al., 2013; Crenshaw, 1991; McCall, 2005; Nash, 2008). Embedded in intersectionality is the elevation of Black women's histories and cultures, another important theme in Black feminist thinking (Collins, 1986).

Black feminist theory allowed me to consider how Black women are simultaneously racialized, gendered, classed (social class), and categorized by their physical/mental ability, religious identity, or sexual orientation. For example, through the idea of interlocking systems of oppression, one could ponder the capitalist economic structure (which encourages competition and individual gain) alongside the patriarchal social structure (that privileges men over women). Then, these structures could be reflected alongside the White supremacist structure, which has privileged and does privilege White people over many groups of Black and Brown people (Kendi, 2016; Leonardo, 2013).

Dialogue as a way to assess knowledge claims: Communication is central to knowledge creation, dissemination, and to social change (Collins, 2000/2009). Dialogue[7] means talk can be used to challenge and "resist domination" (hooks, 1989, p. 131). Not only is dialogue deeply rooted in Afrocentric oral history traditions (Kochman, 1981; Sidran, 1971; Smitherman, 1977), it offers a path toward a new form of humanity in contemporary times, connecting to relationship building and maintenance.

Among Black women authors, dialogue among self and others has been used as a tool in poetry, political essays, empirical studies, and literature (e.g., Chisholm, 2010; Hansberry, 1959; Hurston, 1984; Ladson-Billings, 1994; Lorde, 2012; Sherrard, 2017; Stewart, 1831/1995; Woodson, 2014). Much of this writing transcends boundaries and offers a form of dialogue between the humanities, social sciences, literature, and empirical research, a hallmark of critical research (Bronner & Kellner, 1989; Cannella et al., 2016). Dialogue has also been employed to demonstrate the way in which

Black women have, for generations, viewed themselves as intimately linked to relationships with other human beings (Collins, 2000/2009).[8] Dialogue, a longstanding tradition among Black women knowledge creators, is a part of the *We*.

An ethic of caring for others: Collins (2000/2009) argued that care[9] must not be a claim toward blind communalism with no individuality. Care for oneself must be in tandem with care of others (Collins, 2000/2009). Using the metaphor of quilting (Brown, 1989), Collins described the way that individual pieces of the quilt are an enrichment of the entire quilt. Care[10] is about empathy, compassion, listening, and attentiveness to self-expression. Care is assumed to be a relational act, centered on interactions between people who are in some type of community. Care was often present in the women's depictions of the *Chosen We*.

The notion of love or care must not be subordinating oneself to others and it should not supplant care/love of oneself. Some ideas of love or care are presented in gendered ways that assume that women should love and care for others above and beyond the care that they offer themselves, exemplified by the Black superwoman ideal where one is meant to be strong and typified by caring for others even to one's own detriment (Woods-Giscombé, 2010). Dialogue, emotions, and accountability all come together as part of knowledge. For Collins (2000/2009) accountability and personal responsibility are one of the ways that the notion of love and care can be liberatory.

Care in the process of working with Black women means that I consistently put the women's ideas and comfort ahead of the research itself. For example, while I did eventually collect 105 oral histories across five metropolitan areas, the stories in this book hardly cover the number of trips or conversations that I collected over a dozen years. There were dozens of times where I sat down with Black women and they opted not to have me include the conversation as an oral history in the book. In these instances, we had a lovely conversation and sometimes created a lasting relationship but never recorded our conversations as interviews. Sometimes these conversations led to other people being involved in the project and sometimes they did not. The relationships I created, both those recorded in this book and those that went unrecorded still shaped my thinking and approach. My hope is that these conversations were positive for the women involved too.

An ethic of personal responsibility: Action is important within critique of society. There is no room for one to make claims toward equity without living those claims in one's life (Collins, 2000/2009). There would be no such thing as a value-neutral or objective set of knowledge claims because values would already be embedded in the claims. Many Black feminist thinkers have echoed the importance of Black women in the struggle for racial justice (Jones, 1949/1995; Murray, 1970/1995). Not only is personal responsibility a claim to personal ethics, but there is an inherent claim to care for oneself.[11]

Black women as agents of knowledge: Black women have the authority as agents of knowledge[12] and must be centered as the purveyors, generators, and disseminators of knowledge (Collins, 2000/2009). Writing with and about Black women is knowledge creation in this case. Therefore, I cannot set aside Black feminist thinking and epistemology even though I am not personally a Black woman. The oral histories that represent the *We* in this book are a new form of knowledge as Black women tell, gather, and disseminate their experience-as-knowledge.

Black feminist thinking and epistemology will lead to different ends than would other ways of knowing, according to hooks (2000). Hegemony, the social, political, economic, cultural, or ideological influence of one group as dominant over another, could be shifted by a new way of knowing from the minds of Black women. According to hooks (2000), in starting from a different set of experiences and knowledge(s), Black women have the power to reshape the power structure altogether.

hooks maintained the importance of collective, shared responsibility in this reshaping of power that can come from Black feminist thought: "The formation of a liberatory feminist theory and praxis is a collective responsibility, one that must be shared" (p. 17). While hooks (2000) clearly linked feminist theory and liberation to a collective responsibility, she rejected what she called the "model of Sisterhood created by bourgeois women's liberationists" (p. 45). By this, she meant that many White feminists used a notion of "sisterhood" that was dependent on collective victimization, using this victimization to bond women together. hooks maintained that many strong, assertive, self-initiated women were left out of the feminist movement and the bonding that resulted from it. But hooks went further to claim that in identifying as "victims," White women abdicated their shared responsibility for continuing to maintain racist, classist, patriarchal structures (see also McRae, 2018). Instead of a reliance on victimization as the source of bonding, hooks called for defining one's terms. Rather than building "sisterhood" out of an identity that is dependent on victimization and oppression, hooks asserted, "We can be sisters united by shared interests and beliefs, united in our appreciation for diversity, united in our struggle to end sexist oppression, united in political solidarity" (p. 67). hooks called for solidarity for the cause of equity and the fight for justice. It is a *We* that is built not out of common oppression but a keen understanding of the way in which all people are in the fight for the same justice.

Many Black feminist authors have asserted that in discussions about race there is often an implicit assumption that the focus is on men (i.e., Black men), while in discussions about gender or sex there is an assumption that the emphasis is on White women (Collins, 2000/2009; Cooper, 1988/1892; Davis, 1971; King, 1988; Lorde, 2012). Ultimately, Black women are not highlighted in either discussion, and this has serious consequences for the way that Black women are studied and the way that their challenges and success are understood (Ladner, 1986; Moses, 1989; Winkle-Wagner, 2015). Black feminists have long asserted the need for Black women to be able to self-define and self-value for this very reason (e.g., Anna Julia Cooper, 1988/1892; Patricia Hill Collins, 2002; Angela Davis, 1971; Claudia Jones, 1949; Audre Lorde, 2012). Without self-definition, Black women are often framed in ways that may not connect with their experiences.

Collins (1986) called for the elevation of Black women's cultures and histories. One effort to value this culture and history is to consider entirely different ways of knowing, such as the knowledge that stems from emotion. Poet, activist, and Black feminist theorist Audre Lorde (2012) initiated a different kind of theory in precisely this way, claiming, "The master's tools will never dismantle the master's house" (p. 112). She continued, "They may allow us temporarily to beat him at his own game, but they will never enable us to bring about genuine change" (p. 112). Interrogating the White male philosophical tradition in her late 1970s essay entitled "Poetry Is Not a Luxury," Lorde argued for the inclusion of emotion alongside rationale thought (p. 38): "The White fathers told us: I think, therefore I am. The Black mother within each of us—the poet—whispers in our dreams: I feel, therefore I can be free. Poetry coins the language to express and charter this revolutionary demand, the implantation of that freedom." Lorde continued to explain why the inclusion of emotion, and writing such as poetry, were particularly important for Black women:

> Women have survived. As poets. And there are no new pains. We have felt them all already. We have hidden that fact in the same place where we have hidden our power. They surface in our dreams, and it is our dreams that point the way to freedom. Those dreams are made realizable through our poems

that give us the strength and courage to see, to feel, to speak, and to dare. For there are no new ideas. There are only new ways of making them felt . . .

Through her claims that women have already felt all the possible pain in this world, Lorde made clear that it is a new way of thinking, being, writing, and "daring" that must be introduced in order to fully explain Black women's lives. Lorde argued for the inclusion of affect, of emotion, in our thinking about Black women. Feeling—alongside thinking—must be part of the story.

In this book, Black women's voices, ideas, thinking, and experiences are elevated in ways that are consistent with how Black women define and describe themselves, even to the point where some have coauthored their own histories. Additionally, if a woman took issue with a way she was being represented, I always went with her assertion of self over my own analysis. Self-definition and self-valuation ideas provide a powerful way to check the authority and credibility of my work. Does the work elevate Black women's wisdom, voices, and experiences? Or do I elevate my own voice as a White woman too much (appendix A)? These are questions that I can ask of my own work and that others can ask of me as they read, and it is a way to use Black feminist theorizing as a validation tool.

Finally, rather than continually comparing Black women to other groups as has been done in much of the research about them (see Winkle-Wagner, 2015), the idea of centering Black women and their lives means that Black women can be the center and sole group within a study about them. Additionally, this idea of the importance of Black women as agents of knowledge suggests that research and writers who work with Black women must also take care to understand the cultural norms from which Black women historically and contemporarily have arisen. That is, it would not be enough to simply hear the stories of Black women without putting those stories in the context of larger structural, social, and cultural norms.

What Is Black Feminist Thinking Doing in a White Writer's Mind?

Black feminist thought is theorized by and for Black women (Collins, 1986, 2000/2009). This line of thinking is applied directly to Black women's lives, bodies, histories, and futures and many of the top thinkers assert that the purpose of this work is to elevate Black women. Some Black feminist thinkers maintain that this kind of theorizing should only be produced by and for Black women. I meet this as a conundrum in my own work because I am a White woman (appendix A).

My work is centered on Black women's lives and experiences (Kelly & Winkle-Wagner, 2017; Kennedy & Winkle-Wagner, 2014; Patton & Winkle-Wagner, 2012; Winkle-Wagner, 2008, 2009a, 2009b, 2010, 2015). For over a decade, I decided not to engage Black feminist theories because I worried that I might be perpetrating theories that were not really by or *for* me. I gravitated toward critical theories that helped to reveal oppression and possible remedies to oppressive forces such as those put forth by Habermas (1984, 1987). Yet the critical theories that I employed were largely written by White men (i.e., Habermas) and lacked in-depth treatments of race and racism (Winkle-Wagner, 2009a). Appropriately, my early work was criticized for not contending with Black feminist thinking (Chambers, 2011; Tyson, 2010).

Even when my work was critiqued for the absence of Black feminist theories, I viewed them with much trepidation. They were not *for, about, or by me.* That fact remains. *Black feminist thought is not about me.* Black feminist theorizing should not be authored by me either—*I do not wish to be cited as a "Black feminist thinker."*

In the end, how can I write with and about Black women's lives without centering the theories that bring those lives into focus? I chose Black feminist thought because it is the theorizing that *best captures the lives of the women whose stories are highlighted in this book.* I chose Black feminist thought because it is one of the few philosophical traditions that truly *centers Black women.* Black feminist thinking centers Black women and their experiences in the writing and analysis (Collins, 2000/2009; Dill, 1979; Hull et al., 1982). Additionally, Black feminist thought uncovers the simultaneity or intersection of oppression related to race, class, gender, or other categories (Collins, 2000/2009; hooks, 2000). Black feminist thinking offers a challenge to those who are working closely with Black women in their research. For my own writing and research, I use these ideas to think about the credibility and authenticity of my work, particularly as a White woman (appendix A; appendix C for other publications from the project).

To the *Chosen We*

The 105 Black women in this book were manifold. They were teachers, professors, chemists, politicians, artists, consultants, social workers, engineers, journalists, biologists, mothers, grandmothers, and leaders in business. They had written books, memoirs, manifestos, reports, grants, brochures, movie scripts, poems, and stories. Some women marched alongside Martin Luther King Jr. or Malcolm X. Some identified as Black Panthers. Some were members of elite Black social organizations like the Links, Jack and Jill, and the Urban League. The women were Christian, Muslim, atheist, agnostic, and spiritual without a religious affiliation. While many women identified as Democrats, some were avid Republicans or registered Independents. They were straight, lesbian, bisexual, or questioning their sexuality. While the women in this study represented multiple, complex lives, they shared an important commonality that connected their stories: They were all Black women who grew up and made their lives in the US, a place that constantly made salient their race, gender, class, and difference. While some of them knew one another, and some did not, there were startling similarities in their stories, even amid the unique elements of their varied lives. Not only have many of these similarities been ignored by scholars and by popular media but Black women's ways of knowing (Collins, 2000/2009) have been silenced in broader society. I attempt to shed light on Black feminist epistemology because many of the women in this book described their experiences in ways that resonated with Black feminist ideas.

What follows is a story of adversity, resistance, and triumph. It is at once a contemporary story and one that is part of the legacy of prior generations of Black women. There is a thread that runs through the oral histories in this book that connects them to the larger quilt that is the experience of being a Black woman in the United States. Countless times, a contemporary experience evokes the collective memory and history of Black and African American women for generations. As the primary narrator and author of the book, I attempt to weave the thread that connects the women in this book to one another and to Black feminist writers and Black women who are their contemporaries and who came before them. *The Chosen We*, as a whole, chronicles, as Audre Lorde (2012) so brilliantly put it, "the possibilities of support and connection for which we all yearn, and about which we dream so often" (p. 152).

Chapter 2

From the Unchosen Me to the Chosen We

Black Women Elevating Black Women

> I am of strong opinion that the day on which we unite heart and soul, and turn our attention to the knowledge and improvement, that day the hissing and reproach among the nations of the earth against us will cease. . . . It is of no use for us to sit with our hands folded, hanging our heads like bulrushes, lamenting our wretched condition; but let us make a mighty effort, and arise, and if no one will promote or respect us, let us promote and respect ourselves.
>
> —Maria Miller Stewart, 1832, lecture delivered at the African American Female Intelligence Society in Boston

Black feminist thinkers like Maria Miller Stewart (1832/1987) asserted that society had abdicated responsibility for and respect of Black women. As evidenced in this book, Black women have been successful, both within and outside of education, in supporting, leading, and lifting one another up even amid the societal void of support for Black women. As such, Black women were and are the unsung sheroes for each other, and for their families, communities, schools, churches, social movements, and academic institutions.

Black women still carry a heavy load in the uplifting of their communities and in their own liberation in the absence of support from other groups (Jones, 2009). Black and White women's relationships in the United States are fraught and burdened with a long history of conflict and competition (Dace, 2012; Patton & Winkle-Wagner, 2012). White women perpetuated enslavement (Ware, 2015), led the fight *against* racial integration in schools, and deliberately worked so that Black children were framed as deficient within mainstream school curriculums and textbooks (McRae, 2018). Even within the feminist movement, White women opted to fight for their own liberation to the exclusion or to the deliberate sub-jugation of Black women (Frankenberg, 1993; McRae, 2018; Ware, 2015).

As a White woman, the history between Black and White women entered before me and traveled with me as I journeyed across the country sitting in offices, living rooms, coffee shops, classrooms, and restaurants with the Black women (Patton & Winkle-Wagner, 2012).[1] To pretend it was not there would be to reinforce the very patterns I wanted to break. We met this history together as we entered a dialogue together. Sometimes we were able to transcend this history and create trust, and other times we just let that history sit in the room with us as a realistic reminder of the difficulties we would have in forming a relationship.

When I met Patrice Kenyatta in her office in the Atlanta area, she had been living there for a handful of years and was working on a PhD in a nearby institution. Patrice had identified a national organization of Black women in which she felt at home. She had raised three Black chil-dren who were charting their own paths. Patrice had been able to craft meaning and healing from some of her negative experiences by creating a Pan-African Institute to support Black women from all backgrounds.

When we shook hands, I could tell that she was eyeing me warily. She knew I would be White because I had asked the mutual acquaintance who introduced us to make that clear. As I sat down, Patrice looked at me squarely and asked, "So, why should I talk to *you* about my life?" I looked back at her and said, "Well, you may not want to. That is completely okay." She asked again, "Why should I trust you with my experience as a Black woman?" Patrice's question, her calling out the baggage we brought into the room, led us to have a long and honest conversation about the work that I was doing. I told Patrice that every moment that I am doing these interviews is a chance for me to either earn or betray the trust of the people I am interviewing. I admitted that my credibility is always vulnerable, and that this vulnerability makes me work very hard to meet my obligation to do well by and with the people with whom I work. I was honest about my views of times when White women were not on the right side of justice and perpetrated violence against Black women. White women have often gotten it wrong. I confided that while White women took hold of the feminist movement and left Black women out, it is my view that Black women would not have done the same. As I became more vulnerable to Patrice, I felt the suspicion and mistrust giving way to a bit of shared space and understanding. After nearly 45 minutes of talking, which included many questions that Patrice had prepared for me, she was ready to begin telling me her story. The starting point with Patrice was a common starting point in many interviews. We often had to meet the baggage between Black and White women before we could move forward into sharing narratives of our lives (Patton & Winkle-Wagner, 2012).

As the other oral histories in this book confirm, Black women have always known that their liberation is tied to one another. Patrice Kenyatta's life illustrates the transition from imposed individual (*Me*) identities to those that are *chosen* and community-oriented (*We*) identities. In college she felt immense pressure to meet the expectations, stereotypes, and identity impositions that others had for her (*Unchosen Me* pressures) (Winkle-Wagner, 2009a). She found community with other Black women, moving toward the *Chosen We*, and feeling as if she was able to choose her *self*, her way of being Black, and her idea of womanhood. This chapter offers a theoretical basis for the *Chosen We*, which is a way to maintain an individual sense of self (*Me*) alongside a collectivist, empowering group identity (*We*).

From Feeling *Unchosen* to Choosing a *We*:
Patrice Kenyatta's Story

Patrice Kenyatta's oral history was one of pain, isolation, and eventual redemption as she negotiated Blackness, class, and gender. In many ways her identity was imposed on her during college. She found herself having to fight against a Black identity that her peers assumed of her. As a child of an affluent Black family, Patrice found her class status difficult to negotiate in college because of the stereotypical assumption that if she was Black, she must also be from a low-income background. She also didn't fit with White affluent peers.

In the middle of the civil rights movement, Patrice transferred from the small private women's college where she began her postsecondary education, attending Immaculate Heart College[2] in Los Angeles, a private Catholic liberal arts college. While Patrice graduated from Immaculate Heart with a major in the humanities in the late 1960s, she also took courses at Loyola University and the University of California, Los Angeles. Later, she earned a master's degree in social sciences from Lipscomb University in Nashville, Tennessee. Patrice's undergraduate years coincided with a raging battle for Black humanity, and she was met with the growing Black Nationalist movements in the United States.

A Family of "Lawyers and Judges [and Activists] for Generations"

Patrice Kenyatta grew up as a debutante in California, mingling with Los Angeles's most affluent and accomplished African American families. Her mother had a PhD, and her father earned a JD. Class and status were big issues for Patrice throughout her educational experiences. "I come from lawyers and judges for generations, which is unusual. My grandmother was a judge. My grandfather and my father were civil rights attorneys. My mother's brother was an attorney." Patrice's family history is a remarkable story of 1950s and 1960s Black lawyers and judges who led the civil rights movement (Mack, 2012). Her family was part of Black migration from southern to northern states and cities on the West Coast where millions of Black people moved from southern states in which oppressive Jim Crow laws limited social mobility or opportunity and permitted state-sponsored racism, brutality, and hostility (Wilkerson, 2010). Some of those who migrated to LA became upper-class Black families who participated in a set of carefully crafted social events, organizations, and education (Graham, 2000; Wilkerson, 2010). Patrice had some resistance to officially joining some of the organizations, unsure of some of the politics within them.

> Back in the day, the way I grew up, you had to be in the AKA sorority. You had to be presented as a debutante by the Links organization, and that's only by invitation. You had to be in the Jack and Jill Club. I didn't [join AKA] and I still do not want to. It wasn't at Immaculate Heart. My mother was an AKA, my grandmother was a national officer, my other grandmother was a national officer. Growing up you were in Jack and Jill up until you finish high school. And Links is when you're 17, you're presented. I wasn't in Links. I was presented by Links members. But I never wanted to join Links. It is a very contentious group. Most of the people I know who are in it are dropping out. There's a lot of political stuff inside the organization. I'm just not interested in all of that. No.

I came from a very political family. My father was an activist and worked for Dr. King. So, I was conscious. But the movement, so to speak, had changed a lot when my generation got involved. My mother was traveling and doing all kinds of things. My grandfather was head of the Urban League for 25 years in [a mid-South city] during the heyday of the Urban League and he was very well known for being a community organizer. He had a radio show about politics, a beautiful booming voice. He was eloquent like Martin Luther King. I have been active. I was a board member for years in a couple of cities with the Urban League and the NAACP.

The social groups Patrice mentioned—sororities, the Links, and Jack and Jill—were created to provide communities, which I call *Chosen We* communities, to affluent Black families and their children (Graham, 2000). These groups were chosen in that one can opt whether to join if invited or in a legacy with family already involved. Patrice ultimately chose not to participate in these groups, but she still felt an obligation to be a part of a larger community of Black people.

Patrice entered college armed with a history of activism, leadership, validation, and self-love. But Patrice entered PWIs that did not have the same values or history. She described the way that her family, particularly her father, taught her self-love and validation of her Blackness. Patrice also took seriously her responsibility to uphold her family reputation, which she continued to do with her grandchildren. Patrice entered a firestorm of racial unrest in college—not of her choosing.

"Arm Yourself and Prepare for a Revolution" and Get a Degree

The first chapter is arriving at Bennington College where I went freshman year before I went to Immaculate Heart. I was a fish out of water. It was a great school, but I was not prepared for a school of 350 women where seven were African American. None of the 350 had been exposed to African American people. Very, very affluent community, all women, and boys from our brother school, who had never been around African

American people. So, the race issue, it was a huge elephant in the room for everyone. Plus, this was an environment that considered itself very progressive and liberal. There were lots of contradictions and it was very difficult for those of us who came from a different background. I handled it for a year and couldn't wait to get out. I left and came back home to LA.

I had been exposed to high culture. I came from a very cultured family, and I was a classical pianist at an early age and danced and did a lot of things. But this was a whole new ball game. I was not prepared, and I was on the defensive. I was justifying, proving, validating myself as best I could. I was warding off constant sexual advances from girls and boys. I felt very alone.

Even the other African American girls, the other six, for the most part, had not come from the degree of privilege I had. They were "affirmative action" kids. They were sort of there on that basis, they were being given an opportunity. So, there was tension between us. We had our own hierarchies and class issues and competitions that made another little culture group. That has happened everywhere I've been in school.

I remember a [White] boy told me when I was at Bennington, he was a boy from [a nearby college] who came over to campus. He said, "I want to take you out, I want to take you home." He was from Boston. "But I can only take you in the kitchen and pretend you're the new maid." He told me that and laughed and his friends laughed. I was so hurt. Later, I got angry. But I was so wounded and ashamed. I felt like he had just dumped poop all over me. It was humiliating. But being who I am now, I would handle it very differently. There was [no support] at Bennington.

Bennington College was a place of isolation, racism, and sexism for Patrice. While she felt overwhelmed with the wealth and class privilege of other White students, she also did not connect well with her Black peers. The many impositions on who Patrice could be at Bennington closely align with the idea of the *Unchosen Me* from my earlier work, a designation used to describe Black women who had a difficult time asserting their unique identities at predominantly White institutions (PWIs). Through a year-long ethnographic study during which I met with young Black women in small groups that they called "sister circles," I learned that they did not experience a sense of choice when it came to their identity on a White campus (Winkle-Wagner, 2009a). Rather, the women described feeling pushed and pulled between poles of identity. Some women described constantly negotiating the possibility that they might be "too White" to fit in with their Black peers because of the way that they dressed, the music that they liked, or how they spoke or thought. Those same women explained that if they altered their behavior too much to represent what seemed to be acceptable as "Blackness," they might be viewed as "too Black" by their White peers and not fit with the majority groups (i.e., White students) of the campus.

The young Black women (ages 18–22) in *The Unchosen Me* ultimately felt as if they constantly had to change their behavior, appearance, preferences in music/art/activities, speech patterns, or the way they thought in order to fit between the poles of identity that were prescribed to them on campus. This notion of feeling pushed and pulled between dichotomous ideas of race also played out with gender. The women felt they could either be a "good woman" that was primarily passive, quiet, and indecisive; or they could be a "bad woman" that was overly aggressive or loud (Winkle-Wagner, 2008, 2009a). Of course, as the women experienced the tensions between identity poles, they seldom felt as if they had the opportunity to just *be* whoever they were becoming or to act, think, appear, or to figure out their tastes in music, clothes, art, or popular culture (Winkle-Wagner et al., 2018). I called this lack of identity choice the *Unchosen Me* (Winkle-Wagner, 2009a, 2009b).

Patrice eventually transferred to Immaculate Heart College, which was initiated in 1916 by nuns who were part of a Spanish order (Caspary, 2003). The nuns were so politically progressive that they seceded from Spain and began a Californian order. In the 1970s, the Immaculate Heart Community became independent and separated from the Catholic Church in order to embrace people of multiple faiths, sexual orientations, and backgrounds (Caspary, 2003).[3] From the Immaculate Heart Community came a form of humanistic psychology that embraced justice in a way that could also be secular (Kugelmann, 2005). The nuns were activist against the Vietnam War, and they were connected to priests who had a long history of social activism too (Coy, 1988).

> We were very proud of the commitment to activism. I was in the middle of all of it. I started the first Black student organization [at Immaculate Heart]. That was taking things a little far for the community. It's one thing to claim an identity of

"progressive liberal thought" and it's another to have to deal with a Black student organization on your campus. We were very passive, but we asked hard questions. We had forums and invited some of the more controversial political leaders in Los Angeles to come and speak, and actors and writers. I was very proud to be bringing the discourse to the campus. Outside of the campus, I was still a debutante bourgeois. On campus, I was the person pushing back and leading others to do the same. So, there were contradictions in my identity, according to those around me.

While the nuns at Immaculate Heart may have been progressive, this did not necessarily mean that the institution was completely open to the Black students' fight for equal rights.

I think in general, academic institutions want a kind of open balanced democratic discourse going on in their communities. In theory, this is what they want. But I don't think there really is a true commitment to seeing that people who come from different walks of life are heard and seen and that their needs are all met. Those people feel it. It came through loud and clear when I was at Immaculate Heart.

When I started the Black student organization, a major endowment was threatened to be withdrawn from the Sargent Shriver family, married to Eunice Kennedy,[4] because they thought automatically that if there was a Black student organization, we were going to break the new louver windows in the student union. One of the nuns quietly told me that. She thought it was absurd and she wanted me to know. I wasn't getting permission to do basic things, to have meetings and events and things.

While the Shriver and the Kennedy family both had strong civil rights ties, there was apparent discomfort in watching Black students standing up for their own rights. "[It was as if] we were going to tear up the campus. We're just a bunch of girls. I did cut my hair off and had an Afro, but I was still a debutante. I was still me. The organization continued but it didn't have any fire under it. We felt threatened."

Patrice began to find a *Chosen We* type of community of like-minded people in the Black student organization, which resonates with many of the examples of similar communities in part 2 of this book. These *Chosen We* communities offer a new sense of self that is deeply connected with others such that one begins to feel included, less isolated, and like they deeply belong. While Patrice gave and felt support in the group, she ultimately did not feel supported by her campus. It was almost as if, when she associated with the *Chosen We* community that she had built, the campus made it clear that she was not as welcome. She mentioned that she had changed her appearance to wear her hair naturally, suggesting that this was also a choice that was outside of the mainstream on her campus. Yet she still identified herself as a debutante representing her affluent background. The racial tensions did not stop with her Black student organization.

> I became homecoming queen at Loyola University in '67 when I was in undergrad at Immaculate Heart. Boys at Loyola dropped out [of Homecoming] in protest. They did not want a "Negro queen who did not represent American womanhood." That's a direct quote. It was very controversial then. I wasn't allowed to preside over my court. I wasn't allowed to be part of the ceremony where you give the crown. They came to my house a long distance from where the university was and demanded the crown and retrieved it from me. I was treated horribly. This is a community that claims to be a progressive liberal institution.

Immaculate Heart had a partnership with a nearby coeducational institution, Loyola University, to share a homecoming celebration. The Homecoming experience became a symbol of college for her relative to the race and class tensions she experienced. The Homecoming crown was a symbol of how, even after she built and associated with a *Chosen We* community in her Black student organization, she still received a loud message from her college that she could not represent her campus as their queen. It was not until decades later that the institution apologized. "Being Black in those years was always a major part of my identity. No one forgot it, I didn't forget it. I wasn't just a student ever. I represented people who were struggling in different ways in society, struggling politically, economically. I had to speak for people. I had an obligation. It was a heavy burden for someone who really wasn't prepared."

Patrice described the whole of her undergraduate college experience.

> That was the most difficult time in my life. I know now that I was suffering with severe depression. I didn't know what it was and there was no one to talk to about this. Black people don't talk about things like that. In those years, we did not go for therapy. I remember my mother had me talking to a nun at Immaculate Heart. Sister Violet, God bless her. She didn't know what to do with me. I just cried. I would be in class, and I would cry and run out of class and I couldn't explain it. I remember sitting on a hill overlooking the main road that would curve around the university just in tears. Still, I finished my work at Immaculate Heart.

Immaculate Heart was the location of contradictions for Patrice. It is not that surprising that Patrice suffered from depression during this time, although her mental health challenges were left untreated because of the stigma surrounding getting help.

After a tumultuous undergraduate experience, Patrice decided to go to graduate and then law school, which were also racially charged experiences. Patrice enrolled in a master's program at UCLA, but she left that program, in part because of the racial hostility she encountered but also because of the impositions on her identity as a Black woman (see also Winkle-Wagner, 2009a).

She then enrolled in law school at UCLA.

> This is 1971. UCLA had this new affirmative action program. So, if you wanted to come to UCLA law school, you could only come in as an affirmative action student. I'm the daughter of a practicing attorney, [a] well-known civil rights attorney, and the granddaughter of judges. Still, I had to come in as one of the people, lumped in with the people recruited from Watts, South Central LA, from gang life, from jail. They just pulled us and that was the only way you could be accepted.

Patrice's background led to tensions with her peers and the administrators that were difficult to manage.

I was accepted, I was a student, and my life was hell the whole time I was there.

When I got to UCLA, I was very proud of my work there. But I was disconnected from it, I wasn't invested. Law school was a very scary place, that whole experience. There was nowhere to go for help at home nor at the university. There was no therapy to be had. I understand better now, all these years later, I can see that there were class issues. There were economic differences that defined us that were exacerbated during the very aggressive political movement which was on the verge of real violence all the time. So, the question of where I stood was always a big issue. I had been this activist in two private colleges. I had brought the movement to these colleges, but it wasn't enough. I was still this, as we say, "bougie girl,"[5] this debutante girl who had traveled. I had lived abroad; my family had lived in Istanbul. I didn't fit anything. It was very lonely.

Amid her own struggles to fit into UCLA, Patrice was also confronted with the growing Black Nationalist movement. "The Black Panthers were a strong influence. All these organizations were trying to take over academic departments because grant money was coming in. And the murder at UCLA happened when I was a student." Alprentice "Bunchy" Carter was the founder of the Southern California Black Panther Party. He was shot in 1969, along with his compatriot in the Black Panthers, Johnny Huggins, by rival Black Nationalist group members from "Organization US" (Bloom & Martin, 2013). The rivalry between the Black Nationalist groups played out on the UCLA campus because the Panthers and Organization US supported different prospective candidates for the new Afro-American Studies Center.

I didn't finish [at UCLA]. They were starting the Black Studies Department or African American Studies Department. There was grant money pouring into UCLA and the Black Panthers wanted to control that and to be part of redesigning the culture at UCLA. They became very aggressive. My brother was [a leader] of the Black Student Alliance then, and he was very respected, conservative, but still very political. He was on a hit list to be murdered by the Black Panthers. He had the flu the day they did come and two of those Panthers were murdered.

There was a big shootout. My brother was to be killed that day and he survived and went into hiding for weeks. To this day, I don't know where he went. He would never say, all these years later, I had to deliver a weapon. My father's old German Luger gun from World War II I had in a shoebox. I took it on a bus to a pickup point where some of my brother's colleagues picked it up and took it. I took food, clothes, and stuff to my brother. We were terrified.

He was hiding for a while. It all quelled. The two Panthers were murdered. That calmed down their brethren and the tension subsided, and things went back to normal in time. But it was a very sobering experience to be going to class. We even had the National Guard on campus in full combat gear, guns, the whole thing. You're walking past them trying to get to your lecture.

Those were unusual times, very unusual times. But to be Black meant those National Guard soldiers were the enemy to us personally. We felt that at any point making the wrong move, something could go down. Then we had our political adversaries who were also Black like the Panthers. If you were not defining yourself as part of a grassroots movement and not actively sympathetic enough, meaning you weren't willing to arm yourself and prepare for revolution, and I wasn't, then you were a suspect. You're balancing all of these relationships in the context of an academic institution. Those were very interesting times. That was the 1960s, into the '70s.

I had a very hard time. I was very depressed, very suicidal. I tried to act on that and didn't have the courage but tried a lot. It was a difficult time. I can't blame it all on race, but it was a big factor, trying to navigate the challenges of life from the vantage point of, and through brown skin and trying to compete and distinguish myself and do well.

The loneliness, isolation, and separation were likely key reasons why Patrice did not leave UCLA with a law degree.

By the time Patrice and I spent the afternoon together, she was well into her PhD program and starting a Pan-African Scholars Institute to try to remedy some of the isolation she felt in college for future Black students. She had been married for a long time, had three children who had successfully attended Hampton University (an HBCU), Morehouse College (a private, men's HBCU), and Yale University (an Ivy League PWI). Later, she was divorced. Reflecting on all of her postsecondary educational experiences and how difficult they had been in terms of race and class, Patrice concluded, "Sometimes it's just hard to put your finger on this veil of separation. And we have to fight for our credibility. We have to fight for recognition." The "veil of separation" is a reference to Du Bois's (1903) idea of the "veil" that Black people in the United States live behind. Black people have historically been put behind the veil, because of the initiation of the United States as a colonized country built on the backs of enslaved people. Du Bois's veil assumes that African American people must know both what it means to be Black in America and what it means to be White. Du Bois calls the notion of grappling with Blackness and Whiteness simultaneously "double consciousness." The notion of having to deal with two ways of being at once can be difficult and even damaging for some people, as it certainly seemed to be for Patrice.

The veil is perhaps one reason why Black national organizations were created, as ways to support affluent Black families (Graham, 2000). One way that Patrice contemplated Blackness was through the national organizations in which her family had participated. Through her family history of participation in elite Black organizations such as Jack and Jill and the Links, these groups did not feel right to Patrice.

> I'm in one organization now I've been in about 25 years that is very selective and very unpretentious. But everybody in it is a very high achiever including the ex-mayor of Atlanta and people in politics and the arts who are from all kinds of backgrounds but they're all at the top of their game. It's called the National Smart Set. It's only 23 to 25 members in a chapter. Many cities have them. The group here is just fantastic. They're just amazing. They're so down to earth and so fun. They're like aunts and grandmas to me and daughters to me. We're very close. We take care of each other through divorces, deaths, whatever. It's not a social service group. It's purely social. We have our conclave coming up in October. We have a black-tie party, we play golf, we have a good time. They're world travelers, they're political leaders, they're just fascinating people. So that group is still solid gold. But there isn't much of that left in the Black community. The world has changed a lot.

Patrice's life and educational experiences led to the need for healing. As she began to create a unique space for herself, Patrice found a way to move beyond the imposed identities of the *Unchosen Me*, identities that nearly drove her to suicide, toward finding a community to which she deeply belongs, the *Chosen We*.

The Problem with Being *Unchosen*

The Unchosen Me (Winkle-Wagner, 2009a; Winkle-Wagner et al., 2018) offered a way to think about how Black women often experience pressures on their identity in higher education (impositions on ways they should act, think, or look). I was initially interested in how Black women described their identity within a PWI (Winkle-Wagner, 2008, 2009a, 2009b, 2010a, 2010b). The *Unchosen Me* idea blended theoretical ideas that are seldom combined such as the identity work of George Herbert Mead (1934) and Sheldon Stryker (1980) with the ideas of recognition from Hegel (1807/1952/1977). While I was working closely with Black women in the creation of these ideas, as a White woman, I propelled away from Black feminist thinking at that time because I thought I could not use those theories without somehow exploiting or perpetrating them. Yet the lack of incorporation of Black feminist theorizing in my work was an important critique (Chambers, 2011; Dàvila, 2012; Hernandez, 2010; Tyson, 2010) and one I have spent subsequent years attempting to remedy.

The Unchosen Me allowed for exploration of the aspects of identity that one experiences as outside of the realm of choice (Winkle-Wagner, 2009a). For example, one's sex, at least initially, is determined at birth, labeled as "male" or "female," even while some individuals never identify with the sex or gender identities they are assigned at birth. While some people may self-identify, at least in part, their gender (whether they express themselves as feminine or masculine or nonbinary, etc.), people still must contend with a lifetime of being associated with "male" or "female" and all the traditional stereotypes that come along with it. Depending on one's family and community, a girl may be taught that being a girl means being passive, pretty, submissive, caring (of others before herself), and sweet. If that girl is Black, she may also have to contend with hundreds of years of assumptions that she is a superwoman—that she must be resilient, strong, and that she can carry the weight of her family, community, and perhaps even the world, on her shoulders (Huddleston-Mattai, 1995; Leath, Jones,

& Butler-Barnes, 2022; Porter & Byrd, 2021; Reynolds-Dobbs et al., 2008; Wallace, 1990; Woods-Giscombé, 2010). Patrice invoked the metaphor of feeling as if she were fighting against the world.

Like one's sex (as biological) and gender (as an identity that is expressed as feminine/masculine/etc.), race is also largely *unchosen*, at least initially. When a child is born, they are grouped into a particular racial category, usually based on the phenotype (skin color) and the ascribed racial category(ies) of the parents. For instance, on the US certificate of live birth, there is a place to list the racial categories of the mother and the father.[6] While infants are not listed as a particular "race," the concept of race becomes real for the child as soon as they are born because of the categories listed for the child's parents. Without consent, the child is assumed to be a particular configuration of "race," and while the US birth certificate expanded the options for racial categories in 2003,[7] they still resonate with traditional color-coded racial categories of Black, White, Asian, or Native American. Thus, the *Unchosen Me* is a part of identity with which most people can relate, at least in part. Typically, there are limits to how much choice people feel they have in who they get to be in society.

I argued that the *Unchosen Me* brought together privilege, oppression, and choice to specify impositions on identity. In the study upon which the *Unchosen Me* was based (Winkle-Wagner, 2009a), the identity impositions for undergraduate Black women at a PWI came from multiple actors on campus and they were largely experienced as pressures to conform to preset notions of self, in many of the same ways that were mentioned by Patrice. The Black women in the study experienced pressures from both White peers and from other students of color to avoid being "too White" or "too Black." From faculty and staff, the women experienced a constant imposition that they would either be "spotlighted" and overly visible in the classroom (if they spoke out too much) or treated as "invisible" (if they did not speak out enough). From their families, peers, and campus faculty or staff, the women in *The Unchosen Me* also felt gender impositions to either be a "good woman" or a "bad woman" as described earlier. There were few interactions where the women did not feel identity pressure and where they could be "authentic" (Winkle-Wagner et al., 2018).

While the *Unchosen Me* articulated the lack of choice that Black women felt relative to their identity (the *Me*[8] part of self) on a predominantly White campus, I had a nagging worry that agency was not central in the concept. The idea that Black women were somehow unable to resist identity impositions continued to bother me, not only because it painted a sad portrait of education within PWIs, but also because I kept wondering if I had somehow misinterpreted the women and the data. I went back to the data and reanalyzed it, looking for resistance, times when the women pushed back on the impositions that they described. Aside from some tacit claims that were made in the sister circle groups, resistance and agency were behaviors I could not find in my data, other than the inference toward needing community within the sister circle groups. That is, when I had initially started the data collection for *The Unchosen Me*, I had intended for the focus groups to last for maybe one or two meetings. Some of the groups became very bonded and continued to want to meet for over a year, and the women called their groups "sister circles," inferring a need for familial connection and community with one another.

I initiated numerous extended conversations with colleagues who work closely with Black women as colleagues or students, and who conduct research on Black women in college (Chambers, 2011; Commodore et al., 2018; Kelly et al., 2019; Kennedy & Winkle-Wagner, 2014; Patton & Croom, 2017; Patton & Haynes, 2018; Patton & Winkle-Wagner, 2012; Porter & Byrd, 2021; Porter & Dean, 2015; Stewart, 2008; Watt, 2006; West et al., 2016; Willie, 2003). I surmised that one reason for the lack of direct agency and resistance in *The Unchosen Me* was because the women were very young during the study. The oldest woman in the study was 22, and the bulk were between the ages of 18 and 21. In this book, I turned to older women to explicitly explore the use of agency as it is more likely that as older women they would have had more time to reflect on their lives and the agency they activated at specific moments.

Ultimately, as I transitioned to the study of what became *The Chosen We*, I began to ask: What if, by continuing to emphasize the individual self (the *Me*), we are putting too much focus on the parts (through individuals) and never realizing the whole? Would a better way to understand the *whole* be to understand how one views oneself as intimately and inextricably linked to others, as was suggested in the sister circles? I had to first engage a process of understanding individual selves in *The Unchosen Me* to begin to understand the bigger *whole* of the *We*. The *We* has been there all along, and people have referred to it in collectivist writings as I show later—but the ability to process and discuss with others the idea of a *We* might be something that comes with age.

In this book, I inquire whether the emphasis on individualistic notions of identity, the predominant vantage point of most sociologists, psychologists, and philosophers, have obscured a tradition of viewing oneself as a collectivity alongside others. I certainly have considered identity as relatively individualistic in my own work too. For example, in my book *The Unchosen Me*, while I was studying Black women who were in community with one another in sister circle groups that met on a biweekly basis, the way that I explored their identities was still about the individual (Winkle-Wagner, 2009a). One reason for using Black feminist thinking in this book is that thinkers like Anna Julia Cooper (1988/1892), Patricia Hill Collins (2002/2009), bell hooks (2000), and many more, offer a collective angle of identity where one's identities are viewed in community with others, or where one's identities are impossible to untangle from one's communities. As such, by using Black feminist theorizing here, I am turning to ideas, like the *We*, that were there all along, even when they were ignored by canonical (mainstream, dominant) scholarship and theorizing (Patton & Haynes, 2018).

The Chosen We: Theorizing the Simultaneity of Collective and Individual Identities

The theoretical idea of the *Chosen We* is a way to consider how collective identities are cultivated alongside a strong and stable sense of individual identity. Individual identity has been the topic of a vast body of scholarship in social psychology. Arguably, the field of psychology centers the idea of generalizable individual identity development (Hogg et al., 1995; Stets & Burke, 2000; Stryker & Burke, 2000; Winkle-Wagner, 2012). Though sociological claims about identity develop from the social structure, they still emphasize the way in which individuals put together their sense of self (Hogg et al., 1995; Stets & Burke, 2000; Stryker & Burke, 2000; Winkle-Wagner, 2012). Research in social psychology (Stryker & Burke, 2000; Tajfel, 1974) and political theory (Gutmann, 2009)[9] has tried to point out the possibility of group identities and some authors even refer to a We (Banks, 2014; Dawes et al., 1988; Dovidio et al., 2008). Much of the work on group identity contemplates ideas like in-groups and out-groups (Dovidio, & Gaertner, 2000; Dovidio et al., 2003; Tajfel, 1974; Theiss-Morse, 2009), attempting to carve out how people find belonging, if they do. Some scholarship contemplates collective identity and how these group identities relate to self-representation and action (Ashmore et al., 2004; Brewer & Gardner, 1996) or social movements (Polletta, &

Jasper, 2001). Others consider group identity or collective identity relative to political behavior or action (Gutmann, 2009; Schlesinger, 1991; Simon & Klandermans, 2001).

The *We* is so comprehensive that it encapsulates a way of being in and of itself.[10] Or, the *We* could be a way of being that is intimately linked to one's individual identity (*Me*) without supplanting that individuality. In other words, as is evidenced in this book, the *We* can thrive alongside and not in place of the *Me*, or one's individual sense of self. While there are many treatments of collective or group identities, there remain many questions as to how these identities function over time and influence people's larger sense of self, particularly in college. Some of the work on collective identities takes a "colorblind" approach, avoiding the discussion of race and racial group belonging altogether, which leads to further racial hostility and discrimination (Dovidio et al., 2016). There is a limited understanding as to how group identity and collectivism function in everyday relationships among communities of color, for example. Yet, there is a body of research on Africanist and Afrocentric traditions that considers these questions (Bell, 2002). The two bodies of research often do not come into dialogue with one another as I am attempting to do here.

The *We* is a pathway to understanding a form of collective identity. Collective identity is part and parcel to many diverse cultural traditions. The idea of communalism permeates many of the unique African traditions across the 54 countries and hundreds of distinct groups and languages on the immense continent (Henrich et al., 2010; Bell, 2002; Imbo, 1998; Winkle-Wagner, 2006). In some of these indigenous ideas of communalism within the continent of Africa, the group is prioritized over the individual in a way that does not necessarily impede one's individuality (Bell, 2002; Senghor, 1998) but in a way that one clearly becomes an individual within a tightly woven community. There are examples of these collective identities from Ghana (Wiredu, 1996) down to Sub-Saharan countries like Namibia or Botswana (Winkle-Wagner, 2006; Menkiti, 1984).[11]

While there are examples of multiple groups in African nations who have contemplated collective identities, Bell (2002) cautions against what he calls "unamism," or the idea that all people from a group have a singular set of thoughts, voices, or experiences (p. 60). That is, even within traditions that are more collectivist, there are still varied and dynamic experiences among people within those groups. Collective identities as they are theorized in Afrocentric or Africanist scholarship are sometimes considered in opposition to other identities. As Appiah's (1992) theorizing suggests where there is still an element of inclusion and exclusion (alive vs. dead; part of the group vs. not part of the group; Native African vs. born outside of an African country; etc.) even when there is a sense of collectivism.

Modernist thinking, stemming out of scholarly, White, male minds of Western Europe and well-known philosophers like Hegel (1807/1952/1977),[12] Heidegger (1953/1927),[26] and Habermas (1984, 1987), was afforded credit for developing the thinking of contemporary times, the basis upon which was built my own initial theoretical understanding of critical theory. Some of these thinkers also spoke to a shared social experience that could become part of people's identities, such as a collective consciousness (Durkheim 1893/1984; 1895/1964; 1897/1951), collective essence in Marx (Sabia, 1988), and collective identity (Weber, 1922/1978). While Black feminist thinking was ignored by many and completely pushed aside by still others (Guy-Sheftall, 1995), the thinking of theorists such as Marx, Weber, Durkheim, Hegel, and Heidegger[13] became canonized, held up as sacred, evolved, and settled into the collective minds of Western nations and into the "canon" (or body of knowledge deemed most important) of many academic disciplines (Luker, 2009). I have deliberately, and as often as possible, moved much of the thought of these White men theorists into notes and appendices to flip this trend. Here, I am placing Black feminist writers at the forefront to show ideas that were born alongside those that became canonized (Luker, 2009), even if they were ignored at the time.

I chose to elevate Black feminist epistemology (Collins, 2000/2009), or ways of knowing, while contemplating how to identify the way in which the *We* emerged in this analysis. In so doing, it should be clear that while it is not always expressly articulated, the *We* is always and already connected to historical and cultural notions of the concept, many of which were identified in Black feminist theorizing. As Black feminist thinker Gloria Joseph (1988) maintained, history influences all of humanity. For many Black feminist theorists, connecting history to contemporary times is a way to consider the parts (e.g., individuals) and a way to understand a larger whole (e.g., a group or larger social structure) (Collins, 2000/2009).[14]

The *We*, as I am considering it here, is centrally concerned with the continual interplay between the "whole" and the "parts." And it resonates with some Hegelian (1807/1952/1977) ideas in that way.[15] I use this idea in connection with a Black feminist epistemology (Collins, 2000/2009) as a rationale for the theoretical importance of studying a specific group of people, Black women in this case, and their relationship to the *We*, or the idea that the individual cannot be separated from a larger group, or from those who came before, one's ancestors, lineage, or history (Collins, 1986, 2002/2009; hooks, 2000; Lorde, 2012). To understand identities, I draw on and critique Mead's (1934) ideas of the development of self. I mention it briefly here as a way to offer the history of my own thinking that led to the *Chosen We*.

The *Me* Part of Identities and How They Relate to the *We*

My idea of *The Unchosen Me* (Winkle-Wagner, 2009a) specified *Me* parts of identities that were not entirely chosen by an individual. The idea of the *Me*, or the notion of individual identity that I am using here, is an adaptation of the theory of the self-initiated by George Herbert Mead's (1934) behaviorist,[16] American pragmatist philosophy. While I move beyond his way of constructing knowledge in my own scholarship, Mead's specification of the multifaceted nature of identities and how they relate to actions is useful here. Put simply, the *Me* is the location of objectified identities, parts of self that one develops from an understanding of what is recognizable/acceptable within a given social context.[17]

Mead's (1934) theory of the self is comprised of an *I* and a *Me* part of self. The *I* part of self can be classified best as pure subjectivity (i.e., the way one surprises oneself, the reflective, less tangible part of oneself) and it is a location of volition and agency. The *I* part of self is in continual dialogue with an objectified part of self that is often associated with the roles that people take, called the *Me*. While the *I* part of self is important to consider relative to reflection, agency, and choice, it is nearly impossible to empirically study because studying it would be a process of objectification and the idea of the *I* is not objectifiable (as soon as the *I* is objectified, it would become a *Me*). The *I* part of self reflects on whether one fits within a *We* community too. I am using the *Me*, the objectified idea of identities that is more suited for empirical study to think about individual identities and how those identities develop out of and are ultimately dependent on social contexts. The *Me* initiates through social interaction and reflects socialized roles. One has many *Me* parts of self, reflective of the roles one may take on in various social settings.[18]

A compilation of *Me* identities, and the compilation of the attitudes of those *Me* identities, becomes what Mead called the "generalized other."[19] One takes the "generalized other" into oneself as a sort of socially constructed puppeteer for one's possible actions, and for one's possible ways of being in the world. For instance, if one were involved in multiple social groups, the "generalized other" would be constituted of the collectivity of the norms of all those groups put together. The generalized other assumes that one's identities are at least in some ways, conformist, an attempt to be an individual amid the community.[20] In my prior work (Winkle-Wagner, 2009a), I used the Hegelian ideas of recognition desires for uniqueness and conformity alongside Mead's generalized other to understand both the need for individuality and community.[21] Mead's notion of community is not theorized relative to how an individual might fit into that community. Rather, the notion of community is theorized more to explain the possibilities and norms that are or are not present in a particular group.

While Mead presented the generalized other as a singular accumulation of social roles, norms, and possibilities, I argue that this is one of the limitations of his initial theorizing. For many people, there are likely to be multiple generalized others, multiple accumulated social norms/roles/responsibilities that may or may not connect well. There could be serious and important ways in which generalized others conflict. For instance, a Black person on a predominantly White college campus may simultaneously experience the norms of Blackness and that generalized other alongside the often oppressive and suffocating norms of Whiteness in the predominantly White campus space.

In this book, I adapt Mead's (1934) ideas to specify the *We* notion of identities. The *We* as I conceive of it here can be an extension of Mead's (1934) generalized other, if that generalized other were plural. In so doing, the *Me* identities are in constant interaction with one's *I* part of self and are constantly influenced by the generalized other(s) (figure 1). It is in this constant interaction between the *I* and the *Me* where one may associate with a *Chosen We* community or communities in ways that are liberating and not coercive.

Mead has been criticized as not being concerned with a pluralistic, increasingly global society, particularly the kind of diversity that exists in contemporary society in the United States (Habermas, 1984; Stryker, 2008; Winkle-Wagner, 2009a). The homogenous societal perspective is particularly problematic relative to race and racial history in the American context. Collective identity, or the idea of a possible *We*, manifests for Mead (1934) as a "generalized other" that would be like a nameless, faceless, almost omnipresent set of norms for how one should act and think between and across social settings. But the idea of a collective notion of identity that

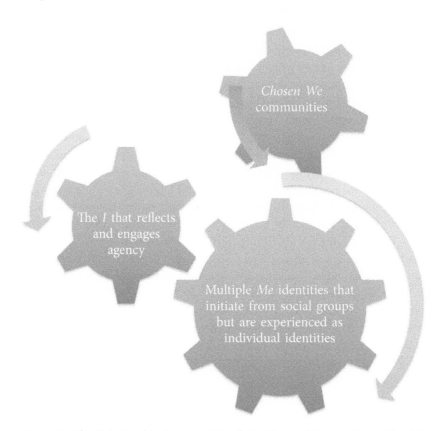

Figure 1. The Relationship between Mead's I, Me, and Generalized Other(s). *Source*: Author-created.

could appear differently across the various subgroups within a society was not within the bounds of Mead's theorizing.[22] My understanding of the limits of Mead's theory is another important reason that I moved toward Black feminist thinking as a way of conceptualizing knowledge of the *We*.

In *The Unchosen Me*, I studied the implications of the "generalized other" with regard to choice (Winkle-Wagner, 2009a). I argued that there is a limited scope of choice when it comes to identity because of the social constraints that are assumed by the "generalized other." I asserted that Mead did not allow for explorations of the existing stratification in society. Subgroups have experienced longstanding oppression and exploitation in the US, and this means that the starting points for identities are not the same. Some identities are viewed as innately better or more advantaged than others. In my ethnographic project with currently enrolled Black women in college, I found that the women may have been contending with multiple, conflicting "generalized others" that made it very difficult for them to make choices about their own identities. The Black women in *The Unchosen Me* described having to constantly choose between predetermined categories of identity, to choose between predetermined *Me* identities. I was left wondering whether there could be collective identity, and even resistance, rooted in the notion of the "generalized other." Could one develop a collective notion of identity that was in direct opposition to oppressive social structures? The *Chosen We* is a way to explore the idea of a collective identity that is at once connected to and divergent from a mainstream generalized other or generalized others.

The *Chosen We*

The *Chosen We* is a theoretical idea that both extends and challenges the *Unchosen Me* (Winkle-Wagner, 2009a). While the *Unchosen Me* points out the limits of choice when it comes to one's identities, the *Chosen We* emphasizes deliberation, choice, resistance, and empowerment. Being "chosen" connotes that an individual, or the community in which one is choosing to engage, is special, unique, and perhaps even entitled to the rights and privileges that are afforded to those who get the special responsibility of being selected. Chosen-ness can also be a state of personal empowerment where one has achieved a sense of stillness and acceptance with oneself: one has chosen one's self sometimes despite the negative and stereotypical predictions and expectations of others or society. The idea of finding an "authentic" sense of self could be a type of chosen identity (Winkle-Wagner et al., 2018). I assert four important characteristics of *Chosen We* communities:

1. The *Chosen We* is created and continued through dialogue and interaction within a group.

2. One must be able to voluntarily *choose* when and how one associates with a *Chosen We* community free of coercion.

3. A *Chosen We* community must allow for a plurality of identities and perspectives even if there is an identity-sharing element to the group.

4. The *Chosen We* (collective, community identity) and the *Me* can coexist.

There is a plurality and sense of community connoted by the *We* form of identity. Rather than viewing identity projects as only singular and individual, with the *Chosen We* I am elaborating on a part of self that is initiated and maintained in community with others. If one chooses the *We*, one can voluntary associate or disassociate with the community at any time. The *We* is an idea of identity that not only initiates in a social group but also is continued through the dialogue and interaction within that group. Given the emphasis on interaction and dialogue, one must have the freedom to interact within the group. If one feels silenced, unheard, or as if their ideas do not matter, the community may not be *chosen* because, ideally, the *Chosen We* is free of coercive forces. One must be able to be in dialogue, to state one's views, and to disagree without coercion.[23]

The *Chosen We* allows a person freedom to opt into and out of a group at their will.[24] In contemplating a type of identity that gains recognition as an alternative identity, the question arises as to whether that identity could still become oppressive when working against existing social structures (see, for example, MacLeod, 1987/2008; Willis, 2017). If a counterculture that at first represented a way to find fuller recognition of one's identities became prescriptive or ultimately leads to one's oppression, it is no longer the *Chosen We*. By this I mean that the moment when one no longer feels a sense of agency, choice, and the ability to voluntary come and go from the *Chosen We* identity, it is no longer chosen. If there were a counterculture that developed because people were feeling misrecognized in other settings, but that counterculture eventually demanded that people only ascribe to that group and not associate with any other people, this would no longer be a *Chosen We*.

The *Chosen We* as it emerged from these oral histories cannot be born out of coercion, oppression, and force, as also specified earlier in the characteristics of the concept. The *Chosen We* may initiate based on a shared understanding of the need to resist, dissent, and protest oppression. The *Chosen We* could be a counterculture or an alternative set of individual identities (*Me* identities). The *Chosen We* could be related to an affirmation of cultural, racial, or ethnic identities. But if one's subscription to any identities were to become dogmatic and oppressive, it would no longer be the *Chosen We* as I am conceiving of it. That is, as these oral histories indicate, the *Chosen We* can transcend the oppressive and dogmatic notion of following norms or ways of being. The *Chosen We* is a voluntary, collective notion of inclusion, acceptance, and recognition.[25]

The *Chosen We* may feel like a deep sense of belonging or inclusion. The *Chosen We* community may offer affirmation and validation of one's background, one's identities, and one's aspirations for the future. If a person were to grow beyond the confines of the group in ways that ultimately lead the person in a new direction, one must be able to voluntarily disassociate from the community without violence or coercion for it to be a *Chosen We*. That is, *Chosen We* communities are antithetical to coercive groups such as cults, abusive relationships, or dysfunctional relationships that deny a person the choice to leave without severe repercussions (the forced loss of family after leaving, harm, violence, expulsion, etc.).

Within a *Chosen We* community, there should and can be a plurality of identities, even if there is a larger identity-sharing group (a Black student union that elevates being Black). For example, while one might associate with a Black student organization on campus, the *Chosen We* community offered by that organization does not necessarily assume that all students in the group experience or identify their Blackness or racial identities in the same ways. One could feel a deep sense of community and belonging while also building a strong sense of individuality as I explain later regarding the way in which the *Me* and the *We* can coexist. If, for example, one felt as if one completely lost all individuality within a group, this would not be a *Chosen We*.

It is possible that one set of individuals may experience a community as a *Chosen We* community, while for others, the same community may not feel as deeply engaging. In other words, there are likely limits to the plurality of identities that might feel completely included within a single *Chosen We* community. A Black student union that placed a lot of emphasis on activism may be a *Chosen We* for some Black students as suggested in multiple chapters in this book. But other Black students may not feel the same sense of connection and belonging to that group and may find their *Chosen We* communities elsewhere. Not only must there be an acceptance of a plurality of identities within a *Chosen We* community, but there must be a variety of *Chosen We* communities from which to choose. It would be an error to think that a single Black student organization would be supportive of *all* Black students on a college campus.

As suggested in the subsequent chapters of this book, the *Chosen We* collective identity is paired with an individual identity—both the *We* and the *Me* can coexist. The *We* is simultaneously an extended development of the notion of a generalized other and an expansion of the

Me forms of identity. The *Me* is the objectified part of self. Immediately manifold, the *Me* can emerge as roles and the many identities that one may take in different contexts and social locations.[26] Anna Julia Cooper (1892/1988) often discussed the multifaceted identities of Black women relative to race and gender, pointing to the way in which these identities sometimes conflict or are not recognized together. Cooper (1892/1988) also described ways in which Black women needed to present parts of themselves to men, White people, and to women (both White and Black). A decade *later*, Du Bois (1903) highlighted the way that people navigated multiple identities in his notion of double consciousness or a two-ness that a Black person might experience within the United States. Double consciousness assumes that a person must act, think, or be different among Black people and among White people. Others have adapted this as the notion of *shifting*, which is a form of altering one's behavior (e.g., decisions one makes, dress, style of speaking, etc.) in social settings such as work (Jones & Shorter-Gooden, 2004).

Finally, one could associate with multiple *Chosen We* communities simultaneously.[27] For instance, in a White supremacist society where White people are historically and continually privileged, a Black person might feel more connection with a *Chosen We* that is associated with positive ideas of Blackness. The opposite could also be the case where a Black person who was deeply socialized into the norms of a White supremacist society might embrace *Chosen We* communities that are more associated with Whiteness. A strong identification with a *Chosen We* community or communities may ultimately shift the way that the *Me* emerges for an individual. One may ultimately possess an identity in an individual way (taking on a *Me*, individual role or identity) and in a collective (*We*) way.

For some cultures and contexts, the notion that one is first and foremost a *We* before they are (or if they are) a *Me* is not foreign as it might seem in Eurocentric traditions that consistently emphasize individuality. See, for instance, the higher education institutional motto at the historically Black Paul Quinn College, which claims, "We over me" (Conrad & Gasman, 2015). It is only in the Westernized world that people have so forcefully asserted the notion of individuality as more important than community.

Through the *Chosen We* concept, I can chronicle in this book how oral histories are connected to larger, social structural issues and social history. I attempt to elevate the rich tradition of Black feminist thought where collective identity, sisterhood, and group empowerment are emphasized while not co-opting that work as my own (Collins, 2000/2009). Through

Black feminist thought, I can honor Black women's existence, lives, and wisdom. The idea of recognition is crucial to my conception of identity, and I adapt Hegelian ideas of recognition desires in my conception of recognition. The *Chosen We* also evolves Mead's ideas about the self being comprised of interactions between the *I* and the *Me*. I advance the idea of the *Me* within group contexts such that one could both have an individually recognizable sense of identity (an identity that one can claim as roles, *Me*) while simultaneously maintaining an inseparable interaction with the *I* (pure subjectivity and reflection) and a deep and lasting connection to a group identity, the *We*. I do so in a way that resolves some of the challenges with the *Unchosen Me*.

Summary:
Moving beyond the *Unchosen Me* to the *Chosen We*

A problem that I identified with the *Unchosen Me* is that the *Me* parts of self are not often fully chosen. Rather, there are *Me* identities and roles that are likely prescribed, expected, or that one feels pressure to exemplify. The *Unchosen Me* is the epitome of lacking choice and agency in identities. The *Unchosen Me* also represented some coercion and pressure surrounding identities that can be oppressive or at least not feel particularly useful to individuals (Winkle-Wagner, 2009a). The idea that identities are *Unchosen* stems from a lack of recognition. Even if one might try to assert alternative identities to those that feel oppressive, if those identities are not recognizable in a particular setting, it will be very hard to present that identity (Winkle-Wagner, 2009a). The sense that one's possible identities or alternative identities are not fully recognized, or are misrecognized, in a particular setting leads to the feeling that the identities that one *can* assert are *Unchosen*. It is likely that a person who feels as if her identities cannot be fully recognized in a particular setting will either leave that setting, opt to accept *Unchosen* parts of self, or continually search for recognition in other places.

The *Chosen We* is the chosen collective community. The *Chosen We* represents that location where one has finally found a sense of recognition of one's fuller self or one's alternative or previously unrecognized parts of identity. The *We* is a separate objectified identity that is at once communal and individual.[28] The *We* is communal in that others also draw upon it and influence it. The *We* is individual in that one's recognition and acceptance of it may differ from that of another individual who shares identities with the same *We*. In this way, the *Chosen We* can be a location of agency, empowerment, and choice. Thus, the *Chosen We* can offer a pathway to recognition.

The *Chosen We* circles back to generations of thought that came before it where humanity and the people that make up that humanity are inseparable. The idea of a voluntary (Gutmann, 2009), universalist (Hegel, 1807/1952/1977; Knapp, 1986) self where the actions of one person deeply resonate and effect the life of another has been both intimated and fiercely asserted without much empirical specification. Black feminist thinkers have repeatedly spoken of sisterhood and collective identities (Collins, 2000/2009). Indigenous and tribal thinkers have named collectivities and intimate human interrelationship as the basis of human experience (Anzaldúa, 1987; Mignolo, 2012).

The *Chosen We* elevates liberation, freedom, community, and sometimes healing. The *Chosen We* offers agency even in spaces where choice seems difficult to recognize. Sometimes, as seen in these chapters, the *Chosen We* is connected to active resistance and larger social movements aimed at transforming and reforming society. Sometimes the *Chosen We* is more subtle, a relationship or set of relationships that offers solace, hope, and empowerment when those ideas may seem difficult to identify on one's own. In other instances, the *Chosen We* is carefully and deliberately crafted by institutions so that most of the people within that institution feel affirmed, as if they deeply belong. Throughout, the *Chosen We* is an important way in which Black women activate their liberation as connected to the liberation of others, as is shown in the pages of this book.

Part II

From Individualism to Transformative Community at Predominantly White Institutions (PWIs)

Predominantly White institutions (PWIs), those colleges and universities with a majority population of White students, were never intended to be supportive and welcoming spaces for Black students (Anderson, 1988; Thelin, 2011). Most colleges and universities in the United States were created by and for White men. John Thelin's (2011) history of American higher education elucidated the notion of education for "Christian Gentlemen" and later, for "Gentleman Scholars" to create a "colonial elite" (p. 25). PWIs were created with race and gender exclusion baked into the architecture, artifacts, curriculum, and admissions policies (Blackshear & Hollis, 2021; Harper et al., 2009; Winkle-Wagner & Locks, 2020).

Land-grant institutions, those campuses in each of the 50 states that were given land upon which to build universities to serve each state's citizenry, were created with the first Morrill Act of 1862 (Thelin, 2011) three years before enslavement was made illegal. These land-grant institutions became some of the elite institutions, often referred to as PWIs in contemporary times. By the state's citizenry, the first Morrill Act meant college access for the White people living in each state and not the *actual* population, which also included Black, Brown, and indigenous peoples. It was not until the second Morrill Act of 1890 that many of the states' African American, Black, and Brown populations were considered as part of the national higher education landscape. With the second Morrill Act *segregated* higher education spaces were created, leading to the establishment of historically Black colleges and universities (HBCUs) in 17 of the southern states with the highest populations of African American students (Thelin, 2011). But even the development of federally funded historically Black colleges and universities is a reminder of the brutal national history of legal racial segregation and exclusion. According to Roebuck and Murty's (1993) analysis, the creation of HBCUs was really "to get millions of dollars in federal funds for the development of White land-grant universities, to limit African American education to vocational training, and to prevent African American students from attending white land-grant colleges" (p. 27).

There were only a few institutions with majority White student populations that admitted African American or Black students in the 1800s, and these were small liberal arts colleges in the New England area such as Amherst College, Bowdoin College, and Middlebury College (Harper et al., 2009). Oberlin College also graduated the first African American woman, Mary Jane Patterson, in 1862 (Katz, 1969). Despite these advancements, it is important to note that by 1950, over 90 percent of African American college graduates had been educated at HBCUs (Fleming, 1984; Harper et al., 2009). However, HBCUs have been and continue to be underresourced as compared to their predominantly White counterparts. In states with both a predominantly White land-grant state institution and a historically Black land-grant state institution, the HBCUs consistently received, on average, at least 12 percent less money (Hoffman, 1996; see also Kim & Conrad, 2006)[1] and funding has been severely diminished in contemporary times too (Boland & Gasman, 2014). By the 2000s, most Black students were being educated in PWIs (Harper et al., 2009), which is one reason why I included so many PWI graduates in this study, as a representation of the national landscape.

A Brief Description of the PWI Alumnae in This Study

The alumnae in this book are highly educated and highly accomplished women. Out of the 105 total women in the study, 69 attended PWIs for their undergraduate degrees (table 1). There were 36 women who attended HBCUs for their bachelor's degrees who are discussed in the next part of the book. Twenty of those HBCU alumnae attended PWIs for graduate school after attending a historically Black institution for undergraduate degrees. Thus, the total number of women who attended a PWI for *any*

Table 1. Demographics of the PWI Alumnae

TOTAL Number of PWI alumnae (undergraduate *and* graduate degrees)	82 women (105 women in the study)
Number of women who attended PWIs for undergraduate degrees	69 women
Number of women who attend PWIs for graduate-level degrees (who attended HBCUs for undergraduate degrees)	13
First-generation status (first in the family to attend college)	33 women
Number of PWI undergraduate alumnae who earned graduate degrees at PWIs	41 master's degrees earned 18 terminal degrees earned (PhD, JD, MD, etc.)
Number of PWI undergraduate alumnae who earned graduate degrees at HBCUs	4 alumnae

Source: Author-created.

of their degrees (including graduate degrees) was 82. Of the 20 women who attended a PWI for graduate school after earning their first degree at a PWI, 13 alumnae attended a PWI for their master's degree and 7 HBCU alumnae attended a PWI for their terminal degrees (e.g., PhD, JD, MD, etc.). As table 1 identifies, 33 of the 82 women who graduated from PWIs were the first in their families to attend college. More than half of the alumnae from PWIs earned at least a master's degree (41 women) and 18 women earned a terminal degree such as a PhD, JD, MD, or similar. Four alums opted to attend an HBCU for their graduate degrees.

The 82 predominantly White institution graduates (which includes those who attended *either* undergraduate or graduate programs at PWIs) attended 49 institutions. Of those, there were 13 PWIs that were only attended by graduate students; they are noted in table 2 as "graduate only," meaning that there was not a woman in this study who attended that institution for her undergraduate degree. Table 2 provides the names of the institutions, including their status as private or public.

Table 2. Predominantly White Institutions by Private or Public Status

Name of Institution	Location	Private or Public
1. George Washington University (graduate only)	Washington, DC	Private
2. Harvard University (graduate only)	Cambridge, Massachusetts	Private
3. Hofstra University	Hempstead (Long Island, NY)	Private
4. Illinois State University	Normal, Illinois	Public
5. Indiana University at Bloomington	Bloomington, Indiana	Public
6. James Madison University	Harrisonburg, Virginia	Public
7. Loyola University	Chicago, Illinois	Private
8. Madonna University	Livonia, Michigan	Private
9. Mary Grove College (graduate only)	Detroit, Michigan	Private
10. Miami University–Ohio	Oxford, Ohio	Public
11. Michigan State University	East Lansing, Michigan	Public
12. Northern Arizona University	Flagstaff, Arizona	Public
13. North Central College	Naperville, Illinois	Private
14. Northwestern University (graduate only)	Evanston, Illinois	Private
15. Oakland University	Rochester, Michigan	Public
16. Ohio State University (graduate only)	Columbus, Ohio	Public
17. Ohio University	Athens, Ohio	Public
18. Peru State University	Peru, Nebraska	Public
19. Rutgers University	New Brunswick, New Jersey	Public
20. Saint Louis University (graduate only)	St. Louis, Missouri	Private
21. Stanford University	Stanford, California	Private
22. State University of New York (SUNY) Buffalo (graduate only)	Buffalo, New York	Public
23. Truman State University	Kirksville, Missouri	Public
24. University of Alabama	Tuscaloosa, Alabama	Public
25. University of California–Berkeley	Berkeley, California	Public

Name of Institution	Location	Private or Public
26. University of Chicago	Chicago, Illinois	Private
27. University of Cincinnati	Cincinnati, Ohio	Public
28. University of Connecticut	Mansfield, Connecticut	Public
29. University of Detroit–Mercy (graduate only)	Detroit, Michigan	Private
30. University of Georgia–Athens (graduate only)	Athens, Georgia	Public
31. University of Illinois–Urbana-Champaign	Urbana-Champaign, Illinois	Public
32. University of Iowa	Iowa City, Iowa	Public
33. University of Kansas	Lawrence, Kansas	Public
34. University of Mary Washington	Fredericksburg, Virginia	Public
35. University of Michigan–Ann Arbor	Ann Arbor, Michigan	Public
36. University of Michigan–Dearborn	Dearborn, Michigan	Public
37. University of Missouri–Kansas City (graduate only)	Kansas City, Missouri	Public
38. University of Nebraska–Lincoln	Lincoln, Nebraska	Public
39. University of Nebraska–Omaha (graduate only)	Omaha, Nebraska	Public
40. University of New Hampshire	Durham, New Hampshire	Public
41. University of New Orleans (graduate only)	New Orleans, Louisiana	Public
42. University of South Alabama	Mobile, Alabama	Public
43. University of Southern California (graduate only)	Los Angeles, California	Private
44. University of Wisconsin–Madison (graduate only)	Madison, Wisconsin	Public
45. University of Wisconsin–Whitewater	Whitewater, Wisconsin	Public
46. Walsh College (graduate only)	Troy, Michigan	Public
47. Wayne State University	Detroit, Michigan	Public
48. Western Michigan University	Kalamazoo, Michigan	Public
49. Whitworth University	Spokane, Washington	Private

Source: Author-created.

The Long Impact of Racial Exclusion in PWIs

Even while more Black students are now admitted to and graduate from state, land-grant, and the nation's most elite institutions, there remain serious questions as to whether racial *inclusion* has ever been achieved (Minor, 2008).[2] Black students at PWIs often report isolation and exclusion (Allen, 1992; Davis et al., 2004; Feagin et al., 2014/1996; Fields et al., 2022; Fleming, 1984; Harper et al., 2009; Loo & Rollison, 1986; Winkle-Wagner, 2009a, 2009b).

Given the history of racial exclusion in higher education, many of the PWI alumnae had an inclination that it might be marginalizing to be on a campus where they were constantly put in the position of being minoritized, which the research has chronicled for decades (Allen, 1992; Davis et al., 2004; Feagin et al., 2014/1996; Fleming, 1984; Harper et al., 2009; Johnson et al., 2022; Loo & Rollison, 1986; Winkle-Wagner, 2009a, 2009b, 2015). However, the level of isolation that was still experienced is shocking. In this part, I highlight how alumnae coped with hostile, racist campus experiences.

Among the alumnae from PWIs, in all five cities and across generations, the women overwhelmingly identified "oasis" spaces as facilitating their success in college. Two types of oasis spaces emerged and are summarized in table 3: 1) Informal relational spaces: informal friendships or places where women connected with predominantly Black groups of students and created relationships that provided community with faculty, administrator, families, or communities; and 2) Formal organizational

Table 3. Black Spaces by Type and Formality

		Type of Space	
		Physical	Relational
Formality of Space	**Informal**	Informal peer spaces	Informal peer, faculty, administrator, family, or community space
	Formal	Formal organizational organizational space	Formal organizational space

Source: Author-created.

spaces: formal student organizations like Black sororities, Black student unions (physical spaces), or academic organizations for Black students (relational spaces).

As figure 2 suggests, the alumnae overwhelming experienced contested racial and gender identities when they came to predominantly White campuses. Racial identities were contested in classes where faculty questioned if the women had done their own work, on campus where peers often acted in racially hostile ways, or in the communities where the campuses were located as women experienced racial microaggressions in public spaces (e.g., being followed by store owners when shopping, being stopped by police for no apparent reason, etc.). The contestation of identity, which was highlighted in chapter 2, was a type of *Unchosen Me* with which the women had to contend constantly. Gender was often contested as well. Professors occasionally said sexist things in classes (e.g., claiming that women could not do things, etc.). Peers sometimes echoed these sexist statements, too. Clearly, race and gender worked together in a unique way for Black women, demonstrating Black feminist ideas of intersectionality (Collins, 2002). Class was likely an issue too, although as I maintained in chapter 2, among many of the alums, particularly in Chicago and Atlanta, class was not discussed as explicitly. In Detroit, class was a bigger issue for many of the women because there were many women whose parents worked for the auto industry and who were the first in their families to attend college.

Figure 2 offers a visual representation of some of the complexities that women faced at PWIs. It is important to note that while a figure cannot fully represent the nuance and dynamic process that Black alumnae experienced, it is a way to understand the larger idea of what is described in coming chapters. As the figure suggests, I am asserting that all experiences on PWI campuses are rooted in and affected by the racial history of the United States. It is this racial history that leads to contested or misrecognized identities, experienced as individual identities or *Me* parts of the self. The racial history of the US also has tended toward a need for collective identities for Black people as people have come together in solidarity for survival, for community, and for recognition of their experiences.

The country's racial history manifested on college campuses such that Black women often felt their identities were contested or misrecognized (figure 2). The contestation of their identities often led women to cultivate or find collectivist spaces where they could experience a meaningful recognition and embracing of their identities and backgrounds. The middle of the figure shows the mechanisms by which Black alumnae described the successful experiences where they thrived in PWIs. The subsequent chapters tease them out in more detail, but Black alumnae described two important ways that they flourished within PWIs: 1) through relational oasis spaces such as informal friendships, mentoring relationships (with staff, faculty, or peers), or through maintaining their relationships with their families and communities; and 2) through engaging in formal organizational spaces that were associated with positive ideas of Blackness such as Black student unions, sororities, or academic clubs that embraced Black intellectualism. These informal relational spaces and formal organizational spaces were mutually reinforcing and beneficial as represented by the arrows going both ways.

Ultimately, it was through these collectivist, community relationships and organizations that Black women seemed to achieve more positive ideas of themselves during college as represented by the possible positive individual identities (*Mes*). Finally, while not particularly well represented in a figure, it is necessary to mention that alumnae were able to achieve *both* individual positive ideas of identities (*Mes*) while also engaging in *We* spaces that were chosen by them. These *Chosen We* identities and spaces influenced positive ideas of self. For example, by introducing oneself to positive and nuanced ideas of Blackness in a group (*Chosen We* spaces), students could initiate individual ideas of Blackness that were unique (possible positive *Me* parts of self).

To bring the figure to life, imagine that as Black women transitioned to their campuses, they were typically met with highly individualistic norms on campus. The campus norms were embedded within a larger social history of race and racism in the United States (figure 2). Predominantly White campuses often represented Eurocentric ideas of individualism. White campuses were also part of the racial exclusion of Black people in education (Wilder, 2015). Black women's backgrounds and identities were contested, misrecognized, and questioned. As Black women asserted their individual identities in predominantly White spaces, and those identities were at least partially contested or misrecognized, they turned to collectivist *Chosen We* spaces. The *Chosen We* spaces were both formal organizations and informal relationships and support networks. At times, the *Chosen We* spaces were physical spaces (e.g., the student union, a particular room), and sometimes they were relational spaces that were not attached to physical places. *Chosen We* spaces were voluntary; one could choose to engage or not engage at various times during their degree programs. It

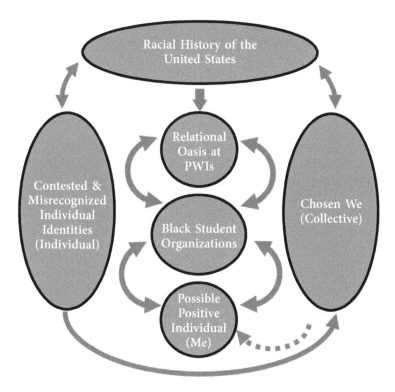

Figure 2. Racial History and Collective/Individual Identities at PWIs. *Source*: Author-created.

was through those *Chosen We* spaces that Black women claimed to create more authentic and positive ideas of who they could be in and after college. The subsequent chapters demonstrate that while some policies and practices have changed within PWIs, there are some eerily similar narratives on contemporary college campuses.

The Structure of Part 2

There was an implicit, unstated assumption across PWI alumnae that many predominantly White campuses are similar. Additionally, as will be evidenced in chapters 3 and 4, PWIs were often demonstrated to be similar even in different states or regions. Racial isolation and racial stress were common experiences across PWIs. Another commonality was that they were often highly individualistic places, as opposed to institutions that are more community focused such as HBCUs (chapters 5–6). Given the strong commonalities across PWIs, I present chapters 3 and 4 thematically, meaning that the chapters contemplate oral histories within PWIs across common topics and themes that the women identified. While individual predominantly White institutions are named, the themes cut across the institutions, demonstrating the need to create or find community spaces within PWIs, either as informal friendships (chapter 3) or through formal organizations like clubs (chapter 4).

Chapter 3

Creating an Oasis Out of Isolation

Relationships That Provided Solace on White Campuses

> The communion in love our souls seek is the most heroic and divine quest any human can take. . . . Learning to love has made it possible for us to care for souls and to rediscover the spiritual vision quests of female ancestors who offer us their guidance and wisdom. Every woman should have, in her circle of love, companions of her soul. Soul nourishment sustains us when all the trappings of power, success and material well-being lose meaning.
>
> —bell hooks, *Communion*

Black feminist thinker bell hooks (2003a) asserted the crucial and unending need for Black women to find relationships of all kinds that offer the unity, nourishment, and care that can help them cope and flourish in racist spaces. hooks centered love as the thread that weaves together relationships and speaks to many relationship types, friendships, and even relationships that one has with oneself. In considering what she refers to as "communion," hooks (2003a) called upon a long tradition of centering an ethic of care within Black feminist thinking (Collins, 1986, 2002).

hooks (2003) critiqued the shortcomings of feminism that often excluded Black women altogether and that also upheld the White supremacist, heteronormative patriarchy,[1] structural oppression that Black women also encountered on college campuses. In contrast to this idea of communion with others, Black women have reported fierce isolation in predominantly White spaces, including PWIs (Feagin et al., 2014/1996; Gregory, 2001; Kelly & Winkle-Wagner, 2017; Winkle-Wagner, 2009a, 2009b; Terhune, 2008). Isolation often increases for Black women who are highly successful in academics, or who are leaders on campus (Fries-Britt, 1998). Black women who have excelled in higher education have had to contend with persistent stereotypes, impositions on who they should be, and expectations of who they are on and off campus (Fordham, 1993; Winkle-Wagner, 2009a, 2015; Winkle-Wagner et al., 2018).

One reason for the stereotypes and impositions that Black women face at PWIs is that White students and students of color are often brought together in ways that are not intended to benefit *both* groups. As Tiffany Thomas, an alum of Wichita State University in Wichita, Kansas, put it, "I would say that a lot of the people who say that it is best for students of color to be involved in the mainstream say it mostly because it's actually best for White students." Empirical evidence concurs that sometimes racial/ethnic diversity on college campuses becomes the primary benefit of White students who do receive cognitive and social/emotional benefits of that diversity (Hikido & Murray, 2016; Park, 2009). It is not the case that integration is a necessarily negative thing, but that campuses and those who lead them must be more aware of how inclusion is fostered. The large majority of the alumnae interviewed for this book did not perceive predominantly White campuses to be that inclusive or willing to be reshaped.

It is crucial to find and build community in these White spaces, as the alumnae, echoing Black feminist thought, asserted repeatedly within their oral histories (Collins, 1986, 2002; Lorde, 2012). Bonnie Thornton Dill (1979) described a "dialectics of Black womanhood" that necessitated community relative to gender and racial oppression. Collins (1990) referred to this as a "both/and" conceptual orientation, a clear link to the concept of intersectionality, where one must simultaneously consider race *and* gender *and* other categories such as class, sexual orientation, or religions (pp. 53–54). Here, Black women built community with informal friendships, faculty, or administrators often because of their "both/and" experiences of isolation by race, gender, and other identities (e.g., class, sexual orientation, etc.).

The communities of support that Black alumnae built and maintained in college were informal physical and relational spaces that they chose on campuses. Informal physical *Chosen We* spaces were demonstrated by locations such as the student union, particular tables in the cafeteria, or a specific residence hall floor where Black women knew that they could find supportive people, usually other Black students. These spaces were "chosen" in that women could freely come and go from them, and they had a choice relative to when and how they engaged in those spaces. Relational *Chosen We* spaces were more fluid. In the case of friendships, these relationships transcended physical contexts and often were important for long periods of time. Alumnae also built relational spaces with faculty and administrators, people to whom they could go to find support and to navigate what were often hostile and difficult campus experiences. Similarly, relational spaces were chosen in that alumnae selected when, how, and for how long they engaged in these relationships.

Friendships and campus organizations can foster community for Black students (Borr, 2019; Leath et al., 2022; Thelamour et al., 2019). Friendships may positively influence women's ability to succeed in college (Martinez Alemán, 2010; Patton, 2009; Sims, 2008). For women of color in particular, friendships can serve as a type of "respite" from stress and anxiety in college (Leath et al., 2022; Martinez Alemán, 2010; McCabe, 2016). Sometimes peer relationships supplant missing faculty, administrative, and institutional support at PWIs (Borr, 2019; Patton, 2009; Thelamour et al., 2019).

Within the critical oral histories that emphasized community fostered by friendships and other relationships, there was a relatively clear demarcation between peer oases, which were clearly a place of solace for Black women, and mentoring relationships with faculty and staff, which were *not* typically described in the same way. Faculty and staff mentoring relationships were clearly shaped by unequal power and they were viewed more deferentially than peer relationships, which were described in more relaxed terms. Faculty may have had control over students' grades or progress in their degree programs. While the relationships could still be close, and could be considered mentoring relationships, they were not free of the positional power, at least during the time that women were enrolled in college. Some of these mentoring relationships with faculty and administrators persisted beyond college and at that point, the power dynamic likely changed significantly. Still, the mentoring relationships were important during the women's college experiences and offered some respite to campuses that were often not inclusive, comfortable, or were sometimes expressly hostile. But first, peer relationships were paramount in creating a *Chosen We* set of spaces on college campuses.

"It Was Like an Oasis": Informal Peer Oases

Peer oases were created organically as friendships or locations on campus where students could meet up during the day. When describing the most important support they received during their time at PWIs, alumnae often talked about friendships they viewed as crucial to their academic success and to their sense of belonging. These friendships were not only relational oases at PWIs, but they were also often identified with a particular space such as the student union, a certain cafeteria table, or a particular residence hall floor.

A Place to "Get What You Need" to Face the Rest of Campus

Janelle, a graduate of the University of Iowa in the 1960s, reminisced on what it was like to attend a midwestern university during a time period when there were very few Black students on campus. She remembered finding Black women who became close friends with whom she could find support on the extremely White campus: "I was in a residence hall with about 500 other women, and there were only four other Black women. And we *had* to find each other." The two women with whom she initiated a friendship in her first year of college, in part out of survival on the racially isolating campus, became important, long-lasting friends for Janelle as all three women joined the Black student union and a sorority together.

Informal friendships were very important to her sense of belonging and comfort on campus throughout the 60-year time period covered by these oral histories. Princess, a humanities alumna of Hofstra University (a PWI) in the 1980s, reinforced the importance of creating a group of Black women friends, an informal relational space that was facilitated by the physical space of a residence hall floor:

> I lived on a floor with minorities. But then going to class I was definitely outnumbered the majority of the time. It was like, do these people think that I shouldn't be here? What do they think about me? I felt the need to be more quiet, I just sat and kept to myself. I didn't really want to speak up, like that would bring all eyes on me. I was very conscious of being one of the very few Black women on campus. I knew almost all of the Black women on campus.

Princess focused on the isolation that she felt, referring to the White racialized campus norms; the campus seemed to only embrace White students. In response, she changed her behavior (e.g., being quiet). She described what it was like after she became part of a group of Black women:

We used to do study groups and stuff like that. We were all three of us history majors so sometimes we would get together. We tried to make sure that we applied ourselves. My two friends went on to be lawyers in New York and in New Jersey. Outside of all the planning and the activism and being involved in the community, we tried to make sure that we supported each other academically so that we all graduated. That was the thing we wanted to make sure, that everyone who came in matriculated and graduated.

Princess's friends served as a support group. They supported one another and together they gave back to the Black community. The informal, relational space they created countered the isolating White spaces on campus and the three women supported one another's accomplishments. Princess combined these informal friendships with support that she garnered from her involvement in a formal student organization, the African People's Organization (in chapter 4).

Charlie, a first-generation graduate of the University of Alabama in the 1990s with a degree in the social sciences, also recalled a meaningful informal space: "I was really aware of being alone. I'd leave my friends, at the union, "Okay I'm going to class" and I'd go to be by myself for a while. The African American students would hang out in between classes. It was like an oasis. You'd come back and get what you needed so that you could go back and do what you had to do." Charlie called the place where her Black friends hung out an "oasis," indicating that this was a place where she felt safe and comfortable. Charlie's space was both a particular physical space and also a relational space. It tacitly countered the overwhelming Whiteness of the campus.

Tiffany (also called Tiff), who graduated from the predominantly White Oakland University in the Detroit metropolitan area in the 1990s with a degree in the social sciences, reflected on the importance of her friendships with Black women in college:

My friends, all of us were pretty similar. My really close friends, we were hard working. We all had set personal goals for ourselves. Not necessarily that we said it out loud. But we all had the goal of graduating. We would go to tutoring together or we would encourage each other to go to tutoring. We would help each other. If we couldn't help each other, we knew who to talk to on campus to get help. We didn't drink very heavily. We were fairly responsible, no drugging or anything like that. We went to parties on campus and hung out on the weekends. But other than that, we knew we had a goal and we stuck to it.

I asked Tiff where she met those high-achieving close friends. She replied:

We met freshman year in college. I had kind of like two sets of friends. I had a friend who was older than me, she was my roommate and she carried herself a little differently than my other friend. She had a baby, she was older. She would go back and forth between home and staying on campus. So when she was at school, I hung out with her. When she went home, I would hang out with my campus friends. I would eat in the cafeteria with them and hang out. But they didn't necessarily hang out with her. It was kind of funny. I learned a lot from her. I learned a lot from them. It just worked out.

Tiff described two sets of friendships that were not necessarily connected, the traditional college-aged students who were on campus a lot their first year and the friendship with a mother who only came to campus for classes.

Sometimes these friends put Tiff in contact with faculty and staff too. She considered, "I remember hanging around the tutoring center a lot because my friends worked there. I would go over there and talk to faculty and staff and kind of hang out with them all day if I didn't have anything to do." Tiff's friendship group transitioned between academics and her social life, not attached to a single context, and it lasted a long period of time (Thelamour et al., 2019; Winkle-Wagner et al., 2019). She summarized:

We just had our friends, and we had our apartment. A lot of our friends lived in the same complex or right down the street. We were all doing well with school. Looking back on it now, we all had our little space that we fit. We just all complemented each other really well. There were four of us. That close knit group. Then, we had a broader group of maybe 10 of us [too]. So the 10 of us would be like, hey, it's Friday night, let's go to a movie, let's go to dinner. It's spring break, let's all pile up in two cars and go. By junior year, you could kind of see where everyone was going to go. For the most part, people have followed into those paths.

Tiff highlighted the friendship group as a relational space where they "fit" in college. She mentioned the apartment as the physical space where they would congregate and where they lived. She maintained that many people in this group achieved their initial goals. The difference in Tiff's description of her friendship group as compared to others (e.g., Janelle, Princess, or Charlie) was that she did not necessarily counter it to the Whiteness of her campus, even if that was tacitly why they connected. Rather, Tiff implied that these were naturally forming friendships. They may or may not have been formed out of a response to the demographics of campus.

Some PWIs put less emphasis on living in the residence halls and being on campus and this created more of a challenge to create friendship groups. Denise described her experience at Wayne State University in Detroit, where she graduated in the 1990s: "Wayne State is a commuter school. You don't have a lot of campus life." Denise was clearly not that connected to her campus or to her professors during college. She did not identify any professors or staff who felt supportive to her, or with whom she connected as a mentor. When I asked if she had friends in college, she admitted, "Not until I got to the School of Social Work, before, not at all. I was working, going to class, and going home, and that was it." I inquired about the friends she made in her social work courses, and she said, "[We had] some camaraderie, because we were in class together all the time." Once she started to remember those friends, she expanded that she had started those courses in the middle of the year:

> We were kind of on the same track, so we were together because it was a much smaller group so there weren't a lot of options for classes. We were together that spring, summer, and then we picked back up with everybody else that fall. I had two solid semesters of the same people in the same classes, and you're forced to really kind of connect with people. Or choose not to. You can do that too. But you can't spend that much time with people and not have some type of relationships forged. So that required some connection and some relationship building.

Denise remembered those relationships fondly:

> The support. Supporting one another. The study groups, to get through statistics. It was the camaraderie and the mutual support that really helped me get through. There were some ladies who were a little older who were coming back to school who [would] go to class, do the notes, but were still struggling with the study techniques and some of the material and everybody looked out for each other, just did what needed to be done to help support one of their classmates to get through.

Denise's friendships in social work were longer lasting than other relationships she built on campus and were the most memorable. These friendships also helped her succeed academically.

Many of the alumnae described close friendships as primarily relationships with other Black students. It was admittedly very difficult for alumnae to create close relationships with White students. Ayana, who graduated from the University of Michigan in the 1990s, summarized it this way: "I can say in undergrad, my friends outside of class were primarily Black. And then in class, it was whomever was around." Ayana had acquaintances with White students, but it was less likely that those were long-term relationships, at least for her. In prior studies, there is evidence of long-term friendships primarily being with those in one's own racial group (interracial friendships) (Borr, 2019; Leath et al., 2022; Thelamour et al., 2019), whereas relationships across racial groups were more likely to serve short-term instrumental goals such as studying together for a single class (Winkle-Wagner et al., 2019). The comparison between authentic, long-lasting friendships and more instrumental relationships was also made by other alumnae, such as Alianna.

When Alianna considered her experience at Stanford University in the 2000s and her graduate studies at Harvard, she remembered feeling severe isolation during her first year in college. Her response to that isolation was to begin to create community with Black students:

> After my first year when I was super miserable and didn't know anybody, I felt so disconnected. I didn't have true friends that I could just hug and go for a cry with. The second year, I was like I'm going to be the head of social for the Black club. So I'm going to know everybody, I'm going to know everybody's name, I'm gonna do all the grunt work and get people to come

out to stuff and plan stuff. So I could be in that community and have that community. That was my answer. I was like, I'm going to do what makes me happy. I tried the whole "be friends with White people." There's like four that I'm cool with that I actually want to know after B [business] school. And I'm sure I'm still discovering people that went to HBS [Harvard Business School] that are awesome that I just didn't know because I didn't have time. I was like, I'm going with what's comfortable, because I am tired of trying. I ended up being the social chair for AASU [African American Student Union], second year. I am so glad I did because some of the board members who end up running it are the people who care the most and are kind of most aligned that way. They're some of my best friends from school now.

Alianna began college trying to make authentic connections with White students and ended up feeling isolated and exhausted because she didn't feel that they reciprocated. Positive interactions across racial groups have been evidenced as beneficial for students of color and White students (Locks et al., 2008). But, like Alianna's experience, most students of color echo the point that White students at PWIs are often not all that interested in creating meaningful friendships with students of color (Antonio, 2001; McCabe, 2009; Thelamour et al., 2019). Her second year in college, Alianna found longer lasting relationships in her organizations with other Black students.

Dana, a James Madison University (a PWI) graduate in the 2000s with a social science degree, corroborated the point about creating informal physical and relational spaces:

Going about your day, you always went by certain spots on campus. We always hung out on the commons or what we called the Lounge. If you're on your way to class, you might make a detour to go by the Lounge to see who was there, say hello to people, check on folks, hug your friends, then go on to class. It was security. It was a way to know that on this vast campus that went across an interstate, that was huge, when everything else didn't seem familiar, you knew where your oasis was. That's what it was. The Lounge and the commons were like an oasis. It was our place.

Dana affirmed that the lounge was a physical space that ultimately became a relational space because of who could be found there, like Charlie's earlier point about meeting her friends in the student union. It was informal in that the students had created the space and it was not institutionalized, tacitly compared to Whiter parts of campus.

Peer relational oases offered a *Chosen We* that allowed Black students a chance to debrief, process, resist, and find support on their White campuses. Black feminist thinkers asserted that experiences are an important way that knowledge and meaning about one's life are created and understood (Collins, 1986, 2002). *Chosen We* relational spaces were a way that experiences were processed, validated, and valued within PWIs. As shown in the next section in Sonya's oral history, these friendships linked to students' finishing their degrees.

FRIENDSHIPS THAT "REALLY KEEP ME MOTIVATED": SONYA'S STORY

When I met Sonya, she was in medical school at Wayne State University in Detroit, Michigan. She told me about her friendships from college, which she also attended at Wayne State University in the 2000s, and noted that they were crucial to the eventual accomplishments of all the women in the group: "One of my best friends, Rachel. She really encourages me. Then there would be Sam, Teonna, Lucretia, Tasha. They've all completed medical school and their residency programs. Some have even graduated from their programs. They encourage me because they've been through some things that I've been through, of course. But they really, really, really keep me motivated. I know they understand." Sonya's friends were highly accomplished, and she named them as being important motivators. She started by describing one of the friendship groups that she developed during her undergraduate days at Wayne State:

> In one of the classes that I took, one of my four language classes, my Swahili class, we had three semesters of it—we were all united. We all pulled together. We studied. And when we studied, we had a direct plan where every week, various people cooked food, we pot-lucked. We studied for exams together. We all made sure that every single person knew what we needed to know. The entire class. All three semesters. We were the evening class. Every last one of us had an A out of that class, every semester. We just started talking to one another and formed a

study group. That's really how it happened. Everybody would just show up for the study group. We just made a decision that we were ride-or-die. We did it, we made it happen.

Sonya met some of her long-term close friends in her Swahili study group. Some of those important relationships continued in medical school. Sonya countered her undergraduate friendships with medical school:

> Then another shocker was I really thought that because at Wayne State, the amount of African Americans, Black students, that are in medical school, you think that people would pull together and they don't. It's like crabs in a bucket in medical school. Period. Everybody is cutting each other, scrapping to be at the top. Because that's the determining factor for your whole program, especially at the end when you're trying to apply for residency. So, there is a lot of game playing with medical students.

In 2018, Wayne State University had a Black student population that was 17 percent of the study body (57% of the student population was White). Sonya could be making the point about the medical school having more Black students than many institutions, which is accurate. Or, it could be that Sonya still felt isolated and like there were too few Black students in her program. The reference to "crabs in a bucket" is a way to describe people who are willing to claw their way over one another to be successful, much in the same way that multiple crabs in a bucket would attempt to escape. Sonya's existing friendships were important for support and for crucial insights into how to be successful in her medical degree program.

Informal peer relationships and friendships could offer an "oasis" in either a physical way (meeting up with other Black students at a certain location on campus) or a relational way (having people to whom one can turn in order to rest and recuperate on campus). Peer relationships were a *Chosen We* in that they were completely voluntary communities that were informal (not formally recognized through institutions as organizations or named spaces). One could choose when and how to engage with informal peer relationships, and one could also opt to leave those relationships at any time. They offered a *We* in that they were typically congregations of Black students who came together because they felt isolated or different on White campuses. Friendships created community out of a shared phenotype or racial background. The shared experiences within friendship communities offered spaces of care (Collins, 2002). This creation of community does differ from how communities were fostered in locations that were predominantly Black, such as the historically Black colleges and universities (HBCUs) discussed later in this book (chapters 5–6). For example, within HBCUs, community was based almost entirely on interest sharing groups rather than on phenotype (Blackness) since most students at HBCUs were Black.

Faculty, staff, and community "oases" emerged differently than peer relationships. These relationships were often shaped by differences in power (faculty members have power over students for grades, etc.), and as such, they served a different purpose. Still, mentoring relationships were crucial parts of community or *Chosen We* spaces for Black alumnae.

Faculty, Staff, and Community Mentoring Oases

In some instances, community and support were also crafted by professors. Engaged, supportive faculty and administrators at PWIs were not the norm. As is well evidenced, students of color on predominantly White campuses often have a very difficult time finding White faculty and staff to mentor them in positive ways (Cole, 2007; Cole & Griffin, 2013; McCoy et al., 2015; McCoy et al., 2017). The lack of mentoring that some alumnae experienced may have made it more difficult to view themselves as agents of knowledge (Collins, 2002) within the predominantly White academic spaces.

Positive experiences with faculty and administrators were noted as remarkable by alumnae from PWIs. Rendòn (1994) claimed these relationships as a form of validation of students' backgrounds that could offer a new model for how faculty at PWIs might better include students of color. Usually, remarkable mentoring practices were with faculty or administrators of color (see also Griffin, 2012b, 2013; Griffin & Reddick, 2011; Luedke, 2017). Faculty of color are often heavily burdened by mentoring in ways that White faculty are not (Griffin, 2012a, 2012b, 2013; Griffin & Reddick, 2011; Kelly & Winkle-Wagner, 2017). Occasionally there were White faculty who filled that call for mentoring too but it was not as commonly mentioned with these alumnae.

Many of the PWI alumnae even encountered racial hostility and gaps in mentoring, sometimes in ways that shaped their majors and their interests. Diane talked about being in a "bucket of milk" at her small, liberal arts PWI. She remembered leaving her first predominantly White campus (the University of Iowa): "I didn't have a mentor. I didn't have anybody looking over me." The consequences of not having a mentor or a good peer support network were steep as she recalled why she left her the first college she had attended:

> Nobody's telling me [what to do]. I don't have a four-year plan. Nobody's talking to me about the expectations, nobody's talking about getting a tutor, none of that. I got none of that. I had a lot of fun. Well by first semester sophomore year I flunked out, lost my scholarship, and they were going to work with me. They told me go to this community college, Kirkwood, it's not too far from Iowa City. At that time my parents cut me off from financial everything. I think they were disgusted. They cut me off. I had to get a job. I got a job a K-Mart and had to get an apartment. I got an apartment with another girl who was still in college and so I worked, and I went to this junior college to try and get my grades up so that I could get back in.

Diane eventually went to a small, midwestern liberal arts college where she was one of very few Black students there. Perhaps her struggles in the first institution could have been avoided if Diane had a supportive community of peers, faculty, or staff. Diane's example demonstrated what is at stake when there is little mentoring available for students of color navigating white spaces. Diane's story continues in the next chapter as she counters her initial lack of support with the *Chosen We* community she found through her sorority.

"A PRETTY BIG INFLUENCE": THE MIXED IMPACT OF FACULTY AT PWIs

As a 1960s social sciences alum of North Central College in Naperville, Illinois, Tweedy remembered a few professors who left a lasting impression:

> One of the professors, a Japanese professor, Hoshiko, was definitely a very big influence on me. She was very uncompromising in her views, which I thought was really cool. I did film studies with her, and she was very in tune with making sure we were exposed to diverse points of view, realizing what

stereotypes are when you see them in films and why they're bad. She always talked about being a feminist so the little thing I remember from her is the pronoun she always used was "she" in all of her write-ups, very specifically and deliberately. She was a pretty big influence.

It was important for Tweedy to have a positive role model who helped her to see women as worth elevating in her coursework and in her life. Tweedy inferred that her professor, Hoshiko, which appeared to be a first name, was very different than most of her professors. Tweedy continued to reflect on positive instances with her faculty: "I had another professor, Professor Pulham, who was more of a mentor. I had him my last year. By the time you're a fifth year, they're sort of like, 'You're leaving, you already know what you're doing.' There's less hand-holding. So he gave a lot of perspective on sort of life things. 'What do I want to do with my career? Like I'm considering grad school.' He gave me advice and things like that." She continued, thinking of another woman professor:

Another strong influence even though I only had her for a quarter, oh my god. There was this professor, her name was Maxine. And she was the most magnanimous woman I think I've ever met. She was teaching us how to write for our senior thesis. She worked at NASA previously. She studied undergrad English, and aerospace engineering, and she got her graduate degree in graphic design. She had all these amazing jobs and was this super smart woman. She decided to be a stay-at-home mom but now was going back to teach physics. So, her kids were geniuses. She again was also uncompromising. She was like my one advice to women is, "I know I left to be a mother, but don't do that. Or leave some thread of your career because now that my kids are older and I'm trying to get back, it's really hard." Even though it seems crazy because she sends people off into space. She has all these artifacts of things that people had taken out into space for her and then brought back.

Even after many years, Tweedy remained in contact with a couple of her professors, a sign that they left a lasting impact on her during college. Tweedy created a community of faculty mentors during college, a *Chosen We* of Tweedy's making.

Graduating a few years later, Dianna Dean also noted the importance of faculty in college. She attended Truman State University in the 1990s before earning a master's and a PhD from the University of Iowa in the 1990s and 2000s; all degrees were in the same social sciences discipline. When I asked her about mentors during college, she mentioned receiving support from a team of faculty and staff:

> There was a program called the Multicultural Affairs Office. They were a great support system to go to for guidance or assistance with getting resources if you needed. Eventually out of that department developed the McNair Scholar Program. When I was a sophomore, I applied to become a McNair Scholar and was accepted. So, my junior and senior year I was a McNair Scholar and that was a great support in terms of preparing and helping me get into graduate school. Then I was able to develop good social support networks with professors. You were assigned a mentor as a McNair Scholar. I still have a good relationship with my mentor. They did a good job; all of the staff of the Multicultural Affairs Department have done a great job of maintaining those supports and contacts even after we've left. Shortly after graduating, they would call and see how I was doing. Those phone calls started to die down as I got further out from graduation, but they still make contact probably about once a year now. Sometimes I'll get invitations to come back and talk to their current McNair Scholars and stuff like that. I was able to develop good relationships with mentors through that program and from my field of study. I had an advisor in my Psych Department. He was a good resource for me while I was in school. We didn't maintain that contact after I graduated, but he was someone that helped guide me in terms of my studies during the years I was there for my undergrad.

McNair is a federally funded program named after Ronald E. McNair, the second Black astronaut to fly in space, and the program is aimed at offering undergraduate research experiences, training, and mentoring to facilitate graduate school access and enrollment for underrepresented students.[2] I asked Dianna Dean if the McNair mentor was the same as her advisor and she explained:

> I had two mentors, my McNair mentor and my academic advisor. She [my academic advisor] is Caucasian and she was a professor of mine as well, so I didn't want to reveal too much to her because I had to take classes with her. So, for my more stressful personal needs, I would go to the [my McNair mentor], she was part of the McNair program, this lady, she's an African American woman. And she helped run the multicultural office. But I went to her more so for those needs than I did my mentor. My other mentor was more related to academic woes and things like that. It was a benefit to me to go to different people because I was thinking, oh I don't want my professor to think I'm crazy [laughter], or to know I am struggling or something. She might think I can't handle it or I'm not strong or something.

While Dianna mentioned two professors she considered to be mentors, she carefully categorized their mentoring to fit aspects of her career. Her male mentor, who could be assumed to be White since she was clear to mention her African American mentor, was only for her academic projects through the McNair program. Her White woman mentor was a professor in Dianna's academic discipline and Dianna was very clear that she wanted to appear strong, so she did not discuss personal matters with her. In attempting to put on a strong persona for her White woman mentor, Dianna may have been invoking a superwoman idea where Black women are often expected to be overly strong and not show signs of emotional, physical, or mental weakness (see, for example, Woods-Giscombé, 2010). Finally, Dianna had a mentor with whom she could discuss more personal struggles who was an African American woman in the McNair Office on campus. None of the relationships were particularly holistic; Dianna couldn't get mentoring on academics and her personal matters in one place. Instead, Dianna knew that she could get forms of support from each one.

Alumnae often built a community of support rather than assuming one mentor could do it all. Also, positive faculty interactions were often compared to negative ones. As a graduate from Illinois State University in the 2000s with a social sciences degree, Colle later moved to Chicago and earned a master's degree in the same field at the University of Chicago. Colle had a variety of experiences dealing with White faculty: "These professors, it was very Eurocentric for me. I was battling that. That perspective really pushed on my values and how I grew up. My mom was in the Black Panthers and she was very conscious and I grew up that way.

Being in that very Eurocentric environment, it was hard. But then it was also like, okay, well, who holds most of the knowledge? So then having to just deal with it." The professors, curriculum, and way of knowing in her undergraduate and graduate programs were startlingly centered on European and White knowledge and experiences.

Colle remarked that both degrees were markedly different than her upbringing, which was Afrocentric and focused on Black liberation, but she conceded that she would have to find a way to get through her programs because White or Eurocentric knowledge was embraced so completely. Eurocentrism is often considered a vestige of colonization where European nations captured and took over other countries, histories, and traditions (Shohat & Stam, 2014). Eurocentrism in contemporary times is often associated with the power and prestige or the historical dominance of White people over communities of color, particularly in the American context (Shohat & Stam, 2014). I asked her how she dealt with that. She asserted: "I had a cluster of friends that had to deal with it too and being that that's how African American people just have to be, they just have to put on the mask that they can take off when they get home, it's normalized, really. But it took me a while to realize that." Colle grew accustomed to putting on "the mask" and then taking it off later with her peers. Critiques of Eurocentric curriculum and pedagogy are common in Black feminist thinking and Colle echoed these ideas. Collins (1989) referred to the idea that knowledge can only come from certain people or look a particular way as "Eurocentric masculinist epistemology" (p. 772). The pressure to consciously perform a way of thinking or being to succeed in White educational spaces was emphasized by the *Unchosen Me* idea, which highlighted how identities are imposed on students on predominantly White campuses (Winkle-Wagner, 2009a; Winkle-Wagner et al., 2018). While the instances of positive interactions with White faculty were more difficult to identify, Colle did remember one professor who left a good impression on her:

> I had one professor at the Social Work Department that she just, god. She was a White woman, Jewish. We would have rich conversations. She would just be blunt. She said, "Go ahead, be blunt too." That was just a great safe space for me. It made me feel like okay, I can trust some White people. Because at first it was just like, they're all like the police. They all had this "you are not good enough, you're just here because you got affirmative action," this or that.

After her one set of positive interactions with a White faculty member, Colle asserted her identities in other ways: "Sophomore year was a lot of pushing against all these ideas and all of these notions of 'okay, you're a Black woman, this is what you can be.' I joined a lot of organizations. The Black Writers Forum, the Black Student Union, the Caribbean Student Association." Colle described her involvement in formal student organizations that elevated positive ideas of Blackness in the next chapter.

Colle's example of a White faculty member who became an important mentor for her was relatively rare among the alumnae. Most of the women carefully described White faculty members' racial/ethnic backgrounds when discussing negative experiences. For descriptions of their mentors' racial/ethnic background, alumnae took care to note that these were primarily faculty of color. There were very few White faculty who ultimately served as positive mentors for these alumnae in college.

As a graduate in the 2000s from Indiana University in Bloomington, Indiana, an alumna named Keys remembered times she really felt her race on campus:

> I definitely felt it in that women's studies class. Everybody in that class was White except for me. Yes, it's always like a scan. When you go in the classroom. You have to kind of scan the area. Who's gonna be my ally in this class? Are we gonna gel? Teacher was White. So, I scanned the class, and I wasn't doing well in that class either. I was getting a C. I was like; this class is really challenging. I surveyed the area as the only Black student in class. That made me feel some type of way. I was already not doing so well in the class, and I was the only Black student in the area.

Keys compared her women's studies class to classes in ethnic studies to point out how students knew where to find connections with other Black students: "Most of the African American classes, usually all the students in there were Black students. Alright, I want to take this class so I can be in there with the Black professor and my Black peers. This is great." Aside from her African American studies courses, Keys found community with her cohort in her education degree:

> In [education] we started to get in cohorts, it was all the same people so that was actually pretty helpful. There weren't a lot of

Black ed majors in my cohort. A majority of them were White women, because there were hardly any male folks wanting to go into education. But the cohort was nice for me, because I like that structure. I know this course is going to have all the same people and their next classes together. Our professor (Brianna), who's amazing, she really gravitated towards the Black women. She's biracial. But she really, she just made us feel really good about ourselves.

When I asked if the professor, Brianna, did anything in particular to make students feel connected, Keys responded:

One, she gave us her phone number, like her personal phone number. And she actually has a White husband. So, her daughter is fair skinned. She [was] always like, "Oh, my Black child. I wonder if my Black child is gonna come?" like in the summertime when she got darker. I think she liked the idea of having brown girls around her. I want to say when she got on Facebook, I sent her a little message and said, "Brianna, I really appreciate you being there for us." She responded back but I haven't heard from her in a long time. She still has the same picture so maybe she's not on there. She was real genuine, nice, and very encouraging. It was a cohort model for her class as well. She just was nice to everybody, really nice woman.

Keys was on a first-name basis with the faculty member in her education cohort, suggesting that they had some closeness. Additionally, she noted that the professor gave students her home phone number and was comfortable being contacted outside of class. It was clear that this faculty member was a woman of color in the careful description of her White partner and the fair-skinned child who was born of that union.

Vivian was a leader in the Black student union and through this organization she encountered a couple of Black professors who were particularly impactful during her time at the University of Central Florida in the 2000s:

I was part of BSU and spoke on behalf of the club and then became the vice president. I felt like I made my biggest impact as the cultural events coordinator. I impacted not just Black students, but the broader community and tried to look at diversity more broadly than just me and my friends. I always felt like the student voice was heard even if things were not changed immediately. I felt like I was heard, and that action was being taken. I went to a few different meetings with the President's Cabinet. But we then had new professors the next year, a Black woman and a Black man, Joseph, who had been a student. So we had those two people who were both actually really important in my life.

When I asked Vivian to talk about her relationship with these professors, she pondered:

I had a closer relationship with Joseph, only because I had applied to go to Tanzania and he was leading the trip, he led class for us. I had a conflict with one of the classes. He still said it was okay for me to be part of the class and I could still go to Tanzania. He held a separate class that same evening at his house with his family. He was just excited to give us a space off campus where we could be together in fellowship and learn about his culture. But also, we talked about "What are you struggling with on campus?" He was like, "I know it's hard. It's all these White people. Yes, it's challenging." It was also interesting because he had a White wife. I didn't know what that looked like. I was like, "Can I talk to her really openly about what I'm feeling?" And she was really open and receptive and weighed in sometimes. She gave us the space to just talk and not be part of it. It just felt like a safe space to talk about what we were struggling with. I know that he provided a lot of support for the other students.

Venita [the Black woman professor], she was a good person just for me to talk to and share how I was feeling. But we didn't really become closer until probably later in my college career, and not super close. But just another Black woman to check in with. And more as a resource for me as I was thinking about what was next after college.

The two Black faculty that Vivian encountered through the Black student union were very significant to her community and her feeling of belonging on campus. Like many other alumnae, Vivian described a community of faculty who supported her.

"FIND A MENTOR OR MENTORS": PRINCESS'S STORY

Princess spent time recalling a negative experience from her sophomore year at Hofstra University in the 1980s, before countering that recollection with how she was supported by faculty of color:

> I remember that one of my old White political science profes-
> sors accused me of plagiarizing my paper. I knew I did a lot
> of research for this paper, and it was in our presidency class
> for political science. We had to write a research paper on our
> favorite president. I didn't necessarily have a favorite president,
> but I decided I was going to write on Abraham Lincoln and his
> extension of the powers of the executive, and so I did a lot of
> research. I don't know what planet he was on, but he forgot I
> was also a history major. I was using political science theory.
> I was also using history texts that I had read in my courses
> and also some stuff that I had read, because I was also a phi-
> losophy minor on Western political theory. I used some stuff
> from *Leviathan*[3] and other things to talk about what it means
> to have a powerful leader and why that could be, even in war
> time, why that could be particularly dangerous. I talked about
> his [Abraham Lincoln's] suspension of the Habeas Corpus and
> his institution of martial law, that we tend not to think about
> that when we think about Lincoln's presidency.

Even years after the paper had been written, Princess's description of it was highly sophisticated, demonstrating her blend of multiple disciplines and texts. Yet, her professor was suspicious of the paper, as she explained:

> For some reason when he [the professor] gave back the papers
> in class I didn't get my paper. I came up to [him after] class
> and said, "Everybody else got their paper and I didn't get my
> paper." He said, "Well we need to talk." Then [my cousin] asked
> him the same thing and he said, "Well we need to talk." [My
> cousin] had written her paper on LBJ [Lyndon B. Johnson]
> and the Great Society. So, two different centuries, two different

presidents, two different issues, not even closely related. We wind up having our meetings with him separately. Before I had that meeting, I was hysterical because I couldn't understand what was going on and it was clear to me that he thought there was some kind of academic malfeasance or dishonesty. I went and spoke to some of my mentors in history and philosophy and I had one that was in anthropology and they were floored. They said, "Well what are you going to do?" I was like, "I don't know. He said I have to have this meeting with him."

I went and had the meeting with him, and he started off by asking me, "Well what does this word mean?" I think one of them was cataclysmic and I was like, "It means something that is potentially disastrous." He kept asking me all of these vocabulary questions and I'm like, "Okay, am I taking a vocabulary test? What are you asking me?" Then he said, "So where did you go to school again, in Brooklyn?" I said, "No, I didn't go to school in Brooklyn. I went to school here in Long Island." I said, "You're thinking of [my cousin who went to school] in Brooklyn." He said, "Oh yeah." And I said, "Anyway, what does that have to do with it?" He said, "Well you know I read your paper and I wasn't clear you had written it and that you had understood the words, like some of the words that I was using." I said, "But I did write it and I cited it. You know I cited every last source that I used." He said, "Where did you get those books?" I said [laughing], at that point I was dual history major and dual poli sci. I said, "Well some of these books are from my history class." I told him I read them under [another professor] and the other books are from the two classes I took on Western political theory and ethics with [another professor] and I said I borrowed this other book from the female professor who taught Western political theory. Then I said, "The rest of them I got from the library." He said, "Well fine, I'm going to go ahead and give you a B-." So of course I flipped and was like, "Well now that you know I wrote the paper why am I getting a B-?" Then he said some craziness.

Princess still seemed visibly shaken by her experience with her political science professor who not only accused her of plagiarizing her paper, but who also repeatedly confused her with her cousin who was one of the only other people in the class who appeared to be a person of color (Princess's cousin was Puerto Rican and did not identify as Black). Princess was "spotlighted" in a way that was racialized and gendered (Winkle-Wagner, 2009a) such that the interaction was not likely to have happened this way with other students who were not Black women. Hypervisibility or "spotlighting" of Black women in overwhelmingly White classes has been well reported (Winkle-Wagner, 2009a). In their pathbreaking article, Dancy, Edwards, and Earl Davis (2018) called the assumption that Black students are a form of property on White campuses a type of "plantation politics," which perpetuates anti-Blackness and the idea that because a student is Black, they cannot possibly excel academically.

Princess persevered despite her professor:

> I went back and talked to my professors, two of them are African American, one in history and one in anthropology; two were White females, one in history, one in philosophy; and then one who was a White male in philosophy. I was screaming and crying. I didn't make the Dean's list because of this B-. I knew that it was going to bring down my GPA. They were like, "Do you think you have a case?" I'm like, "Yeah, I think I have a case. I feel like this is racism, that he singled us out because we're the only two minorities in the class. We wrote really good, in-depth papers. He accused me first of not writing mine, and then it was clear that I wrote mine, he accused me of writing hers." I was taught to write with a thesaurus and not to use the same words over and over again and so I used a thesaurus.
>
> To make a long story short, my professors that were behind me set up a meeting with the chair of poli sci and he basically read the paper and he said that he's not going to change the grade because it's over-cited. But I said, "Okay, but the main problem with this whole argument is that that is not why he brought me into the room." I said, "He [the political science professor] never said to me, 'Princess, the problem with your paper is you over-cite what too many people say. You have the quotation marks, you have the footnotes, you have all that right, but there's not enough of you in the paper.'" I said, "He accused me of not writing my paper and then he tried to say

I wrote my cousin's paper." I said, "That makes absolutely no sense because the writing styles are entirely different. I did not write [my cousin's] paper. I didn't have time to write her paper. I work."

While Princess made clear points about the unfairness she had experienced, the department chair did not change the decision. Princess responded, "The next day I dropped my major and I had enough credits for it to be my minor. I could not stomach to be around anyone in that department." Princess ultimately left her political science degree behind because of the interaction with that professor. She summarized: "I think the situation with that professor was about race and gender and it was conflation, you study intersectionality, so it was all there. I wasn't just Black, I was a Black female. Those things came together for him to doubt my intellect, right?" After a horribly negative experience, Princess, who was a professor herself at the time we met, encouraged other Black women at PWIs:

Find a mentor or mentors, let me say that. I made it through university because I had great mentors. These are people who stood up for me, they couldn't change the grade I got on that paper and for that class, but they stood up for me and said unequivocally, "She is not a cheater. I've had her in my class this is not how she works." They helped me when I started writing my letters for graduate school and writing to get fellowships and stuff. These were the people who had my back. I think mentors are important. A lot of people have professors, but a lot of them don't have mentors. There's a difference. I say that as someone who's in academia.

While faculty mentoring relationships were important, they were also very complicated by power and the White supremacist, patriarchal contexts of predominantly White campuses. That is, even if Black alumnae had good experiences at their undergraduate institutions, they also often remembered racist and sexist experiences with faculty. Faculty mentoring relationships were commonly contextual, meaning that very few faculty relationships transcended multiple contexts. It is not surprising that some women turned to staff and administrators for mentoring support, to build community.

Relationships with faculty, while not free of power or struggle, were often crucial to students' success, and it is important to consider them because faculty are often the creators and purveyors of knowledge. Additionally, because there is a history of more White faculty in colleges and universities, often this knowledge is Eurocentric and patriarchal. Connecting Collins's (2000) Black feminist epistemology, or way of knowing, that centers Black women's knowledge, and Black women as generators and disseminators of knowledge, the relationship with faculty can at once be a site of struggle and a site of disruption and recreation of knowledge in ways that are more inclusive of Black women's experiences and ways of knowing. For example, while Colle mentioned mostly negative interactions with White faculty members, she did have one White Jewish woman as a faculty member who became a trusted mentor, and subsequently Colle felt like she could assert her ideas. Rooted in some of those interactions, Colle joined the Black writers' forum to continue her writing.

Faculty Mentoring and the *Chosen We*

There is a possibility of building a *Chosen We* community with faculty, but it seemed less likely for most of the alumnae. Due to the distinct power differential between students and faculty, it is difficult to create a completely voluntary community where the student did not feel coerced or as if there could be ramifications for severing the relationship. An exception to these complicating factors might be when the faculty-student interactions and mentoring transcend the classroom. Tweedy's examples all suggested that the faculty with whom she connected went above and beyond their faculty roles in the classroom. Princess's *Chosen We* community of faculty mentors were all faculty members that she was able to contact for support outside of the traditional classroom. An important point about faculty mentoring relationships, even if they can be a form of a *Chosen We*, is that the faculty mentors do not necessarily all connect to one another, which is starkly different from peer relationships. Peer relationships and friendships often seemed to overlap, friends were in community with one another. In contrast, the *Chosen We* faculty relationships appeared to be more singular, one-on-one relationships.

Almost all of the faculty members who rose to the category of "mentor" or a *Chosen We* support system were faculty of color. One reason could be that faculty of color know all too well the need for building community because of their own experiences of isolation within PWIs. But the failure of White faculty to adopt better, more holistic, and authentic mentoring practices with Black women (and other students of color) is also a way that structural disparities are reinforced. Many faculty of color described much larger workloads than White faculty because of mentoring students of color, so much so that the increased labor has been deemed the "Black tax" (Griffin et al., 2013). Structurally, this labor of extra mentoring often goes without pay or recognition in many institutions and can be highly problematic for promotion and tenure for some faculty (Griffin, 2012a; Griffin & Reddick, 2011). Given the complexities of mentoring relationships, it is not that surprising that many students of color turn to staff and administrators for their mentoring needs (Luedke, 2017).

"Like My Surrogate Mom": Mentoring from Staff and Administrators at PWIs

Sometimes when White faculty failed to support students of color, the alumnae noted that they built community with staff and administrators on campus (see also Luedke, 2017). Josephine attended Mills College in the 2000s and she noted that while faculty did not necessarily become great mentors for her, a particular administrator made a huge difference:

> I met Samira Herron. She was my direct supervisor, strong woman. She selected me to be on her staff my sophomore year. I was an RA; I was president of BWC [Black Women's Collective]. We shut the school down. We did all these things. I started to put academics to the side. But I really looked up to Samira in terms of professionalism. I went through my first evaluation meeting with her on this job and it was the first time that I learned what constructive criticism is and I had to process it. She gave me time to process it. I swear I've worked ten times harder because she gave me that information. I've found the value in that too. I was just looking up to strong women who were in my life.
>
> I had to have a meeting with Samira because my position was going to be put on probation. She was like, "What's really going on here? What can we do to help you be successful?" She was like, "You are more than this. I know that. You're

highly intelligent." She really built me up and was just like, "What do I need to do to help you be successful." She really cared about me. I had a real vulnerable moment. Even right now, I'm feeling the energy in that moment. I still remember it like it was yesterday. Because she was so real with me and open, I opened myself to her.

At the time that Josephine met with Samira, she was majoring in math and really struggling with whether that was the right choice:

I said [to Samira], "I don't want to be a math major. I don't want to be an engineer." That's what it is. "Usually if I'm passionate about something, I will fight for it. I've fought for everything else that I have. I'm not willing to fight these professors and make them help me. Because my heart is not in it. Why can't I just do a job like your job? What can I do?" She was like, "Okay, now we're getting somewhere. She was like, you *can* have a job like me." That's when she talked to me about grad school.

Rather than allowing constructive feedback to be devastating for Josephine, Samira turned the conversation into an opportunity to build even bigger aspirations for Josephine's future. Josephine remembered:

In terms of being happy, going to class, working hard. I was getting all A's. Everything changed, everything, my attitude about school, the academics, and my priorities. I was able to graduate from Mills College in four years. I was the happiest I'd ever been.

My junior year, midway into junior year, Samira announces that she's leaving. She went to San Jose State to work. We were all very sad but at that point, I think she really gave me the tools that I needed to be successful for those last two years. Then we got a new dean of students, an African American woman. She also helped me a lot with the job process. Before Samira left, she sat me down and we picked schools that I wanted to go to. She was like, it's my responsibility over the summer to start putting things together such as a resume, cover letter, identify your schools, how much the applications cost, and preparing for GRE. Before she left, I knew what I needed to do to get to grad school. When we had this new dean of students, we had a couple new staff members of color who came in, who were amazing. I was able to get into grad school. [One of the new administrators] gave me my first suit. She just really supported me too.

Josephine continued:

Samira also really helped me in terms of practicing for phone interviews and practicing presentations and things like that. Samira's been a part of every big stage of my life. Changing my major, going to grad school, doing my first job search. Now I'm here working for her professionally. During that year or that time frame that I came out, Samira was also there for me. Other staff members who are still big in my life helped me process that piece as well. I also was encouraged by Samira to look into counseling. She usually was like, "I'm gonna require you to go to at least one session." That was the best thing I ever did in my life because I just unloaded and I released things.

At every point, academically, professionally, and in navigating her identities, Josephine was able to turn to her administrators for lasting support. Josephine recalled the process of coming out as a lesbian in her description of support that the administrator, Samira, and other administrators offered to her during that time. She maintained that she continued to receive mentoring and support from many of those people, likely an important part of her expression of her intersecting racial, gender, and sexuality identities. Given that research often suggests that students who are Black and who identify as lesbian, gay, bisexual, transgender, or queer (LGBTQ+) experience marginalization (Duran, 2019), it was likely crucial for Josephine to have supportive mentors around her.

Alianna talked a lot about what it was like to be a Black woman who also had a second identity as Japanese (her mother was Japanese, and her father was Black). She was a student athlete at Stanford where she earned a scholarship to play a highly competitive sport. One of her significant supporters was in the Athletic Department:

She was the assistant athletic director. She was also half Black and half Japanese. I'm actually going to have dinner with her next week when I go to San Francisco. As an eighteen-year-old, racially I had no idea, boy, I had no idea. I didn't know how to interact socially. She was like the coolest, fun, smart [person]. She had gone to Stanford undergrad, played ball there. Got into Stanford B [business] school. Traveled around the world in finance, went into banking, and then came back. She was the assistant athletic director at Stanford. She would mentor a lot of the young Black athletes that would come in because all of us were lost and insecure. She took a lot of us under her wing, and she was that person to go to. She's like your friend but she's an older person, but you can still talk to her about all the things you can't talk to grownups about. She's super cool. At some point she saw that I was having a lot of issues [in my sport]. She reached out. You could go into her office and just bawl for like an hour.

There were multiple ways that the assistant athletic director supported Alianna in college: in her social interactions with other students, in accepting her racial/ethnic identity, and in her academics and sports participation. Alianna underscored how long lasting the relationship had been too.

When I met Samantha in Chicago, she was working on a Northwestern University graduate degree. She talked about her time as an undergraduate at the University of Michigan in an intergroup dialogue program that aimed to bring students together across racial groups to discuss race and ethnicity. It was the 2000s and she had recently finished her bachelor's degree in the social sciences: "The intergroup dialogue program is rooted in social psychology. The professors were psychologists who I felt like really just provided such great guidance and support. In hindsight though, they were like pillars within my experience." Samantha created community with the faculty and staff in the program and in the African American student library: "If I needed to go study, if I needed downtime, to chill out, I would go there. Like the IGR [Intergroup Dialogue] Office, or the African American student library, it was a small library. The librarian also, she was pivotal. This was an older Black woman who you could talk to about anything. Relationship drama, life. Again. I could study there; I could eat there. I would just go see her. A lot of my close friends would also do that." As Samantha considered the community she built in various spaces on campus, she highlighted the librarian in particular:

She was probably like my surrogate mom when I was there. I remember my senior year, I was dating this guy who was like

a stormy character, and drama. I was so enamored. I remember telling her about it. She was very into horoscopes; she was
just very spiritual. She's like, listen, "I can see it already. He's
not gonna treat you right, he's gonna be a liar." Everything she
said came true. I would come and tell her, and she would help
me through everything. The thing is, over those three years, I
developed such a strong relationship with her where I felt totally
comfortable sharing with her in a nonjudgmental way. She's on
Facebook now and I've reconnected, and she's the same way. The
most beautiful spirit. She's still the librarian. Somebody needs to
do a study on her impact on students. So many people would
just come in there because that was like their little safe space.
She is amazing. She would listen. She was great.

Samantha often told this mentor personal things, emphasizing the importance of the librarian listening and not judging the decisions she was
making.

"He Has Always Been There": Ramycia's Story

Ramycia remembered her important mentors in college at the University
of Wisconsin–Whitewater where she graduated in the 2000s. Her mentors were administrators and she noted that they were African American
men. She began by describing how they continued to mentor her in her
doctoral program at Capella University, which is a for-profit institution
that offers primarily online degrees:

Dr. McCan is one of my life mentors. I know they say while
you're in undergrad, you have to find different mentors
throughout life. A work mentor, a life mentor, an academic
mentor, all these people. Dr. McCan is my fraternity brother
too, he is like a big brother, he is amazing. He goes out of his
way to really help his students. I think that's so imperative to
your college success. You have got to have somebody there
to tell you it is okay. I remember when my phone got cut off
or something and I didn't have an account, my account was
all overdrawn. I would give Dr. McCan cash so he would pay
my phone bill through his card. I did it and he would pay
for it for me. He would do my taxes for me when I was in
college. He has always been there. I couldn't see myself going

forward in my academic life or professional life without him right there. I think that is so important. McCan who is now [in upper administration], he helps me a lot with, even now with my dissertation.

Notably, the administrator supported Ramycia holistically, a style of mentoring that was relatively unusual within PWIs. Ramycia contemplated other mentors:

> Dr. Pearl is also a great mentor. But he has also always been there. I know he bought me my first stocks and bonds for a Christmas gift. When I first got there. He made sure that I was in a lot of things, and I was abreast of a lot of information on campus.
>
> My mom didn't have the money and they threatened to drop my classes. I had to apply for the parent plus loan at the time. Gill Perry was one of the directors of financial aid. So, he made sure I got the loan. They made sure I got work study. He was from Chicago, Black guy, was really cool. He used to teach at Malcolm X. So, he understood my struggle.
>
> I think that's imperative for people to see that you can earn more than just get a bachelor's degree. It's important that someone outside of your family is going to support you. That's what Dr. McCan has been for me, was, and is still to me. They were all about helping me. You go to Whitewater and if you don't succeed for real, that's your fault because there's too many resources there, them being one of them.

Ramycia was grateful to have multiple Black men who mentored her during college, who went above and beyond, understanding and embracing her background. The importance of valuing students' backgrounds in this way cannot be underscored enough (McCoy & Winkle-Wagner, 2015; Winkle-Wagner & McCoy, 2016; Winkle-Wagner, McCoy, & Lee-Johnson, 2019).

Staff and Administrator Mentoring and the *Chosen We*

Staff and administrators were more holistic and multifaceted mentors for alumnae than faculty mentors, a type of *Chosen We* for alumnae. Different from most faculty mentoring relationships, some of the staff and administrator *Chosen We* relationships were connected to one another. For instance, in student affairs units, the staff members often worked together and likely offered a more seamless form of community for students. In this way, the *Chosen We* offered by staff and administrators was more similar to peer relationships. There were a few possible reasons for the differences in these relationships. First, relationships with staff and administrators were almost entirely outside of the traditional classroom environment. These communities already were more likely connected to students' personal lives or lives outside of the classroom. In comparison, faculty only see students during the semester in which a student was enrolled in a particular class. Second, the *Chosen We* that alumnae crafted with staff and administrators was a bit more egalitarian. Administrators or staff may not necessarily have had power over individual students in the way that faculty would in the classroom.

The Importance of Informal, Relational *Chosen We* Oases at PWIs

While predominantly White campuses were not described in particularly warm, nurturing, or friendly ways, Black alumnae created informal relationships that helped to nourish and support them in college. Sometimes these relationships were with peers, in the form of both physical and relational spaces where Black women could go, even for a few moments, and feel like they were validated, supported, and authentically recognized for who they were. These spaces were informal, but clearly identified, such as a particular spot at the student union, a particular floor of a residence hall, or a particular spot on the campus quad where women knew they would see other Black peers. Women described these places as "oases" and spaces of "solace" where they could get nourished and supported and shore up the strength to venture out into the rest of the campus. Many of the friendships that were built were long-lasting and not contextually dependent, meaning that women described these friendships as something they took with them off campus and sometimes throughout their lives.

In addition to peer relational oases, alumnae described mentoring relationships with faculty and administrators on campus. Mentoring relationships meant that these faculty or staff members spent extra time and cared for the student in and outside of the classroom or any official formal capacity (e.g., beyond being an organizational advisor). There were multiple instances where faculty or administrators gave students their phone numbers of where they met with students and checked in on them off campus. As if to point out the exemplars and rarity of these positive relationships with faculty and administrators, most women compared their positive experiences to negative and demoralizing experiences with faculty and staff on campus.

Campus faculty and administrators at PWIs could garner the following lessons based on the oral histories from these alumnae:

1. Create a campus ethos of success where *all* students are encouraged to flourish at the highest level. Make clear the success of students of color is assumed, encouraged, and supported at all levels on campus. If the institutional ethos of success does not deliberately and explicitly refer to underrepresented students, there may be an assumption that these groups of students are not included in the campus success model. It is important to include all students clearly and explicitly in discussions about campus success. In the subsequent chapters on HBCUs, there are some great ideas for how some of these institutions are providing a culture of success to students (see also Conrad & Gasman, 2015). For example, students can be told repeatedly through orientations, campus literature, websites, in classrooms, and in public forums (e.g., public lectures, events, etc.) that the campus views *all* students as capable of success in that institution. Support programs that offer services such as tutoring or study skills should be made available, but there should not be an assumption that only particular types of students need those services. While perhaps controversial, making honors courses available to most students is also a way to promote an ethos of success for all students (e.g., students can opt into those courses without officially being named "Honors" students). Finally, campuses should initiate conversations on "who" is viewed as successful by those in power (faculty, staff, and administrators). These conversations must be fiercely honest and led by highly competent trainers to name stereotypes (e.g., racial/gendered/sexuality/ religious). The purpose of these campuswide conversations would be to emphasize ways that campus conversations

about success might be Eurocentric or assume only White and male students are successful. Reframing of success can happen in campus literature, campus artifacts, public speeches and communication, and in the classroom.

2. Rethink success on campus as a collective good that is built out of community rather than an individualistic, competitive model where one student succeeds to the detriment of others. The primary finding shared among Black alumnae who attended PWIs was the benefit of forming communities on these campuses. One way to form these communities was through organic, informal friendships and through informal mentoring relationships with faculty, staff, and administrators. A second way alumnae built community was through formal organizations such as Black student unions.

3. Fully fund and staff resources toward encouraging Black students to authentically engage with one another. Rather than perceiving Black students' (and other groups of underrepresented students') desire to commune with one another as separatist or a threat to integration, encourage these relationships with full confidence that true inclusion can only happen if students feel that they belong. Many underrepresented students are unlikely to feel a sense of belonging if they are only in integrated spaces where they are likely to be the only or one of the only people of color. Encourage students to find community with those who make them feel included, supported, validated, and a sense of belonging on campus. Campuses can offer fully funded and staffed resources and highlight spaces that allow these communities to form (multicultural centers, Black student unions, etc.). From these spaces of oasis and solace students of color are more likely to feel comfortable engaging in other spaces that are more likely to be predominantly White and the staff within these spaces are likely to claim a large responsibility for contributing to students' success too.

4. Faculty and administrators who are engaged in exemplary mentoring should be rewarded for their efforts because

they have the power to transform campus demographics and who is viewed as successful on campuses. Rewards could be made part of tenure and promotion cases and could also be financial bonuses or merit-based pay raises. To make mentoring count toward tenure, institutions would need to offer official guidelines of what activities counted toward mentoring and how these activities were evaluated. There would be multiple ways to assess mentoring practices including student evaluations, student letters, students' progress through degree programs, or though observation (colleagues can observe mentoring sessions). Relative to possible financial rewards for positive mentoring practices, some institutions offer a base salary raise for faculty who win teaching awards to reward good teaching. A similar structure could be put in place for faculty who offer exemplary mentoring for students of color.

5. Create training programs and other opportunities for faculty and administrators, particularly if they are White and have little experience mentoring students of color, to become better, more culturally sensitive mentors to students of color. Those engaged in creating professional development or those consulting with faculty on their mentoring practices must be financially rewarded to avoid a "tax" (Griffin et al., 2013). Often faculty who have positive mentoring practices and can share their ideas in this regard are more likely to be faculty of color. Professional development on mentoring could be incentivized for faculty who participate (they could receive research money, small stipends, etc.). Participation in professional development about how to better mentor students of color could also be one way to offer evidence that faculty are taking mentoring seriously. It is also important to take seriously any grievances about race or gender that occur in the classroom and create a system of sanctions and rewards for instances of racial or sexual hostility.

6. Recognize that some administrators, particularly those in student services or student affairs, may have more contact with students and may be a crucial part of students' mento-

ring and support systems. Encourage students to reach out to, and to create relationships with, these campus actors. Students could be made more aware of these possible social networks during their orientation programs and campus events. Like faculty reward structures, there could be annual awards for those student affairs administrators or other practitioners who are engaged in exemplary mentoring practices.

According to these oral histories, a *Chosen We* community of support for students of color on college campuses must be multilayered, holistic, and seamless. Informal friendships and mentoring relationships connect to the ethic of care in Black feminist thinking, or the idea that it is important to engage in a caring community that does not put care for others above self-care (Collins, 2002). Mentoring relationships often centered Black women as agents of knowledge, through representation (sometimes seeing faculty or administrators who were also Black people) and through elevating the alumnae and their ideas, voices, and histories (Collins, 1986, 2002).

While the women represented here were self-determined, ambitious, and often created their own communities when those communities were lacking on college campuses, this should not be the norm for predominantly White campuses. Students should not be brought to campus and left to contend with racist and sexist campus policies, programs, and people on their own without institutional responsibility for creating and maintaining inclusive practices, policies, and programs. Campuses must have inclusion embedded into all of their efforts—these efforts cannot be left to just a few (and far between) good actors. If they are, students are likely to experience campuses as unchecked bastions of White supremacy, patriarchy, and exclusion. Or, alternatively, as evidenced here, Black women had to take it upon themselves to find ways to engage and embolden communities of support that have connected and continue to connect Black women to one another and to the larger liberatory quest that has persisted for generations.

A final important point that can be taken from these critical oral histories (see appendix A for methodology) is that community should be normative on predominantly White campuses. These alumnae challenged individualistic ideas of college success (Perna & Thomas, 2008) that assume that students should come to college for their individual upward social mobility and benefit. Rather, in many ways, these alumnae offered a type of map on success that could be adapted by others (see also Commodore et al., 2018; Patton & Haynes, 2018; Porter & Byrd, 2021). These alumnae did experience many individual successes (e.g., progress to graduate programs, high-paying jobs, leadership in their communities), but the vast majority attributed their success in college to their community with others, particularly other students of color and Black women. As hooks (2003a) asserted, communion with others "made it possible for us to care for souls and to rediscover the spiritual vision quests of female ancestors who offer us their guidance and wisdom" (p. 231).

Chapter 4

Unapologetically Embracing Blackness

The Importance of Black Student Organizations on Predominantly White Campuses

In our world, divide and conquer must become define and empower.

—Audre Lorde, *Sister Outsider*

In her book of essays *Sister Outsider*, Black feminist thinker Audre Lorde (2012) asserted the importance of collective liberation. Rather than dividing women by race, class, gender, or sexual differences, Lorde called for the importance of honoring differences while simultaneously finding a pathway toward a collective notion of liberation. That is, in defining oneself and one's unique interests, one can create community with others and then be empowered toward liberation.

In spaces where Black women are isolated it can be difficult to find an empowering self-definition (Collins, 1986, 2002) that embraces nuanced ideas of Black womanhood. On many predominantly White college campuses, Black women must contend with fierce stereotypes and external expectations of who they are and can be in those spaces (Winkle-Wagner, 2009a, 2009b; Winkle-Wagner et al., 2018). To that end, Lorde and many other Black feminist thinkers have long promoted Black sisterhood. As Lorde (2012) argued, "I was not meant to be alone and without you who understand" (p. 153).

For many Black women, entering a predominantly White campus space was like walking in "enemy territory" (Winkle-Wagner, 2009a), particularly in the 1960s and 1970s, although it remains extremely difficult in recent times too. Black women encountered overt racial hostility, sexism, classism, and heterosexism alongside more subtle microaggressions such

105

as comments about their hair being different from their White peers. Alumnae, like Diane, who graduated from a small liberal arts college in Nebraska that was overwhelmingly White, described this experience as feeling like a "fly in a bucket of milk." There were countless stories within the oral histories of negative interactions with White roommates, White peers, White professors and administrators.

As Lorde (2012) maintained, and as the critical oral histories in this book suggest, it is this idea of community with other Black women, or a *Chosen We*, that the Black alumnae described as one of *the* most important elements of their success on predominantly White campuses. These spaces were multifaceted and dynamic, representing many interests and ways of identifying with positive Blackness.

Amid open racial hostility and constant racial microaggressions, as well as a sense that they were living within a general anti-Black environment (Dumas, 2016), Black women were drawn to Black student organizations as a form of "placemaking" on college campuses (Tichavakunda, 2020). Sometimes these Black student organizations countered Whiteness or White supremacy on college campuses and sometimes they offered a source of 'joy" that is absent for Black students in other campus spaces (Tichavakunda, 2021). Counterspaces, or those places on campus where students find a way to counter the White environment and norms, especially in PWIs, are important to facilitate student success (Solórzano et al., 2000; Solórzano & Yosso, 2002a). Counterspaces have been evidenced as helping students to better integrate into campus life (Guiffrida, 2003; Lewis & McKissic, 2009; Patton & Byrd, 2021; Tichavakunda, 2020, 2021). Black culture centers are often considered counterspaces, and they provide emotional and social support for Black students (Howard-Hamilton et al., 2010; Hypolite, 2020a, 2020b; Patton, 2006b, 2010; Tatum, 2003; Tichavakunda, 2020, 2021; Yosso & Lopez, 2010). Greek-letter organizations that are specifically and historically committed to the empowerment of Black college students have also been shown to provide emotional, political, and academic support (Brown et al., 2012; Giddings, 2009; Hughey, 2008; McCabe, 2011; Ray, 2013; Ross, 2001).

Formal organizations, Black organizations, such as Black student unions and other similar formal organizations, provided spaces where Black women could commune and support one another. They were locations of resistance against the stereotypes and identity pressures relative to what a Black woman was supposed to be and become. Sometimes the resistance appeared as protests and sometimes it was more subtle, offering a few moments where alumnae found affirmation of their Blackness. These were spaces where Blackness and sometimes, although admittedly not always, Black womanhood, was embraced and supported.

Formal organizational spaces were sometimes physical spaces (e.g., culture centers), occurring in specific locations on campus. At other times, they were relational spaces (e.g., Black sororities, academic discipline-based groups), connected to the relationships built within people in the groups. Formal organizations connected Black women to role models, like-minded peers, and support structures, and with other Black women. The alumnae often described these organizations in familial terms, as an oasis of close-knit relationships.

The membership and engagement in Black student organizations was importantly voluntary, to create a *Chosen We* sense of community, a sense of solace on campus. The vast majority of the PWI alumnae described involvement in these groups, with only a small handful (5–7) of the 69 alums omitting references to them. However, there is some ambiguity among the answers of the women who did not mention Black student organizational involvement, as some did make subtle references to "groups" or "clubs" that were not well defined. Every other critical oral history from PWI graduates had some element of Black student organizational involvement.

"It Gave Me Solace":
Student Organizations That Embraced Positive Blackness

Across generations, Black women described the necessity of these organizations. Dana, who described the importance of informal friendships with other Black students in chapter 3, summarized the importance of formal physical spaces at James Madison University: "The [Multicultural Center] was a very intentional oasis." Most of these organizations promoted a Black feminist ethic of responsibility for enacting action and change (Collins, 1986, 2002) particularly relative to racial and gender justice. In the following sections, I describe Black political and social organizations and then consider Black academic organizations next.

"It Gave Us Another Oasis of Faces of Color":
Black Student Political and Social Organizations

Black student unions were often initiated during the civil rights movement in the 1960s, as part of the political and social movement for Black voting, basic human rights, and equity in social institutions (Patton, 2006a, 2010; Rogers, 2009, 2012). Janelle, who graduated from the predominantly White University of Iowa in the 1960s and who was one of the founders of the Black student union (BSU) on campus, remembered her time in the BSU: "The BSU was extremely active because the campus was just active. It was just an unbelievably electric place. We were so darn radical. Oh God! I mean we really were. A month later, it's three o'clock in the morning, and I'm in the president's house protesting at 3:00 a.m. We woke him up. We were protesting the fact that some of the football players had gotten arrested downtown at a bar." Recalling a night when there was a conflict in a bar after a football game and only the Black football players were arrested while the White players were not, Janelle described how the BSU protested the inequitable treatment. Members of the BSU went to the president's house in the middle of the night. Rather than turning the students away, Janelle remembered the president's approach fondly: "So, the president opened up his house. As the BSU president's good revolutionaries, he had us all sit. [The president] was bringing in chairs and we said, 'No we'll sit on the floor.' So, all of us sat on the floor, in his living room. The president sat down and said, 'What's the issue? What do you all want? Who have you talked to?' He's still in his robe, still in his robe and his pajamas, and his house shoes." Ultimately, the president at the time encouraged the BSU to identify a subset of students to represent their complaints and he met with them on Monday morning to try to make changes on campus: "Monday, we met. He had somebody from the chief of police there, somebody from the Athletic Department, the [student] dean, and a couple of other folks. We all sat down and came up with almost like a manifesto of disturbances involving students in local establishments. [The president at that time] and I laugh about that to this day. I still know him. I still have a connection with him." Janelle and her colleagues in the BSU continued to work with the president to make the campus more inclusive and safer for Black students. They remained in touch even up through the time of Janelle's oral history interview.

In the late 1960s, civil rights protests were occurring on campuses across the country. But not all presidential responses were about willingness to change campus practices. Janelle contemplated this too: "Clearly in 1969, most presidents would have put us in jail, and stripped us of our scholarships, because almost every one of us was there on the state dime. I don't think there was a person in that room that was paying for school on their own. So, we were definitely on thin ice." During the

1960s, there were campuses that suspended or expelled Black students for protesting about their civil rights. For example, on what became called "Black Thursday," at the now University of Wisconsin–Oshkosh, not all that far from Iowa, where Janelle attended college, 94 African American students silently protested by filling the president's Executive Office.[1] Rather than listening to the students, the African American students were expelled, loaded into moving trucks, and put in prison for protesting in one of the gravest betrayals of their First Amendment rights and their academic freedom. In Wisconsin, there are few outside of the community of Oshkosh who know this history.

While Janelle's experience in the BSU was important for her in the 1960s, there were alumnae across generations who mentioned the crucial support that was offered by organizations that prioritized Black students' needs. Tiffany, who graduated from Oakland University near Detroit in the 1990s with a social sciences degree, recalled her involvement in a Black student group: "The Black student organization (BSO) was just a support system. We met, we hung out together, we organized if we felt African American students weren't being represented or being mistreated. We would try to take a stand in whatever way we could. We also used them for resources when freshmen would come in. We would try to show them the ropes. Also, we mentored children or teenagers back in Detroit. We stood out." The Black student organization represented multiple support structures for Tiffany; it was her friendship group, it was a place to connect with a larger social movement (demonstrated by organizing), and it was a peer-mentoring network on and off campus.

Princess, who offered a narrative of faculty mentoring and stressed the importance of finding a good mentor in the last chapter, graduated from the predominantly White, Hofstra University in the early 1990s. She earned a master's degree in the late 1990s from the predominantly White State University of New York (SUNY), Buffalo University, and a PhD from Buffalo in the same field in the early 2000s. She also joined a Black organization at Hofstra University. With her three experiences, she knew well what it meant to be on a White campus. Her involvement with the African People's Organization allowed her to see how students in that group were treated differently from White students involved in organizations on campus:

I went to a predominantly White college, Hofstra University. I was eating in the lunchroom and some dude walked up to me and was like, "Hey so we're having a meeting, do you want to come?" I considered myself to be socially conscious and race conscious. I went to the first meeting of the APO, which was the African People's Organization. I became an active member in that group. Eventually I became a member on their executive board. I held two different positions. So that was really what made me comfortable. That's when I started meeting a lot of people, had a lot of friends.

We did a lot of social events. I was involved in booking speakers. So one year I got Reverend Floyd Flake[2] to come, who was at that point a congressman and he also was the pastor of the Allen A.M.E. Church in Queens, which is one of the biggest churches, the most successful church, but also was a church that constantly, consciously, made a decision to kind of buy up property in the area so that the church and the community owned a lot of the houses. They also had a senior citizens' home, they had a clinic, health care, they [owned] a nursery. Then they eventually opened an Allen Christian school, which was a K–12 private school. I worked on that.

I also worked on some of the social events: parties, mixers, but also we would invite speakers. I also worked with the women in APO and we worked with young girls in the community centers and talked about self-esteem and self-image and safe sex and all kinds of stuff dealing with body issues and protecting oneself and all of that stuff. We talked to them about being on track for college and so that's what I was doing. It was very active on campus and at times we would be in meetings until midnight.

The African People's Organization provided Princess with friends and people with whom she could feel supported during college. Princess continued, explaining how the APO had helped her to navigate the overwhelming Whiteness of her college campus: "I was very conscious of being one of the very few Black women on campus. Now when I go back to my alma mater there are many more, but I knew almost all of the Black [laughing] women on campus, at least at the undergraduate level." While Princess may have outwardly seemed to be very busy with a job and her classes, she maintained that she *needed* to be involved to help with isolation in her PWI. As an example of the deep divide between Black and White students at the time, Princess recalled one of the speakers she brought to campus in her leadership role within the APO: "There was an event where we brought somebody to campus and there were several people who picketed the person. We were labeled as Black radicals and, all of the stigma that goes with that—that somehow, we're just Black students with an ax to grind and that we're not really there to learn. It was just nonsense." The "Black radical" has a storied history in the United States and often this term is used to connote an association with the Black Panther Party, a political group initiated in 1966 that aimed to liberate Black people by any means necessary, including arming themselves to combat police brutality and other forms of brutality against Black people (Robinson, 2000). The Black Panther Party also did a large amount of good work for Black communities such as free breakfast programs, health care, and fighting against medical discrimination (Nelson, 2011; West, 2010). Black radicals have been framed in both positive (empowering, liberatory) ways and in negative ways that associate Black resistance with violence (Rhodes, 2017; Robinson, 2000). Princess continued:

> White students have brought people to campus that I would consider questionable. As students, we refused to back down and not disinvite this person who was involved in a lot of controversy in New York City. We thought part of academic freedom is bringing people to campus and just hearing what they have to say. If it's controversial it's controversial. But the whole point is that we have academic and intellectual exchange. We weren't bringing rabid racists on campus and stuff like that. But there were certain groups that disagreed with this person's politics and scholarship. We had to have escorts escort us from the union.
>
> Then, this whole thing erupted. We were getting interviewed by the newspaper [tapping hand on table for emphasis]. I just remember thinking, this is insane! People did fear for us. I felt that we were under scrutiny because we're a Black group. Because no other group had ever [had this happen]. They brought controversial people up there all the time, and never in my knowledge, subject to that kind of thing for the years that I was there. If you read the student newspaper when they interviewed our chancellor, or whatever, and they asked him, "Well this person has been coming up here for 10 years in a

row; why this year?" And he couldn't even answer. He went on record stating, "We [are] opposed to this person's visit but we support our student groups and academic freedom and therefore we will not prevent this person from coming to campus."

When I told my mom and my dad about what had happened, my parents were like, "Look, this has always been happening particularly when a lot of these Black student unions started in the '70s. We know now that some of them [the Black student groups] were being monitored by the CIA, particularly [in] the bay, San Francisco area, where you have Panthers. Ours wasn't that crazy, but it also happened in other East Coast campuses where they had police officers." And my mom said, "This is what happens. They have problems with some of the speakers that Black groups would bring up." Even now you see this with some of the Latinos where they want to shut down their programs because they don't want them bringing up people who are talking about organizing and amnesty and stuff. So, it was just one of those moments where I realized that it's not just that we're Black, it's about how we see our Blackness in the types of causes that we embrace, that puts us at odds with the administration. If we were kind of complacent "Negros," we probably wouldn't handle problems. You probably wouldn't have had no problems, but because we weren't just about throwing parties, you know. We came under a lot of fire.

Princess's mom provided insight into some of the historical founding of many Black student groups such as the African People's Organization. During the 1960s civil rights movement, Black enrollment in colleges that are now called predominantly White institutions grew considerably (Anderson, 1988; Patton, 2006a). Many Black student unions/governments stemmed out of civil rights protests where students came to campus and continued to have to fight for equal treatment in both explicit and more subtle ways (Boren, 2013; Patton, 2010). Princess had an empowering notion of Blackness, and she perceived that White students were both threatened and frustrated by the unapologetic pro-Black consciousness of the African People's Organization. There was a clear chasm between Black and White students.

Princess's parents mentioned the Central Intelligence Agency (CIA) phone tapping of Black student groups. Indeed, in the 1960s, investigative journalists suggested that the CIA had phone tapped many Black groups, including Black student unions on college campuses, that the US government saw as a potential threat at the time. Angus Mackenzie (1999) authored a book on the "war waged at home" by the CIA and the Federal Bureau of Investigation (FBI) in their attempts to disband Black power movements and protest against the Vietnam War.[3] Mackenzie claimed that his and many other people's basic rights and freedom of speech were threatened by the government's efforts to quell protests. While some who were involved in the CIA and in the federal government have contested these claims (Rafalko, 2011), there appears to be substantial evidence that the government was involved in some forms of censorship and targeting of people who were protesting in the 1960s and 1970s. Most of the people who were targeted were against the Vietnam War effort or were involved in pro-Black movements (Bloom & Martin, 2013; Franklin, 1994, 2002, 2005; Goldberg, 2008; Mackenzie, 1999).

Princess referred to how some White people wanted Black people to be "seen and not heard," pointing out the White supremacist, racist idea that Black people should not speak unless they are actively encouraged to do so, primarily by a White person. In saying this, Princess was underscoring a possible interpretation of how Black students were treated during college. Princess also felt as if Black resistance was against the norms of the White institution. She used the phrase "complacent Negro" as a derogatory way to infer the slavery era terms and norms for Black people; they should not rise up, even in the face of dramatic oppression and loss of freedom (see Franklin, 1958/1969, 2002, for more examples of Black resistance during and after slavery). In so doing, Princess connected a historical racial trope to her work in the student organization, demonstrating how larger racial histories can be illustrated on college campuses.

Black feminist thinkers have also pointed out the importance of Black women's leadership in promoting Black liberation in ways that are like Princess's assertions. For example, Pauli Murray (1970/1995), a scholar, lawyer, civil rights leader, and ordained minister (Guy-Sheftall, 1995) wrote an essay, "The Liberation of Black Women," in which she questioned, "Would the black struggle have come this far without the indomitable determination of its women?" (Murray, 1970/1995, p. 188).

Leadership, intellectual pursuits that valued Black women's knowledge and histories, and activism often were important companions for many alumnae. Michelle Wilson discussed how Black organizations can be the key ingredient in developing a positive self-image as a Black woman within the world. Michelle was a 1990s alumna in social sciences from the elite, private, predominantly White Cornell University in Ithaca, New York. She earned a JD from Northwestern University in the 2000s. Michelle named her Black organization as helping her to view herself in pro-Black ways that reached across the African diaspora (Black migration across the world):

> I learned. I developed my identity as a person of the African diaspora beyond being Black but just starting to have conversations with other students of color from around the world. I remember I was a part of BSU, which was Black Students United. But every year, people wanted to change the name or start new groups that expanded. Like Students of African Descent United, SADU. Like to fold in more and more students so that we could have a more powerful presence on campus. So, I think that, being [a social sciences] major, which is a very broad major, interdisciplinary, I got to study dance and literature and history and psychology and sociology. So that was really great. I definitely was one of those people, especially as I advanced through school, who got very strong grounding in those communities. But I also felt like it was a very kind of activist, pro-Black kind of consciousness, but a little myopic too. Don't be looking a little hippie or doing something that's considered White or whatever. Suddenly I'm in the scrutiny of that [Black] community. My experience is that if you're such a small minority that can make your definition of what it means to be that minority very extreme because you're in "preserve my culture, preserve my identity" mode. Five hundred Black students, by the way, in that 15,000 [at Cornell]. Then it becomes you're either with us or against us.

Reflecting on what she had just said, Michelle considered: "It's so funny how I went straight to Black identity, which is what I think about first. But as I started studying and started getting interested in womanism and feminism and exploring those topics, the subtle sexism of the male professors I admired so much came to light when we started having conversations about how, if you're with the movement, you have to suppress your woman identity to be with the cause." Michelle described being drawn to other Black students on campus very early in her college career because she was put into a position of being in the minority on her campus. Michelle noted that she had learned a pro-Black consciousness from her involvement in the Black student group and this was likely a type of *Chosen We* for her. But she sometimes felt as if she had to act in particular ways to appear Black enough or not too White. She also recalled feeling as if she had to choose between her womanhood and feminism/womanism and her race in her activism. The women's movement and the civil rights movement are often framed as oppositional and this is partially because the women's movement often excluded Black women from meaningful involvement (Collins, 1996, 2002; Davis, 2016). Other times, White women were unified in direct opposition to racial progress. In her historical account of White women's resistance to racial integration in schools and the larger society (from 1920 to 1970), McRae (2018) demonstrated how organized groups of White women not only left Black women out of the feminist movement but also actively resisted school segregation, social welfare policies, and changed popular culture in ways that were deliberately White supremacist. The women's movement, which was primarily a movement aimed at gaining equal rights and treatment for (White) women, led to feminist and womanist (primarily focused on the needs of women of color) arguments for equal treatment of all women. The civil rights movement was focused on better and equal treatment for Black people in the United States and some scholars have suggested that this excluded gender from the battle (Collins, 2002; Davis, 2016; Lorde, 2012). Black women often found themselves bridging ideas from both movements and serving as leaders and activists for women and people of color (Davis, 2016; Guy-Sheftall, 1995).

While social movements were part of formal organizational life for many Black women, other organizations offered a variety of ways to engage on campus outside of activism. Charlie graduated from the University of Alabama in the 1990s and recalled her involvement in the gospel choir organization during college:

> I became active in the University of Alabama Afro American Gospel Choir. The meetings would happen in the Baptist student union, which was not far off campus, and we would all hang out there and sing. It became a recruitment tool for the

university. That's part of how I decided to go to the university. I remember being a little girl and the choir coming to my church to perform. I'm like "all these kids go to the University? This is great I can do this too." We traveled, competed as a choir, and had really great experiences. My [eventual] husband was president, I was vice president, his sister was sergeant at arms. It gave us another oasis of faces of color. It was wonderful.

The formal gospel choir organization, which focused on a combination of religion, music, and Black community, provided multiple sources of support for Charlie as a relational space and a physical space because it met in the same place each week. The gospel choir is where she celebrated her heritage, found her close friends, and even where she met her husband. Her point that the gospel choir is what introduced her to the university is an example of how organizations can connect with local communities.

Cassie, a social sciences graduate from the University of Nebraska in the 2000s, described her experience in Black student government: "I think I just really appreciated the very small African American community on campus because we did everything together. I mean, if you were involved in [Black student government], that was kind of like the 'fam' you know? So those were the people I partied with, I traveled with, I studied with, I had come home with me for Thanksgiving." Through the Black student government, Cassie identified a sense of having an extended family on campus, both in a relational space of friendships and in the physical space of where the group met. The BSG was an intentional, institutionalized space. It was not clear from her description whether the BSG was a way to counter Whiteness on campus, or whether this group was more about celebrating Blackness (or both).

Black student organizations were also often crucial to women's development of a positive sense of self as Black women. Keisha graduated from the predominantly White Emory University in the 2000s with a social sciences degree. She went on to earn a JD from the University of Arkansas a little later in the 2000s. Having spent most of her educational experiences on predominantly White campuses, she had a good sense for how she and many of her peers navigated that. She explained:

At that time, Emory was about 10 percent Black, out of a school of 10,000. That included the law school, the medical school, all the other graduate programs. So, in the undergraduate college, there was about 100 of us. Maybe 100 is low. Maybe 200. So, you knew everybody. If you didn't know them personally, you knew their name, you saw them. Because they were in everything you did. They were in the gospel choir, they were in the Caribbean Student Association, they were in a fraternity or sorority, or they were in other organizations that were traditionally Black organizations.

Keisha underscored the way in which students were minoritized at Emory such that it felt like a very small community of Black students where everyone knew one another. Keisha's point that she felt as if she knew all the Black students on campus signifies how White the campus felt, and how White it likely was at the time; in 2016, the first-year class only included 8 percent African American students.[4] She identified one organization that connected her to campus in her first year: "There was one thing I did like about Emory. They had a group just for freshmen women of color and freshmen men of color called Ngambika. It was the women's organization. And BAM, which stood for the Brotherhood of Afrocentric Men, which was the male organization. And the upperclassmen would do little activities and workshops and fun things with us. But they also teach us how to step." Black organizations were an important part of traversing the overwhelmingly White campus at Emory. Perhaps in the absence of larger campus support, Black students who were juniors and seniors built culturally responsive support for one another.

Josephine noted a similar experience of finding a Black organization at the very beginning of college that empowered and united her with other Black women. A 2000s social sciences graduate of an elite, predominantly White women's college in California, Mills College, Josephine had progressed to her master's degree in a social sciences field from Seattle University directly after her bachelor's degree. She remembered her friend Julianna, who was her "Big Sister" for her first-year orientation program:

I got introduced to the leadership for Black Women's Collective [BWC]. We started seeing the benefits of what it means to reach out to incoming folks. We had to stick together. That was the mentality. That's what I got from my big sis in that moment. That's how I came from this town where I never had an organization that represented a part of my identity. I thought it was so cool and so did my other friends. I think that all student organizations go through a cycle like these are the good times, we're blooming, burn out, we gotta rebuild. So, we came in right out of we need to rebuild time. And they just threw the positions at us. That's when I started learning what it meant to be an activist within the community and creating change. So, my big sis, that's the activism piece that she brought to us, in terms of people of color. It wasn't just about being Black. It was about all of us uniting. My best friend that I first met at the overnight, her name is Julianna. We both went through the same thing at the same time. I was the president of BWC, she was the president of Unidas Mujeres [a Latina women's organization].

The Black Women's Collective became a space where Josephine was emboldened to pursue her activism and unite with other students of color. The BWC gave her a place to fit on campus and it also offered Josephine positive images of Black womanhood. By focusing on the importance of Black women's ideas and histories, the Black Women's Collective was likely very connected to Black feminist ideas (Collins, 2002).

Shayla, an early 2000s humanities major, was a graduate of the predominantly White University of California, Berkeley. Shayla was involved in a Black student newspaper that helped her to combat the Whiteness of her campus. She earned a humanities master's degree from the predominantly White, state flagship institution, the University of Michigan, right after her undergraduate degree and she continued at Michigan for her PhD in the same discipline, also earning it in the 2000s. She started by naming some of the qualities that were important to her to exhibit during college:

I would say inquisitive would probably be one, passionate or ambitious, and caring about the world and about communities of color, different struggles. The Black newspaper is a really radical newspaper on campus. We participated in something called the Black Out on campus. Soul Plaza was our main quad on campus, and there was an arch there. We joined arms and had a black bandana over our face. Basically, speaking out against the silencing of Black students on campus and some of the demands that had been made years ago that still hadn't been addressed by the administration. It made the front cover of a lot of local papers and news in general. We also went around to different classes on campus, in small groups before we joined arms. Not just talking but just standing in the back. Some professors got scared and tried to call the police on us. And some used it as a teaching moment. So, they said, "These students are protesting against this, so what does that mean?" I remember one professor incorporated us in his class, and responding in that way, as a productive conversation moment.

The Black student newspaper became an activist space, a location for resistance to the Whiteness and White supremacy of campus for Shayla and her peers. While some professors seemed to use the activism to help other students to learn, some faculty perpetuated stereotypes of Black students, calling the police. There is a large body of evidence that outlines the policing of Black and Brown students in education, the assumption that these students are going to be engaged in criminal acts (Alexander, 2012; Harper, 2009; Noguera, 2003; Smith, Allen, & Danley, 2007). By calling the police on Shayla and her colleagues from the Black student newspaper, these professors may have perpetuated stereotypes (McGee & Martin, 2011; Smith, Yosso, & Solórzano, 2007) instead of attempting to resist and disrupt them, which was the aim of the activism.

When I asked Shayla whether she thought that this activism had helped to change the way that students of color were treated at Berkeley, she contended, "Not really, no. The new students have to continue and try again." New generations of students might feel as if they are starting over again and again to create lasting racial justice. The incremental changes could take generations to come to fruition.

Many Black student organizations such as Black newspapers, Black student unions, or Black women's collectives were centered on resisting and protesting the mistreatment and inequalities that Black students faced on White campuses. There is a long history of Black women's involvement in such resistance, and Black feminist thinkers' evaluation of these efforts.

Claudia Jones, a Marxist thinker who was writing in the 1940s, asserted the need to center Black women in the fight for racial and sexual justice, a clear link to the idea of intersectional identities (Guy-Sheftall, 1995). Jones (1949/1995) maintained that Black women were uniquely situated in social movements because of their race and gender. Calling on the social history of Black women in the United States, Jones argued for a collective vision of Black women's experience (what I am referring to here as the *We*). She also put Black women at the epicenter of the fight for justice and emancipation. Other thinkers echoed the importance of Black women in the struggle for racial justice (see also Murray, 1970). For example, Pauli Murray (1970; 1970/1995) asserted in her law review article: "Because Black women have an equal stake in women's liberation and Black liberation, they are key figures at the juncture of these two movements. . . . The lesson of history that all human rights are indivisible and that failure to adhere to this principle jeopardizes the rights of all is particularly applicable here" (pp. 196–197). Ultimately, Murray advocated for Black women and White women to come together in the fight for sexual and racial justice, claiming the indivisibility of humanity and liberation for all people, a goal that has still arguably not been reached. While social organizations were one place to find *Chosen We* spaces within PWIs, some students identified community within academic organizations.

"WE'RE ALL IN THIS TOGETHER": BLACK ACADEMIC ORGANIZATIONS

In addition to formal student organizations, some of the participants mentioned organizations in their academic disciplines that provided Black relational spaces in college. These academic organizations were critically important for fostering connections for Black women who were in many cases gravely underrepresented in their academic fields. In joining the academic organizations that promoted positive notions of Blackness, alumnae began to view themselves as scholars in those areas in ways that they may not have experienced without these groups. These formal organizations were important purveyors of Black women (and Black people more generally) as agents of knowledge (Collins, 1986, 2002). Crystal, a 1990s alum of the PWI Michigan State University, with a degree in the biological sciences, joined an academic, disciplinary organization that focused on building community with other Black students in her field. She reflected:

> I didn't have people that were supportive that I knew of. So, I guess as a student, I didn't really know where I was supposed to go, who was supposed to help me. When I went into engineering, engineering had, as you know, NSBE [National Society of Black Engineers] and they had all these Black organizations to help students get through engineering. I didn't necessarily see another organization that was helping students through school like that. So basically, me and a couple of my other friends just fumbled through until we found something we were able to do.

For Crystal, the presence of formal student organizations that helped support Black students in engineering helped her to choose her major. It is possible that the organization offered a new notion of Blackness as linked to engineering.

For some women, the Black organization in which they were involved was linked to their degree program and to their eventual jobs and long-term career plans. Olivia was an early 2000s graduate of the predominantly White flagship state institution the University of Michigan in a social sciences program (she also earned an MBA from Wayne State University). A critical part of fitting into her major was joining an organization for Black students:

> I joined an organization called the National Association of Black Sociologists. They had a student chapter on campus. I tried to make a connection with people that looked like me and people that were going through the same experiences. My family couldn't provide that for me. So I went, I tried to find a group of other people that were struggling just like me. Leaned a lot on older students that said, okay, this is [college], this is how you get in, this is what you've got to do. There are only eight of us, you've got to make a name for yourself. My class, there were actually 15 of us that got accepted.

The organization that Olivia joined helped connect her to her major in college, to find some of the few other students who looked like her in her major, and to give her not only social connections but also insights into her academic discipline.

Lark had a similar experience, finding Black community in an organization that prepared her for an academic discipline. Lark was an alum in the early 2000s of Georgetown University with a social sciences degree. She also earned an MBA from Northwestern University shortly after receiving her undergraduate degree. She remarked: "I did a program right before business school called MLT, Management Leadership for Tomorrow. It is a minority program. It's a year[long] program you do before business school." Lark indicated the importance of being able to associate and work with people from various racial/ethnic backgrounds. This was one of the lessons she learned in her professional school preparatory program, the Management Leadership for Tomorrow (MLT) group. The MLT is a preparation program that "equips African Americans, Latinos, and Native Americans with the skills, coaching, and connections they need to lead organizations and communities worldwide."[5] The program has been in place since 2000 with the goal of increasing the number of leaders of color in business and other professions. There are precollege programs and programs to prepare people for professional schools including MBA programs, which is the kind of program that Lark completed. As part of the MLT program, Lark was given a mentor (coach) and she attended sessions on leadership and how to garner support as a woman of color. Lark explained:

> No matter what, I'm probably going to always be a part of the BMA [Black Management Association]. I'm Black. We're all going to get along and we're all going to have a great time. But it's gonna be a lot harder for me to infiltrate in a lot of ways, to become a part of another group, if I don't spend time with that group. If they don't understand who I am, if I don't understand who they are. I would never take for granted the support network that I think is BMA.

Lark considered her continued involvement in graduate school:

> I was [in a leadership role in the BMA] at Northwestern. That was my biggest thing. We're all gonna support each other because we're all sort of in this together and give each other enough leeway to push ourselves out there and meet new people and expose them to the intelligent smart Black person that's sitting next to you, and not the mob of Black people that are laughing and making noise. To me, that's how you break down barriers and stereotypes. We're not all crazy and loud. And [people] start to actually think about coming to me for a business idea or to be on a project or to help them launch a company and not just automatically go to people they've known before, people they're comfortable with.

Lark offered an important elaboration on how difficult it can be to find and maintain support as a Black woman, while also learning the necessary skills to engage across racial lines. She found this balance in her undergraduate degree with the help of her professional school preparatory program, MLT, and, in graduate school, with the help of the disciplinary based organization, the Black Management Association (BMA). She was able to receive support and to actively resist stereotypes and eventually engage outside of her racial/ethnic group.

Black organizations such as Black student unions or Black student governments were clearly crucially important to many of the alumnae. Another type of organization, Black Greek-letter organizations (sororities), were often noted as important within the critical oral histories. Some women were involved in both types of groups. Other women chose sorority involvement as their primary connection to campus and to each other.

Supporting "Generation after Generation": Black Sororities, Sisterhood, and Resistance

Like other Black-centered organizations, Black sororities were locations of support, resistance, and community for many of the Black women in this study (see also Giddings, 2009). Women joined Black sororities during their time at both predominantly White and historically Black institutions. Historically Black sororities are part of the National Pan-Hellenic Council, Incorporated (NPHC) and are comprised of nine sororities and fraternities, often referred to as the "Divine Nine" (Giddings, 2009; Kimbrough, 2003; Ross, 2001). Many of the women in this study were actively involved in these NPHC sororities such as: Alpha Kappa Alpha, Inc. (AKA); Delta Sigma Theta, Inc. (often called Delta or Deltas); Zeta Phi Beta, Inc. (often called Zeta or Zetas); or Sigma Gamma Rho.[6] On most campuses, NPHC sororities do not have houses where people live together, but rather they are engaged in community and civic activities alongside social events to help women feel a greater sense of belonging in college (Duran et al., 2022). Many NPHC organizations have a long history of community activism and fighting for racial justice for Black people (Gasman, 2011; Giddings, 2009; Kimbrough, 2003; Ross, 2001). The customs, practices, rituals, nomenclature, and traditions of Black sororities and fraternities have been traced back to many African customs and traditions and are often considered a way to carry forward the traditions that were lost in the involuntary and brutal history of enslavement in the United States (Dickinson, 2005). For example, many Black sororities and fraternities emphasize that they are organizing for the "good of the race" (Dickinson, 2005).

NPHC sororities have a "line" of women, and lines are often relatively small (fewer than 20 women), who pledge and eventually "cross over" into full membership in the sororities (Kimbrough, 2003). The "crossing over" ritual has been linked to the notion of "crossing the burning sands" in ancient Egyptian and West African cultures (Dickinson, 2005). The activities that occur from when a woman begins to pledge the sororities (when she is "on the line" or "on a line") and from when she "crosses over" are held in the strictest of confidence; only those who go through the process are meant to know the lessons and what happens (Brown et al., 2012). This process of pledging and being "on a line" has also been linked to African cultural rituals. In particular, in West African initiations, there were activities such as removing the initiates from regular society for a time (in sororities, those who are pledging might be housed together or meet together very regularly for a time period), having an elder teach the initiates for a while (in the sorority, those pledging would be taught by older students or older members of the sorority who have graduated), and teaching the initiates a new and secret language (in sororities this might be signs, symbols, verbalizations, or handshakes) (Dickinson, 2005).

Sometimes Black fraternities and sororities have received a negative reputation for hazing activities (Parks et al., 2015), and some of the women here referenced some hazing experiences. Yet Black sororities were the vital group in college with whom some alumnae found belonging, a connection to their heritage, sisterhood, and a connection back to their communities. Accounts of sorority involvement often focused on the importance of caring for oneself and one's sisters, Black women's self-definition and self-determination, and the necessity of taking action in the face of injustice, all of which are Black feminist ideas (Collins, 1986, 2002). Many women remained actively involved throughout their lives because of the sense of sisterhood and the strong emphasis on giving back and engaging in the community (see also Greyerbiehl & Mitchell 2014; Kimbrough, 1995, 2003). The sisterhood and connections to self and community were unmatched in other groups during and after college. For many of the women, their Black sororities are where they located their belonging in their careers.

Keisha (2003 alum from Emory University) was heavily involved in a Black student organization her first year during college (a woman's organization called Ngambika, described earlier). Her first-year involvement set the stage for her to join a sorority in her junior year. She described what she learned:[7]

> I feel like the sorority taught me a lot of things that my parents could not. Your parents could tell you to get good grades in school, but they can't tell you how. They can lead you to the water, but they can't tell you strategically how you drink it.

How do you make this move to get this desired result? They [my parents] were just like, "Don't come back pregnant, don't flunk out." That was the main thing. Do not flunk out. I have a cousin who flunked out. In the sorority was the first time I met a Black woman who had a PhD. Now, my sorority is largely teachers. So, I met a lot of people who were teachers and were influential in their schools and their communities. I met people who were therapists and people who were just all of these professions. Even as an undergraduate, I joined my junior year, I would imitate some of the things they did, ask them questions. These kind of people that connected with the school, with my activities associated with the school, also I think helped shape me to where I am today.

Keisha noted that as a first-generation college student (her father did finish college one year after she graduated), the sorority played an important role in helping her to know what strategies would be useful for her to be successful in college, and to gain exposure to professional women in various fields. Thus, the sorority was an important social network, but also an important way to find role models so that Keisha could begin to view herself finishing college and eventually graduating from law school (she earned a JD in 2009 from the University of Arkansas).

Leah (a graduate of the University of Nebraska in the 2000s) highlighted her involvement in a sorority in her reflections about college:

I started seeing Black Greeks on campus and I started to notice how they carried themselves and the things that they did and that involvement that they had and the impact that they had on their community. I really embraced that and I joined Delta Sigma Theta Sorority Incorporated, which really taught me the meaning of being a woman and how to carry yourself, and just how to embrace like that womanhood and sisterhood and doing things for your community and how important that is as a minority. Being around other college-educated women who carried themselves well and just had that respect made me also want to embrace that too. A respectable woman is a woman who walks around with her head high and has confidence, will always speak out on what she believes in, and is involved, is about business.

Leah, who joined the African People's Union early in college her first year, noted that her Black sorority is what helped her to embrace her womanhood. She not only gained a sense of belonging from the group, but she also learned how to serve her community. Leah maintained that connecting to the community was particularly important as a Black woman, reflecting the notion of racial uplift that is often so prominent in Black sororities (also see Gasman, 2011). Her sorority served as a formal, organizational space. It was primarily relational because it was not connected to a particular physical place.

Zeta, who chose her pseudonym because of the importance of her sorority in her life, graduated with a social sciences degree from Oakland University in the Detroit area in the 2000s. She reflected on how she changed after joining the sorority:

> I'm definitely more polished. I think before I speak. I went into college saying what I thought. Like, it's the truth so I should say it. Although I do believe that the truth is certainly important, silence is golden. There are certain things you just keep to yourself. So, I'm a lot more tactful in my approach with people. I think that's come from work and the sorority, dealing with people. You deal with all different kinds of personalities, some you like, some you don't like. But you still have to be professional, you still have a job to do and you have to figure out how to work together.

While most of the women became involved in sororities while they were in college earning undergraduate degrees, some women didn't join until long after college was over. Graduate chapters or alumnae chapters allow women to join at any point in their lives, if they have earned a bachelor's degree. Most organizations require that alumnae women be invited to join by someone who is already a member.

The desire to join a Black sorority after college may illustrate the way in which Black sororities connect to and engage in communities. For example, Diane was a woman who joined a sorority more than a decade after finishing her college degree. Diane was a mid-1990s graduate of a predominantly White, small, liberal arts institution called Cally College,[8] which is in Nebraska. Her path to college was not easy or seamless; she began her college career at Des Moines Area Community College in Des Moines, Iowa, before transferring to the University of Iowa. She left the

University of Iowa after one year and eventually enrolled at Cally College, which is where she earned a degree in the social sciences. She earned a master's degree in the social sciences from the University of Nebraska in the late 1990s. During the time of our interview, Diane was enrolled in a PhD program in the social sciences at the University of Nebraska, completing that degree before this book was written. Diane did not join her sorority until she was in her PhD program, well after completing her undergraduate degree. She explained:

> [I joined] just this last year. I pledged a grad chapter, spring '09. I just pledged Delta Sigma Theta; I've always wanted to be a Delta. But at undergrad, first of all, I messed up in college. You have to have a certain GPA to do it. Then I went to a junior college, and then I went to Cali [California] that had no sororities. I could have pledged and drove all the way to Omaha every week. I was like nope, not doing that, because they had a chapter in Omaha. So, I just never did it. But a really good friend of mine is a Delta. She kind of talked to me about it, she's like, "Have you ever thought about pledging grad chapter?" I was like, "I'm not going through that crap, no no no no no." I do love what they stand for and I love volunteering, giving back to the community, and so I kind of talked myself into doing it, and I did it.

I asked Diane how she was enjoying her new membership in the graduate chapter:

> It's work! Oh, and it's expensive. It's not cheap. But it's been a good experience. The craziest thing about being in a sorority, the coolest thing I think, is I now have this network of [a] gazillion African American—and other races—sisters. I mean historically we are African American, but there are other women who are in the organization that are not all African American. But I have this huge universe. I go somewhere and having a Delta pin and we're, "Hey soror!" We're like sisters. It's a neat, neat experience.
>
> What I love too is that sometimes when I talk to people that don't know me, they always think I sound angry, because I talk loud and I talk passionate. That's what we do culturally.

> But I love when I get with my sisters, because we can talk like
> that and nobody thinks anybody is mad, nobody is thinking
> somebody is getting attitude. Nobody's judging each other. It's
> how we chat with each other. It is nice. I love that. Love it. But
> White people take that sometimes the wrong way. They take
> it as if we're being dominating and powerful. That drives me
> nuts. Or "Diane were you mad?" "No, I was just passionate
> about what we were talking about. I talk loudly because I want
> you to hear what I'm saying."

Diane indicated the importance of the large social network of other
Black women, both in the local community and in the nation. Diane
compared the times when she could relax with sorority members and
express herself in a more robust way with how she was treated by White
people if she spoke in the same way to them. The stereotypes of Black
women as "loud" or "angry" is well established and has a long history
of being debunked and critiqued in academic scholarship as a way that
Black women are misrecognized and misunderstood (Fordham, 1993;
Griffin, 2012a; Koonce, 2012; Walley-Jean, 2009). The sorority provided
a place where Diane could just be herself without the worry of White
people watching her, judging her, or wondering why she was expressing
herself in a gregarious manner. The sorority was a space of resistance to
Whiteness and to stereotypes of Black women.

Finding Places to "Celebrate Being Black" at a PWI: Nosipha's Story

Nosipha began her college degree in social sciences in the 1980s at the
public, liberal arts University of Mary Washington in Fredericksburg,
Virginia. Nosipha went on to earn a master's degree in the same field
from Ohio University in the mid-1990s. She earned a PhD in the same
discipline from Michigan State University in the early 2000s. Nosipha
recalled the importance of being involved in Black organizations at the
very start of her college experience at Mary Washington:

> I started with a summer program that I attended before college,
> which allowed me to do two courses: calculus and biology. I
> got to meet other African American students who were coming
> into the program. There were 13 of us that came in as African

American students at Mary Washington and we formed a bond. We had a mentor named Mr. Henry Banks, and he took us under his wing, and Dr. Madison and June Washington and Mr. Ray Burns. So, we understood what the meaning of Blackness meant in going to a predominantly White university.

[The program] was aimed at students of color to get us acclimated to campus, to introduce us to courses, and to each other, mostly to each other. We would have annual banquets where we would celebrate being Black. There were awards given, we would toast each other and celebrate each other's accomplishments.

The summer program built a sense of community, a *Chosen We* group, before college even began. Starting college with a group of other African American students meant that Nosipha had a built-in community when she began to transition to the predominantly White campus. Importantly, not only were the students offered messaging about positive ideas of Blackness, they were also taught to celebrate one another's accomplishments through yearly banquets.

Nosipha described the importance of the group with which she was involved:

We had a strong consciousness. At that time, apartheid was at its highest, and we got to learn about Nelson Mandela, we got to link what the civil rights movement did in America to what it did in South Africa. A comparison of those two and seeing the African experience as a holistic one, not just separated by borders or by oceans. It was one total experience. We got involved with the Black Student Association. It was [previously] called the Afro-American Student Association; we changed it because we thought "Afro" was a bit outdated. When we had that name, we were first on the name of organizations, so people got to see our name first. We did change it to the Black Student Association, and we took on causes. We even did things with the Nation of Islam, because that was big back then too in the 1980s. I went to college from 1986 to 1990.

Nosipha continually used the word "we" when referring to her experience at Mary Washington, indicating that she saw her experience as deeply connected to the few other Black students she knew on campus. Her partnering the Nation of Islam, an African American political and religious organization that emphasizes the liberation of Black people,[9] may have been controversial at the time. There has been controversy about whether the group promotes self-determination and achievement, or whether it reproduces race, gender, and class categories (Akom, 2003). The Southern Poverty Law Center, a group associated with fighting hate in the United States, has listed the Nation of Islam as a hate group for many years, claiming it is racist, sexist, homophobic, and anti-Semitic.[10] Malcolm X was one of the more famous members of the Nation of Islam and connected it to his work on Black liberation until 1964 when he disavowed the organization and started his own, highlighting Pan-Africanism and Black self-determination (Dyson, 1996; Terrill, 2007). Three members of the Nation of Islam assassinated Malcolm X in 1965 (Dyson, 1996). Nosipha continued:

> Nelson Mandela[11] was really big, you know when Mandela was keeping his name alive, so you would see his image blasted off. There were also marches on Washington that we got to participate in. When the Supreme Court reversed all these decisions which impeded African American progress, we dressed up in all White for women, all Black for men, and we marched and held placards in Washington, DC. And that's a lot to do with Mr. Banks, because he was definitely conscious and always trying to create a comfortable environment for Black students at Mary Washington. In the end, only nine of us graduated, four of us didn't. But some that didn't graduate went on to pharmacy school and stuff like that, and they came back and saw us graduate. We still keep in touch today.

Nosipha underscored how engaged the students were in trying to understand Blackness and racial justice globally with a Pan-African perspective. She also mentioned the importance of South African apartheid in the development of her resistance and activism during college. Apartheid was a legal and governmentally created form of racial segregation that started in South Africa after the election of an all-White government in 1948 (Murray, 1994). Apartheid was in place for nearly 50 years (Price, 1991). The policy separated people by skin color in neighborhoods, schools, the government, and all institutional structures. During apartheid, it was illegal to marry someone with a different skin color, land was forcibly taken from Black South Africans, and there were periods when Black South Africans were forced to always carry paperwork with them (Murray, 1994; Price, 1991). It is not surprising that it took many years to rebuild the country that had been racially segregated for generations (Bond, 2014; Hart, 2002; Mandela, 2011; Meer, 1988).

During Jim Crow, people were separated in education and other social institutions (Woodward, 1955/2002). Jim Crow laws were a legal form of racial segregation after the end of slavery in the US to continue the oppression of Black people, and to try to keep White people from interacting with, marrying, or having children with Black people (at least by consent; many children were born due to the rape of Black women during slavery) (Woodward, 1955/2002). Like South African apartheid, Jim Crow–legalized racial segregation lasted for generations, nearly 75 years. Jim Crow was enforced through local police forces, local officials (judges, lawyers, mayors, etc.), and through acts of terror such as unprosecuted lynchings (horrific and often public murders of Black people).[12]

These histories coincided for Nosipha in a significant way, such that she could use South African apartheid to understand racial history, resistance, and activism in the United States. Knowing this history seemed to help her create a stronger sense of her own power, and the need to assert herself as a Black woman. Nosipha wove together her history and Pan-African history in a way that demonstrated that she saw herself as part of a larger notion of Blackness that transcended her institution, her identity, and the United States. It is likely that Nosipha saw at least some type of global Black *Chosen We* in this global perspective. Ultimately, Nosipha credited her involvement in the Black Student Association as a major reason for her graduation from college and she suggested that it played a large role in the success of her friends too.

While the Black Student Association helped Nosipha to develop a pro-Black consciousness in college, her leadership in the organization came with some challenges. Reflecting on her interest in fighting for racial justice, Nosipha recalled:

> It started with the Black Student Association. I was vice president. I worked my way up from secretary, treasurer, vice president, to president. When I was president we had more of a mixture of ethnic groups. We had Whites join in. Some people were against that. I wanted to be an organization for everybody,

but the causes were for Black people, African American people. An NAACP[13] type of thing, you know.

I stepped down from the presidency because I was being attacked, and I just didn't want to put up with it and I stepped down. Mr. Banks was glad, because he wanted somebody else he thought was more pro-Black than I [was] and he got somebody who was. People were just doing things to sabotage my tenure as president so that I would not look like I was doing anything. I didn't really like limelight, and unfortunately, I was getting too much limelight. So, I was okay with the decision I had to make. I still participated. I just wasn't a leader.

It is unclear what it might have meant to be more "pro-Black" or exactly what happened to make Nosipha's presidency difficult, but it is important to highlight that involvement in organizations can be complicated. While Nosipha did credit the Black Student Association with helping her to become more conscious of her Blackness in positive ways, and with promoting her general success in college, there were still some challenges related to the group. There have been many accounts of Black women perceiving pressure to choose between movements for Black freedom and women's movements (Davis, 2015) so it may be the case that this was part of the issue for Nosipha.

Black Student Academic, Social, and Political Organizations and the Chosen We

PWI alumnae identified formal Black student organizations (academic, social, or political) as integral to their belonging, support, and success during college. It is important to note that there was no single organization or approach that was effective for everyone. Alumnae identified different combinations or types of opportunities that worked for each of them. Not only is it necessary to highlight the importance of Black *Chosen We* organizations and physical spaces on PWI campuses, but it is also crucial to emphasize that there is not a one-size-fits-all prescription for these organizations. One of the elements that makes these communities *Chosen We* spaces is that women could choose if, when, and how to engage these groups. It is highly likely that some graduates of these institutions did *not* engage in these organizations, although that would merit further study that specifically recruited people who were not involved in these groups to see why they selected other opportunities. In this group of alumnae, nearly all of them identified these communities as the primary way that they thrived in college.

Black formal student organizations such as Black student unions, African People's Organizations, sororities, or similar groups served as both social and political *Chosen We* communities for the vast majority of PWI alumnae. These organizations were sites of community, leadership, and often they were also places to launch resistance to racist and White supremacist policies and practices on PWI campuses. Many of the alumnae were leaders in these organizations and subsequently leaders in campus movements for racial justice (Princess, Michelle, Josephine, Jasmine, Nosipha, Vivian, Charlie). Sometimes the leadership in these organizations transcended campus boundaries. For example, Tiffany mentioned mentoring primary and secondary students in the community through her organization. Black student organizations were *Chosen We* spaces because students voluntarily opted to join them and could decide when and how often to engage.

Many women explained formal Black student organizations in communal ways, using familial words like "the fam" (Cassie), or calling the group a "support system" (Tiffany), or saying that Black students really had to "stick together" (Jospehine). There was an emphasis on unity, solidarity, and building a *Chosen We* community that could both help to counter and resist the Eurocentric nature of PWIs. But importantly, these organizations also offered unique, empowering, and dynamic ideas of what it could mean to be Black. Michelle described her involvement in her Black student organization as helping her to begin to view her identity as much larger than just being Black in the United States; she soon saw herself as a Black person who was part of a larger African diaspora and connected to numerous ideas of Blackness globally.

The leadership positions that many women had in college were not without complications and difficulties, however. Sometimes alumnae named specific ways in which campuses treated Black and White student organizations differently. Princess described her group being challenged about a speaker that she tried to bring to campus and noted that she did not see predominantly White organizations being challenged in the same way. Multiple alumnae described feeling as if they had to choose between their gender or their race in these organizations. At times, Black women felt they had to suppress their gender concerns to elevate the fight for racial justice (Michelle).

Black academic organizations were *Chosen We* spaces because alumnae chose to study the academic disciplines associated with these organizations, and the alumnae also opted for voluntary membership in the group. Involvement in these academic spaces provided positive community spaces to identify both role models and peers in particular academic disciplines. In many academic disciplines that alumnae mentioned such as engineering (Crystal), management (Lark), and sociology (Olivia), there seemed to be few, if any, Black scholars. Students who studied these topics might only read scholarship by White male authors.

Even while there has long been important scholarship by Black intellectuals, there is evidence that many Black scholars were systematically left out of the major disciplinary canons in their fields. For example, the first African American man to earn a PhD at Harvard University, W.E.B. Du Bois, is arguably one of the most important founding sociologists (Bonilla-Silva & Baiocchi, 2001; Morris, 2015; Zuberi, 2004), but Du Bois's work is often not included in representations of the sociological "canon" because he was systematically kept from being included as a leader in his discipline because he was Black (Morris, 2015). For Black women, the pathway to being included as leaders of their academic disciplines has been particularly difficult. As an example, 10 years before Du Bois was writing his major works, Anna Julia Cooper (1988/1892) wrote her major work, *A Voice from the South*. Cooper remains relatively unknown by many sociologists, even in contemporary times, even though she made some of the founding assertions about the need to consider race and gender as interconnected identities (Lengermann, & Niebrugge, 2006; May, 2012).

The necessity of Black academic *Chosen We* spaces is emphasized by the fact that some students might journey through college and never take a class from a Black faculty member in their academic discipline. Creating community with other Black intellectuals in disciplines that were traditionally White and male was a necessity to feeling that alumnae could be included, or be leading scholars, in a particular academic area. Involvement in these groups meant that one could break down racial stereotypes that often did not allow much space for Blackness to coincide with academic ideas (see also McGee & Martin, 2011). For those Black alumnae who earned graduate degrees in disciplines that were formerly exclusive to Black women, there can be an important shift in knowledge creation (Collins, 2002).

Sorority membership offered another type of *Chosen We* space on PWI campuses, a close-knit, familial community on college campuses and beyond. Sororities, particularly National Pan-Hellenic Council (NPHC) sororities that are historically mostly Black members, are unique organizations that often bring with the membership an expectation that one will continue active engagement through one's lifetime (Giddings, 2009; Ross, 2001). Women who joined a sorority in college by and large continued their involvement for many years afterward because of the expectation for lifelong engagement (Giddings, 2009) and because the organization provided such a meaningful set of social relationships, support, and community engagement. Sororities were *Chosen We* sites on campuses because women selected whether to join these organizations. Sororities are not open access organizations however, so choice is not all that is required to join. Rather, those interested must be accepted as members by the current membership before they can join. Once a woman opted to pledge a sorority and was accepted, she was offered support, sisterhood, and community engagement. Sometimes sororities purposefully offered concrete support on how to succeed in college and role modeling that families could not, particularly for first-generation college students. It is not that families were not engaged or interested in their students' college experiences. Rather, if family members had not attended college, it would be hard to give specific advice on how to be successful in that realm. Keisha explained that while her family wanted her to earn good grades, the sorority was able to help her understand *how* to achieve these academic successes. Sororities offered crucial social networking and representation. The sorority also often offered important nuances about what it meant to be Black and a woman.

The Importance of Black *Chosen We Spaces* on Predominantly White Campuses

The importance of Black community *Chosen We* spaces on predominantly White campuses cannot be underscored enough. For alumnae, these spaces are a lifeline on campuses that can be outwardly hostile to Black students (Valandra Fields et al., 2022). Or, for those who are not actively feeling alienated, these spaces become necessary self-selected vessels through which a student can choose to navigate the campus. Out of the 69 predominantly White institution alumnae who attended these institutions for their undergraduate degrees, only a handful did not emphasize the importance of Black spaces in college.

It was crucial that there was a variety of types of formal organizations where Blackness was embraced, celebrated, and highlighted. A one-size-fits-all approach could have been limiting, or worse, essentializing toward students, inferring that all Black students have the same interests or needs when they clearly do not. Some women found their "oasis" in Black student government or a Black cultural center, while others found solace in Black academic organizations where they could embrace their academic discipline as a field that might encourage Black participants. Regardless, in order to counter the often overwhelming and alienating Whiteness of these campuses, it was a necessity to have a space that was unapologetically embracing Blackness.

Campuses and administrators within them could take a few important lessons from these critical oral histories of PWI graduates:

1. View healing, nurturing, Black organizations and physical spaces as a central and crucial part of racial justice work at PWIs. To be clear, not *all* Black students will want to engage in these Black spaces or organizations, and no effort toward inclusion should be viewed as a panacea or a one-size-fits-all (Feagin et al., 2014/1996) approach. But Black or racially/ethnically focused spaces should be embraced, elevated, staffed, and funded.

2. Cultivate physical spaces dedicated to the discussion and inclusion of racial/ethnic identities on campus. One way to do this is through providing campus resources to put race-centered spaces in central locations. These physical spaces (Black culture centers) should be sites where students know that they can enter that space and see others who look like them and where their racial identities are embraced through the literature (books, brochures, media) and artifacts (artwork, the people who are held up as models, awards, music, games).

3. Foster academic departments where Black academic disciplinary groups are celebrated to demonstrate that all disciplines can and should have a Black presence and role models who look like students. To do so means taking seriously the hiring of faculty of color in academic disciplines across campus. Additionally, within academic departments, there

should be deliberate and ongoing discussions about the authors and scholars who are centered as part of the "canon" in particular disciplines. Faculty should be encouraged to deliberately build racial diversity into the authors who are cited and read in their syllabi and courses. Departments can also take seriously the artifacts that are represented in the department and be more racially inclusive in this representation. For instance, departments should consider what artwork or books are put up in the department and who is represented by those artifacts (Are scholars or color represented?). Departments should also examine who receives awards for teaching, mentoring, and research to identify why certain kinds of work are demonstrated to be meritorious in the department (Is the work of scholars or students of color identified as meritorious in the department?).

4. Foster openness to the inclusion of NPHC sororities and fraternities on campus that honor the histories, backgrounds, and identities of Black and Brown students. Carefully evaluate the resources given to traditionally White Greek-lettered organizations and those that are African American, Latina/o/x, or Asian to ensure that resources are distributed in such a way as to promote equity (also see Duran et al., 2022).

5. Encourage racial/ethnic organizations and other campus efforts, and those faculty or administrators who advise or support them, to be open to race and gender liberation so that Black women do not perceive a need to choose between fighting for one identity over another.

6. Campus efforts to unapologetically embrace Black formal organizational spaces are not a threat to integration and multiculturalism. Rather, they are a crucial supplement to true inclusion. That is, offering voluntary *Chosen We* spaces that students can opt to engage with (or not) at various times during their degree programs may be one of the most important efforts a campus can undertake to positively demonstrate that the institution is not a bastion of White supremacy and Eurocentrism. A PWI campus can

and should have spaces that clearly and unapologetically promote Blackness (and Brownness, etc.). By promoting and distributing resources (facilities and funding) toward various racial/ethnic organizations, campus administrators can proactively demonstrate a meaningful commitment toward better and more authentic inclusion.

Black organizational spaces are a way to "define and empower," not a way to "divide and conquer" (Lorde, 2012). These organizations allowed Black alumnae spaces for self-definition, resistance, and the elevation of Black women's knowledge, insight, and futures (Collins, 2002). Black formal organizational spaces can be sites of empowerment (Lorde, 2012). Through this empowerment, these alumnae were in many ways able to transform their own ideas of who they could and would be as Black women. They also often transformed their campuses in the process.

Part III

From a Collective Legacy of Racial Uplift to Empowered Individual Identity at Historically Black Colleges and Universities (HBCUs)

Long before there was institutional recognition of it, Black people in the United States were meeting about, constructing, and fighting for educational freedoms (Williams, 2007). Numerous historians have pointed to the deep, unending tenacity and desire to use education as a form of racial uplift among Black communities (Anderson, 1988; Gasman, 2007a, 2007b; Williams, 2007). For example, the "Colored Conventions," which occurred from the 1830s to the 1890s, were a series of state and national meetings among free Black people in which they "strategized about how to achieve educational, labor, and legal justice at a moment when Black rights were constricting nationally and locally."[1] The following chapters focus on higher education's role in racial uplift. Historically Black colleges and universities (HBCUs) are one of the foremost examples of a long tradition of racial uplift through education, created by and for Black people through philanthropy, church support, and eventually, state support (Anderson, 1988; Benton, 2020; Gasman, 2007a; Gasman & Sedgwick, 2005; Lee-Johnson, 2021; Ricard & Brown, 2008).

After the abolishment of enslavement of Black people in the United States, a long and arguably unending process of reconstruction began during which the country attempted to repair the damages done by the insidious practice (Franklin, 1994). However, the enslavement, derogation, and exclusion of Black people persisted for at least another 100 years. Some scholars claim that the country has never been fully reconstructed (Blackmon, 2009; Clark-Pujara, 2016; Wilder, 2014; Williams, 2007). One of the most pervasive questions immediately after the abolishment of enslavement was how to educate Black people who had been systematically and purposefully kept from basic literacy and education (Anderson, 1988; Jones, 1992; Williams, 2005).

Higher education was no exception to racial segregation in education. HBCUs were some of the first institutions that offered an accessible pathway to higher education for African American and Black people in the United States (Ricard & Brown, 2008). HBCUs attempted to meet the rising challenge of providing higher education for thousands of Black students after enslavement (Gasman et al., 2015). In northern states, free Black people received higher education at historically Black colleges, including Cheney University (founded in 1837) and Lincoln University (founded in 1854) in Pennsylvania and Wilberforce University in Ohio (founded in 1856) long before the end of slavery in 1865 (Gasman et al., 2015). It was not until 30 years later that HBCUs would be federally supported.

Through the first Morrill Act, passed in 1865, all 50 states received land and money to build public state universities to make higher education more accessible for White citizens (Thelin, 2011), although arguably, the land that was often "given" was stolen from indigenous populations. The first Morrill Act did little to make higher education accessible to Black people. Only a few of those land-grant institutions were public HBCUs (Gasman et al., 2015). The second Morrill Act was passed in 1890, granting land with which primarily southern states with concentrated Black populations could build public institutions to educate Black citizens (Thelin, 2011). The second Morrill Act led to the creation of 17 southern public land-grant HBCUs. These institutions were funded at a gravely disproportionate level as compared to their predominantly White counterparts (Gasman et al., 2015). The unequal resource distribution to HBCUs has continued to haunt these institutions (Kim & Conrad, 2006). Despite unequal funding, recent scholarship argues for the importance of viewing HBCUs as the asset that they have been and continue to be for many students nationally (Williams et al., 2018). Due to the history of their founding, most HBCUs had some element of racial uplift, perseverance, and social mobility for Black people in their missions and these ethos have persevered over time (Albritton, 2012; Conrad & Gasman, 2015; Gasman et al., 2015), even as these institutions have diversified racially to include an increasing number of White students or students from other racial groups in addition to Black students (Mobley, Johnson, & Drezner, 2022).[2] The alumnae in this study attended HBCUs that are embedded in a larger history of racial uplift and social mobility for Black people.

A Brief Description of the HBCU Alumnae in This Study

Of the 105 women in the larger study, 36 graduated from HBCUs (table 4). Thirty-four women earned a bachelor's degree at an HBCU and two attended a PWI for their undergraduate degree and then earned a graduate degree at an HBCU. Ten of the women who graduated from HBCUs for their undergraduate degrees were the first in their families to earn a college degree (also called first-generation students). The two women who attended HBCUs for their graduate degrees were not first-generation college students. There were two alumnae who earned bachelor's degrees at predominantly White institutions (PWIs) and then chose to attend an HBCU for their graduate programs.

There is often an ethos of graduate school preparation at many HBCUs, as if there is a normative assumption to earn an advanced degree such as a master's degree or a PhD. HBCUs offer exemplary preparation for students to attend graduate programs, even in disciplines that are often very difficult to enter such as science, technology, engineering, and mathematics (STEM) (Boncana et al., 2021; Perna et al., 2009). Related to these trends, of the 36 women who attended HBCUs for their undergraduate degrees, the majority (25 women) went on to complete master's degrees and 12 of the alumnae earned terminal degrees such as PhDs, MDs, or JDs (table 4). Recall that among the 82 PWI alumnae, 41 women earned master's degrees and 18 earned terminal degrees.

In 2016, there were 102 HBCUs[3] located in 19 mostly southern states (Lovett, 2015). The 36 HBCU alumnae in this book attended 10 HBCUs. Many HBCUs that were included in this study do not offer graduate-level degrees (table 5). Of the institutions represented in the book, there were only three where alumnae attended graduate programs: Clark Atlanta University, Howard University, and Tuskegee University (table 5). At both Clark Atlanta and Howard, there were alumnae who earned both bachelor's degrees and graduate degrees. Of the two alumnae who attended HBCUs

Table 4. Demographics of the HBCU Alumnae

TOTAL number of HBCU alumnae (undergraduate *and* graduate degrees)	36 women (105 women in the study)
Number of women who attended HBCUs for undergraduate degrees	34 women
Number of women who attend HBCUs for graduate-level degrees (who attended PWIs for undergraduate degrees)	2 women
First-generation status (first in the family to attend college)	10 women
Number of HBCU undergraduate alumnae who earned graduate degrees at PWIs	25 master's degrees earned 12 terminal degrees earned (PhD, JD, MD, etc.)
Number of HBCU undergraduate alumnae who earned graduate degrees at HBCUs	1 alumna (attended an HBCU for master's, PWI for PhD)

Source: Author-created.

Table 5. Historically Black Institutions by Private or Public Status

Name of Institution	**Location**	**Private or Public**
1. Benedict College	Columbia, South Carolina	Private
2. Clark Atlanta University (formerly Clark College and Atlanta University, undergraduate and graduate)	Atlanta, Georgia	Private
3. Dillard University	New Orleans, Louisiana	Private
4. Fisk University	Nashville, Tennessee	Private
5. Florida A&M University	Tallahassee, Florida	Public
6. Howard University (undergraduate and graduate)	Washington, DC	Private
7. Spelman College	Atlanta, Georgia	Private
8. Southern University and A&M College, Baton Rouge	Baton Rouge, Louisiana	Public
9. Tuskegee University (graduate only)	New Orleans, Louisiana	Private
10. Xavier University of New Orleans	New Orleans, Louisiana	Private

Source: Author-created.

for graduate school after earning an undergraduate degree from a PWI, one attended Tuskegee University for a doctoral degree in veterinary medicine and a second earned a master's degree in social work at Clark Atlanta University. Two alumnae attended public HBCUs (of the 17 public state, land-grant institutions nationally). The other seven institutions from which alumnae graduated are private institutions. Some of the private institutions are storied to be more prestigious institutions among HBCUs (e.g., Spelman College and Howard University) (Lovett, 2015). One of the institutions that alumnae discussed in this book is one of two remaining historically Black women's colleges, Spelman College (the other is Bennett College in Greensboro, North Carolina) (table 5).

Racial Inclusion and Resistance at HBCUs

The findings in the next chapters resonate deeply with the growing body of evidence that maintains that Black students have more positive experiences at HBCUs than at PWIs. HBCUs have served a central role in promoting college access and success for students of color over time (Conrad & Gasman, 2015; Williams et al., 2022). In studies that compare Black students' experiences at HBCUs and PWIs, the importance of historically Black institutions is monumental (Allen et al., 1991; Allen, 1992; Fleming, 1978, 1984; Willie, 2003). Black students have reported better social, emotional, and cognitive learning outcomes and satisfaction at HBCUs as compared to their predominantly White counterparts (Allen, 1992; Allen et al., 1991; Chen et al., 2014; Hardy et al., 2019; McCoy et al., 2017; Mobley & Johnson, 2015). Attending an HBCU has also been linked with positive academic outcomes in fields where Black students are greatly underrepresented, such as within STEM disciplines (Nguyen et al., 2019; Palmer, Davis, & Thompson, 2010; Palmer, Davis, & Maramba, 2010; Palmer & Gasman, 2008; Winkle-Wagner & McCoy, 2016) and in preparation for graduate programs (Boncana et al., 2021; Perna et al., 2009). It is no surprise that scholars have started to suggest that it is important for decision-makers at PWIs to learn from the practices and successes at HBCUs (Arroyo & Gasman, 2014; Conrad & Gasman, 2015; Williams et al., 2022). Among the 36 alumnae accounts in the following chapters, the words "warm" and "nurturing" or a "sisterhood" or "family" were common phrases to describe their HBCU experiences.[4] These words are in stark contrast to PWI alumnae in this book, who emphasized terms such as "isolation" and "culture shock" (part 2).

A Brief Preview of the Findings from HBCU Alumnae

The HBCU graduates whose oral histories are included here span college experiences that occurred from 1954 to 2014. The experiences offer two thematic claims, across generations, institutions, and geographic regions, all of which will be explored in the next two chapters (figure 3). HBCUs offered diverse and nuanced ways of being Black women. By feeling deeply included in a *Chosen We* community that embraced their backgrounds, the alumnae were able to identify their own individuality and uniqueness (their *Me*). The *Chosen We*, a concept about community and belonging, also means that one can be exposed to more viable alternatives for their identities. In contrast, within PWIs, Black women described the constant need to dispel stereotypes and to push back on expectations of who they had to be because there were so few Black students and fewer viable alternatives for who they might become on those campuses (see, for example, Winkle-Wagner et al., 2018). It is not that Black women at PWIs did not identify their individuality. Rather, it was the case that through contested and misrecognized individual identities, Black women at PWIs turned to *Chosen We* communities to *affirm* their identities. At HBCUs, this process was flipped: by being brought into a campus *Chosen We* community that felt deeply affirming (Williams et al., 2022) and offered many versions of what it could mean to be a Black woman, the alumnae then could identify and claim their individuality. There were two claims to how Blackness and womanhood were crafted in HBCUs (table 6):

1. HBCUs offered a perspective of Blackness-as-greatness (chapter 5). HBCUs are examples of a larger, historical legacy of collective identity, a *Chosen We* that is associated with Black excellence. Black women have been important to this legacy in ways that have at times gone unnoticed or have been undermined.

2. Black women felt a deep sense of belonging that is associated with HBCU campuses being a type of "home" or "family" (chapter 6). In becoming part of the *Chosen We* of Black excellence, alumnae identified feeling like they were deeply included in something larger than themselves. Often, this felt so inclusive that women described it in familial terms, and this familial ethos allowed Black women to identify individual identities, or their *Me*.

The emergence of the long legacy of Black excellence in chapter 5 is deeply connected to the Black feminist argument about the need for more emphasis on African American history and culture (Collins, 1986, 2002; Dillard, 2000; Lorde, 2012). The legacy that is referenced, which was initiated by families and communities and reinforced by HBCUs, was a way to bolster Black women's long path to self-knowledge and self-valuing (Collins, 2002; Cooper, 1892). In chapter 6, the connection to HBCUs as a type of home or family also related to the idea of a Black legacy or history of uplift that is represented by these institutions (Collins, 2002; Davis, 1971). Important throughout these chapters is the idea that the identities and experiences of the alumnae were intersectional (Collins, 2002; Williams et al., 2022). The systems in which the women engaged represented intersecting oppressions too. Alumnae discussed public schools that were only partially integrated at best, neighborhoods in larger metropolitan communities that were often segregated, and repeated acts of racism and hostility in predominantly White public spaces. Community was a way to cope and thrive amid overlapping oppressive social structures and institutions. Importantly, as I explored in table 6, the community that was fostered was integrated into many campus activities and norms (e.g., orientation programs, classrooms, pedagogies, events, policies). Additionally, there were overlapping community norms across students, staff, faculty, and alumnae, a noteworthy difference from PWIs where campus norms were not always shared across campus constituencies (table 6).

Finally, because there were 27 women who attended *both* HBCUs and PWIs (either attending an HBCU for an undergraduate degree and a PWI for graduate school of vice versa), the alumnae offered a unique opportunity to reflect on the differences between these two types of institutions (table 6). Comparing the two institutional types, HBCUs may have been better locations for mental and physical health and well-being, at least for the alumnae in this study.

Figure 3 offers a way to visualize the connections between the United States racial history, collective identities, and individual identities at HBCUs. In particular, the figure attempts to demonstrate that

1. HBCUs are examples of a larger, historical legacy of collective identity, a *Chosen We* that is associated with Black excellence and greatness. Black women were brought into collective identity from the moment they arrived on campus. They were deliberately and consistently reminded of their

Table 6. Mechanisms for Establishing Intersectional Black Womanhood at HBCUs

		Definition	Mechanisms for establishing intersectional Black womanhood
Definition of Blackness	Blackness as (Intersectional) Greatness	Blackness was associated with a long history of self-determination and excellence. Included in this definition is a varied idea of gender that intersects with race and other identities and often elevates Black women as leaders.	• Orientation programs • In classes • Campus colloquia and events • By peers, faculty, staff, and alumni
	Blackness as Home	As alumnae were able to identify varied and intersectional definitions of Blackness and womanhood, they described a sense of belonging that made campuses feel like home.	• Campus demographics, artifacts and ethos • Campus norms of the importance of community and collectivism • By peers, faculty, staff, and alumni

Source: Author-created.

place in that community throughout their experiences in and outside of the classroom.

2. In becoming part of the *Chosen We* of Black excellence, Black women felt a deep sense of belonging that is associated with campuses being a type of "home" or "family." The idea of being at home and part of a larger family on

campus both reaffirmed the *Chosen We* of Black excellence while also opening space for developing individuality, or the *Me* parts of identity.

3. The familial ethos of HBCUs made it possible for Black women to identify their unique sense of individual identity, their *Me*. Black women noted that the campus culture felt as if being Black is not monolithic, or being Black was not a particular "label." Rather, the development of individual *Me* identities helped to expand the possibilities for what it can mean to be a Black woman. The familial ethos at HBCUs stood in stark contrast to the experiences that alumnae recounted at PWIs where they were often treated as tokens or representatives of the Black experience.

While a two-dimensional figure cannot fully represent the full complexity of human conditions, general pathways can be structured from it. As figure 3 suggests, the racial history of the United States influences the creation of and experiences within HBCUs, and the way that people develop and experience their identities. As this chapter and the next assert, HBCUs foster an ethos of being deeply included in a collective. I am calling this collective the *Chosen We* because women voluntarily chose to join it, and they also had the volition to leave it if they desired to do so. The *Chosen We* that was cultivated within HBCUs was an important way for women to feel included, and ultimately, it was through that collective identity that the women were able to develop an agentic, empowered sense of individuality.

The pathways from collective to individual identities were the opposite for PWI alumnae. Figure 3 provides a way to visualize how collective and individual identities emerged within HBCUs. Like PWIs, HBCUs cannot be separated from racial history in the United States (part 2). While individual and collective (*We*) identities can resituate history in some ways (for the present moments that eventually become history), what has happened in the past is always shaping the racial present. The alumnae at PWIs repeatedly described a contestation and misrecognition of identities such that they had to turn to collective spaces (both physical and relational) in order to be able to survive and then thrive within their undergraduate programs. In contrast, the alumnae who attended HBCUs strongly maintained the importance of an ethos of collective identity within their undergraduate institutions (figure 3). That is, because alumnae were immediately and continually brought into the community of the campus and treated as if they were being included in a longer history of excellence, they were better able to identify diverse and nuanced ideas of Blackness and womanhood. Identities proceeded from a collective (*We*) to a unique, nuanced, and more individually chosen set of identities (*Me*). Ultimately, the pathways of identities were simple. In HBCUs there was not only a more collective campus culture, but there were also simply more ways of being "Black" and of performing Black womanhood. The arrows in figure 3 go both ways because the process of shaping identities was iterative, often collective, and holistic. The pathways in which alumnae described experiencing collective and authentic individual identities occurred through 1) being brought into the legacy of racial uplift, and 2) feeling a deep sense of belonging such as being at home. It was through the legacy of racial uplift and belonging that alumnae were able to identify unique individual (*Me*) identities.

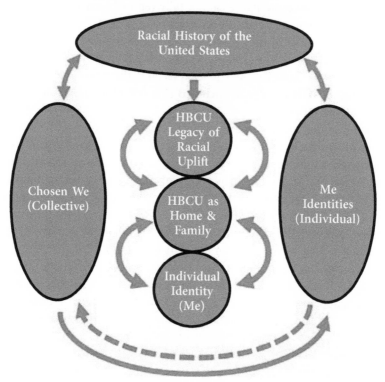

Figure 3. Racial History and Collective/Individual Identities at HBCUs. *Source*: Author-created.

As students enrolled in HBCUs, they were immediately included as part of a much broader legacy of racial uplift. Alumnae reported knowing they were a part of this legacy on their first visits to campus, their orientation programs, and their first weeks as students through campus colloquia and events. The legacy of uplift and Black excellence was repeatedly taught and highlighted throughout degree programs, in classes, activities, campus events, and campus artifacts. It seemed as if most campus actors worked deliberately to perpetuate the sense of inclusion in something larger, a collective idea of Blackness-as-greatness. Peers, faculty, staff, and alumnae all were named as people who helped reinforce this positive messaging. Through this general ethos of Blackness-as-greatness, alumnae were able to begin to see nuanced and intersectional ways of being Black and of being women. The sense of collective identity meant that alumnae felt deeply included in their campuses, even naming these institutions as a type of "home." It was through this process of collective identity and inclusion that alumnae were then able to identify authentic, diverse, and intersectional individual identities (*Mes*).

HBCUs were the epitome of *Chosen We*, collectivist, communities in that they were deeply connected to a long legacy of collective Black greatness. Alumnae chose to become part of these communities when they chose to attend a particular institution. Families, peers, faculty, administrators, and alumnae reinforced and built the *Chosen We* communities during and long after most of the women in this book graduated from college. The HBCU *Chosen We* communities were both relational and physical spaces.

HBCU campuses were physical spaces that provided necessary protections from external hostility, racism, or sexism. Other campuses provided a campus identity through the architecture, quads, or campus artifacts that made it clear that students were entering a sacred space. For instance, at Dillard University, all of the buildings are painted white and constructed in a similar style with lush green lawns separating the buildings, making it clear where the campus begins and ends and that the campus is a special place.

The relational aspect of the *Chosen We* communities at HBCUs was reinforced through orientation programs, campuswide colloquia, coursework, a particularly caring approach from faculty, peer mentoring programs, and campus events. Community was woven into the experience in a seamless way. There may have been students who did *not* perceive that they belonged on these campuses. Some students who identified their gender as nonbinary may have had trouble fitting into some HBCU campuses (Johnson, 2017; Lundy-Wagner & Gasman, 2011; Mobley & Johnson, 2015). But the alumnae represented here identified deeply as part of these *Chosen We* communities.

The Structure of Part 3

The two chapters highlighting narrative, critical oral histories from HBCU alumnae offer thematic claims: 1) HBCUs as being connected to a larger legacy of Black excellence and greatness, and 2) HBCUs as offering a deep sense of belonging that allowed for alumnae to identify nuanced individual identities associated with Blackness and womanhood.

The way in which alumnae connected their experiences to specific institutions was different than at PWIs and the data are presented differently too. In PWIs, alumnae identified highly isolating, individualist experiences that ultimately led them to create and identify communities such as informal friendships and formal student organizational *Chosen We* spaces. The individualist nature of PWIs meant that the findings emerged as a collection of individual histories that were very similar. The emphasis in PWIs was on the experience of being a Black woman on those campuses. The specific institutions were not necessarily as important (e.g., the University of Nebraska, the University of Michigan) as was the predominantly White environment. In other words, an alumna might talk about her experience of navigating racial isolation and identifying community with other students of color and then only mention the specific institution as an afterthought. For this reason, part 2 was presented as a combination of narrative and thematic ideas about PWIs more generally.

Within HBCUs, alumnae were specific about the institutional ethos where the institutional context was always named as important. For most HBCU alums, it was not enough to say that HBCUs were great institutions where they felt like they belonged (which they said). Rather, alumnae described being a "Spelman woman" or a part of the "Dillard family," for example, to talk about HBCUs and their larger experiences. They offered institutionally contextualized ideas as to how the institution fostered an ethos of excellence or belonging. The narratives in the following chapters offer a form of institutional critical oral history (appendix A), like institutional case studies, to contextualize the data to the institution as many of the alumnae did.

Chapter 5

Blackness-as-Greatness

The Normalization of Nuanced Views of Black Excellence within HBCUs

No, you don't look like most of the people out in this world. No, you will not be treated like most of the people out in this world. However, you are still somebody, a person to be contended with. Don't let anybody tell you differently. You are unique, you are special, you are intelligent, you are beautiful.

—Lisa, Spelman College alum, 1990s,
on what she learned from her HBCU

There is a painting by acclaimed Black artist Gilbert Young, in which a Black man is leaning over the side of what looks to be a solid concrete wall, reaching his left arm down to the outstretched Black hand of another person. Reproductions of the painting, aptly called *He Ain't Heavy*, sold well over 1,000,000 copies before the Cleveland, Ohio, based artist passed away in November 2018. That painting is a visual representation of the kind of racial uplift that is associated with historically Black colleges and universities (HBCUs). Entering an HBCU has been described much like the image in this painting, with the institution reaching toward an outstretched Black hand that is reaching up toward a better life. Likewise, the vast majority of HBCU alumnae interviewed for this book described their experience of college as feeling deeply connected to a much longer history of Black racial uplift and mobility.

Some campuses (such as Dillard University, Howard University, Spelman College) hold parting ceremonies that quite literally called upon ancestors to connect students to the long heritage of Black excellence, greatness, and collective uplift. These ceremonies and other practices like them were a way to honor African American traditions, histories, and cultures (Collins, 2002; Cooper, 1892). Typically, parting ceremonies are steeped in a deliberately planned Afrocentric ritual of calling upon one's elders, ancestors, and those who went before to guide them on their pathway through college. Parting ceremonies are also often carefully planned, deeply moving goodbyes to students' parents or loved ones as they give their children over to the institution, which is deeply connected to a long lineage of Black excellence. Many alumnae described parting ceremonies as highly impactful for them and their parents—a ritual they carried with them through and beyond their time on campus. The idea of calling upon one's lineage of excellence was both a personal responsibility to work toward continued greatness, and a reminder of the obligation that one had to offer their education back to their communities in order to continue the long line of uplift. Parting ceremonies and a legacy of Black excellence were part of what made HBCUs starkly different from PWIs.

HBCUs were vitally important in creating access to college for the alumnae in this study. Even after *Brown v. the Board of Education* in 1954, which mandated racial integration in public schools, most primary and secondary schools failed to accomplish the task (Bell, 1980; Feagin, & Barnett, 2004; Pettigrew, 2004). Even districts that attempted to racially integrate often perpetuated disparate educational experiences and outcomes for Black students (Domina et al., 2017; Lewis & Diamond, 2015; Warikoo et al., 2016). Similarly, higher education institutions were racially segregated and slow to racially diversify their campuses (Dancy & Brown, 2008; Harper, Patton, & Wooden, 2009; Orfield et al., 2005; Smith, 2016; Tienda, 2013; Winkle-Wagner & Locks, 2020). HBCUs have been a crucial, steady form of college access for many Black students (Arroyo & Gasman, 2014; Flores & Park, 2013), and they are known to provide culturally affirming experiences for many Black students (Williams et al., 2022).

Bennett College and Spelman College, founded in 1873 and 1881 respectively, offered a major pathway for Black women to attend college (Guy-Sheftall, 1982). However, HBCU narratives have often been centered on men (Jean-Marie, 2006; Lovett, 2015). For instance, emphasis on HBCU alumni, Black intellectuals, artists, community leaders, and social movement leaders, often highlight men (e.g., Martin Luther King Jr., Thurgood Marshall, Booker T. Washington, Jesse Jackson, Samuel L. Jackson, or Spike Lee). Black women are quite often "swept under the rug" (Gasman, 2007b; see also, Brazzell, 1992; Jean-Marie, 2006). Many notable Black women graduated from HBCUs such as Toni Morrison, Oprah Winfrey, Alice Walker, or Marian Wright Edelman, to name a few. Willa Player was the first Black woman to serve in the role of president of an HBCU, becoming president of Bennett College in 1956, and she spoke out consistently for the need to highlight Black women's experiences in HBCUs (Gasman, 2007b). Some scholars have repeatedly called for a more nuanced gender and sexuality analysis at these institutions (Bonner, 2001; Harper et al., 2004; Johnson, 2017; Lundy-Wagner, & Gasman, 2011; Mobley & Johnson, 2015). These oral histories are a way to elevate Black women's histories within HBCUs, to honor their value, wisdom, and significance in history (Collins, 2002; Cooper, 1892).

Many HBCUs were initiated with a mission of racial uplift (Albritton, 2012; Arroyo & Gasman, 2014; Bettez & Suggs, 2012) and have continued to be culturally affirming exemplars as institutions (Williams et al., 2022). Within this mission, according to these alumnae, is a pervasive notion that in joining the HBCU campus community, one is joining the long historical legacy of Black excellence (Dillard, 2000). There is great, assumed responsibility in this legacy too, a need to pay forward the excellence of individual accomplishments. The collective notion of uplift is in part related to the notion that HBCUs are a type of "home" for the women who attended them. Many of the women used familial terms such as "sisterhood" or "family" to refer to their experiences with peers, faculty, and staff at their alma maters. Finally, the idea of Black greatness that is fostered in HBCUs is nuanced and dynamic, not monolithic. Many of the alums referred to "diversity" and the idea that "Blackness has no labels" within HBCUs. A nuanced vision of Black excellence meant that women could at once be part of a historical and contemporary community while also carving out their own sense of individuality, their own sense of Blackness.

This chapter carves out the legacy of Black greatness that was fostered in HBCUs. The combined oral histories detail *how* the legacy of Black greatness and the collective identity, the *Chosen We*, were nurtured within HBCUs. In sum, the idea that women could be successful was promoted from the moment women stepped onto campus, often before they were officially enrolled during summer orientation programs. It was cultivated throughout their time at the institutions, and sometimes even beyond that as they continued with alumni groups. Importantly, it was not just one group on campus that encouraged the sense of belonging to a collective identity. Rather it was students, staff, faculty, administrators, and even alumni of the institutions. Greatness, and the collective identity, the *Chosen We*, was deliberate, consistent, pervasive, and holistic.

The Legacy of Black Greatness in
HBCUs before, during, and after College

While the women in parts 1 and 2 of this book echoed the long history of racial exclusion within many PWIs, in part 3 the women underscore inclusion and community. Across generations and institutions, HBCUs emerged as a powerfully collectivist set of institutions that promoted community, solidarity, a positive sense of self, and high academic standards (*Chosen Wes*). There was a pervasive theme that by joining an HBCU, a woman was joining hands with generations of accomplished and powerful African American people who preceded her (Giddings, 2009). Not once did an alumna describe an HBCU in a way that promoted only her individual accomplishments over those of others. Rather, HBCUs were framed, from the beginning to the end of their experiences, as community-minded institutions, a generational legacy, a *We*. I focus less on *decisions* to attend HBCUs here to allow for a deeper analysis of pathways through college after one enrolled (but see Freeman, 2002; Tobolowsky et al., 2005).

The discussions of Black greatness (Dillard, 2008) in this chapter are from alumnae who not only attended HBCUs but were clearly people who deeply internalized the values of their institutions. While these oral histories demonstrate what HBCUs *can* be and *are* for many people, it is necessary to point out that there are likely some students who attend and perhaps even graduate from HBCUs who may not have felt the same connection to their institutions. For instance, some students who are lesbian, gay, bisexual, transgender, queer, or gender nonbinary have reported complicated, and sometimes less than positive, experiences within HBCUs where gender norms can be traditional (Patton et al., 2020). It would be useful to interview people who felt less connected to their HBCUs or perhaps even those who opted to leave their institutions. Nonetheless, the alumnae here were a group of 36 HBCU alumnae who were deeply committed, continually connected to, and outwardly enamored with their HBCUs.

The specific HBCU institutions, many of which were deeply linked to the communities in which they were located, became paramount to the oral histories of the alumnae. Some alumnae had long family connections to specific HBCUs as alums. The campuses were often highlighted in ways that intersected families, communities, and campuses. An examination of specific institutions was not necessary in the case of PWIs because the oral histories that emerged from the alumnae of those institutions had thematic agreement on topics such as the importance of informal friendships and formal student organizations that spanned across various institutions. Alternatively, HBCU alumnae described examples of institutional culture. As such, the chapter begins with an overview of some of the ways that alumnae connected their families, communities, legacies, and HBCU institutions before offering a narrative, brief oral history of an alumna named Karen who attended Clark Atlanta University, which is a comprehensive, urban, private, coeducational institution in Atlanta, Georgia.

"A Sense of Pride" from Families and Community to HBCU Campuses

HBCUs were often framed as part of a long legacy of Black greatness by alumnae. Erin, who graduated from the private women's Spelman College during the 1950s, recalled the way in which her family prepared her for Spelman: "When I was four years old, 'Baby, you're going to college.' It was not if you go to college but *when* you go to college. That was the family thing. You will go to college. Mama said, 'She's going to Spelman.' I was frequently told, 'Erin, you were so good, keep going, you will be somebody.' That kind of community of support I had at home. The whole community supported me in that." Erin's description of her family and community continually supporting her toward college, and specifically toward going to Spelman, is an important example of how many HBCUs are closely linked to families, communities, and to racial uplift (Luedke, 2020; McCallum, 2017). She continued to reflect on how the sense of community empowerment and uplift were translated on campus at Spelman, saying, "We were always Black and proud at Spelman." Compulsory chapel was a place where the familial and community uplift were translated onto campus. Erin reminisced: "I was excited all of my time at Spelman. I loved it, even compulsory chapel, because I met people, interesting speakers. Spelman opened up a whole new world for me, a little girl from South Georgia, small town. The people who spoke at chapel were highly educated. Many of them became leaders in the civil rights movement. People from South Africa came, White and Black ministers from across the Atlanta area, outstanding people from all over the country." Spelman was the place where the family ideas about uplift were realized. Erin went on to explain that many of the major civil rights leaders of the time were brought to campus to speak to the women as a form of exposure to what was possible after graduating, and to honor the long legacy of Black greatness that Spelman, like many HBCUs, fostered.

During a focus group over dinner in New Orleans, Theresa, who attended the Catholic, private Xavier University in New Orleans, Louisiana, in the 1980s invoked the legacy of uplift and community support: "We were born in the early '60s. We were young children when Martin Luther King died. We were young children when the Black Panthers were a big thing. Civil rights, all that, was when we were born. We were those kids that our parents had that felt that education is your right, and you have to go. This is the only way you're going to make it." Theresa underscored the legacy of education in the civil rights movement and movements for justice and liberation and justice for African American people in the US (Wallenstein, 2008b). Theresa, like other HBCU alumnae, felt as if she was born into that legacy, an intergenerational type of *Chosen We*, with a responsibility to continue it.

Valencia, a 1980s alumna of Howard University with a social sciences degree, asserted how she experienced the institutional norm that all students exhibit greatness:

> They instill such a sense of pride. I saw so many people even before me, who were older than me there, doing wonderful things, doing what it is they wanted to do. All these students, when I first got there, they came from all these very prominent families. I thought, wow, that could be me. Why not? I came from a family that was considered either average or slightly above. I just felt like there was nothing that I could not accomplish. Nothing. I think too having to struggle some was good. I think that was really good. Nothing came easy. We had to really work for everything we attained.

Valencia identified as middle class and she was not the first in her family to attend college. Yet she perceived some students as much more affluent than her, which suggests that at least in her experience there were some upper or upper middle-class students that she encountered at Howard. Had Valencia's background been low-income and/or if she were the first in her family to attend college, she may not have felt as if prominence and affluence were attainable.

Amanda also graduated Howard University two decades later, in the 2000s, with a biological sciences degree. Amanda highlighted Howard's connection to the community: "Howard is also very big on helping the community and that's important to me. I think that's something that not all schools can really say that is something that they do. Especially because Howard is right in the middle of DC, they really don't have a choice but to be involved with the community." There was an important connection between the idea of Black excellence that had permeated many of the homes/communities of many alumnae and the way that HBCU campuses like Howard connected back to those communities. Amanda's example was a way in which she selected a *Chosen We* community surrounding the campus to provide motivation about why her degree mattered.

Mimi, who graduated from Spelman College in the early 1960s with a social sciences degree, emphasized the vital role that HBCUs have played in Black education and uplift. She contemplated younger generations' views:

> You really do believe I can do whatever I choose and set my mind to. But you don't understand. You are aware of the struggles, but you don't value the struggles because you had it so easy. We've given you everything and we've paved the way for you and now you just float on across that stage, get your degree without having any blood, sweat, and tears behind it. There is no appreciation of all that stands for when you say Spelman College or even Morehouse. Some people were sitting in a church basement somewhere making sure that whatever they did was going to make it possible for me, 130 years later, to march across the stage. You better get out of my way, this is important.

As Mimi sat in a church basement reflecting with me and her Spelman alumnae group, she pointed to how generations of Black parents, grandparents, aunts, and uncles sat in church basements to find ways that future generations of their children would have access to opportunities. Historians have corroborated this point, describing the importance of Black educational planning in church basements as one of the major ways that many Black schools and colleges were started (Jones, 1992; Williams, 2007).

Nadia, Spelman alum from the 2000s, whom I met in Chicago, described Spelman with a relatively deep understanding of Mimi's points about the history of racial uplift:

> It's beautiful to see the legacy and see they paved the way for me and I'm paving the way for this class of 2015. It's just

awesome to see that historical connection and to just know the struggle that Black people have had in America. But women, while Black men were afforded the opportunity to vote, Black women were still seen in the shadows. We were in the shadows, they weren't there. To be able to educate a Black woman is a whole other story. So that's what makes it so powerful to know that I'm a part of that legacy and a part of that history. It's something that I don't take for granted. That's what we try to make sure other women know what it means. You need to know the history; you need to know the legacy. This is not a right. It's a privilege. To just be getting an education. Don't take it for granted.

Nadia referenced the deep legacy of Black excellence for Black women at Spelman College. She also pointed out the way that Black women were left out of major social institutions until a shockingly recent time period. Women were not afforded the right to vote until 1920, and even then there were ways in which women were kept from the ballot box (Keyssar, 2009). Of course, when "women" were given the right to vote that meant *White* women could vote but it still excluded Black women. Voting continues to be a racially contested issue in this country. The Voting Rights Act, not enacted until 1965, was an attempt to ensure that Black people were granted their basic right to vote as United States citizens. But there were still dramatic efforts, particularly in southern states, to keep Black people from voting, such as intimidation, violence, or making voter registration overly difficult (Keyssar, 2009). Even in 2008, the United States Supreme Court gave its approval that strict identification laws could be legal in some states (needing to show a driver's license or photo identification to be allowed to vote). The fight continues for *all* people to be able to practice one of the most formative and important citizens' rights. During the writing of this book, there were numerous states that were enacting exclusionary voter identification laws, and there were attempts to make polling places less accessible so voters could not get to the ballot boxes on election day (Mycoff et al., 2009; Wilson et al., 2014). Nadia's point was that in attending an HBCU, she felt embedded in this history of fighting for rights and freedom for Black people.

Nadia reflected a history where Black women were often erased and omitted, even when they were the leaders of movements (Giddings, 2014; Jones, 2009; White, 1999b). Black feminist authors have asserted that in discussions about race, there is often an assumption that the focus is on men (i.e., Black men) while in discussions about gender or sex, there is an emphasis on White women (Collins, 2002; Cooper, 1892; Davis, 1971; Lorde, 2012); Black women are made invisible in both. Black feminists have long asserted Black women's need to be able to self-define for this very reason (e.g., Cooper, 1892; Collins, 2002; Davis, 1971; Jones, 1949/1995; Lorde, 2012). HBCUs can be a space for this self-definition and -valuing.

Marwa started her undergraduate degree at Benedict College, a private liberal arts HBCU in Columbia, South Carolina, during the 1970s. She transferred to the University of South Carolina midway through her bachelor's degree program. She later earned a degree in the humanities from another HBCU, Clark Atlanta University, and a PhD from the University of California, Riverside. She surmised, "The hope that the civil rights movement gave us, the hope, the optimism; we loved each other, we cheered each other on and we expected so much from everybody. We didn't expect anything else." Racial uplift came from "multiple directions": "You had the church telling us that we were the best, that we could be, and then, my father and my mother telling me the same thing. How could it not happen? Now there were some people who fell through the cracks, I'm sure. But how could you not be great with all that was available to you?" Marwa's example of how racial uplift was woven into the fabric of her family, community, church, and later, her HBCU, demonstrated how connected this idea was to the historical legacy of race in the United States. The movement for racial justice that surrounded Marwa reinforced her community of support, her background *Chosen We*.

Benedict College continued the legacy of Black greatness that Marwa had learned from her community growing up: "Oh my God I was so happy, [speaking very rapidly] because you felt grown up. It was just a wonderful experience for me when I first stepped on Benedict's college campus and it touted itself as being the greatest college in the universe. You [laughing] believed it. My first exposure—well, my first exposure outside of high school to poetry—was when Nikki Giovanni came to campus." For Marwa, Nikki Giovanni exemplified excellence. Giovanni, a distinguished university professor at Virginia Tech University, has written three nationally best-selling books of poetry, has won seven NAACP Image Awards, has been nominated for a Grammy, and was a finalist for the National Book Award.[1] At Benedict, Marwa continued to be surrounded by a *Chosen We* community of support. Marwa's web of support was almost entirely made up of Black people supporting other Black people.

Marwa reflected on the importance of her legacy within her family and the broader community that surrounded her before and during college:

> I have to give it to the civil rights movement, seeing Coretta Scott march along with Martin Luther King and Julie Belafonte marching, women marching, being a part of that whole social current. I feel so blessed to be a part of that, to have come on the heels of that. It gave me optimism, it gave me hope, it gave me perspective. It let me know that being in the world was worth being here, because there were people who would lay down their life for me. That's love. I have that kind of social love, social/cultural love. I don't know if this generation has it. I had it. From the musicians to the people marching in the streets, to my church, to my family, to my classmates. I had it.

Marwa called the *Chosen We* support that she encountered while growing up and during college a social/cultural love. It was through this love, through community, knowing that she was part of and surrounded by self-determination and excellence, that she excelled.

Tiffany A. went to a predominantly White high school in Maryland before she opted to go to Spelman where she graduated with a business degree in the 2000s. Tiffany A. connected with what Marwa suggested, but nearly 40 years later. She summarized her reason for going to Spelman, "It's all just, all intelligent Black women who really want to go somewhere." She continued to consider the legacy of promoting Black women in particular, "When you walk on Spelman's campus as a Black woman, you realize, this place was created for me. There aren't many places in this world that you can say, this is created for Black women. You feel it. I loved it." It was from this collective *Chosen We* that Tiffany A. ultimately found her individuality. She remembered her family reflecting on her time there, "It was really like they were embracing Spelman as 'Wow, we can see Tiffany really kind of becoming herself here.'" Tiffany's point that she was finally able to become *herself* is an example of how joining a *Chosen We* legacy of greatness at an HBCU allowed some women to find a unique, individual identity.

Lisa attended Spelman in the 1990s, majoring in the physical sciences. She remembered the legacy of greatness that was taught to her there:

Spelman taught me that no, you don't look like most of the people out in this world. No, you will not be treated like most of the people out in this world. However, you are still somebody, a person to be contended with. Don't let anybody tell you differently. You are unique, you are special, you are intelligent, you are beautiful. So that carried me, for the most part, through the rest of my life. It's something that I still instill to this day.

Lisa attended Northwestern University where she pursued a master's, and later she began a PhD in her science discipline where the experiences were less positive. Yet Spelman messaging stayed with her and instilled self-confidence about her potential. When asked how Spelman managed to send such positive messages to students, Lisa responded:

> It was pretty much almost an everyday thing. It was reinforced in class, it was reinforced walking on the campus, it was reinforced in the artwork. It was reinforced [everywhere]. We had to do a mentoring program our freshman year. I remember some of the people, especially alumnae, who came and spoke to us. It was just like, "you are amazing." That's what I kept hearing. I was only on campus three years because I did a dual degree. But for a solid three years, that's what I heard. I don't know how else to describe it. It was just an amazing experience. I didn't appreciate it as much as I do now while I was there. I appreciate it like I can't even describe now, knowing what I went through when I was there. It helped me become who I am now.

The positive messaging, a way to continually reinforce belonging in the *Chosen We* community, was embedded in campus artifacts such as artwork, the speakers who were invited to talks on campus, in coursework, and in general norms at Spelman and led Lisa to find her uniqueness.

Nina, who graduated from Spelman in the 1980s, observed, "[Spelman is] that environment where people want you to succeed. That is the expectation. That is that ethos there. You're going to succeed." Nina later argued that Spelman deliberately prepared graduates to enter the world:

> My friends and I joke about this. They say when they shake
> your hand on that stage and they slap you on your back, what
> they're doing is they're sticking a titanium rod in your back. So
> as soon as they hit you on your back, your rod is in. As you
> walk out in this world, you kind of look around and the longer
> you stay away from Spelman you get to say, "Oh, I know that.
> I smelled that coming. That's cool, I can be there." That's where
> that anchor comes from. Even when people are trying to be
> however they're going to be, you still have that titanium rod
> in your back that says, "Fine, it's your choice, I'm doing this."

By putting a proverbial "rod" in the backs of graduates, it was as if the
institution was giving a lasting form of support to graduates for the
remainder of their lives. In that way, many of the alumnae felt like they
could take part of their *Chosen We* community (the relationships and
experiences) with them when they graduated. Part of the preparation
that Spelman offered their graduates was aimed toward offering ways to
cope with racial or gender injustices outside the gates of campus. Amid
the extensive evidence about the racist and sexist experiences that Black
women endure in their professional lives (Brewer, 2016; Howard-Hamilton,
2003; Jones & Shorter-Gooden, 2004), HBCUs such as Spelman deliberately
prepared students for it.

Like the Gilbert Young painting that I invoked at the beginning of
the chapter, there was a sense among HBCU alumnae that one should earn
a degree and then reach back and pull up the next generation. The desire
to connect back to one's community in a spirit of uplift and empowerment
is also rooted in Black feminist thinking (Brewer, 2016; Collins, 2002;
Dillard, 2008; hooks, 2000; Lorde, 2012). Similarly, Marwa's oral history
of her experience at Benedict College resonates with this intergenerational
legacy. Other alumnae, like Karen, described attending an HBCU as linked
to this legacy of communal uplift.

GETTING A PIECE OF "HERITAGE" AND "PRIDE" AT CLARK UNIVERSITY: KAREN'S STORY

Karen was from the Kansas City metropolitan area, but she went South
for college, attending the historically Black, land-grant, public institution,
Clark College, which later, in 1988, was merged with Atlanta University to
become Clark Atlanta University, a comprehensive, urban, private, coed-

ucational institution.[2] Karen graduated from Clark with a social science major in 1978 before the two institutions merged. She later returned to the Midwest and attended the predominantly White, urban institution, the University of Missouri–Kansas City (UMKC) where she earned a master's degree and a PhD in the 1990s in two different social science fields.

I met with Karen in her office in Nebraska. As we settled in, she described how she opted for an HBCU:

> In my family, it's real common for us to attend historically Black institutions, and so I had actually visited this school when I was a freshmen in high school, and my sister, one of my older sisters, was teaching and they took a group of kids to visit a lot of the schools in the South and so she took me. I had visited, I saw the setting, and I liked it. Then there was my mom that told me I needed to get that piece of my heritage and background so I could become more of a well-shaped individual. I did and it was the best thing that she ever made me do [laughs]. I have to give her credit today.

Karen's mom encouraged her to move to the South from the Midwest to get the experience of being in an HBCU. When I asked if her mother had also attended an HBCU, Karen responded: "She did. She attended Lincoln University, but going to school back in the late 1940s, there weren't a whole lot of choices in Missouri. So that was kind of the automatic choice for her. She did attend one [an HBCU]." Karen offered a reminder that it was not surprising that her mother had attended an HBCU because there was limited access to any other higher education institutions, as was the case for almost all Black people before the 1950s (Smith, 2016). Karen recalled her mother insisting that all the children in the family take standardized tests (ACT, SAT) to prepare for college. Karen's mother implemented college-bound practices into her family long before it was the norm in high schools (Gullat & Jan, 2003; Robinson & Roksa, 2016) as many Black families have done (Knight et al., 2004; Williams, 2005).

As a Kansas City native, the move to the South, to Atlanta, allowed Karen to see a different idea of Black leadership than she would have seen in her hometown. Like Black feminists who came with her and before her, Karen underscored the importance of seeing people who looked like her in leadership (Brewer, 2016; Howard-Hamilton, 2003; Jones & Shorter-Goodin, 2004):

Growing up as a child in the '60s, I was born in 1960, there was still a lot of racial issues the way they are today, but in the '60s, a lot of blatant issues were going on. That was when you got the whole surge of Black pride. It became a good *thing* to be Black. But I still suffered through a lot of racial issues, in my elementary school and middle school. It really affected my self-esteem. That was one of the ways that my mom felt that going to a city like Atlanta, going to the South, would help me. It would help me to get my self-esteem and it truly did. It did, because I saw people that looked like me that were doing amazing things and they had a lot of self-pride and assertiveness, and I possessed none of that up until that point. Even though I say my parents are role-structured and protective, I was okay in that cocoon in that environment, because you know, I was cushioned from a lot of other things that could have really affected me negatively.

As many students who grew up in the 1960s, Karen experienced racial hostility in her primary and secondary schooling. Many scholars have argued that when racial integration was implemented, far too little attention was paid to how Black students would (or would not in many instances) be welcomed into formerly White schools (Feagin & Sikes, 1994; Fordham, 1996, 2008). The failure to consider Black students' needs in school integration has persisted (Lewis & Diamond, 2015).

Karen reflected on her mother as a driving force for why she went to Clark University, in part to transcend earlier integration experiences:

That's what I used to say, "They don't know what my momma told me, and what I had to do." It's all because I was scared of her, and she was literally the size of a pea. Oh, gosh, she could run the whole house. That's what carries me through my everyday life, Rachelle. I've done the executive MBA and yes, I was the only Black female in my class. You would think a class like that is mostly White men, White men that are vice presidents of Sprint, top engineering firms, corporations like that. But I held my own, because I said, oh, they don't know. I'm here to succeed. I'm not trying to be a crab, in order to get up to where I'm pulling other folks down. But it's just, this is the game plan that I've always had to ascribe to, because that was the family's way of doing things.

Karen described an attitude of hard work as being instilled by her mother. Numerous women reinforced the desire not to "be a crab," desiring not to push each other down instead of lifting one another up. Karen illustrated a clear ethos of uplift. The power of families in subverting racist structures such as schools or universities must be elevated in Karen's story and in so many others' stories too. Black families and communities have consistently resisted and transcended White supremacy, racism, and stereotypes as a way toward uplift through school involvement, parent organizations, and through support of their children's educational aspirations at home (Billingsley & Caldwell, 1991; Collins, 1998; Few, 2007; Posey-Maddox, 2013; Posey-Maddox et al., 2016).

Contemplating what might have happened had she not attended an HBCU, Karen pondered: "I needed that experience, because I had self-esteem in my household and in my family, but in general society, I didn't really have it. I had issues about my complexion as a young girl, and my complexion is very different from the others in my family, the beauty of African American people is we have so many complexions." Karen underscored that in her family she was built up toward having high self-esteem. But she knew that the larger society did not necessarily accept her as a dark-skinned Black woman. Colorism, the idea that those with lighter skin tones are more acceptable or likely to be successful in society, has deep roots in racism and White supremacy (Harris, 2008; Hunter, 2002; Kerr, 2005; Wilder, 2010, 2015). Colorism is also interrogated and resituated in Black feminist work (Few et al., 2003). Attending an HBCU helped Karen to recognize the full range of beauty and skin tones among Black people and this was part of how she gained confidence. Karen cited her HBCU experience as preparing her for her current position at a predominantly White university where she was often the only Black person in meetings. She continued to consider her family and the role that skin color played for them:

> My whole family is the whole spectrum. I grew up with a lot of issues, there was a lot of carryover from slavery and Jim Crow and all those kinds of movements in our history, and so, I had to overcome all of that and feel good about myself, you know,

my level of intellect, my appearance, my beauty, and all those kinds of things. So, I needed that experience, and my mother was so smart in telling me I needed that. If I hadn't had that, I wouldn't be here. I just don't think I would. I share all that with my girls. They have very healthy self-esteem.

Karen connected her own experience to the long national history of racial hostility, terror, and separation in the period of slavery and in the Jim Crow racial segregation policies that followed. This history negatively altered her self-esteem and view of her appearance, abilities, and intellect. Yet the location of the institution normalized Black leadership and excellence for her:

Atlanta was more fast-paced. But it also gave me the opportunity to see more Black people in positions of power, like a Black mayor, a Black city manager, people in all areas of government, and then all those Black professors, so it really gave me just the opportunity to just grab mentors and role models from all different walks of life and that was real encouraging and I had not received so many Black people in their own private businesses. That was real impressive.

Karen witnessed numerous examples of Black leadership and excellence, on campus in her professors and administrators, and off campus in the numerous Black community leaders in Atlanta. Her story is not singular in this way but part of a larger narrative of the importance of role models and examples of Black women's uplift (Brewer, 2016; Howard-Hamilton, 2003; Jones & Shorter-Goodin, 2004).

Karen considered ways that her HBCU continuously cultivated support for students:

They have a week's worth of orientation. A lot of Black schools do this same kind of thing, and they bring the freshmen on campus a week before the upper classmen, so the freshmen get the opportunity to get used to the campus and they're able to bond. At Clark, they put us in what was called clusters. In your cluster, you take all your humanities together. You pretty much take like at least three or four classes together, all your gen-eds with the same people. So those people tend to be your friends.

From the time that students came to campus, they were offered a *Chosen We* community of other first-year students. Not only did they take classes together, but they also took courses from people who were deliberately involved in trying to dispel racial stereotypes:

> In our Math Department, we had Doctor Ibis who is well known for teaching math and removing the fear for African American students within math. Eventually he put this whole program together that MIT and a lot of other schools use. For the longest time he had the reputation of graduating more doctoral level African American students in math than anyone else. He came up with this concept called study tables. You had to go to a study table like three or four days a week. But the study table really was to follow-up to the lecture and help you with your recitations, which is mostly taught by like grad students here [at the university where she worked]. But at Clark it was taught by professors.

There is evidence that suggests that many Black students, and particularly Black women, have been told that they will not do as well at math as White students (specifically White men) (Good et al., 2008; Spencer et al., 1999; Steele, 1997; Steele & Aronson, 1995). Karen's professor was intentionally facing that stereotype before students had a chance to turn away from math or to think that they were not "math people" (see also Nasir & McKinney de Royston, 2013; Nasir et al., 2017).

Karen expanded on what made Clark feel like such a protective place during college and why that was important for her. Faculty members played an important role in creating and maintaining an environment that promoted excellence:

> The thing about attending Clark that is so amazing to me was that environment was still very structured and very protected, because the college professors just assumed the role of the parent as well as the educator and the mentor to you. They still protected you and they really cared about you individually. So, I had a professor in my major and he pushed me. He was relentless, even before I switched to the [social sciences] major, because I started out as a pre-med major.
>
> As a freshman, I left my high school, and I was considered the top girl in science leaving the high school. So, I thought

I knew chemistry. I get to college and I'm lost. My chemistry professor, I'll never forget him, Dr. Reginald Freeman, and he had this real big voice and he would try to get you to respond. But it was a big lecture hall so that part was different for me, and you had to walk all the way down the stairs to the lecture hall. I started out sitting in the back. Well, at Clark, they ingrained in you, the "A" seats are up front. You need to move up front. To this day, I never sit in the back of a class.

He told me one day, "Miss Karen, I need to see you after class." He had this big old deep voice, and I was so scared, I was shaking. I went to his office, and he said, "What is wrong with you?" He asked me where I was from, what were my parents like, what did my parents do, and what I was thinking. I thought, why does he want to be all in my family's business? Then he said, "What did you come to college for?" I said, "Because I want to be a doctor." And he said, "Well, you can't be a doctor without passing my chemistry class." I said, "But they gave me chemistry, and biology, and calculus." He said, "Well, if you're going to be a pre-med major, you have to take all these classes." He said, "Obviously you tested into it, so you must have had the skill level initially." So, he told me my parents would be so disappointed in me and how could I let my family down and my race of people down by not achieving. He said, "Do you know what they call the person that graduates last in the med school class?" I was looking like, "What?" And he said, "They call them a doctor." And that was the "aha." That was my issue. I felt that if I was not at the top and not completely excelling, then I was just a failure. He said, "You are probably going to a doctor right now that somewhere along the way earned a C or a D, but yet, they're your doctor, you have complete faith in them in their skill."

So, he said, "Meet me tomorrow in my lab," and it was like Friday evening and all my friends were going out and everything and he had me in that lab and he took me through every lab we had that week, from like six in the evening to nine. He said, "I can't help you tomorrow because I'm going fishing tomorrow." He said, "Do you know that church over there on the corner across from Miller House?" I said, "Yes, the Baptist Church?" He said, "Yes," he said, "Meet me there on Sunday." So, I made my friends go with me on Sunday, and we get there and he's like one of the deacons or something. Then he comes and he taps me in church, and he said, "I'm glad you made it." He said, "You have some offering?" I was like, "No." He said, "Here," he gave each of me and my friends some offering. So, then he said, "Now stay after church because we feed the college kids." Eventually I did change my major.

Dr. Freeman went well above and beyond classroom teaching to support her. The idea of faculty engaging in the holistic lives of students mirrors an emphasis of the field of student affairs or student services (Evans & Reason, 2001; Thelin, 2011; Winkle-Wagner, 2012).

In loco parentis, or the idea that colleges and universities serve "in place of parents," initially a legal term (Lee, 2011), was an assumed practice in most higher education institutions in the late nineteenth and early twentieth centuries (Thelin, 2011). Evening curfews imposed on students, the practice of staff or faculty calling a student's parents to discuss how the student was doing at college, and other such practices were generally acceptable practices on many campuses when in loco parentis was common practice. Many institutions propelled away from that practice in the 1960s, maintaining that some of those policies conflicted with students' constitutional rights as adults (Lee, 2011; Thelin, 2011). However, HBCUs have a much longer history of deliberately engaging in the full lives of students in a way that might be considered unusual in some PWIs. To be sure, sometimes the notion of "in place of parents" can be sexist, treating women as if they are young girls to be guided instead of people with agency and power (Njoku & Patton, 2017). Perhaps there is a differentiation between some of the constraining policies such as evening curfews and the way in which faculty deliberately engaged the full lives of students. For Karen, having a faculty member take an interest in her as an individual was a turning point where she began to know that she could succeed in her degree.

When I asked Karen if she continued to interact with Dr. Freeman after that first year in college, she responded: "Oh, I did. I did, because you know them, and they know you. They will call you at your dorm, or they'll check on you, and you know, take you to dinner, or take you to their house and bring your laundry." Karen noted faculty as supporting students in ways that transcended the traditional classroom such as taking students to dinner, having students to their homes, or calling students to check in on them. Karen summarized why this approach to student-faculty interactions was useful for her:

> That was the best environment for me. They pushed us from day one that if you attended an HBCU now for undergrad, you'll go to the PWI for graduate school. They always said, "diversify your education, don't do everything here. Mix it up." They will push us toward internships and just all other kinds of experiences. [They] prepped us for the GRE. My psychology professor, he's the one that gave us a ride to the GRE, he paid registration for me and a couple other friends to take the GRE. He took us, he gave us a ride down there after he prepped us for it. So, it was almost assumed, just like college, it was almost assumed, this isn't where you stop. At my school, that's what was ingrained in us in day one. "You're not stopping at the bachelor's," unless that's something you truly wanted to do, but they always taught us to keep going to our terminal degrees.

Faculty were vital in making graduate school seem possible. Not only were faculty members at HBCUs reaching into their own pockets to pay for students to take the Graduate Record Examination (GRE), but they also transported students to take the exams.

Karen reflected on how her HBCU experience helped her feel more confident so she could be successful in PWIs such as the one where she eventually went to graduate school—the University of Missouri in Kansas City:

> UMKC was originally University of Kansas City, and that school was originally built to educate men and White males. So, you still had a lot of that, it had a glass wall effect around it, between UMKC and the community. They really tried to work hard on that, but they still kind of look conclave there within the heart of the city. But the transition wasn't as difficult, because by the time I left Clark, I had enough of that self-assuredness and self-esteem that I could excel and that I didn't feel any inferiority between myself, as an African American, and anyone of any ethnic origin. That was around the time when that book *The Bell Curve* came out and all that craziness.

But by then, I just felt, they just don't know I can really excel. I knew the way they taught us at our schools that they were prepping us for all those kinds of things. I remember when my husband went to KU [University of Kansas], he had some of the exact same texts for his graduate courses that he already had in undergrad, because they were always trying to teach at a higher level [at the HBCUs]. So, I had really no problem with the transition.

You could be competitive, and you could succeed [after Clark]. I had no doubt that I *would* succeed, and it was always a marvel, to other folks. "Well, you're the only African American here." Whatever. "You're the only one we have in our department." It would be just like, "That doesn't matter." I'm the only one in my building where I work now, so, it's like, ah, that's sad. But I'm the first African American to win boss of the year.

Karen remarked that her experience at Clark Atlanta helped prepare her for being the only Black woman in many of the White educational spaces in her graduate programs and in her career.

Karen mentioned *The Bell Curve: Intelligence and Class Structure in American Life* (1994), a very contentious publication by Richard Herrnstein and Charles Murray. The book, called pseudoscience by many social scientists (Fairchild, 1995; Graves & Johnson, 1995), because of its racist implications, claimed that human intelligence is determined by both environmental and biological factors. Herrnstein and Murray (1994) argued that intelligence is at the root of life chances such as later income, educational attainment, or other social factors such as having children before marriage. The most racially charged part of the book was the claim that low intelligence was genetic in Black people. Critics of the book claimed that the book's analysis was not mathematically sound, the interpretation was sloppy and likely driven by a racist agenda, and that Herrnstein and Murray were deliberately attempting to perpetuate racist ideologies (Graves & Johnson, 1995; Graves, 2001; Heckman, 1995). It is noteworthy that Karen pivots from *The Bell Curve* to the self-assuredness she gained at her HBCU. It was as if Clark Atlanta prepared her to contend with race in multiple ways.

Karen considered the reasons why the HBCU experience was particularly important for her and the development of her confidence:

I think I could have come out of this whole experience on a whole different side, and a different level of understanding and I'll say not at the level of awareness and where I am today, which I think helps me to walk in that building that I do over there every day and being the only Black person, and in an essence being the representative of African American people every day, with some of the little comments and the innuendo and the things. I endure and can handle it. I think that the HBCU makes a huge difference. When other people try to come in, have that strength inside there [pointing to her heart].

Karen and others echoed the long legacy of so many Black feminist thinkers who went before them and described ways to carry self-determination and support even in the face of racism, sexism, and other adversities (Cooper, 1892; Collins, 2002; hooks, 2000; Lorde, 2012). Karen identified the HBCU as the turning point for her, the place that instilled confidence, which she was able to use in her future education and career opportunities. By pointing to her chest, she indicated that she took the confidence learned at Clark into other spaces. Like the idea of putting a "rod" in one's back at graduation at Spelman, Karen suggested that she carried her *Chosen We* community and support from Clark with her in her chest.

THE CHOSEN WE AND INTERSECTIONAL BLACK GREATNESS AT HBCUs

The legacy of Black excellence was a community and familial construct. Alumnae described holistic support and socialization where they were continually raised up into the *Chosen We* communities of their families, neighborhood, church communities, and local groups. These narratives highlight a way in which families and communities surround these women in Black excellence. Families/communities identified their own *Chosen We* legacy of excellence on which to raise the next generation. The alumnae turned to the support of their communities and families as a shield to the White supremacist and racist schools and cities that surrounded them (see also Dillard, 2008).

One does not necessarily get to select one's initial family. But these alumnae described continuing to turn to those communities and to their families. Thus, while they were born into a family or community and perhaps did not initially *choose* their families and communities of origin, they did continue to choose to turn back to them. I would argue that these *Chosen We* communities that were initially chosen *for* the alumnae by their parents or community members were important foundations for most of the alumnae here. Over time, the alumnae chose their *Chosen We* communities of home, family, and community for themselves. This is exhibited in the way that some alumnae saw the choice of their institutions and degrees as intimately connected to giving back and connecting with communities (Valencia and Amanda at Howard; many of the Spelman alumnae; Karen at Clark Atlanta University).

An important connection to the *Chosen We* idea here is that the HBCUs were viewed by almost all the HBCU alumnae as continuing the legacy of greatness that had been started in their families and communities. They entered HBCUs, new *Chosen We* communities, that often deliberately connected like bridges their family/community histories, racial identities, and backgrounds. Once on HBCU campuses, women were socialized into their *Chosen We* communities. They chose their specific institutions, and they continued to choose to engage in the larger campus spaces and smaller groups on campus too. Alumnae noted that they were taught what it meant to belong in these *Chosen We* spaces in very holistic and seamless ways: through orientation programs, campus events, coursework, and by multiple campus actors (peers, faculty, administrators, alumnae, etc.).

Conclusions on Greatness

The sense of greatness and a larger collective identity, or the *Chosen We*, was pervasive within the HBCU according to these alumnae. The alums offered specific ideas for how the practice of promoting community and greatness was implemented. Campuses and administrators, even those at PWIs or other institutions, could take a few important lessons from these critical oral histories of alumnae from HBCUs, such as:

1. Root campus practices with Black students (and perhaps other groups of underrepresented students too) in a historical legacy of excellence. Within HBCUs, all ideas about greatness and Black excellence were grounded in a historical legacy, building a community, where one generation directly connected to the next. Not only was this historical legacy a reframing of possible stereotypes of deficit thinking (i.e.,

coming from greatness instead of coming from a deficiency) but it was also deeply connected to students' families and communities of origin. Alumnae described seeing connections in how they were raised in their families, churches, and communities and the general ethos of their HBCU campuses. Starting all practices with students of color from the perspective of amplifying existing greatness is a reversal of many common support services that aim to fill in gaps, deficiencies, or ways in which students are perceived to be lacking. It would mean that practices, programs, and policies would be created in such a way to promote success for all students.

2. Connect campuses to communities and families. Multiple alumnae asserted that the reason they were earning their degree was to offer their knowledge and skills back to their communities. The more that campuses can actively engage the communities in which they are located, the more likely that students will feel connected to their own roots and legacies of greatness too. Programs that offer students stipends or internships in the community are one way to engage this community connection. Also, opening parent-family offices on campuses where they do not exist could be a way to better connect with students' families such that students can continue to feel as if their campuses are connected back to their families. These offices could hold professional development events to help families who do not have college backgrounds to understand what their students are experiencing, for example.

3. Offer orientation programs that engage community building and connection to excellence on campus. Orientation programs at HBCUs were more than one day and introduced students to the community in which women were entering so that they immediately saw themselves as part of something bigger than their individual selves. Rather than sending a message that some students will make it on campus if they follow certain rules or prescriptions, the orientations at HBCUs elevated ways in which students were assumed to

be successful on campuses (e.g., one is being brought into community where excellence is assumed). Crafting orientation programs that are long enough for students to develop relationships with other students and communities on campus would mean students enter their experience with some built-in friendships that could sustain them. But, carefully creating the messaging of orientation programs to promote students' success on campus is paramount to socializing students into the possibility of their success in that space.

4. Develop discipline-based or interest-based cohorts for students to engage smaller communities on campus. Once on campus, there were either cohorts of students who took classes together (e.g., general education courses taken together at Clark) or students were enrolled in specific coursework that educated women about their legacy of greatness and how to continue it (e.g., African Diaspora and the World at Spelman). In all instances, an important element of these cohorts was the emphasis on excellence and thriving on campus. Cohorts that have a similar discipline or interests can help to offer exposure to new ideas, academic areas, or interests that can then become important communities for students to engage.

5. Expect that faculty provide high standards alongside care. Faculty at these HBCUs demanded excellence and offered intrusive mentoring and teaching that transcended traditional classrooms (e.g., approaching all students as "their" students on and off campus, insisting that women could exhibit high standards and excellence in classes, etc.). Within both PWIs and HBCUs, it is possible to create reward structures to encourage good mentoring practices such as mentoring awards or merit-based salary raises for faculty that demonstrate these highly engaged mentoring practices. Additionally, some faculty who may not have the skills for holistic mentoring practices may need professional development. Campuses could make this professional development accessible (i.e., free) for faculty and even encourage involvement by offering small stipends to faculty.

6. Engage the power of peers on campuses. Peers on HBCU campuses promoted the greatness and community that they had been taught as students. Providing peer mentoring programs for students to support one another would be useful. Also, offering students a voice within decisions about new programs, policies, and practices would be valuable to create more seamless messaging about the goals of the campus to support the success of all students.

As Angela Davis (1971) proclaimed, "The Black women of today . . . as heirs to a tradition of supreme perseverance and heroic resistance, we must hasten to take our place where our people are forging toward freedom" (p. 91). The alumnae viewed their college experiences and their futures after college as deeply connected to the legacy of the Black women and men who came before them. There is perhaps no better example of the *Chosen We* than this connection to community. Community was holistic across the experiences within HBCUs. Because multiple campus actors (faculty, staff, peers, alumnae) elevated the community they were trying to build, students experienced a meaningful and lasting sense of belonging within HBCUs, as if they were part of the family. Being a part of the legacy meant becoming a part of a "family" in college and this was a starkly different way of framing the college experience as compared to PWIs. As the next chapter asserts, the familial ethos of HBCUs quite purposefully connected to the legacy of community within these institutions.

Chapter 6

HBCUs as Home and Family

Embracing Intersectional and Nuanced Blackness through Inclusion

Let's just start the college in your living room.

—Mary McLeod Bethune quoted in George Yancy,
On Race: 34 Conversations in a Time of Crisis

Born in rural South Carolina in 1875 during the country's attempts at Reconstruction after hundreds of years of enslavement, Mary McLeod Bethune[1] was a Black feminist activist, scholar, and leader. Her parents were formerly enslaved and she was the only person in her family to attend school as a child. In 1904, with the intent of educating Black girls and women in particular, Bethune founded what eventually became Bethune-Cookman College[2] (now Bethune-Cookman University) in Daytona, Florida, and she also presided as one of the first Black women to be president of a historically Black college or university (HBCU). Bethune's educational uplift was not only constantly aspiring upward but also reaching back to communities and families to bring them up in turn.

It is no surprise that HBCUs have long been considered "nurturing" and "warm" as compared to PWIs (Arroyo & Gasman, 2014; McCoy et al., 2017; Palmer et al., 2013; Winkle-Wagner & McCoy, 2016). Many of the alumnae from HBCUs referred to the institutions as "home," using familial words to describe their relationships in college, claiming a deep sense of inclusion and belonging within these campuses. Alumnae emphasized feeling at home on campus, as if students had joined a *Chosen We* campus family. Alumnae felt that their backgrounds, families, and communities were affirmed within these institutions (also see Williams et al., 2022). Unlike PWIs, where Black women experienced contestation and constant misrecognition of their identities, at HBCUs, Black women felt as if the institutions were created for them. One alumna, Tiffany A., who graduated from Spelman College asserted that the institutions was "created for me." Like chapter 5, this chapter proceeds with institutionally bounded narratives. After illustrating some thematic agreements about experiences of feeling at "home," I offer a critical oral history from Jordan, an alumna of Dillard University in New Orleans, Louisiana. Then, rooted in the sense of inclusion that alumnae felt on their campuses, I consider how alumnae identified individuality, unique aspects of their identity, presenting a narrative from a Spelman College (Atlanta, Georgia) alumna, Nicole.

HBCUs are a "Home" and "Family"

In stark contrast to the alumnae experiences in PWIs, the alumnae from HBCUs often felt affirmed in their backgrounds and racial identities upon entering campuses. This is not to say that some did not experience challenges in college, or that they did not encounter difficulties relative to their gender, racial, sexual, or religious identities. But, for the most part, the alumnae at HBCUs repeatedly used the word "home," and used familial terms to describe their relationships with friends, faculty, and administrators (referring to people as sisters, mothers, etc.) when talking about their campus experience.

"Like Being at Home": The Familial Inclusion of HBCUs

HBCUs had an ethos of affirming students' backgrounds while emphasizing their likelihood for success (Arroyo & Gasman, 2014; Conrad & Gasman, 2015; Williams et al., 2022). Tweedy attended a PWI (University of Chicago) for her undergraduate degree in the 1960s and 1970s. She encouraged her two children to consider attending HBCUs because she wanted them to have a more nurturing experience: "I always say I got the best of both worlds, being able to go to both [PWIs and HBCUs] because my daughter went to North Carolina A&T. She got so nurtured at North Carolina A&T and did really well." While her own college experience was rife with racial isolation, Tweedy felt some comfort in having been able to vicariously experience the warmth of an HBCU through her daughter's college experience.

Elaine, who attended Dillard University, a private HBCU in New Orleans, Louisiana, in the late 1980s and early 1990s, described her peers, staff, and faculty at Dillard University as a "family":

> Once I got there and got situated and met some people, it turned out to be the best place for me because the setting was so small. There was really a sense of caring from the faculty and staff outside of the classroom. My freshman year, I lived on campus. We had a room mother in our dorm who was an older woman, who was really maternal. "You're not supposed to do that, what would your mother say?" She was awesome and great. She was watching out for us. We had curfew. If we would miss curfew, she would call our parents. She was really on top of things.

Historically, higher education institutions have often practiced "in loco parentis"—the notion that the institution is serving "in place of the parents" (Thelin, 2011) included curfews, rules about visitation of the opposite sex in residence halls, and guidelines for appearance and dress. While these policies were no longer in favor in many PWIs by the 1980s, HBCUs continued many of these practices for years afterward.

The faculty at Dillard University promoted familial norms too. Elaine remembered:

> Another thing my freshman year that solidified for me that I had made the right decision was my biology teacher at the time would come and pick us up from the dorm on Sundays if we wanted to go to church with her. We would meet her out on the main street on Sunday morning and she would come pick us up and take us to church, and then bring us back home. Sometimes she would take us back to her house and feed us. [There was] a lot of that going on in school.

It was as if faculty viewed students as part of a family that they were responsible to nurture and lead. Elaine continued:

> When I got into my major, there was no way that you were going to fail. We had to pass our exam in order to get our teaching license. One of my instructors, there were about five of us, she would make us come to her house to study. "Okay,

you guys are coming too, it's not an option. I want you there at such-and-such a time and you're going to study." She would teach us how to make things. She taught us how to make pecan pie.

Elaine's example demonstrated that faculty saw their role as holistically involved in students' lives, both in and outside of the classroom. Elaine summarized her experience at Dillard: "The experience was great because it was a balance. It was that sense of family at the school but then on the academic side, they gave us all that we needed as well. I don't think I could've picked a better [place] for me." The small class sizes, the faculty who were deeply involved in students' success and willing to show their humanity to students, and the friendships, all made Dillard seem like "family" to Elaine.

Amanda, a 2010 biological sciences graduate of Howard University in Washington, DC, and who later earned a graduate degree at Georgia State University, compared PWIs and HBCUs:

In general, my experience at Howard was just kind of like being at home. It's very comforting and nurturing. It's just not a feeling that I got at Georgia State but it may have been because I was at the graduate level and I wasn't seeking the same kind of things. Just come to campus, do what you have to do, progress your career, and go on. Whereas at Howard, I'm making connections, building relationships, establishing a legacy, hopefully, for my future kids. Two very different settings. But I'm certain that going to an HBCU had a lot to do with it and had a lot to do with the reasons why I feel so connected and why I cherish the experience a little bit differently than I think a lot of my friends do. A lot of my friends who didn't go to an HBCU, they have different feelings about their experiences. I'm glad I made the choice that I made but I also understand it's not the choice for everybody.

Amanda noted that her HBCU experience was about building a legacy for the future.

Like Amanda, Nicole, a 2004 alumna from Spelman College whose narrative is included in this chapter, described her institution in familial terms:

Spelman is a sisterhood. It is a sisterhood. I was talking to a girl this morning on the phone who is not from Spelman, but I was connected to her through another person. And she was trying to figure out what she wants to do in psychology. I was like, "Oh, I know like five people who do this kind of psychology. They're all from Spelman. I can call them and they'll all talk to you." I don't even have to say, "Let me check and see. I know they'll talk to you." Because that's just how it works, right?

The "sisterhood" clearly invoked a familial feel at Spelman for Nicole.

Reinforcing the idea of a lifelong familial type of bond, Erin, a Spelman alum from the 1950s, considered how she had engaged with Spelman students and alumnae throughout her life: "The friends I met are still my friends, lifelong friends. Of course, my affiliation with the young ones at Spelman is significant. I enjoy meeting all the younger folks. They're my little sisters. There is a lifelong bond from that experience of going to Spelman." Erin simultaneously continued her friendships from Spelman and viewed current students in a familial way, as younger sisters.

Acra, a Spelman alum from the 2000s, echoed the feelings of her Spelman sisters regarding the familial feel the institution fostered for its students:

> The one instance that really stood out to me about Spelman and really encouraged the sisterhood of the institution was during freshman week. We'd all kind of heard that they may be waking us up in the middle of the night and making us all go to the chapel. But we didn't really know. They woke us up. We have a Spelman hymn that we sing. They made us hold hands and walk to the chapel singing the song over and over and over again until we just knew it front to back. And then they got us in there and they talked to us and they talked to us about our journey and I think that was a really enlightening moment of the journey that I was about to start on. It was really great and when I went to the reunion and after our convocation for the reunion, we all stood up, we locked hands. We started singing the hymn. I think all of us can remember how Spelman gave us that sense of sisterhood and belonging and knowing that we're all going to be okay, and that we're on this journey together.

The midnight convocation was clearly a way that the institutional ethos of sisterhood was fostered, demonstrating a way that she experienced the *Chosen We* community at Spelman. Acra considered initiatives that Spelman used to foster a sense of community: "There's an organization that does all the activities now. They actually have more things now that I've been involved in since I've become an alum. There's a history and tradition session. They bring back alumnae to talk to the students and talk about our history with the college. We tell about what we've been through with our roommates and everything that we experienced. They can ask questions." Having experienced the power of the *Chosen We* community immediately when she came to campus, Acra felt a responsibility to return to campus as an alumna, to welcome new students into the sisterhood. She realized that this was not the case for all who went to college: "I talked to some of my peers from back home, the ones that did go away to college, and their experiences were not the same. I don't think they were as fulfilled as I was." Acra realized that her Spelman experience and the sisterhood that she felt there were not the norm, particularly at PWIs.

Brynn attended Florida A&M in the 2000s and graduated with a social sciences degree. Describing the best things about the institution, she responded: "The unity. We were always really excited for homecoming and football games, convocation, we would all go and just really hear what was being said. Being involved in the community other than student government. It was just a lot of fun. Socially, there was always something to do. There's a sense of unity I got there I don't think I would've gotten anywhere else." Brynn saw her institution as a place to which she deeply belonged. The idea that people are all connected to something greater than themselves is tied to the notion of a collective sense of identity, institution-wide *Chosen Wes*. Jordan's narrative continues the idea of institutional connection that feels like family.

"It's Like Having Another Family" at Dillard: Jordan's Story

Dillard University, in New Orleans, Louisiana, is a private, liberal arts institution affiliated with both the United Methodist Church and United Church of Christ. The campus is known for its whitewashed buildings with grassy quads in between. Many of the women who attended Dillard talked about the physical beauty of the campus and the sense that coming to the campus meant that they were and would become something special, an idea that was continually reinforced through campus programming.

Hurricane Katrina decimated parts of New Orleans in 2005 and flooded most of the buildings on campus. It was one of the worst, most costly, and deadliest hurricanes that the United States has ever experienced (Hartman, 2006). Even over a dozen years after Katrina's impact, parts of the city were still scarred with abandoned buildings that still bore the marks of the federal agencies that went through them to find missing people and to remove bodies. Campuses all over the city were flooded. Some took months and years to fully reopen. Dillard was particularly affected because of its proximity to one of the major levies that broke; most of the campus was covered in well over eight feet of water. For nearly two years after Hurricane Katrina, most of the returning students had to live and go to class in a Hilton Hotel in downtown New Orleans while the Dillard campus was restored. Many of the students had to leave the city during the storm and they lost all their possessions. When I visited years after the flood, there were still water marks eight feet high on multiple campus buildings.

Jordan graduated from Dillard University with a biological sciences degree in the 2000s. She started out by connecting the institution to her own biological family: "My first day on campus, I wanted to go back home almost immediately. Then they do a really good job here of transitioning you. The first couple of days, orientation is really family oriented, so my mom and my grandma and my two younger brothers were in town for the weekend." She continued:

> They do a program; it's called a parting ceremony. It's where you've had these three days with your family here. Now, the idea of the parting ceremony is that your parents turn you over to the school, literally turn you over. There's a program outside on the lawn, and you walk through the doors, and you can't come back out of the doors after. After you go through the beams and you walk in the doors, you can't come back out. You start your strictly student orientation.

The parting ceremony helped students transition from their families to their new campus family at Dillard.

Relatively soon after Jordan transitioned to campus, the city of New Orleans was devastated by Hurricane Katrina. Thousands of people were displaced and relocated to Houston, Texas, or other cities in Louisiana. Many never came back. She retold her own experience of displacement from the disaster, having come back to campus early to train as a resident assistant in the residence halls:

> That year was the start of my sophomore year. I was back early. I had only been here maybe a week or so, because we had RA orientation, I was a resident assistant. I moved in and Katrina hit. That was a learning experience. I went back home, after we went all the way around the world to get home. I left, I went to Houston. I wasn't able to get back to [my city in Alabama]. Maybe, over the course of two weeks, I drove from New Orleans to Houston, flew from Houston to Birmingham and then drove from Birmingham to [my hometown] because there was no way to go east, so you kind of had to circle around New Orleans just to get back to the other side.

Jordan continued her recollection of Katrina, remembering that she did not have a car at the time and so she needed to find transportation out of the city, taking a ride with a friend during the forced evacuation. Leaving campus in a rush, Jordan did not know how long she would be gone from campus. After leaving Dillard for what was supposed to be a few days, Jordan found herself not able to get back. Jordan and her friends spent a week and a half in a hotel in Houston before getting a flight to Birmingham where Jordan's godmother met them and drove Jordan and her friend home. Jordan remembered how disruptive the hurricane was to her program:

> That was August. Everybody thought Dillard was opening back up. It didn't open until January. From August until January, Dillard wasn't open. All these schools were accepting students from this area. Back home, the University of South Alabama was accepting students. The day after I got home, they were doing their registration. I went there and I enrolled. I got back in school there. I was in school for about two weeks there and I just decided, I just couldn't do it. I just didn't want to be in school, and it wasn't even long term, it was right after Katrina.

After going through so much loss at the start of her second year in college, it seemed nearly impossible for Jordan to try to switch institutions to attend a PWI. Jordan felt strongly that she did not want to settle for less than the "family" she had at Dillard: "I'll just wait on Dillard to open back and when Dillard opens, I'll go back. That's when I realized too, the family feel that Dillard had. You just didn't want to go anywhere else. I didn't want to transfer to another school. I just wanted to come back here. I just worked at the mall from September until January. Dillard opened in January, and we were back here." Jordan remembered what it was like going back to Dillard, the place she longed to be during the months it was closed for rebuilding:

> Katrina was the most memorable experience of my college career. We were in school in the Hilton-Dillard contract. They had a contract with the Hilton, to where we lived there. We lived in the room up one floor. There was a little diner downstairs in the Hilton that was our cafeteria. Dillard contracted that out; that was our cafeteria. The conference rooms, in the ballrooms at the Hilton, we had rows and rows of partitions, we turned the ballrooms into mini-class rooms. Right next door to the Hilton is the World Trade Center. Dillard contracted with them, because they had rooms, offices, with computers and that's where any computer-based classes were. We just built a makeshift university from January until July. We did accelerated semesters. We did two semesters from January until July, to make up from the hurricane. We called it Spring 1 and Spring 2. The first semester was from January until May, and then from May until July. We did class every day and just made up two semesters in two months.

The way that Jordan described going back to Dillard was framed in collective ways. She felt deeply connected to the institution, the aftermath of the hurricane, the rebuilding, and the way that the spirit of the Dillard family persevered despite one of the worst natural disasters to have ever hit the city of New Orleans. Jordan described all this as "The aftermath. Then getting back here and half the university wasn't built. Our building wasn't ready, so we had classes wherever we could find an empty classroom. All our labs, for about two years, we contracted with Xavier University, so we would travel over to their labs. It lasted for a really long time. The city itself and the university is still recovering.

That's probably one of the biggest things I've experienced. That's really life changing."

The campus completely changed after Katrina: "A lot of people didn't come back. My two best friends that I met here, they both came back. We all graduated from here. But a lot of people didn't. We had maybe 2,100 students my freshmen year. When we came back to campus, maybe the whole university had like 700? Enrollment was way down." Not only was the campus cut in half by the disaster, but many students did not ever fully recover their damaged property. While the federal agencies like FEMA were supposed to offer financial assistance, to get the claim filed people had to meet with an inspector in the site of the damage. Most students were not able to get onto the campus to get their claims filed, which meant they simply lost all their material possessions on campus. When Jordan got back to campus, her building had been gutted and everything was gone. Despite the loss, Jordan still maintained that her ties to campus kept pulling her back: "I desired to come back to Dillard. I had just fallen in love with the institution itself, like the atmosphere. The desire to come back to Dillard was just like what I knew I had left behind, just the close-knit family here." The familial feel of Dillard persisted even though the institution was underwater and recovering from devastation for the larger part of Jordan's degree program. Having experienced such a monumental experience together meant that those who returned to campus were even more bonded than they were initially. Jordan remembered:

> College, always had been my way out to do something, like to do anything better. I was always called a nerd in high school. That was my ticket, my meal ticket. So that was the big motivator. I just knew I had to finish.
>
> We have all these shirts, there's like 10 ways you know you went to Dillard. We listed them all on the back of the shirt, these little things that you know, that were unique to Dillard. We came back and the relationship between the students was like never before. I remember pulling up to the Hilton turned into this really big reunion before anybody actually got anything done.

There is perhaps no greater tribute to the enactment of an institutional idea of family than the way in which Dillard was rebuilt, by students, staff, and faculty after Hurricane Katrina. Those who returned, like Jordan, likely came back because they just did not want to be without the campus family they had created—and while the campus was a disaster for months and years afterward, it was the sense of community that pulled people through to graduation. As Jordan noted, the "family" remained long after they graduated.

THE *CHOSEN WE* AND THE EXPERIENCE OF BEING AT HOME WITHIN HBCUs

Institutional *Chosen We* communities were fostered by affirming students' backgrounds and connecting to those backgrounds. Not only did HBCUs offer orientation programs that often explicitly connected the campuses to students' families and communities, but once students transitioned to campus, they were constantly reminded of their belonging. The sense that one belonged on campus was built through constant affirmation that students' backgrounds were the norm and were fully accepted. Part of the normalization of racial identity was related to the demographics at HBCUs as compared to the demographics at PWIs. In contrast to PWIs where Black women often felt like they were the anomaly, at HBCU students could look around and see people who looked like them as peers, faculty, and in the leadership of the institutions.

The *Chosen We* of HBCUs was intimately connected to the sense that the campus was an extension of one's family or community. Some alumnae had family members who also attended the same HBCU and that deepened the idea that the campus was a *Chosen We* that affirmed one's background. By choosing to enroll in a particular HBCU, a student was also deciding to become part of the larger *Chosen We* family or home-like community of the campus. The initial feeling that one could be so deeply included as to be at "home" remained an important institutional ethos, a *Chosen We*, on these campuses. As students entered HBCU campuses they were also met with the normalcy of diverse ideas of what it could mean to be a Black woman. One's background can be affirmed while also allowing space to express individuality, as the next narratives maintain.

Finally, Not "On the Fringe": Finding a Nuanced Individuality at HBCUs

A crucial aspect of the *Chosen We* within HBCUs was that part of identifying with a larger community of Black students meant that alumnae could eventually identify their individuality. While nearly all the women described being brought into a community of excellence within their respective HBCUs, there was a nuanced vision of identity in these institutions. Background identities, communities, and families were largely affirmed at HBCUs, making it less likely that students had to encounter identity contestations and misrecognitions in the way that they did within PWIs. The affirmation of one's background and identities prior to coming to college seemed to allow alumnae to experience more opportunities to move from a sense of belonging within a *Chosen We* community on campus toward the identification of their unique *Me* identities.

Alumnae asserted their individuality in a few ways: 1) through a recognition that one was connected to a larger legacy from which one could begin to individuate; 2) through appearance such as hair, clothing, or a unique sense of style; 3) by embracing the diverse ways of being a Black woman that one could ultimately choose; and 4) by asserting other identities that could intersect with one's identities as a Black woman. A few examples follow to demonstrate how alumnae from various institutions described the individual *Me* parts of identity that they were ultimately able to assert.

Marwa provided an example of how an individual can use a *Chosen We* community as a safe location from which to individuate. She attended Benedict College in the 1960s and 1970s. She reflected, "There were people who would lay down their life for me. That's love. I have that kind of social love." Marwa carried that love with her to college and it helped her to excel. She also recalled having done some important work on her individual identities during this time:

> Once you leave home, even though I was staying at home when I was in college, still, you go through a kind of identity reevaluation of crises. I think maybe I worried about it more than most people. Well, I was a young woman trying to find herself, you know, find her identity. What's my purpose? What am I going to do? What is my future? Even though I was in college, and I was getting my degree. What does all of this mean? I made it. What is all of this? Where do I go from here? College was not hard to me because I just loved it.

After coming to campus, Marwa began to ask questions about her own individuality. While Benedict provided a community for her, she used her experience to identify and assert her own sense of individuality, as a Black woman who was both deeply connected to her community and individually self-possessed. As she explained later: "I'm a Black woman. I never thought of myself as anything else. It's just like that file cabinet [pointed to the cabinet in the room, laughing]. I just had such a solid African American community." While the questions she asked herself during college were about her individual identity, she returned to the deep grounding force of her home community, that was affirmed in college, and this enabled her to explore who she was as an individual within that community. Marwa's notation of developing individuality is very different from women who attended PWIs and found their identities as Black women contested or misrecognized (see also Winkle-Wagner et al., 2018).

Sunshine grew up in the Midwest, in a small town in Iowa. She attended Fisk University in Nashville, Tennessee, in the 1990s and early 2000s where she earned a social sciences degree. Sunshine later earned a master's degree in social sciences from the University of Nebraska in 2009. During our time together in Lincoln, Sunshine was enrolled in a doctoral program, which she finished during the writing of this book. She remembered why she selected Fisk, so far from her hometown and an institution that would be so different from her predominantly White high school: "I wanted to go to an all-Black school. I didn't have that. I didn't have any kind of all-Black experience except church, but it wasn't enough. I got really ridiculed by my friends who didn't understand why I wanted to go to an all-Black school. They all went to school in Iowa." Sunshine selected Fisk in part because she already felt included in a campuswide *Chosen We* with her Black identity in a way that had not happened for her in Iowa.

Sunshine recalled her sense of joining *Chosen We* subcommunities on campus to assert some of her interests and identities:

> It wasn't probably until my junior or senior year I was really active. My senior year I was really active in gospel choir, I was the president, and I was copresident with my other friend Maxine. I lived in a sorority by then. I joined a sorority my sophomore year. When I became a part of a sorority that opened me up to a whole different set of people. There was a level of physical affirmation. There's a high level of scholarship associated with my sorority as well so now you had to look the part, which was more so than just what my school expected. I was bitter about that, so I cut off my long hair and I started

an afro. That's totally against what my sorority would say is appropriate. I had to prove to myself that I'm still beautiful even if I don't have a long perm. I cut my hair off my spring semester of my second year.

One way that Sunshine asserted her uniqueness amid the *Chosen We* communities of her HBCU campus and her sorority was through her hairstyle. She strongly wanted to push back on the expectation that she could only be beautiful if she met a Eurocentric standard of beauty where her hair was long and straightened with a perm.

In her free time during college, Sunshine worked in an orthopedic shoe store. One of her coworkers invited Sunshine to church and that proved to be a transformative experience. Sunshine reflected: "[The coworker] asked me if I wanted to study the Bible and I felt like that was the answer that God was giving me. We started studying the Bible and she was teaching me all these things about the Bible that I had never known. I was so excited, and I would call my mom and tell her things that I was learning. I ended up getting baptized May 27, 2001." Sunshine identified her adult baptism as an important moment of developing her individual sense of self. She remembered how it felt to assert her religion as an important part of her identities:

> I felt like I finally didn't have to wear those faces, like my life was different because I had a standard. It was a mind-blowing experience because now there were all these races in my church. We were partnered up in discipleship partners and so an older spiritual person would help the younger and vice versa. It helped me to be able to overcome my stereotypes, because the more I've been in my all-Black school, with this all-Black stuff, the more I hated White people.

Sunshine noted that she wanted to move beyond hatred of White people. As she pondered, "I didn't feel like I could believe in God and feel all these things in my heart, just all the stereotypes that I had in my mind."

By the end of her time in college, Sunshine described bringing her religious identity and her campus identity together. "I would just try to make my worlds go together, and so right before I moved here, I feel like everything was good, like it was coming together." Sunshine developed her individuality by bringing together her racial identity, her gender identity, her religious identity, and her other identities. While she seemed to enjoy her time at Fisk University, it was the joining of her HBCU experience with her church experience that seemed to make her time in college meaningful for her.

Nzinga, who graduated from Spelman during a similar time period in the 2000s, recalled ways that she began to individualize her appearance. She talked about how she felt like she had to change her hair in secondary school. When I asked her what she thought she should have done with her hair, she explained, "Straight, long, 'good' hair, or curly, or pretty much anything non-Black or non–African American, non-nappy, non-course hair. I think growing up it was like, I kind of want hair like that." Essentially, Nzinga felt as if she had to do whatever it took to minimize her hair and to make it meet Eurocentric standards. All of that changed when she went to an HBCU for college because there were so many different women with so many different types of hairstyles. She recalled the relief she felt when she discovered that there were many ways to perform and present her Black womanhood in college:

> When I got to college, I realized I could embrace what I have, like my hair. It is who I am and there shouldn't be an excuse for it. I'm African American so why don't you expect me to just have regular [African American hair]? It's not super curly, it has these natural curls, it's not really straight, it's coarse, it can get thick, it needs to be moisturized. It's regular old Black hair. It's just what it is. I think while I was in college, I began to embrace it. I think it helped that I was in a larger city, and that I was at a school where there were so many different types of women there. Everyone had different looks. I was able to see the beauty within it. Like, I am not saying that long hair isn't beautiful or curly hair isn't beautiful. While I was at college, I was able to embrace the beauty within different types. And how women carry themselves differently. Everyone has a different style. While I was in college, I was able to be part of that different style and embrace other people's style and images of beauty and I loved it.

Being around so many kinds of Black women offered Nzinga important alternatives to what she could be too. It was as if being part of an intersectional, nuanced *Chosen We* allowed Nzinga to find her own uniqueness.

When I asked Nzinga about the pressure she felt to present her hair and appearance in ways that were Eurocentric earlier in her life, she noted:

> That was definitely trying for me. I never really had a problem with my skin complexion. But I know my sister, who is dark skinned, always told me there would be guys who would talk to her and would be like, "You're pretty for a dark-skinned girl." She hated that. So, it's the moments when they said something like that she wouldn't talk to them ever again because she felt that "My skin is beautiful the way it is, and it shouldn't be an excuse or I shouldn't be pretty 'for' (emphasis on for) [a dark-skinned girl]." It shouldn't be like that. It should just be "You're beautiful because you're beautiful." I learned those different things. You know, those types of lessons.

After being around myriad hair types, skin tones, and appearances of Blackness at Spelman, she began to accept herself in a new way. By being brought into a larger *Chosen We* community that affirmed her background and her appearance, she was able to identify her own unique way of presenting her appearance and her womanhood.

Nzinga summarized her time at Spelman as helping her to develop individuality:

> My time in college really shaped me as a female and as an individual. I learned a lot about myself. I would start just where I was in high school. How I thought as a girl in high school, or a young lady in high school. Then I might end in how I think as a woman now, and kind of in between fill in the gaps of how I've grown and how certain experiences have helped my ideas in the world.

It was the community of Spelman that helped Nzinga develop her individuality. Through embracing the diversity around her, Nzinga was empowered to find her uniqueness. This was very different from Black women's experiences at PWIs where there were very limited ways to be a Black woman.

Other alumnae echoed the assertion that HBCUs offered diverse ways of being a Black woman, highlighting differences in geographic or regional identity (see also Daché-Gerbino, 2018; Daché, 2022; Daché et al., 2022).

Brynn grew up in Georgia and wanted to attend an institution that was away from home but still close enough to visit. She graduated from Florida A&M University (FAMU) in 2005 with a degree in the social sciences. She described how diverse it felt:

> Freshman year is a lot of fun because everything is really new and you're meeting people from different places. It was kind of like camp with classes because we were all living on campus and going to class, eating on campus. None of us had cars or anything. I think freshman year was probably the most exciting because everything was just so new. I wasn't that far from home. About five hours, right on the Georgia/Florida border. It was a good enough distance where I could have some independence but if I wanted to go home, that wasn't a problem. I really enjoyed freshman year, learned a lot. I went to a historically black college. The dynamics can be a little bit different. I feel like there was a lot of unity there and socially, there was always something to do, something to get involved in. It was just very diverse. Although it was a predominantly African American campus, everyone was from pretty much everywhere. People [were] from Michigan and California and Chicago and Detroit, DC, Virginia, Maryland area, Florida, Texas. Each state pretty much had their own club.

Being at FAMU helped Brynn to realize that there were various ways to consider diversity, even geographic region. While there may have been a larger sense of "unity" at FAMU, students all belonged to the *Chosen We* of campus, there remained important differences between them.

Another way in which alumnae experienced a sense of being in a familial type of social network in college was through their involvement in student organizations within their HBCUs. Student organizations such as student government or sororities were a manifestation of the nuanced possibilities for who one could be and how one could present oneself. In addition to her regional affiliation with other students who were from Georgia, Brynn remembered finding other ways of developing her individual interests and ideas on campus while building close relationships with her peers:

I was a psychology major. I was involved in psychology club. I did some volunteer work in the community in Tallahassee, volunteering with other kids' programs, running groups. I was involved in student government my last two years of college. I really enjoyed that too, being able to hear the concerns of the students and being involved on that level. I had a pretty prominent position, senate secretary. You're responsible for all recordings and meetings and minutes and things like that. That was on a weekly basis for a whole year.

Brynn later joined a sorority during her graduate program at the University of Wisconsin and she found a lot of solace in that community to deflect the overwhelming Whiteness of that campus.

Elle was a 2000s graduate of Spelman College with a major in a humanities discipline. Coming from a low-income background in her home state of Mississippi, Elle particularly noticed class differences at Spelman and sometimes that made her feel as if she did not belong on campus. She remembered transitioning to campus:

I thought that I had it all figured out. I didn't at all. When I came into Spelman, I realized that. I thought that I was a very knowledgeable person, very well read. I knew I wasn't well traveled. But I didn't think that it mattered because I read a lot and I was likeable, and I succeeded in high school. What I had done in high school was nothing compared to what some of the women that I went to college with, what they had done in high school and the experiences that they had. That was really intimidating. I also felt like I didn't have anything to bring to the table. I grew up feeling like if you don't have anything to bring to the table, you really don't matter. I wasn't rich. I wasn't particularly fashionable or cutting edge. When you're in college, all of those things matter. Even the girls that weren't rich, they were very different. They wore their hair different, and they had different names. Their parents were hippies. They'd been to Guadalajara, or all these different places. Even if they weren't rich, they were rich in experiences. I just felt like I didn't fit in. I was from Mississippi. I thought I was smart. Obviously not that smart. It was hard to go from being at the top to going to a college where everyone that went to that college was at the top of their game. They were all really smart or they all were really well connected or really well traveled. I felt like I didn't fit in.

It is likely that there were other students from the Deep South and also from low-income backgrounds, but Elle did not feel like there were many people like her on campus.

Elle eventually joined a sorority, which made all the difference to her sense of inclusion. Her involvement was an extension of familial bonds for her because her mom had joined a sorority at Tuskegee University and her cousins also were in sororities during college:

> When I got to Spelman the women that were in the sorority that I joined, they were flavorful. I liked the way they carried themselves on campus. I liked the type of programs that they offered. They were all very smart, all very well put together. They seemed very natural. They didn't try too hard to be, they just were very classy women. I decided to see about joining. Once I expressed my interest to one of the chapter members, things got real.
>
> I definitely built some good relationships with my sisters. I went to college with all women so there are definitely going to be some cliques and some snobs. I think it's always shocking to people when they find out you can actually go to an institution all for women and really not have to deal with a whole lot of cattiness. I didn't really deal with a lot of attitudes and mean girl mentalities. There was plenty of ambitious, smart, go-getting women who would happily welcome you into their friendship at Spelman. I guess I was scared to try to reach out for that. But me pledging my sorority opened those doors for me.
>
> I would say, even now in my job today, it's a lot about building relationships. If my boss was here, I would introduce you to her, and she would tell you that within this office, I'm the strongest person in terms of building relationships with people. She will seek me out if she needs someone to come present a panel. If she needs a connection in the governor's office in Tennessee or the speaker's office in Mississippi, she knows that my relationships that I've built and the network

that I've created would help her get that contact. And that was all learned through my experiences pledging my sorority. I would say that a lot of good came out of that.

One of the main things that Elle highlighted as beneficial in her sorority membership was the large social network that it offered to her, not just at Spelman but nationally.

Sorority involvement at PWIs and HBCUs differed slightly even though they were the same organizations. Within PWIs, sororities would have been locations where Black women could engage with other Black women in a way that might have been difficult in other locations on campus due to the sheer Whiteness of the demographics. That is, sororities were likely safe spaces, or locations that at least partially resisted the Whiteness of the rest of the campus. In some instances, women described HBCUs as heavily involved in Greek-letter organizations such that it would be difficult to feel like one truly belonged on campus without becoming involved in a sorority. In other instances, there were more ways of being involved at HBCUs than there were at PWIs making sorority involvement not as vital to a feeling of belonging on campus.

Nicole's story follows, and it suggests another way of finding one's individuality and uniqueness within an HBCU. Her narrative provides a variation on how one comes to individuality within the *Chosen We* of an HBCU.

FINDING A DIVERSE AND SELF-ACCEPTING BLACKNESS AT SPELMAN: NICOLE'S STORY

Nicole grew up in a military family and had lived in multiple cities by the time she went to college, but she mostly claimed Texas as her home state. She graduated from Spelman College in the early 2000s with a social sciences degree. She earned a master's degree in the same social sciences discipline from the predominantly White public institution of the University of South Florida in 2005 and continued for her PhD there, completing her doctorate in 2009.
Nicole's dad encouraged her to consider attending an HBCU. Nicole remembered:

I did not want to attend an HBCU initially. I was a military kid and so we lived all over. I did not think that I would do well at an HBCU because I had never gone to school with a lot of other African American people. I had an experience unfortunately where I was perceived to be a certain kind of way because of the way that I spoke, the interests that I had, because I could sometimes be classified as a little bit of a weird kid. I wore fishnet stockings and liked to go with some of my friends to mosh pits. I was a little bit interesting for an African American kid. I was ostracized by other African American people that I knew. Outside of my family, when I was in my own community, I felt like I was on the fringes because I heard stupid comments from people. Things like you talk this way, you listen to this music, you're not really that Black.

I asked Nicole how she coped:

I just brushed it off. I wasn't assertive back then like I am now. But I internalized it. I struggled with maybe I should be different. I just really wasn't secure in my identity. When you think about stages of cultural identity, I was not secure in my identity at all even though my parents constantly told me, "It's okay to be Black. There isn't a dichotomy. You can't say I'm Black so I can't like that." But they were my parents. I felt like, "Yeah but you're not going to school. This is what I'm hearing at school." I had a best friend who was African American just like me. She also had the same experience. That's why we were best friends. That was our social circle.

In her primary and secondary schooling, Nicole did not feel like she fit in with other Black students because of her musical tastes, her taste in clothing, and her other interests. She felt isolated and struggled with her identity as a Black woman because she did not feel like she could signal what she perceived as the appropriate form of Blackness to fit in with most of her Black peers. She remembered not initially considering an HBCU:

When it came time [to be] looking at colleges, the majority of colleges I selected were predominantly White institutions. My father was like, "I think you should also put an HBCU on that list." I was like, "I don't want to go to an HBCU. Why would I choose to go to a school that's predominantly Black when I've had such bad experiences? That would be stupid." That was the kind of view that I had back then. My father had initially started off at an HBCU and then joined the military and then ended up graduating from a predominantly White institution through the military. But he loved his HBCU experience. He was like, "Let's just go visit Spelman because we're right here in Atlanta. I'm telling you, I've met people from Spelman, I work with people from Spelman. These women, they come out, they're so poised and so articulate and driven. It'd be a great experience for you." I'm like, "Whatever." I ended up applying [to Spelman] because my father wouldn't get off my back.

Finally, Nicole gave in and, "I decided I was going to go to Spelbound." Spelbound[3] is the Spelman College recruitment event for newly admitted, prospective college students where they come to campus for two days in the spring semester before they begin college in the fall. The women stay in the residence halls and attend multiple events to become more familiar with campus, and to get to know currently enrolled Spelman students. Nicole remembered:

I went to Spelbound and still kind was like "uh, whatever." I stayed with two girls, one who actually ended up coming to Spelman too. I went there and the girls that I stayed with were super nice. I remember one of the girls, she's very into the arts and things like that. She had these earrings all down her ear and she had a nose ring. Again, I had a very narrow view of what it was like to be African American. She had these colored tips in her dreadlocks. Coming from San Antonio, I hadn't even really seen anybody with dreadlocks. Again, this is a very narrow view, saying this sounds really weird now. But I hadn't seen that. She was vegan. I was like, "Wow. She's comfortable in her skin," which I clearly was not. She was super nice. She also had a tongue ring. The other three girls that were visiting were also really nice girls. I had an amazing time there with the girls in the room. I had gotten these phrases that I'm basically this Black, White-girl.

Spelman offered Nicole a place where she could pursue multiple interests because there were many ways to be Black in that space. She explained her revelation of Blackness as multifaceted that came from her freshman orientation program:

> At Spelbound, first of all, seeing the other girl who did not fit this narrow idea I had of what it was to be Black, made me like, okay, she's not fitting into this little narrowly defined concept. I met other girls while I was there who were at Spelman and did not [fit] either. I looked around and saw a lot of people who, I guess you could say, looked similar, but were also different. And it's likely because I just had a very small population to sample. I didn't know there were so many people that were so different, but also the same.

Nicole contemplated why it was such a revelation to see different ways of being Black. Black women on campus had different interests, ideas, and tastes and that was accepted:

> There were four [Black women] in my [high school] class. It's not really much to judge off of [just a few people], right? And then in the community when I went places, the Black side of town, at my church and things like that, that was that experience I was kind of generalizing to everything else, and that's a shame. But that was really just lack of exposure. That was, for me, one thing that I was like, "Hmm, interesting," that I was really surprised about.

After realizing that Spelman could introduce her to entirely new ways of thinking about her Blackness, Nicole reflected on what was so special and unique about the Spelman College orientation program, and ultimately, what prompted her to accept her admission:

> I heard over and over again at Spelbound about how supported you were at Spelman. "Everyone is a sister and you're not going to fail. It's our goal to make sure everyone comes out successful and that you all are supporting each other." Even though I hadn't been accepted to Spelman at that time, during that weekend, it already felt like I was supported by the girls who were the hosts. They were like, "This is why I love Spelman." Everybody was exuding why they love Spelman so

much. "Spelman is so supportive. It's completely changed my life." I had not heard that in any of the tours—hearing all of these talks about how you just feel inspired and you feel that you can change the world. Literally you go in as whatever kind of girl you are, and you come out as this Spelman woman.

Nicole contemplated the change that happened for her once she enrolled on the campus: "[My dad] was ecstatic. He was like, 'College is not just about the education. It's about the experience that it builds for you as a person, and you need this experience to solidify the kind of woman that you are called to be. If you can't feel comfortable in yourself with yourself, then it's going to shape your entire future.' Everything he said was true." Nicole's dad was deeply invested in her attending an HBCU. While Nicole initially pushed back on his advice, once she accepted her admission to Spelman, she felt affirmed and able to explore a more nuanced version of her identity. She reflected: "I went as an insecure girl who did not feel comfortable in her identity, who was ashamed to say that she loved Journey and her and her mother listened to Janice Joplin and she wore fishnets. I was ashamed of those things, which is so silly now. But then I was. I went to Spelbound and did not feel like I was on the fringe." Spelman provided an experience where Blackness and womanhood were not monolithic or treated as just one way of behaving or one set of interests. Ultimately, because Spelman allowed Nicole to express herself in multiple ways as a Black woman, the experience did much more than offer her a college education: Spelman gave Nicole a place to find and express her uniqueness. Contemplating what her HBCU experience meant for the way she saw herself, Nicole asserted:

> Now I'm like, yes, I'm African American and that's very much a part of my identity. Being African American does not have a label to it. I can say this to other young girls who I know struggle with those same things. You don't have to be classified by that. In fact, I'm a psychologist. I had a girl recently, she is Chinese, but she goes to a predominantly White middle school. And she says how kids turn to her and they pull their eyes and say how much she loves math. She's like, "I'm not even good in math." She's like, "I hate my school and they make me feel ashamed of being Chinese and I wish I wasn't Chinese." I can sit there and be like, "I'm not Chinese but I understand

what it's like not to be secure in your identity." And talk about some degree of that process of what it takes to get support to be comfortable with who you are. Spelman did that for me. It did that. It provided me with not only that experience with my cultural identity and making me feel comfortable and helping me continue to solidify that we are all different women that have different walks of life. Solidified that even more when I got my roommate who was a girl from New Jersey, grew up in Newark. She told me on the phone she thought I wasn't African American when she talked to me. She was like, my roommate is one of the girls who are not African American. Her eyes were opened about a lot of different things. So, we all had different walks of life but we all came out being transformed.

For Nicole, it was Spelman that helped her to develop into a positive and confident person who did not have to be constrained by stereotypical notions of Black womanhood.

Nicole also spoke about the way in which Spelman made her want to do more for her community once she graduated in the early 2000s. She compared her positive experience at Spelman to her negative experience at the University of South Florida in graduate school:

Those early experiences have shaped who I am today in terms of wanting to mentor and talking to others, especially with graduate school, the fact that I made it through that, because it was a very tough experience. I made it through that. Knowing I had the support from Spelman and that built me up to be a better person. Where I am today, now, which is I own my own practice. I work for myself. I felt like I could do those things because I was confident in myself, which was shaped by Spelman. I felt like if I could make it through some of that tough stuff I [experienced] in grad school, why can't I make it through this? Right? All those experiences, tough, good, bad, whatever, all of them shape exactly who I am today in terms of my professional self. I mean, I'm not going to really change anything. It would've been great not to have to have that kind of experience at USF. But it shaped who I was today. Now I have students who were in that program who were like not only did you graduate with a professor that they all still know but now you own your own business, you're doing well, you like what you do. Maybe there is hope I can make it through this program too. I learned from Spelman; I have to help.

Nicole attributed her confidence and her desire to help others to her time at Spelman. In comparison, her graduate program at USF was something she described as surviving, in part because of the strength she garnered from her time at Spelman.

The Chosen We and Developing Individuality through Diversity at HBCUs

Through inclusion at HBCUs, alumnae asserted their individuality. By attending institutions where students were culturally and racially affirmed on campus, alumnae recalled feeling empowered to choose to represent and perform their identities in diverse ways. Rather than being presented with a single, often stereotypical idea of Black womanhood as can be the case on PWI campuses, the HBCU alumnae argued that they were exposed to nuanced ways of expressing their identities. For some alumnae, finally being in a space where there were many ways of being Black and a woman was liberating in ways they had not previously encountered. This is not to say that some alumnae did not have struggles at HBCUs. While the data here are overwhelmingly positive about HBCU experiences, there were still identity struggles like some of the ones mentioned earlier (e.g., Elle's struggles with class differences). Yet there were simply more options, more *Chosen We* possibilities, at HBCUs. While one might feel included within the larger campus *Chosen We*, there were also many other options for choosing to identify with diverse groups (e.g., organizations, sororities, clubs) on campus.

Conclusion on Nuanced Individuality through the *Chosen We* at HBCUs

The oral histories from HBCU alumnae suggest that HBCUs can be culturally affirming and empowering spaces in which to earn a degree. Alumnae experienced a deep sense of belonging within *Chosen We* communities on these campuses. The campuses were *Chosen We* spaces in that the alumnae selected the institutions often knowing that HBCUs would affirm their backgrounds. Sometimes HBCUs were already an important part of the women's family histories; their parents, aunts, uncles, or siblings had attended HBCUs for generations. Thus, when alumnae described HBCUs as being another home or an extension of their family, sometimes it was the case that attending a particular institution was a continuation of a familial legacy. It was through the sense of belonging that alumnae then were able to see the nuances and diversity within the institutions. It was often described like a breath of fresh air for alumnae to have realized that there were many ways to present their racial and/or gender identities; there were many ways to be Black women at HBCUs. On that note, there are not as many stories here about women who identify as lesbian, gay, bisexual, or transgender. It is likely that gender may have still been constrained in some ways on these campuses even if this set of oral histories does not discuss that, aside from a few exceptions. Still, the overwhelming presence of claims to being included in a larger community and then finding a way toward individuality in these oral histories is worth noting.

The importance of community and being able to see oneself as unique within that community provides some important implications that may be adaptable at other HBCUs or PWIs:

1. Elevate campus efforts to create meaningful spaces of inclusion that students can associate as another type of "home" or family." While campuses might not be able to create a campuswide sense that the community is a home away from home, campus actors can deliberately foster inclusive spaces or subgroups on the larger campus. For instance, while at HBCUs there might be unity over the mission and some of the campus practices such as orientations or assemblies, on larger campuses or at PWIs, these "home" spaces might be multicultural student centers or campus events that promote inclusion for students of color.

2. Promote the affirmation of students' backgrounds on campus. One of the reasons that students felt at home at HBCUs is because they encountered campus practices and demographics that were more likely to affirm students' backgrounds. The affirmation of students' backgrounds can happen at orientations, campus events, in classrooms, and in campus artifacts. At campuses where there are students from

many backgrounds, as is the case at most PWIs, it would be necessary to affirm students' many backgrounds deliberately and actively. For instance, at PWIs, campus actors could try to include people from multiple backgrounds in the creation of policies, programs, and practices as one way to try to create messages and actions that students might interpret as affirming of their backgrounds.

3. It is important to elevate the diversity at HBCUs relative to geography, socioeconomic differences between students, cultural background differences, language differences, differences in gender identity or gender expression, or other differences. The alumnae were able to individuate after feeling affirmed and included on campus and it was helpful for the alumnae to see the many nuanced and intersectional identities that they could exhibit and still be positively recognized on campus.

4. It is necessary to highlight more than one model for being a student of color or a Black student on campus and to avoid stereotypical definitions, practices, or programs that treat Black students as a monolithic group. A unique characteristic of many of these oral histories is that the alumnae can personally identify the differences in their experiences at PWIs and HBCUs because many of the women attended both types of institutions at some point during their educational careers. It is not so much that one kind of institution is wholly good while the other is indefensible. Rather, it is the case that PWIs are highly individualistic, competitive, and steeped in Eurocentric norms and values. Sometimes these institutions can be positive places for Black students. But often, students who attend PWIs still experience racial hostility and isolation. HBCUs were warm, nurturing, and more community-oriented. That type of institution, with an emphasis on being a part of a community, is likely not for everyone either, although the alumnae here seemed to have relatively positive experiences.

At both HBCUs and PWIs, alumnae were able to identify both community and individual ideas of their identity. The alumnae in this book coped with the isolation of PWIs by creating *Chosen We* communities even if they did not formerly exist. Out of individualistic norms at PWIs, community *Chosen We* spaces offer an alternative and powerful way to identify one's sense of self at PWIs. Alternatively, at HBCUs, alumnae considered enrollment in these institutions as a way of joining an existing *Chosen We* community. Out of the *Chosen We* community of HBCUs, alumnae were able to individuate and identify a unique sense of self.

Part IV

Embodying Race, Institutional Memory, and the *Chosen We*

The White supremacist history that led to the creation of historically Black and predominantly White colleges and universities has influenced both historical and contemporary experiences at these institutions. The racist history of legal exclusion of Black students from state, public institutions (Smith, 2016) means that these institutions were not created to support students who were not White and male. There is a growing body of research that points to the persistent history of exclusion and isolation within predominantly White institutions (PWIs) (Brooms, 2019; Feagin et al., 2014; Fleming, 1985; Fries-Britt & Turner, 2001; Thelamour et al., 2019; Winkle-Wagner, 2009a). Historically Black colleges and universities (HBCUs), on the contrary, are often found to be warm, nurturing, and supportive campuses for the students who attend those institutions (Allen et al., 2007; Gasman & Arroyo, 2019; Mobley, 2017; Williams & Johnson, 2018; Williams et al., 2018). Given this history, it is not surprising that the narratives in these next chapters suggest that when alumnae transitioned from an HBCU to a PWI (e.g., from a bachelor's degree to a graduate program), they were often faced with culture shock, isolation, and racial stress. Yet HBCUs offered environments that were so affirming that many of the alumnae were able to carry these positive affirmations with them (see also Boncana et al., 2021; Nguyen et al., 2019; Perna et al., 2009; Williams et al., 2022).

In part 4, I present narratives of alumnae who experienced *both* predominantly White and historically Black campuses during their educational careers. The alumnae who attended both PWIs and HBCUs were able to make direct comparisons between these institutions in a unique and important way. There have been prior comparisons between Black students who are attending HBCUs and PWIs in the same time period (Allen, 1992; Kim & Conrad, 2006; Fleming, 1985; McCoy et al., 2017; McCoy et al., 2015; Reeder & Schmitt, 2013). Often these comparisons find HBCUs to be warmer, more nurturing places than PWIs (Arroyo & Gasman, 2014; Conrad & Gasman, 2014; Winkle-Wagner & McCoy, 2017). HBCUs have also been identified as more likely to promote upward social mobility as compared to PWIs (Hardy et al., 2019). Most of the comparisons take a particular moment in time and examine Black students who opted to attend *either* a PWI or an HBCU, and then there is a comparison of the dissidences in how Black students describe their experiences. While these explorations have gone a long way toward explicating some of the important differences and student outcomes between HBCUs and PWIs, it is still relatively unclear how students who were enabled to attend both types of institutions might identify the differences for themselves. In offering this perspective of those who traversed both types of institutions, this portion of the book allows for a previously unseen analysis.

A Brief Description of the Alumnae
Who Attended Both HBCUs and PWIs

Approximately one-quarter of the alumnae in this book (29 women) attended both HBCUs and PWIs during their educational journeys (table 7). Of those who attended both institutional types, 25 alumnae first earned a bachelor's degree at an HBCU before choosing to attend a PWI for their master's degrees (table 7). Some of those same alumnae then pursued a PhD, MD, or JD after earning a master's degree. There were 12 alumnae who earned terminal degrees at PWIs after first having graduated from an HBCU (table 7). There were considerably fewer alumnae who opted to attend an HBCU for their graduate or professional programs after having earned a bachelor's degree at a PWI (4 alumnae total). One reason for this trend could be that there are relatively few HBCUs that offer graduate-level professional programs compared to PWIs.

Table 7. Demographics of the Alumnae Who Attended Both HBCUs and PWIs

Number of HBCU undergraduate alumnae who earned graduate degrees at PWIs	25 graduate or professional degrees earned: 25 master's degrees (some en route to a terminal degree); 12 terminal degrees (PhD, JD, MD)
Number of PWI undergraduate alumnae who earned graduate degrees at HBCUs	4 alumnae
TOTAL number of alumnae who attended both HBCUs and PWIs	29 total alumnae

Source: Author-created.

Brief Comparisons between HBCUs and PWIs

There were a few claims that emerged from the data where alumnae actively compared their experiences between PWIs and HBCUs:

1. HBCUs were designated as more community-oriented campuses than PWIs. Often words like "unity" or "solidarity" were used to illustrate the focus on community within HBCU campuses (chapters 7 and 8). Similarly, words like "warm" or "nurturing" were also used to identify the norms of HBCU campuses. When comparing across the two types of institutions, metaphors like "hot and cold" were used to connote the dramatic differences in both racial demographics and in campus norms.

2. HBCUs provided affirming experiences that alumnae could take with them to empower them in other contexts. Several of the alumnae discussed the importance of having attended an HBCU *before* attending a PWI because they were able to shore up the affirmation of their identities and backgrounds in such a way that they were able to take that confidence with them into circumstances that were less welcoming to them as Black women (chapter 7).

3. Attending an HBCU after a PWI could be a form of "culture shock" even if the experience was positive. For those alumnae who first attended a PWI for their bachelor's degrees and then transitioned to an HBCU for graduate or professional school, the experience could be a bit of a "shock" to suddenly be in a predominantly Black environment. Additionally, some of these alumnae mentioned a type of stigma or feeling that HBCUs might not be as rigorous as some PWIs, even if that was just a perception and not based in evidence from the institutions.

4. Alumnae who attended PWIs for their undergraduate degrees seemed more likely to experience major health crises in or soon after college. While one can only make inferences from this data because it was not initially a part of the study, it was the case that numerous alumnae from PWIs included health crises as crucial points in their oral histories about college. Not one of the HBCU alumnae mentioned a health crisis during or soon after college.

The Structure of Part 4

In the final portion of the book, the 29 alumnae who attended both PWIs and HBCUs shared their stories about the differences between these institutions. In chapter 7, I explored what it was like for alumnae to have transitioned from HBCUs (for their undergraduate degree) into PWIs for their graduate and professional programs before considering the handful of alumnae who had the opposite transition, from PWIs to HBCUs for graduate or professional programs. HBCUs were identified as focused on building community and creating inclusion. Thus, HBCUs were referred to as "warm," "nurturing," and places where "unity" could be cultivated. PWIs were demonstrated to be good academic institutions, but they were also rife with racial stereotypes and racial stress, and sometimes that felt isolating to the alumnae. In both types of institutions, the alumnae identified *Chosen We* communities as important parts of their experiences and eventual success in their degree programs. In the case of PWIs, these *Chosen We* communities were like those mentioned in part 2 of the book: informal friendships and formal student organizations that elevated racial/ethnic identities. At HBCUs, as demonstrated in part 3 of the book, the entire campus was crafted as a type of *Chosen We* community to which students could deeply belong.

After offering some of the general comparisons between the two types of institutions, in chapter 8, I reflect on an inferred theme from the alumnae who attended PWIs for their undergraduate degrees. There were multiple instances where PWI alumnae identified health crises as significant parts of their undergraduate experiences. What captured my attention was that there were no comparable histories from HBCU graduates—not one of the alumnae mentioned a health crisis during or soon after college. I end by comparing how *Chosen We* communities were framed differently in PWIs and HBCUs, even if these communities were consistently identified as vital to eventual college success.

.

Chapter 7

From "Unity" to "Isolation"

Comparing Experiences within HBCUs and PWIs

Sisters are more than the sum of their relative disadvantages: they are active agents who craft meaning out of their circumstances and do so in complicated and diverse ways.

—Melissa Harris-Perry, *Sister Citizen*

Black education, particularly in the southern United States, was essentially taken from Black people and then created by and for the main benefit of White people in the United States (Anderson, 1988; Watkins, 2001). For example, before racial integration in schools, there were numerous Black teachers and administrators who carefully crafted their curricula and pedagogy for their Black students (Anderson, 1988). The lesson to be garnered from this history is *not* that integration should not have happened in public schools or in higher education. Rather, the lesson is that Black people should have been part of the conversations and included in a meaningful way in the decisions that were made about the education of Black students. HBCUs offer a natural test case of the hope and possibility that can stem from the deep and lasting involvement in higher education that was created by and for Black people. The research on historically Black institutions of higher education offers comparisons between Black students who attended PWIs and those who attended HBCUs (Allen, 1991; Allen et al., 1992; Hardy et al., 2019; Kim & Conrad, 2006). More recently, some scholarship has focused on comparisons between HBCUs and other types of minority-serving institutions such as tribal colleges, Hispanic serving institutions, and Asian American Pacific Islander serving institutions (Conrad & Gasman, 2015). Most comparisons between HBCUs and PWIs are comparisons of similar students at both institutional types at one moment in time. For instance, many studies examine Black students at a similar stage who are enrolled in degree programs at predominantly White and historically Black institutions (Hardy et al., 2019; McCoy et al., 2017). Yet there is a gap in understanding of how individuals can attend both types of institutions during their educational careers and then reflect on the differences from their own multifaceted experiences. This chapter attempts to begin to fill this gap, by contemplating how Black alumnae pondered their experiences in *both* institutional types during their educational careers. While the level of education is obviously different relative to the disciplinary focus in graduate school versus the attempt to focus on breadth in undergraduate programs, there is still a meaningful understanding to be gained by those who have ventured to earn degrees at both types of campuses. Within the narratives of those who attended both PWIs and HBCUs in their educational careers, there emerged an important inference relative to the ways in which different institutional types may influence the health and well-being of alumna, which I consider in chapter 8.

It Was "Almost Like Hot and Cold": Comparing HBCUs and PWIs

For those who were able to compare their own experiences at PWIs and HBCUs, there were typically unambiguous metaphors in the way they crafted their accounts. Often the transition between institutions was framed as a "shock" or in a metaphor for the degree of warmth such as "hot" and "cold." It was as if there could hardly be enough emphasis on the differences between the two types of institutions. For many alumnae, the huge shift in racial demographics between the two types of institutions was enough to create dissonance for them in how they viewed themselves and their experiences. But in addition to the racial demographics, the institutional norms and types of support that were offered within those institutions were also quite starkly contrasted. In this chapter I provide some alumnae illustrations, across multiple oral histories, of what it was like to go from an HBCU for an undergraduate degree to a PWI for graduate or professional programs. Then, I consider the reverse transition, to understand what it was like for those alumnae who earned undergraduate degrees at

PWIs and then transitioned to an HBCU. The chapter ends with an oral history from a participant called Brynn.

"It Was a Culture Shock": Transitioning from an HBCU to a PWI for Graduate School

Brie's comparison between Florida A&M (FAMU) and the University of Michigan was clearly an illustration of the blunt difference between PWIs and HBCUs. She attended Florida A&M University for her undergraduate degree in the physical sciences. After college, Brie earned admission into a graduate program at the University of Michigan where she earned a PhD in the physical sciences in the early 2000s. She compared the two campuses:

> For my graduate school experience my greatest takeaway is that the two experiences were quite different, significantly more different than I expected. Whereas the undergraduate experience was broader even when the focus narrowed within a major, the graduate experience was immediately narrow and continued to narrow with time. There was minimal diversity in the content to learn unless one specifically sought it out in graduate school. I was incredibly grateful to have the opportunity to take classes in public policy while at Michigan. If I wasn't proactive, my only classes would have been in [the physical sciences]. Given the type of institution Michigan is, I felt it was important to take advantage of opportunities to step beyond my graduate study focus. Non-core activities seemed like an easier and more welcome (by professors, advisors) endeavor with my undergraduate experience.

Not only was the academic content different relative to depth (in graduate school) versus breadth (in undergraduate programs), but Brie noted the lack of diversity in the content within her PWI Michigan program, which likely refers to lacking readings or topics that related to scholars and communities that were not White. She continued:

> The greatest difference between my HBCU and PWI experience was the sense of community, specifically fostered by my professors. At FAMU I felt that professors cared about me and invested in getting to know me personally. They inquired

about my whereabouts if I missed class. They questioned me when they felt that I wasn't performing up to what they knew I could do. I did not have the same experience at Michigan. While classes were similar size, if not smaller, teaching was not the highlight. Professors, who were also research advisors, were primarily concerned with the graduate students working in their laboratory and on their research. Getting to know students outside of that small group wasn't a frequent event.

Brie specifically noticed differences in how professors worked with students. At the HBCU, faculty held students to high standards and seemed to insert themselves into students' lives if students were not performing well. To be sure, Brie was still successful, but it did not seem that she felt a tremendous amount of support at her PWI.

Like Brie, Nadia emphasized the importance of mentoring in comparing the differences between PWIs and HBCUs. At Spelman College and many other HBCUs, there was an assumption that many of the students would attend graduate school. After finishing her undergraduate degree at Spelman, Nadia completed a master's degree in the social sciences at Old Dominion University in the 2000s. At the time when we met in Chicago, she was currently enrolled in a PhD program at Loyola University–Chicago, pursuing studies in a social sciences discipline. When it came time for her to pursue a PhD, she credited the mentoring she received at Spelman as helping her to prepare:

> I worked for five years after getting my master's in 2008. And I've always known that I wanted to pursue my PhD. Education is paramount to just my values and my value system, different from different family members in my family. But for me, it was kind of my escape from urban society in America. And I knew that if I wanted to achieve anything, I needed to have an education to do so. I admired my vice president at Spelman. She had a doctorate. Our president, she had a doctorate. So, all of these wonderful role models are providing examples for me of what is going to be helpful to get to those next levels. So, I knew that I wanted, I needed to have some practical experience. Because how many tangible experiences, how are you applying the theory in practice, and so I worked. It just felt right at that time to start to pursue researching programs.

And Loyola was one of my top choices because of its social justice mission. The faculty and my research interests, and the program itself is structured in a way that I felt supported and nurtured. And even though I'm in the minority, I don't feel that way within my program.

When asked why she did not feel like a "minority" in her academic program at Loyola, Nadia considered the importance of representation and mentoring:

I can start back with my childhood mentors. I would credit them for putting me on the path for wanting to be education-ally and spiritually grounded. They were through my church. But they had a youth mentoring program called an [Achieve] program. They were actually at my wedding a month ago. But their program allowed us inner city children to see different things around us in the world, exposed us to things we probably would not have been privy to. For that, I am forever grateful because they definitely took us on conferences and etiquette classes and public speaking classes and things that just cre-ated a desire to want to do better and present a better self for ourselves, not just for other people. So that was kind of in my younger years, and something that kept me grounded through middle school and high school. I've always just been driven to exceed my own expectations and just kind of do things with a spirit of excellency because I felt like that was part of me accepting the challenge. I accepted the challenge to be spiritually faithful and accepted the challenge to be academically astute and accepted the challenge to help my fellow peers around me. So, I've just always had that in my mind about how I wanted to move forward and how I wanted to engage. So, as I do my journey, I have to say that they were the foundation for that mentorship example.

Thinking about how these mentorship experiences then translated to her experiences at Spelman and in her master's program, Nadia reflected:

In college, I admired the vice president. She was not my direct mentor. But just being around her and seeing her leadership, showed me some things that I kept in the back of my mind. Like okay, take notes. This is good to know, this is good to see. I would say then, when I got to graduate school, I got a formal mentor. She is a woman of color who was very honest and open with us personally and academically, just kind of challenging us and pushing us. Letting us feel comfortable but also knowing that it may not be easy. "You're still a minority individual. Your social identities are going to always be seen first. So, you need to make sure that your work speaks for itself as well as for who you want to be known as." That always encouraged me. I never was ashamed to be articulate and to address concerns and just to have that voice. She encouraged that and made sure that we didn't feel that that voice was a bad voice. Just hearing her story about being a mom of three, trying to finish her PhD. And she did it and she's a tenured faculty member. It can be done. You might hear some of the trauma stories. People who are childless and depressed. But I've seen in my own eyes that it can be done. I look at my current advisor here at Loyola and she's also a woman of color. So, I'm very blessed to be able to have women of color who see my potential who also know that I am destined to do something, probably bigger than I can even imagine for myself. They want to make that happen because they see that there is a void and there is a need and there's not enough representation. Especially at the professor level. It's encouraging to know that I can tap into my master's [degree program] mentor. Or you know, the relationship that I'm fostering right now with my current advisor, to have that support and that encouragement. Well, ODU is a lot more diverse than Loyola is. But Loyola is very, predominantly white.

Nadia ruminated on the differences between the three institutions that she attended for her undergraduate, master's, and PhD degrees:

They're both two different experiences from Spelman. Where I can look to my left, look to my front, look to my back and I can see my sisters and I can see someone that looks like me, whose story may be similar to mine. So, I think that experience by itself, it empowers you to a whole different level. I don't know if I would be the same person that I am today if I went to a different institution for undergrad. Because that experience alone, like I said, just shaped and contributed to shaping this person today. I think I have a different level of comfort because I already got my foundation. I've already defined for myself, who I was, and what I wanted out of life. To be put into a majority environment when I am in the minority, I still feel empowered and I still feel like I have a voice and I still feel like my voice matters. I don't feel threatened. Whereas I've interacted with some of my other women of color friends who went to predominantly White schools for undergrad or all through. And it's a whole different thing. They feel isolated. They feel different. I don't have that feeling. But I think that that's greatly contributed to the empowering support that I received from my undergrad experience.

Having attended Spelman and cultivated sisterhood and support, Nadia felt more empowered and ready to enter the PWIs that she attended for her master's and PhD degrees. It seemed important to Nadia to point out that she saw other women of color who had attended PWIs from undergraduate programs through graduate school struggle differently with finding their voice and dealing with isolation. Nadia asserted the crucial importance of building an empowering foundation, comfort, and the sense that she and her voice mattered. She seemed to take the experience of empowerment at Spelman with her and it changed how she viewed her PWI experience.

Amanda made similar comparisons to Nadia about the women of color who did not ever attend an HBCU during their educational career. After graduating from Howard University, Amanda pursued a master's degree at Georgia State University in a biological sciences discipline. She compared the two:

My experience at Howard was like really being at home, just not at home. It's very comforting and nurturing. It's not a feeling that I got at Georgia State, but it may have been because I was at the graduate level and I wasn't seeking the same kind of things. Just kind of, come to campus, do what you gotta do. Progress your career and go on. Whereas at Howard, I'm like, making connections, building relationships, establishing a legacy, hopefully, for my future kids. Two very different settings. But I'm certain that going to an HBCU had a lot to do with it and had a lot to do with the reasons why I feel so connected and why I cherish the experience a little bit differently than I think a lot of my friends do. A lot of my friends who didn't go to an HBCU, they have different feelings about their experiences. So, I'm glad I made the choice that I made but I also understand it's not the choice for everybody as well.

Amanda implied some of the differences between institutional types relative to how individualistic the PWI campus was where everyone just came and went to class and then left. She also reflected on the way in which undergraduate and graduate degrees differed in terms of the focus that students need in graduate programs compared to the breadth of study in undergraduate degrees.

Perhaps because of her field of study, which was in the biological sciences, gender became a bigger issue for Amanda once she started her studies at Georgia State:

> For me, gender has just become within maybe the past two to three years something that's been obvious. The differences and the issues that women face have just become more obvious to me. I can't help but wonder if it's because the differences I've noticed were between going to an HBCU and then when I went to get my master's, I went to Georgia State. Which honestly, I don't think they could still be called a predominantly White institution. But at one point, they were. That's when I saw the differences in how I was treated or talked to with my gender. I do wonder why that is because I have experienced some microaggressions, as many people like to call them, from Black men. But for the most part, I wasn't seeing them until I entered a field where it was mostly dominated by White males.

At the graduate level, it still may have seemed as if White men dominated her department and field too. Amanda offered an example:

> When I first started the program at Georgia State, I was the only Black female in the program. And then there was another [woman], there was one other White female, and a Black guy.

Then everyone else were White males. For the most part, we would study together and there were never any really like intimidating or aggressive moments. But there would be little comments after we would take tests. I mean, I studied, I like to do well on my tests and in my classes, so I would get good grades. I would get little comments like, "Well, how did you do better than me on the test?" I'm like, "Well, I studied. I don't know how I did better than you. I just did. I don't want to say I'm smarter than you. But I'm not exactly sure what you're getting at." I would get that question more than once from the same person. So, it was almost like okay, are you accusing me of something? Or are you saying I should not be capable? Or maybe you don't mean any harm and you just truly don't understand. But there is a reason why I'm getting that question and you're not asking anybody else that, because I'm not the only one who did better. Those are the kinds of things where I had never experienced anything like that.

Activating stereotypes about gender and race, her peers seemed to imply that as a Black woman, Amanda must be inherently less intellectually capable. Amanda thought back to her time at Howard:

When I was at Howard, it was just very different. Like, we—me and my classmates—we worked together on our projects, we took our tests. If somebody did better, they just did better. And maybe, in that setting, maybe the gender differences, just presented themselves differently. Maybe it wasn't in an academic setting, maybe it was more so socially. I would probably have to think a little bit harder to come up with any kind of example for that. But definitely, I didn't start seeing those things where I could really point it out until I got to Georgia State.

After reflecting on gender differences in her two experiences, Amanda contemplated differences in racial experiences and treatment at the two institutions:

Socially, they're different just because you have different groups. Georgia State is interesting because once upon a time, I don't know the exact numbers now, it was a PWI. But now, honestly, if you combine all the different minority groups together, I'm almost certain that they're the majority. So, if you walk around Georgia State, it's not the same as if you walk around UGA [University of Georgia–Athens]. It's different. I could still obviously see the differences. The classroom, the overall campus setting, might still look kind of diverse. But then when I get specifically to my classes, which are the [biological science] classes, upper level, I'm mostly looking at one group. I had to deal more with conversations that probably made me a little more uncomfortable. Like I never really had to deal with that before. I had many friends, one of my best friends who went to UGA and her freshman week, she moved in the same time we moved in. She called me crying because she had to deal with a very upsetting blatantly racist experience. And I never at any point through my four years at Howard had to deal with anything remotely like that. So going to Georgia State, finally coming to a point where I was like okay, now I have to actually deal with these things that some of my other friends are telling me happened. I knew they happened. I didn't not believe it. Because I mean, I had dealt with things in childhood or whatever. So, I knew those kind of things happened. But actually, dealing with it and having to really feel uncomfortable about it, that was definitely a first. And for it to not be something that just happened one time or two times, it just takes you back a little bit. Because you're never really prepared, I don't think, for that.

Even within an institution that had a relatively high percentage of students of color on campus, Amanda noticed that her academic discipline did not share that diversity. At the time of writing this book, Georgia State University was not listed as a minority serving institution with the Office of Civil Rights. But the institution does boast a 42 percent Black population on campus and White students are in the minority, as only 25 percent of the institution.[1] Most of Amanda's descriptions about her graduate school experience were about feeling isolated, dealing with gender issues, and dealing (or helping friends to deal) with racial hostility or sexism, which likely influenced her ability to fully focus on her learning. She recalled who made the bulk of the problematic comments:

It was usually just with peers. Sometimes I would get comments about my hair. Normally my hair is really big. So, I get comments about my hair. Or again, comments about my ability to do well. That stopped pretty much after the first year because I was with the same students. So finally, they were like, "Okay, she's capable." And so eventually that stopped. The other little comments didn't really stop. People asking questions, wanting you to explain things for an entire race. I'm like, "I can't do that for you, sorry." Those kind of things never really did stop. And it was pretty much mostly with peers.

The constancy of the request to represent one's entire race and answer questions about one's racial background can lead to racial battle fatigue, the feeling that one is simply worn out from having to battle racial issues all the time (Smith, 2014). Racial battle fatigue can be particularly salient in some disciplines such as those in science, technology, engineering, and mathematics (STEM) fields (McGee, 2016). At the graduate level, because students work in concentrated ways with a small group of peers and faculty, it can be very difficult to find a break from racism and sexism (Blackshear & Hollis, 2021; Dortch, 2016; Shavers & Moore, 2019).

While mostly peers were the ones making sexist or racist comments in her graduate program, Amanda remembered one faculty member who said something offensive to her:

I never really experienced, except for once, having a faculty member say something that made me a little uncomfortable. But I did have one in class one time. We were having a class discussion about faith-based exercise interventions. My professor said something about, "I don't know what it is with you guys, but it seems like you're in church all day long." And it's kind of funny because I would say that to my friends. But you don't expect to hear it from your professor. So, you're like, "Oh wait. What should I say? Should I be offended right now? Should I not?" What am I supposed to say or what am I supposed to do because this person who is in charge of my grade made a comment that made me feel a little bit uncomfortable. I don't want to say it's malicious. They don't mean anything by it. But sometimes you would just like for people to take a second to think about what they're about to say before they say it and how it might be interpreted. There is a better way that she could have said it that would have come across a little bit better. It was easy for her to open her mouth and say it because she really didn't have to worry about a whole lot of people in the class feeling any kind of way about it.

While Amanda did identify as Christian, the professor had clearly just assumed that she knew Amanda's religious affiliation because of Amanda's medium brown complexion and her identity as a Black woman. While the Georgia State experience had been less positive than her time at Howard, Amanda still summarized that she was glad to have attended Georgia State because of what it meant for her ability to figure out what she wanted to do individually: "Honestly, my experience with the program, as much as it opened my eyes to different things that might not be positive, it also has pointed me to where I feel like I'm meant to be." Ultimately, Amanda took her experiences at Howard and at Georgia State and used them to help her identify her own niche in her discipline. When we met for our interview, she was working in the field for which she had completed her master's program and she was using her experiences to do advocacy work for people of color in that discipline.

Nicole recalled her transition from Spelman to the predominantly White University of South Florida where she earned her master's degree and her PhD:

They were all White. They were all White. For example, if you wanted to do this research study here? If you wanted to do a research study on something related to students of color or anything related to people of color, it wasn't supported. Students would pretty much tell you, if you do that, you're pretty much not going to finish because they don't support that. So, I felt like I went from this really great supportive experience to now I just have to play this game to finish. I struggled with this whole question, should I leave? If I would've wanted to be a faculty member, I probably would have needed to leave. But I knew I wanted to be a clinician and to be a psychologist, you have to have a PhD. So, I thought, I know I want to be a clinician and maybe teach on the side. So, I felt like I wasn't killing myself if I wasn't able to do the research that was related to people of color. That sounds really bad. But I didn't really

know how else to get out. It was just not a good experience
like Spelman at all. But I got out.

Nicole reiterated how White her graduate program felt by saying it twice.
She saw her path to a PhD as wholly instrumental. She simply needed to
finish her degree to have the career she desired and so she finished her
program while making large sacrifices about what she wanted to study.
When I asked how she might talk with others who desired to attend the
University of South Florida for graduate school, she rejoined:

> To students that call me and they're like, "How do I get out
> of here?" I wouldn't ever tell anybody to go to my program.
> I would not tell anybody that's a student of color and that's a
> male because they've never graduated a male student of color,
> ever. I was liked in the program because I worked hard, and
> I did really well. I was liked. Unfortunately, in some ways, it's
> a bad thing. Because they can say, "Look how this African
> American woman did well in the program." I'm kind of used
> as that model that made it through the program. But it's like,
> what part did I have to give of myself? And probably because
> I had already lived that role before, I knew how to just flip
> that back on again. I wouldn't encourage everybody to go
> there because not all students of color can do that and just
> shut that part of themself off to make it through the program.
> If you aren't that kind of student, you're not going to make it
> through. So, because I was liked, I started finding out a lot of
> stuff about the program. Other faculty members who were not
> in my department, would tell me, faculty members of color
> told me. You guys have never graduated a male of color. They
> come but they never finish. Every single one. I'm not sure
> how APA, which is the American Psychological Association,
> has not dinged them on that. But they've managed to get out
> of that somehow.

Nicole considered her time in graduate school to be like shutting a part of
herself down to survive. She had to change what she wanted to study and
felt the need to keep her focus on White people and away from studying
people of color. There are other studies that have found that students of
color often feel as if they must act, think, or appear in particular ways

226 | The Chosen We

on PWI campuses (Winkle-Wagner, 2009a; Winkle-Wagner et al., 2018). Nicole recognized that the department could be critiqued nationally for never having graduated a man of color from the program. This kind of critique is a potential sign that Nicole was able to resist some of the program norms, at least after she graduated, which could demonstrate a way in which she had crafted an individual identity. Lisa's story about her transition from Spelman College to Boston University, and then to Northwestern University for her graduate degree, corroborates many of the previous themes.

After attending Spelman for her first three years of college, Lisa needed to attend Spelman's partner institution, Boston University, in order to complete her degree in a highly specialized type of engineering. The two institutions were paired such that her general education and early science and math courses were at Spelman, but she could only complete the engineering specialization by finishing her last year in Boston. After earning her undergraduate degree, Lisa earned a master's degree in a biological sciences field at Northwestern University. When I asked her to compare her historically Black and predominantly White experiences, she responded:

> What I like to tell people about my experience there, it was almost like hot and cold. Boston in general was a very cold city, weather wise, people wise. Atlanta is very hot, friendly. That, in a lot of ways, translated to life on campus. BU is very much a city campus. It's right in the middle of everything, right near Fenway Park and everything. So even though you would be on campus, it's very much like you would interact with the city as you would outside of campus. People just didn't talk to each other. I'm from the South. I was used to talking to everybody. But nobody said hi when you walked by. I came so late I was kind of considered as an outsider. They weren't quite familiar with who I was. I'll speak to you but I'm not that type A personality where I'm just going to be in your face all the time. I think in a lot of ways, people didn't know what to think of me. They didn't know how to accept me or take me at all. Whereas Spelman was very different. They pull you in, in a sense. Obviously, I just didn't get that at BU. As far as research and everything is concerned, again, BU, it was like, "We're the best." Spelman was like, "We're the best. If we're

not the best, we're trying to be the best." So, in a lot of ways, that was very similar. As far as attitudes toward the outside world was concerned.

When Lisa talked about Boston University, she used a singular, individual way of speaking about it, speaking to only her own individual experience. When recalling Spelman, she named it as a collective group to which to belong, in saying "they pull you in." Yet she identified an important similarity that both Spelman and Boston University had an attitude of being, or trying to be, the best academic institutions. She continued:

> The population demographics were totally different. The class-rooms were different. Spelman is very small. So, at the most, we would have 20 to 25 students. One of my largest classes at BU was probably about 80 or 90 students. So, the professors didn't know your name. I do remember one professor, one of my electrical engineering professors. I remember it was a semi-conductor class. I remember I got the best grade on the test during one of the class periods. And he was like, "Good job, Lisa." But it was one of those situations where I think it was like wow, she knows that she's talking about. At BU I felt like I constantly had to prove who I was, how smart I was, what I could do. Whereas at Spelman, we didn't have to do that. Of course, that's been my experience ever since I left Spelman. I feel like in everything I do, I have to constantly prove that I'm competent, that I'm intelligent enough, that I'm able to do the job like you want me to do.

A crucial difference between the PWI and HBCU experiences for Lisa was the perceived need to prove herself as a Black woman.

In addition to her time at Boston University, Lisa also did a domestic exchange program for a semester at Stanford University, so she had another predominantly White campus experience to compare to her time at Spelman. She explained: "So basically, it was an exchange between the schools. They sent some students to Spelman and we sent students to Stanford. So, I got a semester at Stanford. That was very different from BU. At Stanford, especially the Black students, were like, 'How is everything? All of us wanted to go to an HBCU but when we got into Stanford, it was like, "it's Stanford." Did we make the right decision?' So, a lot of times I got that question." When I asked Lisa what she told students who asked this question, she replied:

> I don't know. I see benefits of both. I see good and bad of both. I loved Stanford. I loved it. But at the same time, I just don't know because I followed up with a couple students from there. I really didn't keep in touch with too many. But they're doing big things, huge things. I don't necessarily know if they would be doing those same big, huge things had they not gone there. So I used to tell them, "I don't know. I can't tell you a straight answer on that." I appreciated that experience because it allowed me to get a taste of life on the proverbial other side versus what I dealt with. Just as far as the students on that campus were concerned based on my experience, they were very close knit. It was very much a familial type of thing on their campus. Which I neglected to say at Northwestern, I had the same thing among the student body with the Black students. That's half the reason I was still pretty sane after eight years of being there because the classmates of mine, especially the Black classmates, they were my grounding force. They kept me sane. Those are the ones that I still keep in touch with now. They're mostly professors now. But had I not had them, I don't know where I would be right now. I would've never made it through Northwestern had I not had them. That's the kind of, that same kind of unified body, that's what I felt at Stanford at the time. Which is what I think they were craving by not going to an HBCU.

Lisa emphasized the necessity of *Chosen We* communities within both HBCUs and PWIs. She noticed that the way that she flourished within the PWIs was to create community with other Black students, primarily through informal friendship groups on campus. Like students who attended PWIs for their entire experience, it did not seem to be the case that institutions were playing a particular leadership role in creating the collective space for Black students. Rather, students were creating collective spaces on their own to be successful within PWIs.

Taken together, Lisa contemplated important differences in the geographic location and the culture of the different types of institutions:

I tell everybody when I first went to Atlanta, it was a culture shock, mostly because it was hard, I wasn't used to seeing Black faces everywhere. Like in Atlanta, Black people are everywhere. I mean, they were the mayor, they were politicians, they were in stores. Then I went to Boston my last year of college. It was completely different and plus, the weather was different. Boston is an ancient city in comparison to a lot of cities in the US. Just culture wise, I was shocked. But I appreciated that experience as well because it taught me. It kicked me out of that idyllic world that Spelman had put me in.

Having grown up primarily in the Chicago area in the Midwest, Lisa first felt culture shock in going to Atlanta because there were more Black people in positions of power in the city, and there were many more Black students on campus than she had encountered in her high school. The move to Boston brought another geographic shock, both because of the weather and because it was another huge demographic shift compared to Atlanta. In the following excerpt she revealed another form of shock in her transition to Northwestern University for graduate school. Lisa contemplated how her transition from an HBCU to a PWI influenced her identity:

That was my first case of really trying to assert my identity and who I was, because I got a lot of pushback when I went to BU. Number one, they didn't know who I was, they didn't know anything about Spelman. They could care less. And here I am this Black girl. I was one of, I think at the time, two or three Black people in my department. That was undergrad and so I had a lot to prove. Some of it, I did end up proving, others I didn't prove like I should have. But I remember specifically a professor yelled at me for an assignment I didn't turn in. I took it at first. It was unexpected. But after I walked away, I was like, "I should've gone off on him. Who is he to yell at me and scream at me and say you should've known better?" Like, I wanted to curse him out like, "Who the fuck are you?" Excuse my language. Again, that was that whole Spelman mentality. Because I think had I not gone through that, I probably would've walked away crying like he just killed my spirit, he just lowered my self-esteem. That was one of my first learning experiences with the difference between HBCUs and versus PWIs.

Spelman had given Lisa a mentality that she and her ideas mattered, and that she did not deserve to be treated as inferior. Lisa considered:

> Next came grad school. When I got to Northwestern especially, entering into grad school, it was again a different ball game. At the time, BU was still on the cusp of reaching the Research I institution. But Northwestern was a Research I. "We're in Chicago and we try to compete with the Stanfords and the University of Chicagos of the world, and the Harvards, and the Dukes of the world." It was another shock that I don't think I was quite prepared for. But what I really wasn't prepared for was the lack of support that I received from, or didn't receive, I should say, from my department. I was an NSF [National Science Foundation] scholar. How much do I have to prove? How much do I have to show that I'm good enough?

Even though Lisa had earned a highly competitive and prestigious source of funding, she felt as if she had to prove a lot in graduate school. Lisa reflected:

> They should've been fighting to keep me. They should've been fighting to just make sure I graduated. Again, you live and learn. So, I started this off saying grad school was the next chapter. Grad school, fell in love, got married. So, the things with grad school I had to learn was about establishing myself as an adult. At the time, I also had recently bought a condo. So, I had property for the first time in my life. I had real responsibility. I soon met my boyfriend, which became my then husband. And so, all these things were going on in my life. It's like how do you balance student, woman, asserting your womanhood, property owner now, and then wife? He [my husband] also had children so I was also a stepmother. It was very tough to deal with. Especially with the lack of support that I got at the time with my department because my advisor wasn't the most supportive person on the planet.

I don't think it had anything to do with race or anything. He just didn't know how to advise students.

Lisa admitted that she had a lot of life transitions occurring at the same that she entered her graduate program, transitions that many students might face during graduate programs (Gardner, 2008; Gardner & Holley, 2011; Golde, 2005; Nettles & Millett, 2006). Lisa spent four more years in her doctoral program with little support from her advisor or anyone else in her program. At one point, her advisor tried to present Lisa's research at a conference without citing her for the work. Soon after that, her funding ran out so she could no longer afford to finance her doctoral program. The toll her doctoral program took on her was very heavy and Lisa eventually decided to leave her program without the PhD (also see Shavers & Moore, 2019). Lisa reflected on the hardship that her doctoral program brought her:

> I remember talking to a career counselor on campus. I broke down in her office at least twice, from what I can remember. I was like, "I'm supposed to be the one that gets the Nobel Prize. This is the pressure that was put it on me as a child." Like, "Lisa is the Einstein of our neighborhood. She's supposed to get the Nobel Prize." One of my nicknames from childhood was Einstein. Of course, at the time, I wasn't thinking about it as pressure. But it was a lot of pressure, a lot, a lot of pressure on me. And I just saw myself as a failure. Even though I had gotten by that time, three degrees, I didn't get the PhD. I was supposed to be the scientist. I was supposed to be the smart one, to finish, and go and do these big things, make all this money. [The counselor] finally said, "Well, what are some of the things you want to do, or you've always wanted to do in your life but you haven't been able to because you've been in school." I said, "I've always wanted to own my own business." And so, she was like, "Well, what else do you like to do?" I was like, "I like to cook. I love to bake." She was like, "Have you ever thought about a baking business?" I was like, "No, I haven't." So as part of my resurgence, I guess, and a way to get my mind off of things, I ended up starting a catering business. Which was actually pretty successful if I must say so myself. I was still reeling from leaving graduate school.

I ended up with the job at [the design school] where I am now. So that school is very much about the creative process, creative living, creative work, which I appreciated because that's one thing that I enjoyed about the baking business. I remember telling people, I've been a scientist for so long, I forgot I used to like to draw. I'm not the greatest artist in the world but I did like that. I liked creative things. I liked making things. Even if this is something insignificant, it was stuff that I created with my hands. So, I was able to get a little bit of both. I teach math at [the design school]. So, I'm still in the creative environment because the students are so different from Northwestern students. I mean, just in the dress, the conversations they have, their attitudes in general. It's so, so different and it's so relaxed. That's what I appreciate about that environment. Because even though I'm teaching math, I still get that science portion. But at the same time, it's a very flexible relaxed situation. My colleagues are great, the ones that I talk to. That's part-time. In the meantime, I'm still looking for full-time work.

Given that her decision to stop pursuing her PhD had been relatively recent, I asked Lisa if she had considered going back at some point in the future to finish:

I've toyed with the idea, especially lately. I don't know if it's the economy, I don't know if it's because I've been out of school for so long and people just don't necessarily trust my experience anymore. I don't know if it's the answer to the rest of my life and my career goals. Because of course all my friends, for the most part, are professors. I talk with one frequently. She's a professor at University of Tennessee. And even though I'm at a smaller liberal arts school, we commiserate all the time about our students. Even though she enjoys her life, and she enjoys the life it affords her, I don't think that's necessarily the life for me. And I have a few other friends around the country who are professors. I never wanted to be a professor when I was in grad school. I wanted a PhD but never wanted to be a professor.

While Lisa's story is perhaps unfinished, it is important to note the dramatically different ways that she experienced support within her HBCU and the PWIs, both at the undergraduate and graduate levels. Continuing the comparisons between HBCUs and PWIs, next I highlight the reverse, those alumnae who first attended a PWI for their undergraduate degree and then opted for an HBCU for graduate school.

"I Thought I Died and Gone to Heaven":
Choosing an HBCU for Graduate School after
Attending a PWI

There were four alumnae who opted to attend an HBCU for graduate or professional school after having completed an undergraduate degree at a PWI. The depictions of the transition from a PWI to an HBCU still had elements of "shock" that mirrored some of the transitions of those who attended an HBCU for an undergraduate degree—although the racial demographic surprise was reversed. Given the comparisons between HBCUs and PWIs so far, it may seem likely that attending an HBCU for graduate school after having earned a degree at a PWI might be unequivocally positive. Yet those alumnae who followed this path found the transition from a PWI to an HBCU to be more complicated than that. There were positive elements and complicated negative elements too.

The child of two professors who worked at the historically Black Tuskegee University, Maciel decided to attend a predominantly White institution, Emory University in Atlanta, Georgia, for her undergraduate degree where she earned her bachelor's degree in the 2000s. She recalled:

> Tuskegee is pretty much 99.9 percent African American students. Then I went to the extreme. While I was at Emory, I loved the campus, I enjoyed my experience. But the African American students there, it was very interesting interacting with them because it was almost like there were a few that I really connected with because they were just really secure about themselves at the school. But then you had those that were trying to overcompensate because the AUC [Atlanta University Consortium] was right around the corner. They felt like they had to be a certain way, or you had to be down a certain kind of way. It's kind of like, for me, it was like, look, I'm from

Tuskegee, Alabama. My parents teach at an HBCU. I'm here at school. We're not really doing this. But that was something that at Emory, you saw that tension all the time. You had those that were the richie rich kids, you had to be on their level. Or you had those that were trying to be down but really, they were just overcompensating, and they didn't seem secure. You're at Emory. It is what it is. We're in Atlanta. That's a Black mecca here in the South. What's your problem? I'm okay with it. I wasn't as involved in extracurricular activities especially with African American students on campus. I didn't feel comfortable because I just felt like it was going to be pulling my identity all kinds of ways. College is a place where you evolve. Not go backwards. So that's something I would definitely say my expectations weren't met there. But I was grateful that Emory was in Atlanta. So, I was able to get the culture aspect and the bigger scheme of things just because of the city.

Having grown up around an HBCU, after finishing her bachelor's degree at a PWI, Maciel opted to attend an HBCU for her graduate degree. She remembered:

I went back to grad school in Tuskegee for grad school. Going back to Tuskegee for grad school inside of myself, and this is just me being honest, I kind of felt disappointed. It's almost kind of like I went from here and kind of came down here. And this is something, this is a type of conversation that you have. Like sometimes, you don't want to say it. But I know why I say that. So, one, resources, of course. At Emory, the resources are just completely different from Tuskegee University. And of course, depending on the department or whatever. But just on the grand scheme of things, they are completely different. Also, a little bit, it was going back to what I said I had already outgrown. So even though I tell people, I say even though I'm from Tuskegee, I'm not *of* Tuskegee.

When I asked her what she meant, Maciel replied:

I felt like I was the token in the Black school. I was the smartest one there. Everybody was looking at me like, "you're from

Emory." All of them graduated from Tuskegee undergrad. So, when you're in class, you kind of feel like my ceiling is low because everybody's looking at me. I'm in grad school though. I need somebody to push me. I felt like the drive that I had at Emory, it dropped a little bit because the expectations were completely different. I don't want to say lower or better or whatever but different. I didn't feel like I was growing. Like I said, I was already home. I fought that for a little bit, even accepting that. I struggled. I struggled going back. The greatest thing was that my parents worked there so I went to school for free.

It is hard to know what role going to the institution where her parents both were professors might have played in her views of going back to Tuskegee.

Ayana earned a Doctor of Veterinary Medicine degree from Tuskegee University after she completed her bachelor's degree at the University of Michigan in the 1990s. When I inquired about the transition from a public, predominantly White campus to a private HBCU in the South, she named the experience, "Interesting. Interesting because it's an HBCU." She continued:

When I went to my interview for Tuskegee, they said, "You have never experienced rural communities, do you think you're going to survive?" And I'm like, "I can survive anywhere." They said, "There is no movie theater, there is no shopping center. There's none of these things. They're nearby, a half-hour drive. Do you think you can do it?" I'm like, "I can do it." Tuskegee in terms of it being HBCU, the vet school really wasn't. It was maybe 60 percent Black, maybe even less now. So, it wasn't like in class, everybody was all Black. Honestly, when I first got there, I was calling home and I was like, "This is like a third world country. It's so rural." But I had a cousin. She was 35 minutes away from me, which made it easier.

The main source of shock in Ayana's transition from her PWI to the HBCU for graduate school seemed to be the geographic location of the institution, in a very small southern town. Ayana created support for herself in veterinary school through her cousin and by getting close to a study partner. Ayana spoke in great detail about her study partner, who passed away unexpectedly in their fourth year in a tragic car accident. The tragedy was extremely difficult for Ayana, but she tried hard to make the best of it. She asserted, "In the end, I graduated first in my class because of him." She carried her study partner with her throughout her program and into her career as a source of motivation.

Marwa remembered how it felt to transition from Benedict College, an HBCU, to the University of South Carolina, a predominantly White campus, which she did midway through her undergraduate degree. She admitted, "I felt I had failed by leaving Benedict College and going to the University of South Carolina." Perhaps this is one reason Marwa selected to attend an HBCU for graduate school. Marwa graduated from Clark Atlanta University with a master's degree in the 1990s about a decade after earning her undergraduate degree. She summarized, "When I enrolled at Clark Atlanta University, and I thought I had died and gone to heaven." When I asked Marwa what she meant by that description, she responded, "Oh my God, it's the most exciting thing I had ever done. It was fabulous." Having had a somewhat difficult experience in two predominantly White institutions in her undergraduate degree, Marwa compared the support she encountered at Clark Atlanta:

> I was getting my master's and I didn't know what I was going to do. [A professor and I] were walking. She walked me to the car and we were just talking, talking, talking. She says, "Marwa, you are a scholar. You do your work; your work is on time." I was just listening to her out in the parking lot, she just happened to say that. And I said, "You know I could do this. We can either go to law school or we can go get a PhD." That's when I decided to go get a doctorate.

Marwa's professor at Clark Atlanta held up a mirror to her in a lot of ways. Marwa named this as the moment when she knew she would earn a PhD, which she did eventually earn at the predominantly White University of California–Riverside.

Ultimately, the transition from a PWI in undergraduate programs, into a graduate program at an HBCU was multifaceted. While the HBCU was often experienced as warm, the direction of the transition (PWI to HBCU) was a bit less common, at least in this set of oral histories. Thus, to consider more in-depth understanding of the comparisons of those who had been in both types of institutions, this chapter ends with a brief oral history from an alum named Brynn who transitioned from an HBCU in her undergraduate program to a PWI in graduate school.

The "Culture Shock" of Transitioning from an HBCU to a PWI: Brynn's Story

Brynn knew early in her undergraduate program at Florida A&M University (FAMU) that she would attend a graduate program. At FAMU, at least in her program, it was almost an expectation that students would pursue more education after their bachelor's degree. At the end of Brynn's undergraduate experience at FAMU, she applied for graduate programs and ultimately decided to attend the University of Wisconsin–Madison for her master's degree. Her parents had attended UW–Madison and had lived in Madison earlier in Brynn's life before they relocated to Georgia, which was where Brynn spent her childhood. She explained how the pathway from an HBCU to a PWI was encouraged in her undergraduate institution: "At FAMU, they had a program called the Graduate Feeder Program. So, they have relationships with certain schools to have slots for students and University of Wisconsin–Madison was one of them. [My parents] did play a little bit of a part because my parents, they never really went back. [My mom] had some good friends from there but she never really talked about the university, going to school there. But she was happy that I did." Brynn described what it was like to transition from an HBCU in undergraduate to a PWI in graduate school: "I remember when I got there it was just very isolating. Even the campus was kind of overwhelming. I think UW has 40,000 students. I think mine [at FAMU] only had like 13,000. Even as a graduate student, my focus and my goals were different, it still felt very overwhelming. I was like, God, I wonder how a freshman must feel. When I got to UW, I had such culture shock." Not only was the institution much larger than her undergraduate HBCU institution, but also, most students were White.

The size and the Whiteness of campus together are part of what likely led to Brynn's sense of "culture shock." It is also probable that Brynn noticed the difference in the ethos of campus where the PWI was highly individualistic and her HBCU had been much more community oriented. I asked Brynn about a specific moment when she felt culture shock during her time at the PWI: "I think my first taste of culture shock was when I went to Target. I swear, I was like, I wonder if I'm the only one. I really genuinely felt like I was probably the only black person in the entire store."

It was not just the campus at UW–Madison that felt like culture shock to Brynn. The community surrounding the campus was also overwhelmingly White to her, and that enhanced the sense of culture shock that Brynn already felt. She compared her culture shock to what she had left behind at FAMU: "The unity. We were always really excited for homecoming and games, football games, convocation, we would all go and just really hear what was being said. Being involved in the community other than student government. It was just a lot of fun. Socially, there was always something to do. I just feel like there's a sense of unity I got there. I don't think I would've gotten anywhere else." Brynn continued to describe the feeling of "unity" from her HBCU experience, a norm that I would associate with a *Chosen We* community at FAMU. In contrast to the community Brynn encountered at FAMU, she recalled her transition to the predominantly White, UW–Madison campus:

> I felt kind of isolated. When I went up there, I didn't know anybody. It was just a big culture shock, going from the South to the Midwest, a historically black college to a predominantly White one. I just felt isolated in my program and not because of anything that happened, just because I didn't know anybody. But I felt very fortunate because my program was actually really diverse. There were about 16 of us, half were Caucasian, half were Asian, Latino, biracial. So that helped a lot. I feel like as a cohort, we were kind of close too. So actually, I'm going to see some of them next week when I go up there. Just being diverse but also not necessarily doing things like I should've done then.

Along with the geographic differences, Brynn reiterated her sense of culture shock and isolation in both the larger campus and in her program at the PWI. When I asked what she meant in saying she had done things in graduate school she should not have done, Brynn responded:

> Well, I missed class a few times, and not necessarily realizing how that would've impacted my grade especially because class is only like 15 weeks. I was told I wasn't going to be going on to do my internship the next year. That was very difficult because I felt isolated and singled out because of that, and because no one told me that it was going to play out like that.

No one told me, "Well, if you don't do this, there's a chance you won't do an internship." I feel like someone should've told me that or someone should've sat me down. I don't feel like that was very clear. Not to say that there should've been clarity about actions and consequences. It was more the fact that someone didn't come to me and express their concern to me in a clear-cut way. So that was difficult. I took an extra year and did my internship. I needed some more funding, so I started working as a nanny. Just took some other classes, I think. It is what it is.

While Brynn was ultimately successful at UW–Madison, earning a master's degree in a social sciences field in the 2000s, she described the experience as one that was rife with untold norms and rules. Some of these unknown norms and rules were ultimately transformative, such as needing to add an extra year to her degree program. The financial cost of an extra year in her of graduate school was an added burden that no one communicated to Brynn and that she did not understand until it happened. There is evidence that faculty at HBCUs are often more hands on, meaning that they are more likely to reach out to students to communicate rules, expectations, and guidelines than are faculty at PWIs (McCoy et al., 2017).

For Brynn, being held back an extra year before being able to complete the internship she needed to finish her program was difficult in other ways too. She pondered: "With the situation where I was kept back, there was only me and one other Black girl in the program. I didn't feel like I was being singled out, but I definitely felt like my race was more salient. I didn't want to perpetuate a stereotype about African American students not doing well in graduate school. I was concerned about that, concerned I was letting people down. So that was difficult." Brynn highlighted how she felt as if she had to represent her race in graduate school in a way that most of her White peers were unlikely to have felt the need to do. I asked Brynn from where the pressure to represent herself in a particular way at the PWI came. She considered: "I think it was more internalizing. People always asked where I was from. I think people just assumed I was from Milwaukee or Chicago. I'm like, "No, I'm from Atlanta." So, people weren't really used to that or meeting another person of color who was in the graduate school program. I didn't really see the big deal about it." Brynn had to constantly reassert her hometown. She noticed that perhaps people were not accustomed to seeing women of color in graduate programs at UW–Madison.

Reflecting on the overview of her experience in the PWI for graduate school at UW–Madison, Brynn argued:

> For the most part, it was a pretty good experience. I definitely didn't see myself living there forever. Looking back now, it was nice to have a lot of access to the resources that UW had. It was a good experience, just because I was able to form my own tight-knit circle of friends there. Some of the sorority members, they were in graduate school too. So that's how we got to know each other a little bit better, at graduate school events and just hanging out socially. I don't think I'd move back. I contemplated moving back. I think that part of my life is ended, that chapter is closed.

Brynn made the best of her experience at the PWI, gravitating toward close friends, most of whom were women of color and some who were in the same sorority. Perhaps knowing that the time at the PWI was finite was important too.

The Chosen We and Attending Both an HBCU and a PWI

Across the oral histories and across institutional types, alumnae maintained the importance of identifying, creating, or activating *Chosen We* spaces to thrive in college. For those who attended an HBCU for their undergraduate degrees and an PWI for graduate education, there were some differences in how the *Chosen We* spaces functioned and appeared in these different campus contexts. Coming from an HBCU where the entire campus may have felt like a type of *Chosen We* space that embraced and elevated Blackness or Black students, the shock was particularly acute because of the vast differences that people encountered at PWIs. Across the oral histories of those who transitioned from PWIs in undergraduate degree programs, into HBCUs in graduate programs, there was a sense of struggle to find community. That is, it appeared to be quite difficult to transition from an institutional ethos of community where the institution may have been a *Chosen We* type of community, to an institution that was highly individualistic. Also, in graduate programs, students might be less inclined to join organizations (e.g., Black student unions) that may have allowed for community but were primarily targeted toward under-graduate students. Thus, it may have been quite a bit harder to find the community that was available to undergraduate students within PWIs. Nonetheless, a few of the oral histories did offer insight into ways that alumnae pursued *Chosen We* groups within the PWIs to make these campuses feel less isolating and more supportive. For example, Lisa described being highly involved in Black student organizations during her graduate program. Brynn connected with her sorority during graduate school to find support. Or, at times, alumnae created informal support networks through friendships in their doctoral programs or professional programs such as study groups. Sonya (in chapter 3) talked about the importance of friendships during her doctoral program, for instance. *Chosen We* spaces and groups were necessary in both HBCUs and PWIs even if they manifested in different ways.

Conclusions on the Transition between an HBCU and a PWI

The comparison between HBCUs and PWIs was quite stark with metaphors such as "hot and cold" to underscore the differences between experiences within these institutions. Commonly, HBCUs were framed as warmer and more nurturing places. A remarkable element to many of the oral histories of alumnae who attended both PWIs and HBCUs is that alumnae asserted that they took the confidence and self-esteem that was built up in them during their HBCU experiences with them into their time at PWIs. For instance, Nadia talked explicitly about the way in which Spelman College had fostered such a sense of empowering self-confidence in her that when she encountered isolation at Old Dominion University in her graduate program, she was able to reassert her worth. Lisa mentioned a similar sense of understanding her own value when she encountered isolation at Boston University.

Notably, while HBCUs and PWIs were framed in very different ways by alumnae, there was still a sense that the overall experience was good at *both* types of institutions for some alumnae. For instance, Brynn ultimately suggested that she was glad to have attended both FAMU and UW–Madison. Lisa's undergraduate experiences at Spelman, Boston College, and Stanford University all had positive elements, even though she saw big differences in these opportunities. I understand the idea that some alumnae ultimately framed their PWI experiences in positive ways to mean that experiences can be different for individual students. Also, it is not accurate to simply say that all experiences at PWIs are negative or that all experiences at HBCUs are positive. Rather, there were important implications of these oral histories for both types of institutions. I explore one such implication here in part from inferences that were made in the data and in part as a pathway for future research.

To be sure, for students who transitioned from undergraduate institutions at HBCUs to graduate programs at PWIs, it is not all that surprising that there might be multiple levels of shock in the experience. Graduate or professional educational programs are highly specialized, and the stakes often feel very high for the students who enroll in these programs (Cohen & Miller, 2009; Grant-Vallone & Ensher, 2000). There is evidence that many graduate and professional students suffer from anxiety and depression or other mental health issues during their programs (Hyun et al., 2007). Coupled with typical stressors of entering a highly specialized and difficult course of educational training, the transition from a predominantly Black to a predominantly White campus can be particularly difficult. It is possible that the culture shock and racial stress that many alumnae encountered in this transition from an HBCU to a PWI was exacerbated by the profound differences in racial demographics and institutional norms of the campuses.

Alumnae experiences in comparing HBCUs and PWI do offer some important implications for practice that might be translatable toward other campuses:

1. PWIs could offer transition support services in their graduate and professional programs that are specifically aimed at supporting students of color in their transitions to campus, given that it is likely that students may have attended other types of institutions for their undergraduate programs.

2. HBCUs that have pathway programs that connect students to predominantly White campuses could incorporate support for the shock that students may encounter. Offering students coping strategies (e.g., ways to reduce stress, positive self-talk, self-esteem building activities) would be useful to prepare students to make the transition to PWIs.

3. HBCUs could arrange the pathways programs to work as cluster programs, meaning that HBCUs could send small

groups (5–12 students) into specific partner graduate programs at PWIs as part of the program. For students who
come to graduate programs within PWIs in small groups,
they are likely to be a bit less isolated if they matriculate
with other students from their undergraduate institutions.

4. PWIs should focus on cluster recruitment and admissions
for graduate and professional programs. Students of color
could be recruited and admitted to programs in small
groups (2–5 students per year depending on the size of the
graduate or professional program) so that there would be
some way to make sure that students of color feel a little
less isolated within the programs. The cluster recruitment
and admissions process would also go a long way to diver-
sifying programs in meaningful and sustainable ways.

5. PWIs could learn from the inclusive, warm, and nurturing
practices at HBCUs that promote students as successful.
Alumnae from HBCUs identified administrators and faculty
as highly supportive, as if success was assumed on those
campuses. Predominantly White campuses could certainly
adopt this model of students-as-successful and encourage
this success in orientation programming, campus transition
programming, and in campuswide events, assemblies, and
artifacts.

Given the very different institutional contexts and norms, it is quite
likely that alumnae's emotional, mental, and physical responses to these
institutional contexts may vary quite dramatically. While the alumnae
did not speak directly to their mental or physical health, it was clear that
the transition from an HBCU to a PWI was not particularly easy. When
alumnae used words like "isolation" or "culture shock" as labels for their
experiences in PWIs, it seemed that these words were meant to invoke the
relative difficulty of the transition from a predominantly Black environment
to a predominantly White environment. For some alumnae more than
others, it seemed that the transition between institutional types may have
taken a toll on them. In admitting it was difficult but they just "got out"
of their programs in the way that Nicole did in this chapter, for example,
in explaining what it was like for her at the University of South Florida, a
sense of the difficulty of some PWI experiences began to emerge. Coupled

with the experiences of alumnae who attended only PWIs throughout their educational careers, in the next chapter, I consider the way that mental and physical health may have been affected by educational experiences.

Chapter 8

In Sickness and Health on Campus

The Health Inferences of College Contexts and Health in 60 Years of Oral History

Caring for myself is not self-indulgence, it is self-preservation, and that is an act of political warfare.

—Audre Lorde, *A Burst of Light: Essays*

Reflecting on living with cancer toward the end of her life as a Black feminist theorist, writer, and activist, Audre Lorde (1988) aptly summarized the need for care of her physical, emotional, and mental health. Like many Black, highly accomplished women who came before and after her, she was diagnosed with a life-threatening illness (Geronimus et al., 2010; Simons et al., 2016). In so doing, she also provided a clarion call not only for the end of her own life, but for the lives of so many Black women who accomplish and achieve so much, sometimes at the expense of their own health and well-being. The question of the educational cost to one's well-being has haunted me in the finishing of this project, as it will continue to for years and projects yet to come.

After having spent a decade meeting with Black women in five different cities in the United States, I set about the onerous task of analyzing the data, knitting together the histories, asking questions of the alumnae as to whether my interpretations were correct, and trying to piece together the very large puzzle that thousands of pages of data can present. While I had never asked the question explicitly in any of the interviews, an inference began to emerge—and it was not something I set out to study or consider when starting this effort. Black women who attended predominantly White institutions for the bulk of their educational career (i.e., undergraduate degrees) seemed more likely to get sick. That is, although it had not been something I was studying or anything that was on my radar to consider at all, I realized that there were stories of illness, life-threatening disease, and breakdowns from some of the women who attended predominantly White institutions. There were no such instances that were reported from the alumnae who attended HBCUs for their undergraduate degree programs. Admittedly, given that I did not explicitly ask questions about health or sickness, it is possible that women at HBCUs had more positive experiences such that it did not occur to people to share stories of illness. But it is also possible that women who graduated from HBCUs really were less likely to suffer from the same health crises that women from PWIs seemed to endure. I can only infer on this point. It is not something I set out to study, nor was it something that I realized until long after I had completed all the oral histories. But what follows is what I did notice from the data, along with a call for more study on this crucially important insight that was given to me by the alumnae represented in the histories here.

The alumnae, particularly the 69 women who graduated from predominantly White institutions (PWIs), talked about health, wellness, and sickness quite a lot. In a word search in the oral histories, there were 125 references to health across the data. Some women dedicated their lives to women's health. There were two instances where women used the word "illness" in their oral histories. During the oral histories, there were 99 references to "sickness" or being "sick" or appearing "sickly" and all of them came during the recounting of predominantly White campus experiences. In comparison, there were only 11 instances where alumnae used the word "wellness" and these instances were primarily among HBCU alumnae. Yet I still refer to these instances where women described their health, or times when they were sick, as *inferences* for a couple of important reasons. First, because I did not explicitly ask questions about health, I am unable to compare health or instances of sickness across all the oral histories. There is a possibility that people were either sicker than it appears (i.e., more people became ill during college or immediately after). Alternatively, there is also a possibility that the illnesses may have occurred regardless of the institutions that women attended, or that other parts of their lives may have led to social or racial stresses that ultimately made them more likely to become ill. Regardless, the clear differences between those who attended HBCUs and those who attended PWIs relative to the predominance of a "sickness story" is striking enough that I am opting to share some examples here.

Some alumnae hesitated to tell me that they had been sick during college. There was a clear emergent theme of alumnae feeling as if it was simply not possible to take time off or to admit any kind of weakness. It was as if the admission of any type of powerlessness could abruptly end one's higher education journey and the risk of that was too great. There was a clear assertion that "failure was not an option" or that "stopping was not a possibility." The fierce tenacity of these alumnae is remarkable and likely one of the reasons that these women are so accomplished. Yet there is a worrisome trend in these stories of pressing forward in the face of illness. It was as if some of these women needed to be "superwomen" to complete their degrees, particularly on predominantly White campuses. The superwoman idea asserts that Black women often feel as if they must consistently present strength in the face of all adversity and that care should go to those around them before it goes to oneself (Abrams et al., 2014; Beauboeuf-Lafontant, 2007; Donovan & West, 2015; Woods-Giscombé, 2010). While presenting oneself as a superwoman might be a path toward high accomplishment, there is also evidence that it can relate to higher rates of depression, anxiety, binge eating, and other deleterious health outcomes (e.g., cancers, diabetes, etc.) (Donovan & West, 2015; Harrington et al., 2010; Leath, Jones, & Butler-Barnes, 2022; Watson & Hunter, 2015).

The women in this book are highly accomplished and awe-inspiring leaders in their disciplines, families, and communities. But there are also some troubling signs that these accomplishments may come at some personal costs for those who achieve. Janelle Johnson, a University of Iowa graduate from the 1960s, became ill with an unknown sickness of some kind and was forced to leave the University of Iowa early during her first year of college, before completing her final exams. She indicated that her body was simply worn out from the studying, protesting for civil rights, and from socializing with her friends. Recalling how Janelle described her illness:

> I got sick and I had to leave school at the end of my freshmen year. I took incompletes and had to leave school about a month before classes were over. For seven and a half months, I had just completely run my system raggedy. It took a good

month before I could keep food down well, before I didn't have vertigo when I stood up. I was in bad shape. I don't remember the drive home. I was just exhausted. I didn't have mono. But whatever I had it just was not going to let me loose until I stopped. If I stayed in school, it wasn't going to stop.

Janelle did not seem to have ever been told what it was that she had, but she was very sick, and it took weeks and weeks for her to recover enough to even process what had happened. Yet despite her illness, as I later realized was the case with all the women who had a health crisis during college, Janelle was deeply committed to returning to school the second she was well enough to travel. She said it this way, "There was never really an option for me that I wasn't going to come back." It was Janelle's oral history that prompted me to return to the data and to understand alumnae had experienced similar illnesses. As evidenced in this chapter, Janelle was certainly not alone in finding that her health could derail her degree program, at least in part.

Tiff had a similar illness to Janelle, although she graduated from Oakland University in the Detroit metropolitan area many years later, in the 1990s. When I asked Tiff about any obstacles that she had faced during college, she started by saying, "To be honest, I didn't really have any obstacles." Then, as she thought about it a bit longer, Tiff admitted: "One issue I ran into was my health. I got sick. I had to stop classes for about a month or two. That hurt me because I did depend on work-study to pay for that. I wasn't working. I forget what I did in that case. I just took out a loan." Tiff seemed a bit resistant to discussing any challenges she had experienced in college, as if she felt the need to put on a strong face about her experience. Or, perhaps Tiff saw others around her struggling in ways that seemed to be more serious. Tiff did not expand upon what kind of illness she had that made her need to leave classes for a period of time. When I asked her specifically, it seemed that she may not have known, like Janelle. I still wondered if Janelle and Tiff might be the only women who experienced these isolated illnesses. But unfortunately, there were others, all of whom attended PWIs. Some, like Faygen, simply remembered a time where they had to leave their college path at a PWI to recover.

Faygen graduated from the University of Cincinnati in the 2000s. But her college experience did not begin that easily. She remembered getting sick after being on campus only a short time for a precollege program:

I had done a summer program there a couple years prior. I think it was great because it was about eight weeks long. I didn't get to participate in all of it because I got sick partway through, and I had to leave. But I made some really great friends that I kept all through and got me familiar with the campus. And because we were still high school students, we couldn't take as many of the programs that we wanted to that pertained to our major. Especially me, mine's very specialized. So, I got a couple of my history courses out of the way and things like that. It didn't necessarily change what I was going to go into but it made me feel a little bit better about it.

For Faygen, she became too ill to stay for her entire precollege program and had to leave. She did not elaborate on what type of sickness she had, like Janelle and Tiff.

Long before Gen attended and graduated from the University of Michigan in the 1990s, she had been shouldering significant responsibilities in her family, often using part-time jobs to help financially and taking care of her seven siblings. She remembered how her family situation almost kept her from going to college:

I almost didn't go to U of M because I was so afraid about what will happen if I leave the other seven. So that was really hard. So even in school, I was working and sending money home to them, trying to take care of my siblings. I had a different role as well, trying to be torn between [school and family]. And things were falling apart even more. My brother started running away. I was just like, oh my god, what's going to happen? So, you've got all these other worries that you're thinking about and trying to go to school at the same time. Then I ended up getting meningitis. I got hit by a car. So, there was a whole bunch of things that happened during this span of time. I remember getting sick with meningitis. A counselor, in fact a White counselor, when I met with this counselor, the counselor was like, "Well, maybe you should take a semester or a year off." But I remember, it didn't matter if I was sick or I was just having a hard time; that was their recommendation. If I was struggling with a class, the recommendation was to take some time off. I remember older students saying, Black students saying, "Okay, be careful, because the minute you say something is wrong, they're going to tell you to take some time off." And sure enough, that was the answer. In my mind, that was never an option, never an option to take time off. It didn't matter if my grades were dropping. Take time off? No, I'm going to finish this. I did end up switching counselors and going to, they had a program, which is more of a minority group that really helps pay attention to minority students. So, they actually had minority counselors who gave me totally different advice. When I started going to those counselors it was like, "Okay, let's just lessen your workload. Who told you to take 20 credits?" I was like, "Oh, you're not supposed to?" "No, you should have like 12 to such-and-such." It was just a mess.

After having worked exceptionally hard to get to college, Gen nearly did not go because she felt such intense family responsibilities. All through college, she worked part-time jobs and sent most of her money home to her seven siblings. When her body finally gave out and she contracted meningitis, she may have really needed a break. Gen had such negative experiences with White counselors who always encouraged her to leave campus that she did not feel she could trust the advice to leave campus, even with meningitis. She elaborated:

I had a serious battiness. I had meningitis. You stay sick for a minute with that, if you live. And then, I got hit by a car, so I had knee surgery. It was just nuts. So during this span of my time, I had a lot of misfortune. However, I don't ever remember thinking that I was not going to graduate, that I was going to drop out, ever. That was never, ever, ever a thought. It was just, okay, bad things happen, keep moving, keep going. I think I would highlight those events and the physical therapy and getting back, you know.

Gen barely took a break, even with her significant physical and cognitive limitations during this time: "I was in the hospital. Even when you come out, it took at least three months to even get back to normal because I was just out of it. Like, you're exhausted. It was just bad. The professors postponed the exams. I was able to finish the exams later and get the grade without dropping out or anything like that." While Gen did have professors who were willing to postpone exams and let her finish course-work as she recovered from her meningitis and knee surgery, she did not experience all that much support from the larger institution and neither did her friends who came with her to Michigan:

> My two best friends ended up losing money. So, they didn't continue. So, then you've got the one best friend, her mom couldn't afford to send her anymore, so she went back, after sophomore year. Then the other one, she lost her scholarship and so her parents couldn't afford it, so she went back. Then it's like, just me. By junior year, it's me. What's crazy, your first orientation day, and I don't know if all schools do this, but they said, "Look to your left, look to your right, there's only one of you going to be here for graduation." And I remember specifically I looked at my one best friend and my other best friend. And I said it won't be me, I guarantee you that, and they said the same thing. But both of them were not there at graduation. I remember thinking, "Why would somebody say that?" I thought that was the worst thing, in my mind, for someone to tell an 18-year-old. I remember thinking that would not be me, and it wasn't me. Even though my two best friends said it, it was them. And one ended up going to U of M Flint and graduating years later. And the other one, I don't think, ever went back. She was doing things, drinking, smoking. I never did. That just wasn't my thing. So, it kind of messed our relationship up a little bit. Right, right. And they were both Black.

Highlighting the oft-described approach at PWIs, Gen remembered being explicitly told that two out of three students would leave college without a degree. Given that Gen went to college in a group of three Black women, it is particularly noteworthy that the institution seemed to have an approach of little responsibility for their success from the very first day on campus. It was quite literally as if they were being told that the campus was a highly individualistic place and they would be lucky to survive it. Gen continued:

> I switched majors several times. I went from pre-med to nursing. And in fact, let me just tell you why I switched my

pre-med. I got sick. I suffered really bad throughout with very bad migraines, I mean, excruciating migraines throughout my college. And actually, it started like the year before I went to college. I don't know what triggered it but I was having really bad migraines, to the point where you just can't move. I remember getting medicine and getting put on all these different medications. And one medication, I had a reaction to. When I went to the ER and I remember I got questioned like I was on drugs and like I was a thug, by another Black physician, which was even more shocking. However, I would wear bandannas. I remember thinking to myself, why would he question me? Because I said I think I'm having a reaction. Well, why would you think that? And I remember feeling like he thought I was in there to get drugs. And I was just like, you are horrible. He wouldn't do anything. So, the next morning, I went to my primary doctor, and she was like, you're having a reaction. Because I had went to ER to get the medicine and I had a reaction. Which she said they should've caught anyway. I remember thinking, if they can make that mistake, I remember getting fearful of being a physician and making a mistake and jeopardizing someone's life. And I remember thinking no, I don't want to be that person. So then I was like, but I can do law. And if I do mess up, I can probably go back and fight for that person to get out. So, I switched to pre-law. I was like, I can be an advocate, I can talk my way into anything, I thought. But then, the whole time I'm in college, I'm working.

Ultimately, some of Gen's heath challenges prompted her to change her major because she had such a bad experience in the emergency room when she had a bad reaction to her migraine medication. Gen summarized her college experience at Michigan: "To go through the challenges like being sick and pray to get well. All of that shaped who I am. And to realize you're on your own. You really are on your own." Gen realized that at her PWI, she would be on her own and have little institutional support to help her, regardless of what medical conditions she faced. While Gen felt isolated during college, she was not alone in experiencing health challenges that altered her experience even though it took many years to knit together these experiences. Freedom had a similar experience within a Michigan institution only about an hour away from Gen, even though they did not know one another at that time.

Freedom started her educational journey at a local community college, Wayne County Community College, in the Detroit metropolitan area where she grew up. It was the only institution that seemed accessible to her financially and geographically when it was time for her to consider college (see also Daché-Gerbino, 2018; Daché, 2022; Daché et al., 2022). Her family originated from Louisiana but migrated to the Detroit area before Freedom was born in the hopes of obtaining jobs in the auto industry, where both of her parents worked for the remainder of their careers. When I asked Freedom if her parents had attended college, she looked surprised and told me that they not only did not attend college, but they also had not completed high school. Postsecondary education was a new path, filled with new hopes of social mobility, for Freedom and for her family.

After earning her associate's degree, Freedom eventually transferred to a four-year institution, the University of Michigan–Dearborn, as a nontraditional-aged college student (above the age of 24) where she earned a bachelor's degree in the 2000s. UM–Dearborn is in the Detroit metropolitan area and so the mission and vision of the institution is well connected to outreach in that community. While UM–Dearborn was more diverse than some PWIs, with a 26 percent undergraduate student of color population, the campus was still approximately 75 percent White students when Freedom attended. She suffered the loss of a family member and became ill partway through her degree program:

> I had a class, a statistics class. My sister passed away during the same time. Statistics kicked my butt. But even though my sister had passed away I didn't stop. I kept going. I was doing online. It was supposed to be, you did online one day, and you did one day in the classroom. But the professor worked with me during that time to plan her funeral and all that stuff. I didn't stop. That's when I knew, if I can get through this, dealing with my sister's death and statistics that's kicking my butt, I can make it. I can keep going. I knew I must love school because this is my excuse, this is my escape. If I want to get out, nobody would fault me for leaving now. But all I could do was think about what I was going to do to make

sure that I went to school. And another thing was that I had gotten sick in school. I had to have surgery. I was so ill. I was so ill. I had fibroid tumors so I was bleeding terribly. I would have to put on pads and tampons and put on all these clothes to make sure. Because it would just come out and it would just be everywhere. It would look like a murder scene. But I didn't want to miss school. I was so anemic, I couldn't walk. I could barely just walk. I would have to stop and catch my breath because I was so out of breath. But I wouldn't give up. Because I wanted to go to school. So those are the things that come back to my mind when I think about it. Just how determined I was. I was not giving up.

Around the same time that she lost her sister, Freedom developed fibroid tumors in her uterus and had to have surgery to get them removed. She was in her 30s at the time of her diagnosis with uterine fibroids. While many women develop uterine fibroids as they age, Black women are disproportionately more likely to develop fibroids before the age of 40 and this diagnosis can impact fertility and overall health in extremely negative ways (Eltoukhi et al., 2014; Stewart et al., 2013). Even when she was experiencing tremendous pain and bleeding from the tumors and the recovery, Freedom continued to attend classes and make progress. After recovering from the fibroid tumors and the surgery, she continued with her degree. She remembered:

At one point, I thought I might have had cancer because they found a lump in my breast. The only thing I was thinking about was, can you go to school and have chemo? That's what I was thinking. I wasn't thinking that I *wasn't* going to go. I was just thinking, how was I going to go. I never thought I wouldn't go. I was just thinking, dang, I hope I'm not sick. That was my only concern. I don't want to miss class. Because I'm going to school. When I had that surgery, I had to be out for six or eight weeks. The whole time, I was just preparing for going back to school, I'm going back. It didn't matter. I was going to be sitting there sick. I was so ill before that surgery, really, I shouldn't have been in school. I don't know how my mind even functioned. But there was never a time I didn't think I would go back. Nothing was going to stop me from going to school. The only thing that could've stopped me was my kids because I had to care for them. But I waited till they were old enough. I didn't start until my baby went to kindergarten.

Freedom's remarkable tenacity to remain in school regardless of her illness did result in her finishing her degree. Freedom's experiences also connect with research on how Black women often feel as if they must act like superwomen (Abrams et al., 2014; Beauboeuf-Lafontant, 2007; Donovan & West, 2015; Leath, Jones, & Butler-Barnes, 2022; Woods-Giscombé, 2010), as if there is not time for rest, illness, or recovery. It is likely the exhaustion of raising five children, the youngest of whom was 15 when we sat down for our interview, attending college as the first in her family, and doing so while ill all took a toll on Freedom that might be difficult to fully measure. Freedom's children did see college as available to them. She remarked about her children's reactions to her degree, which she earned while her children were teenagers and in their 20s:

They were so happy. They were so proud. That really has been great for my children, all of my children, even my boys, even though they're so much older. For my daughters especially, it's like, "of course I'm going to college." There's no break for them. They don't think any differently. Academically, they're very strong. Their life is so different than my life was. They're avid readers. They read stacks of books and they're proud. My daughter wrote a paper. And she can write so doggone good. She wrote a paper about what she wanted to do when she grows up and she said she wants to go to U of M like her mom.

Comparing her younger children to her older three children, Freedom noted that they had such a different life than hers, in part because of her college degree. It was clear that Freedom's younger children, who witnessed her working hard for her college degree, also saw college as a viable and realistic option. Based on her experiences having persevered through college, even when ill, Freedom offered:

When I was sick, they didn't mind giving me a withdrawal, an incomplete, and then working with me because they knew that I was a sincere student. So, get to know your professors and talk to them. Participate in class. Don't sit in the back of the classroom. Sit in the front of the classroom. Raise your hand and say something. Just ask a question. If you don't have anything to share, ask a question. Just let them know that you're there. I think that makes a very big difference.

Ultimately, Freedom pointed to the need for self-valuing and asserting one's presence and knowledge to be successful in college, both themes among Black feminist thinkers (Collins, 2002). It is another story and another inquiry altogether to understand what role the institution might have played in Freedom's continual illnesses during her four-year degree program. As a nontraditional student who was a mother of five and over the age of 25 when she attended college as the first in her family to do so, Freedom likely had other stressors in her life before coming to campus. Yet it is worth pointing out once again that HBCU alumnae did not report these kinds of health crises during college. The different between HBCU and PWI alumnae could be coincidence, but it is still worth exploring deeper how institutions might influence students' health in college, as Sonya's narrative demonstrates.

"Failure Was Not an Option": Sonya's Story

Sonya attended Wayne State University in the Detroit area for all three of her degrees (bachelor's, master's, and MD) in the same social sciences discipline. When we met for her interview in Detroit, she was nearing the end of her medical degree. She summarized her undergraduate college experience: "When I finished up with my bachelor's degree, I was overjoyed because it was an accomplishment that I successfully achieved. It was hard. It was difficult. I went through a lot of sickness. I had very understanding teachers though. In undergrad, I had cancer. I was diagnosed with cancer twice. But I was still determined so I did it." I asked her how she was able to cope with that and still earn her degrees. She specified: "You have to do it if that's what you set your mind to doing. Failure was not an option, period. I had to do it. And having that determination and that drive and having college is also what helped me get through dealing with cancer because I had something else to put my mind on. I could focus on other things. It was hard. It was challenging. But I did it." Sonya did not say what kind of cancer she had battled but she suggested that college may have helped to distract her from her health concerns, which may have helped her to fight her illness. Sonya continued to reflect on her journey through college and with reaching remission for her cancer:

> You can't imagine it because you haven't been put in those shoes. If you're put in those shoes and you have a determining spirit, you'll do it. You will do it if it's something you really want. Everything in this life, to me, is about how bad do you want it? How bad do you want to get it? What will you do to get it? So, it was just, you jump in or you continue to stay in the race and you do what you have to do. You learn different strategies along the way. There are times when I fell short. But I looked at where I fell short and decided where do I go from here? How do I pick up the pieces? Where does this piece of the puzzle fit? You make yourself do it.

I asked Sonya how the cancer might have influenced her to attend medical school to earn a medical degree. She replied:

> I wanted to help people. It's not necessarily the degree. I wanted the knowledge. The degree is just something that hangs on the wall, something in the Records Department of a school, the university. But what I have as far as knowledge and what I carry in my heart, that is what will make the change. Because having the knowledge and having the passion and the concern, that is when it is in operative use, that is what I was concerned with. Because that is what will say this is what you can do.

Sonya recalled how she initially did not see becoming a doctor as available to her:

> I always knew it as a kid but I didn't think I was smart enough to do it. When I was coming up, you heard doctors and lawyers are so smart, they're just geniuses. I didn't think I fit in that category. Which I still don't believe I fit in that category. I fit in the category of anybody else that's out there trying to make it happen for themselves. Some people are born just smart like that. However, most people in society, we're smart or we're bright or intelligent because we have the determination. You

will yourself to do it. It's about being determined. It's just about being determined and dedicated. I just became determined and dedicated to do what it is that was in my heart to do.

Growing up Sonya was not often told that she was smart. Her mother compared her to her sister a lot and the comparison was not particularly favorable to Sonya. Still, Sonya persisted through her bachelor's and master's degrees into a medical degree program. Sonya considered her experience in medical school, summarizing:

About med school, it's the hardest thing I've ever done in my life. It's way different, it's extremely different. It's a shocker to you because you're kind of used to maybe writing papers or even the mindset of undergrad. And when it comes to medical school, you have exams like your first year, your blocks, your exams are every three months. So, [you might] think, oh, okay, I don't have to really study. Until you take that exam, and you don't pass it. Even in medical school, a whole lot that you wouldn't think that takes place in medical school. You have a lot of people that still goof around, and you have a lot of people that are very serious. There is no in between. I didn't know about a lot of the parties and stuff. I didn't know people get high. You think in medical school that people are so concerned with health.

Sonya experienced shock in a few ways during medical school. She was surprised that students partied as much as they did, and particularly that they took drugs that were illegal at that time. But Sonya was also surprised that she did not feel supported by other Black students who were in medical school with her. Earlier, Sonya used the metaphor that her peers were like crabs in a bucket to demonstrate the lack of support she felt. She seemed to feel as if her peers were more interested in pulling one another down than they were in helping one another to succeed.

Sonya explained that she had not passed her board exam the first time that she took it, which meant that she would need to wait six months to retake the exam and that she would have to remain in medical school for an extra year. It was clear that medical school and her exams had been a major source of stress for her:

Not passing a board exam, especially when you see you didn't pass by a margin of one point. It's not just that but it's also, we have to pay for these exams. When you have a limited income, almost no income, it's hard to come up with the money. Then just the whole mental state of the failure of it. I didn't pass. You just feel unworthy like you don't belong. Am I the only one going through this? So that can be heavy. Really, really heavy. I'm doing the extra year, which is hard, the embarrassment of it. I think that's the biggest part is just the embarrassment of it. I had to borrow extra money because it's not free. That extra year is not free. You have to pay for it.

It was obvious that Sonya was still under significant stress in her medical degree program and that the stress would not let up until she was able to pass her board exams and enter residency. Summarizing her educational journey and her medical school experience in particular, Sonya noted:

Well, I've been through a lot of sickness. A lot of sickness. I had a gastric bypass and I was sick right after I had the surgery. I was in and out of the hospital a lot. A whole lot. And then they thought that I had cancer again. So that was a battle. Then I got married. Then I went through a divorce. I got pregnant when I was married, and I lost my children. I had huge milestones.

Having already survived cancer during her undergraduate degree program, Sonya continued to encounter significant challenges in medical school. Sonya suffered multiple miscarriages before ending her marriage, all during her medical school degree program. The cancer scares also were a source of significant stress during her medical degree. I inquired how Sonya had managed to persevere, given all her health crises and the difficult times in her personal life. She responded unflinchingly:

My relationship with Christ. Prayer. Prayer. He made it happen. Gave me peace, gave me inner peace, gave me joy, a forgiving heart, a loving heart. That's how He did it. Love. Love. Love. Love and more love. Forgiveness, teaching me forgiveness and understanding. I wouldn't have made it. Absolutely not.

There was a lady that lived across the street. Miss Monroe. She was like a second mother to me. And she just started telling me over and over and over about how different I was and how special I was and how I had all of these gifts and talents and do what you like to do, do what you like to do. I started telling her, I don't even know how. Because I had lived my whole life trying to be and do what everybody else wanted me to do. One day, we were having a conversation and she said, "You just have to do it." I'm like, well, "How do you just do it?" And she said, "You'll figure out a way." And I figured out a way. I just literally one day was like, okay, I'll try this. And I tried it. It went just like a domino effect. It just went from exploring one gift and talent to the next. That's how it happened.

Through a combination of her religious faith and her close relationship with a close mother-figure type of friend, Sonya persisted. But it did not seem that she was able to take a break to heal, even when she was very sick.

Another way that Sonya found support during her degree programs was by finding or creating *Chosen We* communities. Sonya talked about these communities as a positive aspect of both her undergraduate and professional programs, such as her previously mentioned Swahili class study group.

Given that the community did not exist prior to taking the class, I asked Sonya how the students built the community together. She considered: "We just started one person at a time, just talking to one another. We formed a study group. That's really how it happened. Everybody would just show up for the study group. We just made a decision that we were ride or die. We did it, we just did it, we made it happen." Sonya's study group in her Swahili classes during her undergraduate degree became a type of *Chosen We* community for her. The students in these courses studied together, ate together, and helped each other to pass the courses, making sure that every single one of them succeeded in the class. Sonya noted that it was an unusual experience, and it did not happen again in her degree programs.

During medical school, while Sonya characterized the experience as hugely competitive and not particularly community-oriented, she still found *Chosen We* communities from where she drew support. I had asked her of a time she felt supported during medical school. She quickly responded with a few examples:

When I joined (MAPS), which is an association for Black medical students, Black pre-medical students, becoming a part of that, and seeing that there were African American students that were really doing what it takes to get into medical school. Just to see the opportunities that were actually available. Because I didn't know. I had no one to show me at that time. Then I became a part of Psi Chi, which is a national honor society for psychology. Becoming a part of that was rewarding. Because I really saw my hard work and becoming a part of the research groups.

I inquired as to why these groups were particularly beneficial to her. Sonya considered: "I definitely learned how to research. Just to be in a setting of people that were striving for success and professionalism was just very rewarding to see. I was able to see myself not where I was but where I'm going to be. I was able to see it." While it is unclear whether her involvement helped Sonya to navigate her health crisis, it did seem to be the case that she felt supported and as if her goals mattered when she joined these organizations.

Finally, while Sonya had been through major health crises throughout her educational journey, I began to wonder how she continued to stay motivated to finishing her degrees. When I asked her this question, she replied:

Serving the community, especially the underserved communities. I want to help as many people as I can, health wise and with learning materials and programs and outreach programs. I want to be able to find as many programs as I can to be able to help people. People that are willing to volunteer just to help. I think that's a problem with society, with this world as a whole. We don't help one another enough. I think that there is a lot of selfishness. People tend to look at people and they judge them. I think that people make wrong, inaccurate conclusions about other people. I think that a lot of judgment is off. This is why a part of the world is the way that it is because there's such a lack of love, there's such a lack of compassion, such a lack. I think that if people learned to really love one another, if people act really, really with a heart of compassion and with a heart of love, I don't think that the world would be like it is now. If people would stop being so selfish, so self-righteous and so self-centered, I think that there would not be as much poverty. There would not be as much hunger. There would not be such a lack of education. There would be so much more greatness. I think that if we came outside of ourselves and really made a true effort to help other people, that in that, you can help other people pull out the greatness that's in them. And then they can see what they can do. And they start doing. And then they can help the next person. And the next person. I think that that's a significant part of what this world needs. And aside from that, I think all of us need a stronger relationship with God. Because if we had a stronger relationship with the Lord, then I know that we would love a lot more. And love is the center thing.

Love for one another and oneself seemed to become the root of Sonya's—and many other alumnae's—stories in the end.

The Chosen We and the Possible Health Consequences of Institutional Types

Alumnae found or created *Chosen We* communities across institutional types, as evidenced by parts 2 and 3 of this book. Within PWIs, these *Chosen We* communities were primarily informal friendship groups or formal student organizations such as Black student unions. Alumnae who attended HBCUs framed those institutions as *Chosen We* spaces where women felt affirmed particularly in their racial identities and the diversity of ways to be Black on those campuses. It is an open question as to whether *Chosen We* communities may play a role in mediating the mental, physical, and emotional stress of going to college. But it is worth underscoring that the alumnae who identified health crises during or shortly after college were all from PWIs. Would the alumnae have experienced worse or more negative health outcomes had they not been able to find or create *Chosen We* communities? Again, this is a question that begs for further consideration but not necessarily one that can be answered by this data. It could be that institutional *Chosen We* communities where one feels deeply connected to and affirmed within a campus might be healthier relative to the physical, emotional, and social stress on students' bodies.

But at this point, I can only infer from the data on these points. There is however a clear path toward future research to understand whether *Chosen We* communities might be a possible intervention into the stress and negative health effects of being on particular campuses.

Conclusions on the Health Inferences between HBCUs and PWIs

There are clear differences in experiences between PWIs and HBCUs. The size of institutions are often quite different, where PWIs tend to be larger than most HBCUs, particularly state, land-grant, public PWIs. But the most obvious difference between these institutional types are the racial demographics and the campus norms on what backgrounds are valued and affirmed. HBCUs are becoming more diverse with an increasing number of White students attending them (Closson & Henry, 2008; Hall & Closson, 2005; Mobley et al., 2022). But there remains in many of these institutions a predominantly Black student population allowing for Black students to be on campuses that have the potential to embrace multiple ways of being Black. One's background as a Black or African American student is not the anomaly, but the norm. Additionally, HBCUs often have an ethos of promoting *all* students as successful rather than the individualistic focus on competition that is so pervasive at PWIs (Conrad & Gasman, 2015).

The solution to the health inferences here is not to suggest that only one type of institution is appropriate for Black women. There are, however, some relevant ideas related to the health and well-being of students that can be garnered from these oral histories that could be applicable in both HBCUs and PWIs:

1. Examine how success is promoted and framed on campuses as linked to physical, mental, and emotional health. Faculty and administrators within both HBCUs and PWIs should carefully examine notions of success within their institutions to understand whether ideas of success are manifesting a superwoman ideal. That is, might there be an assumption that one should achieve at all costs that is promoted in campus events, orientations, classrooms, and artifacts? If stated ideas of success do seem to have super-

woman ideas embedded in them, campus leaders should create campuswide efforts to reframe success in ways that also honor students' health and well-being.

2. Promote and make available mental health services to all students. Mental health services should be financially covered by students' fees so that students have access to these services regardless of their financial positioning. By making mental health resources a normative and typical part of students' experiences, some of the stigma that can be associated with mental health on campus might be removed and Black women may begin to get some of the mental health support that they need. Additionally, campuses should carefully monitor who mental health practitioners are on campus and give careful attention to hiring counselors who are Black women or who are women of color because there is evidence that Black students are more likely to reach out to and feel more comfortable with mental health practitioners who are of the same racial group (Goode-Cross & Grim, 2016).

3. Create or support campus policies that allow for students to take medical leave when needed without penalty to their degree programs and progress. For alumnae who became dangerously ill with cancer or other illnesses, medical leave was a necessity for them to finish their degree programs; had there been clear policies in place for them to take this leave and then transition back to campus, a source of further stress would have been alleviated.

4. Elevate *Chosen We* community spaces that allow for students to be vulnerable and to relax sometimes. By offering organizations, physical spaces, and campus resources toward rest and restoration spaces with others, not only might students feel better supported but they also could begin to rest a bit.

5. Promote wellness as a normative part of one's college experience. Student affairs practitioners could be particularly useful in presenting programming and services that help students to understand nutrition, the role of sleep and rest

in their health, exercise, and other positive ways of coping with stress (e.g., spirituality, religion, meditation, etc.). These messages should also be part of faculty mentoring and advising and within graduate and professional school training too.

FINAL THOUGHTS ON HEALTH OUTCOMES OF COLLEGE-GOING

The health and well-being of Black women and other groups of women was a major emphasis of the oral histories of Black women's lives, both professionally and personally. Without identifying the exact professions, which could betray confidentiality, there were 10 of the 105 women whose careers were directly dedicated toward fostering women's mental and physical health as social workers, doctors, counselors, psychologists, and attorneys who focused on women's legal justice. For example, Charlie, a graduate of the University of Alabama in the 1990s, created a career where she spends the bulk of her time working in group counseling for Black women. Viviane, a University of Central Florida graduate from the 2000s, has dedicated her career to public health issues with an emphasis on women's health. For women whose professional careers were not specifically focused on women's wellness, there were many, many women who were actively involved in women's emotional, social, legal, educational, and physical well-being and justice through community organizations such as sororities, philanthropic organizations, global nongovernmental organizations that focused on women, educational access nonprofits, and community outreach and service groups.

Conclusions on the *Chosen We* among Black Women

Black women have, for generations, understood that their liberation is intimately tied to one another. They have practiced this knowledge in their elevation of one another, in their uplift of their families and communities, in their own accomplishments that hardly, if ever, have been only for their own individual accolades. In the face of oppression, enslavement, segregation, and education that dehumanized them, Black women have built and created sacred communities, what I refer to as *Chosen We* communities.

The narrative oral histories in this book have echoed generations of Black feminist thinking that described Black women's support of one another as a type of "homeplace" (hooks, 1990), Black educational spaces that serve as fugitive spaces[1] to gain freedom from racial hostility (Grant et al., 2020; Nxumalo & Ross, 2019; Tichavakunda, 2020). While the word was not often used, these fugitive, home spaces were often a source of what some authors refers to as "Black joy," with the idea that joy can be a sustaining tool too (Tichavakunda, 2021). In the oral histories in this book, *Chosen We* communities were sometimes crafted by Black women in predominantly White campus spaces that were racially hostile and exclusive to them. Sometimes these *Chosen We* communities were formal student organizations that affirmed Black women's identities, offered sites for resistance and protest, provided intellectual space of other Black scholars with similar interests, or perhaps blended all these roles.

Within HBCUs, the alumnae in this book found something else entirely: they encountered a campus space that was built for them, their histories, and their futures. As such, the experiences within HBCUs were overwhelmingly positive. That is not to say that the alumnae did not encounter challenges within HBCUs, nor is it to minimize the complex college experiences they had in those institutions, some of which were likely not always positive. Yet, when HBCUs are compared to PWIs, the contrast was stark and HBCUs clearly offered more nurturing, welcoming, and inclusive overall environments for Black women who graduated from these institutions.

Black women have, for generations, stood up for one another and stood together. It is remarkable, and can be a lesson to others, particularly those who are not Black women, that community can foster success. Yet there remains an enduring question as to why no one else aside from Black women has been standing for and with Black women. As legal scholar and Black feminist theorist Pauli Murray (1987) put it: "To thrive, I need a society hospitable to all comers—Black as well as white, women as well as men, the lame, the deaf, the blind, the brown and yellows and red—a society in which individuals were free to express their multiple origins and to share their variety of cultural strains without being forced in a categorical mold" (p. 391). Murray's point is that if other populations supported one another and supported Black women, not only would she (and Black women) be more likely to feel more fulfilled, but others would be more authentic and liberated too.

The women in this book were remarkably accomplished. They were college graduates, and most of the alumnae had also earned PhDs, JDs, MDs, and other advanced degrees. These women were leaders in their respective professional fields and in their families and communities. Yet there were costs to this greatness in the form of stress and health consequences too. There were costs too in the idea that only Black women were there to support other Black women. Imagine what Black women might be able to achieve if others stood with them. Imagine the liberation that could be accomplished if those who do not identify as Black women—people with an embodiment like my own as a White woman for example—understood that collective liberation is a path to greatness for all. Imagine if the *Chosen We* could be reframed to where all felt the obligation of the *We* of our collective humanity. Imagine if all Black women felt unequivocally *chosen* by higher education institutions, those within them, and by the larger society in the way that they chose and elevated one another unendingly and unequivocally, often lacking support from the rest of society, for generations. It is high time for higher education and society to do the same for Black women.

Black women have long understood their liberation is bound to one another. And those of us who do not identify as Black women have often failed to realize our *own* liberation is bound to the *liberation of Black women*. Choosing Black women—supporting them, learning with them, creating community with them, elevating their knowledge, ideas, joy, and leadership—is a path to liberation for everyone.

Appendix A

Putting Black Women at the Center as a White Woman:
An Oral History Methodology

The Black Women's Alumnae Project was a labor of love that took me nearly 12 years to complete in part because of my strong commitment to attempting, as a White woman, to put Black women at the center of the study from its inception to the present volume. Here I reflect on the process of gathering the critical oral histories that are compiled in this book—and I consider the triumphs and challenges of doing this work that I have long called "my heart's work," as a White woman. Importantly, I chose time, care, and authenticity over using this project as a path toward tenure or promotion as a scholar. In part this was because of the time it took to complete the work in the way that I felt was credible. But also, it was important to me that I was not personally benefiting (in the way of my career advancement toward promotion and tenure) from Black women's lives as a White woman. I am a full professor with tenure at the University of Wisconsin–Madison and this book was not part of any of my promotion or tenure materials. Not to be taken lightly is the way in which, during the writing of this book, impressions changed about who should even do research with Black women and other historically minoritized populations too.

In each of the five phases of the collection of oral histories for the project, I had to contemplate anew the possibilities for how (and whether) me doing the work was appropriate. In this appendix I talk about how I did it—but I do so with the strong understanding that even by the time the words I write go to print, the ideas around who can and should do research across lines of difference may have shifted. I committed to a moral compass for doing the work that I outline here—and I did the very best work that I could *only* with the strong support, collaboration, and wisdom-sharing with Black women with whom I have built community over the past 20 years. One reason for the length of time it took to publish this book was my commitment to the importance of publishing with all who worked on the project in each of the five cities before writing this book. All data for those articles are *not* in this book; see appendix C for other publications from the project. Making the choice to publish articles from the project with those who were involved in it *before* publishing this book was the right ethical decision. I would recommend this approach for anyone doing research across lines of difference. Those involved who *are* part of the communities being elevated in the work must benefit first and foremost from the project. Finally, relative to collaboration, many of the oral histories in this book were collaborative writing efforts with participants in the project, although all participants in these pages elected to remain anonymous (see appendix B for participants quoted in the book).

The Black Women's Alumnae Project was an oral history project (Atkinson, 1998; Carspecken, 2014/1996; Lemley, 2017; Williams, 2018) about Black women college alumnae who graduated from college between 1954 and 2014. The blending of critical inquiry and oral history allowed for a focus on racial uplift, agency, and the sharing of wisdom, advice, and stories that have been passed down between generations within many Black families and communities (Honey, 2002; Rogers, 2009, 2012). The critical aspect of the oral history methodology relies on roots in critical theories (Carspecken, 2014/1996) such as Black feminist thought, the theoretical perspective of this project (hooks, 1990, 2003a, 2003b, 2014).

Connecting the oral history and Black feminist traditions, I rooted the methodology in the scholarship of scholars of color who used experience, dialogue, and wisdom-sharing as a path to transform the way knowledge is created (Ahmad, 2020; Castillo-Montoya & Torres-Guzmán, 2012; Espino et al., 2010; Fries-Britt & Kelly, 2005). Many of the scholars who authored pathbreaking work to fundamentally question how knowledge is created were peer reviewers/advisors on this project. As such, the critical oral history methodology, as I crafted it here, is meant to create findings that stand in contrast to the essentializing, monolithic ways in which Black women are often represented in the research about them (Commodore et al., 2018; Winkle-Wagner, 2015; Winkle-Wagner et al., 2018). The critical oral history methodology here builds on a long tradition among communities of color of racial uplift through wisdom/oral history sharing that has been applied to higher education, where Black college students have been encouraged to give advice to future college-going generations (Luedke, 2020; McCallum 2017).

While each of the introductions to the parts of the book offer the most insight into the participants' demographic characteristics and alma mater institutions, I offer some general ideas of the participant recruitment process here. There were 105 total participants in the study who were living or working in five metropolitan areas in the US (Atlanta, GA; Chicago, IL; Detroit, MI; Lincoln, NE; New Orleans, LA) and graduated from college between 1954 and 2014 (a 60-year time period). The metropolitan areas were the focus of the study because they all have concentrated populations of Black people. In the following section, I reflect on the process of data collection and analysis.

Putting Black Women at the Center as a White Woman

I began the project with a keen awareness of the possible difficulty that I would have recruiting Black women alumnae to complete oral history interviews with me, as a White woman. My prior recruitment efforts and reflections on conducting research across racial lines served as an important guide for what would be necessary to build trust and recruit participants to the study (Patton & Winkle-Wagner, 2012; Winkle-Wagner, 2009a, 2009c, 2015). As a White woman who has done research with Black women for my career, I knew from experience that my ability to navigate various metropolitan areas for the study would hinge on my own authenticity and relationships with Black women living and working in those cities. As is always the case, as a White woman doing this work, race has often entered the room long before I meet with Black women for the project, meaning that the history of relationships (positive, and often negative) between Black and White women is invoked in my efforts to build trust (Patton & Winkle-Wagner, 2012). Not only would it be important to enter the field carefully, but every single moment of the project was a chance to build or betray trust with the Black woman who I aimed to elevate and support through the findings (Winkle-Wagner, 2009a, 2009c). Specifically, it was only through authentic and close relationships with Black women who were already deeply embedded in the cities of interest for the study that I could do the work. In each city, I first worked to secure:

1. Black women with deep roots in the metropolitan areas who could serve as gatekeepers to groups and individuals in the city to help me build relationships (see appendix C for a reading list of publications with gatekeepers).

2. Black women who could serve as advisors and peer reviewers on the work I was doing in the city and/or in the analysis and interpretation processes.

3. Black women who could serve as collaborators in the short- and long-term on the data collection, analysis, and interpretation of the data from each city for the project (and some served in multiple cities).

Admittedly, to set this benchmark for how to proceed authentically in the cross-racial research that I was doing meant that the project took many years longer than it might have had I *not* met these three goals. Yet I am convinced about the deep importance of putting Black women at the center of not just the topic of study, but of the project itself regardless of the time it took to complete the project because of it. *To be clear, I would caution other researchers, particularly White women (or anyone who is doing cross-racial work), against choosing speed of completion of a study over the authenticity, humanity, and credibility of attempting to conduct cross-racial research in humanizing ways.*

Throughout the project, I moved slowly and carefully in adding metropolitan areas to the study so that I could secure Black women–led gatekeepers (those who had access to providing relationship starters to Black communities and groups within a city) and Black women–led advisory groups, collaborators, and peer reviewers of the analysis and interpretations from the project. Admittedly, the process worked a bit differently in each metropolitan area as I acquired funding for the project and because the people serving as gatekeepers, collaborators, and peer reviewers were typically not the same people. For this reason, it is worth noting that the gatekeeper(s) in each city served in different capacities based on their own needs or desires and career stages. For example, I offered anyone serving as a gatekeeper an opportunity to collect some of the interviews and to coauthor and publish from the data (see appendix C for a reading list of publications with gatekeepers). Some gatekeepers were interested in that, and others were not at various points in the project.

The Inception of the Project and Data Collection

As I indicated in the acknowledgments of the book, the entire project started from a conversation I had with Diana Slaughter Kotzin. I am hugely indebted to her for the idea and for her wisdom throughout the process. The trajectory of the various cities in the project unfolded over time as did my approach to entering cities, collaborations, and understanding of the work. I started with a "solo scholar" model (where I was planning to be the only researcher doing the entire project) and I ended in a much more community-scholarship approach, meaning that, as I learned from participants, I reshaped my approaches.

For each of the five cities in the project, I initiated data collection in a particular metropolitan area usually with the crucial assistance of gatekeepers, collected oral histories, and one city often led to the next. Gatekeepers in each city would send emails and make phone calls to people in their social networks, and then I asked each participant if they would do the same to expand the various networks of people included in the project. While I was engaged in one city, I often started planning, identifying possible gatekeepers who would be able to help me contact participants and trying to raise money for trips to the next city—and I sometimes initiated contact with prospective alumnae too. Otherwise, I mostly completed data collection in one city before traveling to the next in part because of time and resources, and because it allowed me to spend more time contemplating differences between the cities.

There were no monetary incentives for those participating in the project. While I did often purchase coffee, food, or snacks as a small sign of my gratitude, I did not have grant funding to incentivize participation in the project with gift cards or cash. While I did receive internal grants at the University of Nebraska and the University of Wisconsin, a large portion of the project was paid for by my own income (e.g., travel expenses, transcription costs, copyediting costs), which is now more unusual and certainly made the project take longer too. I did feel a deeper level of obligation to participants, because of the lack of monetary incentives, to offer opportunities for their participation and to offer other ways to show my gratefulness, such as thank you notes after each interview, continued engagement with many participants, mentoring some participants toward or through graduate programs, connecting participants to those in my own social network who might be good contacts for them, and so forth. In some ways, the obligation to create a deeper relationship may have been more useful for participants and for the project (e.g., no one was participating to simply acquire an incentive). Also, from an ethical standpoint, the women in this project all were working full-time positions and were not in immediate financial need (many identified as upper middle class or identified themselves as relatively affluent). Had the participants been low-income, or in immediate financial need (e.g., needing housing, food, etc.), my lack of monetary incentives might have been a different ethical question for the project than I felt that it was, given the social status of this group of people.

Lincoln/Omaha, Nebraska

I started the project while I was working at the University of Nebraska–Lincoln as an assistant professor in a tenure-track faculty position. My gatekeepers for Lincoln and Omaha, Nebraska, were Black faculty members on campus who wished to remain anonymous here. I also chose to combine these two cities even though they are 45 miles apart because identifying Black women and their degree levels in either city could run the risk of betraying confidentiality since both cities are locations where some educated Black women have chosen to move for their jobs. That is, while there are concentrated Black communities in both cities, those communities are highly visible and identifiable. I must admit that at the start of the project, I did not offer publishable collaboration opportunities for the participants or for the gatekeepers in part because I was still struggling with how I would get tenure myself and I had certainly been trained to think about solo authorship as important. I am a bit embarrassed about this now, but it is important to note the ways the project changed over time. As such, I did not ask gatekeepers for their labor beyond emailing prospective participants (i.e., they did not collect interviews or do any analysis on that part of the study). I do regret that choice now because it would have made the work better and more authentic. But I was a bit wrapped up in trying to keep my own position at that time. Thankfully, I waited to publish from the project until I had more data from other cities and then I did collaborate more.

Early in my time at Nebraska, it was made clear to me while on the tenure track at the University of Nebraska that much of my research with Black women was not a tenurable choice. The senior faculty who encouraged me to abandon my research line with Black women in search for tenure have since retired. But, having to stand up for the importance of Black women's lives and for this work was an important part of my commitment to the project and this work. I continued to pursue the work, knowing that tenure could not be the goal of the work but that I should do it anyway knowing that the work would not be part of my tenure case. But it slowed my progress on the project and made me less collaborative in the beginning of the project too because I felt like I was constantly defending the work (and my ability to stay in academia).

I moved to the University of Wisconsin–Madison (UW–Madison) shortly after starting the project. My role with participants in Lincoln and Omaha was multifaceted too. There were five participants who had not yet earned an advanced degree when I interviewed them and we stayed in close contact while I coached them, and in some cases closely mentored them, toward doctoral programs. All five of those participants have earned their PhD at this point and I did collaborate and continue to work with many of them for years after I stopped collecting data in these cities. I have chosen to protect these participants' anonymity and so I am not naming them here. Some of the costs of the project for the Lincoln/Omaha, Nebraska, phase were funded by an internal institutional grant from the University of Nebraska, the University of Nebraska Layman Research Award.

New Orleans, Louisiana

In New Orleans, I worked with a close friend and collaborator from graduate school, Carla Morelon, to gain access to participants and to the city. Morelon was crafting an ambitious career in higher education administration at the time, so when I asked her if she wanted to help in data collection and analysis and publish together from the data, she opted not to do so at that time. I do wish I had circled back to possible collaborations with her later because I deeply value her as a friend, colleague, and collaborator. All the participants in New Orleans came from or were connected to Morelon (e.g., some participants introduced me to other people after our oral history interview). I collected and analyzed all of the oral histories in New Orleans on my own. The Layman Research Award funded my travel to New Orleans and other associated costs for this phase of the project. While I continued to work with my longtime colleagues and collaborators as advisors (for data collection processes, analysis, and interpretation) on this phase of the project, my limited funding at the time meant that I was not able to travel repeatedly to New Orleans and my relationships with participants were more limited to email. I did not develop collaborative (i.e., publishing or mentoring—either receiving or giving mentoring) relationships with participants in New Orleans. Most of this data was also collected during my time on the faculty at the University of Nebraska before the spirit of the project had fully developed in the way that it did in Chicago, Detroit, and Atlanta.

Chicago, Illinois

After receiving an internal grant at UW–Madison, the Fall Research Competition award through the Wisconsin Alumni Research Fund (WARF), I hired Tangela Blakely Reavis as my research assistant (she was also my doctoral advisee at the time). Reavis became my first gatekeeper for data collection in Chicago, Illinois, and later became a longtime collaborator on the project too (appendix C).

Soon after, I reached out to Bridget Turner Kelly for ideas on the project because she was living and working in Chicago at the time, and she was senior to me in academia. Kelly became a second gatekeeper on the project, a longtime collaborator, and friend (appendix C). Finally, with another doctoral student, Courtney Luedke, as my teaching assistant, with whom I had frequently collaborated on other projects, I had built a phenomenal team to significantly expand the project into Chicago.

All four of us collected data in Chicago and so we were able to gather more oral histories, spread ourselves across the city, and dialogue about analysis and interpretation. Because of geographic proximity and because I had more grant funding at the time, I was able to travel to Chicago multiple times to work with participants and with the gatekeeper team. Some of the participants in Chicago encouraged us to open a phase of the project in Atlanta, Georgia, because they had migrated from there. Also, two of the gatekeepers, Reavis and Kelly, both had contacts in Atlanta too. Thus, Chicago and Atlanta became connected parts of the project. As a team, we had many conversations about our identities related to those of participants—Reavis and Kelly identify as Black women; Luedke identifies as a multiracial woman; and I identify as White. We each identified our racial identities to participants before the interviews. The conversation often contemplated how participants disclosed and what our processes were for building trust.

Detroit, Michigan

Soon after data collection began in Chicago, I contacted a collaborator and longtime colleague, Carmen McCallum, about the possibility of opening a phase of the project in Detroit. McCallum, who identifies as a Black woman, has deep roots in Detroit, having grown up there, and she agreed to be a gatekeeper on the project. We had already collaborated on other projects by this point. McCallum continued to collect some of the Detroit interviews with the team, and she was a major collaborator on the project too (appendix C). The enthusiasm we had built as a team in Chicago meant that some team members also were able to travel to Detroit with me—Reavis and Luedke. Between McCallum's initial gatekeeping work and participants' connecting us to other alumnae in the area, we shared the data collection process in Detroit (e.g., I collected approximately one-quarter of the interviews in Detroit). Like the Chicago team, we all disclosed our identities to participants before the interviews. As a team, we dialogued about the process of collecting oral history interviews, given our varied identities.

Atlanta, Georgia

Closely after the Detroit phase of the project began, the gatekeeper team traveled to Atlanta, Georgia, to begin making relationships with Black women alumnae there. Bridget Kelly and Tangela Blakely Reavis were key gatekeepers alongside a handful of the Chicago participants in the project. Luedke, Kelly, and Reavis all came to Atlanta to collect oral histories there. Like the processes in Detroit and Chicago, we all disclosed our racial identities to participants before the oral history interviews. As in Chicago, we each collected approximately one-quarter of the interviews in Atlanta. We also dialogued about the process of collecting those oral histories, the analysis and interpretation of that Atlanta data (see appendix C for other publications from the project).

The Critical Oral History Interviews

I started the interview protocol in the Lincoln/Omaha and New Orleans phases of the project. As members of the research team joined the project, we trained together for a series of weeks before entering the field to collect the oral histories. I was the only person collecting in-person oral histories in Lincoln/Omaha and New Orleans. For Chicago, Atlanta, and Detroit, members of the research team traveled together to each city to collect in-person oral history interviews (Kelly, Reavis, Luedke, and McCallum—appendix C).

We used an unstructured, opened-ended interview protocol that I adapted from Atkinson's (1998) life story methodology toward an oral history approach that considers the person's experiences to tell history. The rationale for an open-ended interview protocol was to allow participants full authority on crafting the stories/oral histories of their lives. As such, the alumnae chose the chronology of their stories, the significant moments to share (or not share), the direction we took in the interview, and the boundaries of their own stories—where their "history" stopped and started. The open-ended structure was a way both to promote a more egalitarian approach (Carspecken, 2014/1996) and to decenter my own voice, authority, or expertise as a White woman leading the project. I did not want to assume that I knew the order, direction, or paths that Black women would want to share.

We asked one question to guide the beginning of the interview: If your college experience were a book and each significant moment were to be a chapter, where would your story start? From there, alumnae then could speak in the chronology that they chose rather than having that chronology imposed on them. Because we encouraged participants to start in the place of their story that they desired, the interviews would sometimes launch from childhood and participants could consider "chapters" (i.e., significant moments) into adulthood. Or some participants would start from their current location (e.g., job, etc.) and go backward. Those gatekeepers who collected some of the interviews trained with me in a series of sessions so that we could come to consensus on how to ask follow-up questions and what directions to pursue in the interviews. We had a list of possible areas about which to prompt participants: relationships, advice for success in college, ways college may have shaped their lives (or not), support networks, involvement/activities outside of the classroom, academic experiences, racism/sexism/heterosexism/etc., and identity (however the participants defined identity—we did not assume a definition beforehand). The unstructured, open-ended interview method encouraged a shared authority between the interviewer and the interviewee, connecting to a component of critical oral history, to make visible the histories that the participants want to tell from their perspective in a way that rights history (Lemley, 2017). Given the unstructured approach, some interviews lasted more than three hours and other interviews were closer to 90 minutes in length. We recorded all interviews, and I paid one professional transcriber to transcribe all the interviews to have consistency in how data were transcribed.

Data Analysis

In starting to analyze data, I began with a six-month process of emergent data analysis individually (without help from student researchers or the gatekeepers). From the more than 3,000 pages of data, I coded 500 pages of the data (across cities—100 pages from each city) using this a low-level, "in vivo" coding approach. In Word documents, I coded paragraphs or sentences of the data with a three- to six-word "code" to the side that was crafted in the participants' words. Each transcript elicited approximately 150 codes. I then took those emergent codes and put them in a separate document to cluster the codes under categories that eventually became themes. I proceeded this way for the first 100 pages of analysis for each city (500 pages of data were analyzed this way) and then compared the clustered code/category lists across transcripts and cities. From this first-round analysis, I created a codebook.

For the next round of analysis, I presented the codebook to Reavis, Luedke, and another graduate student who was a paid research assistant for me at the time and who became a close collaborator, Jamila Lee-Johnson. We discussed the codes in the code list until we reached consensus (e.g., I would show the code and which data supported the code, we discussed it, and the team raised questions or concerns). I also showed the code list to other peer reviewers who are Black women and colleagues of mine to garner additional feedback. Once the code list was solidified after two months of discussion and review, we began to enter data into analysis software, NVivo. We used the code list to code the entire body of data (including the 500 pages that were initially coded).

After all data were coded in the NVivo coding software, I ran a data query and then reanalyzed the sets of data on my own that are separated into chapters in this book using Carspecken's (2014/1996) meaning field and reconstructive horizon analysis on any data that seemed to have much deeper meaning (about one-third of the data). Meaning field analysis allows for the range of possible meanings to emerge from the data where a phrase that was said by a participant is then considered for other meanings with the words "and," "or," or "and/or" between them. For example, if one were to say, "I needed to find other Black women for support," I might construct a meaning field like: "I needed to find other Black women for support AND there were not many Black women AND/OR I was not supported by people who were not Black women AND/OR I was not supported by men." One continues with the meaning field until it seems that the range of meanings has been teased out. Then, I conducted a reconstructive horizon analysis where I deconstructed a phrase of data into the possible "objective" (shared meaning, the ways that objective reality might be shared), "subjective" (restricted meaning, often in the participants' mind), "normative" (claims about ethics or morals), and "identity" (claims about oneself).

During the process of this analysis, I worked often with various peer debriefers on my research team, discussing the findings of the analysis with collaborators (for other projects) locally and nationally for their perspectives on my interpretations.

For any data *not* presented in this book, the larger research team engaged in a separate analysis process described in those published works (appendix C). For gatekeepers in the study, I offered the third round of analysis of the data to them first before offering it to students. We met as a gatekeeper team to discuss interests and then ran queries in the coding software for those topics and reanalyzed the data based on the topic of the article (appendix C). Then, once the gatekeeper team had authored multiple papers, I started to use the dataset toward training doctoral students and to offer them analysis and publishing opportunities. I ran queries on a topic of the data within the coding software (e.g., friendships) and then used the third-round analysis process to train doctoral students on analysis for that area of data (e.g., for between 20 and 100 pages of data not used in the book) to write separate conference papers or articles. Data in the articles with gatekeepers and students do not appear in the book (appendix C).

Data Validation

In addition to the consistent process of reflexivity that I personally engaged through journaling, field notes, and conversations, I also completed multiple forms of data validation. Each participant had the opportunity to review the transcript for their oral history in a process of member checking (Carspecken, 2014/1996). After alumnae reviewed their transcripts, I made changes to transcripts based on participants' suggestions. After the participant returned the transcript, I offered the opportunity for participants to continue to be involved in whatever way suited their needs and/or prior commitments. Some participants *only* reviewed their transcript. Others were in continued contact with me regarding ways that I was writing and positioning their oral histories. Still other participants revised their oral histories and I kept their revisions here in these pages. Again, the participants in this book wished to remain anonymous so, while they are not named, they were offered the opportunity if they desired, and many had a hand in writing their own histories.

I engaged in peer debriefing (Carspecken, 2014/1996) throughout the process of data collection, analysis, and interpretation. In addition to the peer debriefing that happened on data collection teams in each phase of the project where we initiated conversations about gaining trust, cross-racial research (and within-group research since gatekeepers were mostly Black women), and technical aspects of what was or was not working well, I also turned to many colleagues for their perspectives on my analysis and interpretation. While I claim any errors here, many people spent time discussing and/or reading my work on this project. I had multiple, extended conversations about this project, the data collection, analysis, and interpretations with Thandi Sulè, Dorian McCoy, Courtney Luedke, Dina Maramba, Milagros Castillo-Montoya, Bridget Turner Kelly, Cherene Sherrard-Johnson, Jamila Lee-Johnson, Tangela Blakely Reavis, Deborah Faye Carter, Angela Locks, Carmen McCallum, Mike Wagner, and Clif Conrad. During the writing of this book, I was on sabbatical at the Institute for Research in the Humanities at UW–Madison and I am grateful for the many conversations I had there, including during a book talk I gave as part of my fellowship on how to properly write history. Additionally, there were many people who reviewed the writing at multiple points, reading my interpretations to offer insight—and all these reviews were invaluable in helping me to think and rethink my positioning, the presentation and writing of the oral histories, and the study itself. To name a few of these reviewers here, I am hugely grateful to: Diana Kotzin, Christy Clark-Pujara, Xueli Wang, Dorian McCoy, Courtney Luedke, Cherene Sherrard-Johnson, Linn Posey-Maddox, and Mike Wagner.

Throughout the data collection and analysis process, I engaged in field note writing and reflective journaling about my own positioning with participants and with the data (and with members of the research team). After each interview, I would journal about my skills as an interviewer and about ways I was or perhaps was not able to achieve trust with the participant (at least from my own vantage point). The field notes and journaling were useful as I contemplated the findings in this book, providing context and details about sites and my own shifting role throughout the project. It is possible that at certain points I became overly self-reflective, making the book harder to write and to put out into the world (e.g., asking whether I should write the book as a White woman, asking whether I should continue, etc.). The process of journaling did help me contemplate ways to make the project a bit less about me and my own processing or changes I noticed in myself during the research so that I could try to elevate participants. It was also through the reflective journaling that I realized I needed to spend a year reading Black feminist theories, which I did after the first round of analysis. I journaled during that reading too to continue to interrogate how I could and could not use the theory (i.e., I ultimately was informed by Black feminist theories but could not *be* a theorist in this area).

Triangulation (Carspecken, 2014/1996) occurred through the multiple research sites (five metropolitan areas) and through multiple rounds of data analysis. I compared across research sites and across generations (10-year periods of time) in the data, allowing for me to contemplate when time and region might have shaped the oral histories. The multiple rounds of data analysis allowed for me to check my interpretations (e.g., Were the themes the same or different and why?). If interpretations were different across rounds of analysis, I conducted additional analyses on that part of the data until I could work through conflict or different interpretations on the data. Sometimes writing out oral histories as I did here was a way to check interpretations too (i.e., Did the interpretation in the writing mirror the interpretation I had in earlier analysis?).

In the end, it is with great vulnerability that I offer up this book to readers. It is now up to the readers to ascertain whether I have met the goals for authentic and humanizing, cross-racial research that I laid out earlier. I hope to have met these goals and have spent more than a decade trying. But I also know that there are errors—both in the writing and in my judgment. I carry my embodied Whiteness and my White-womanness always, both in the field and in the writing and I know that it does change the work that I do too. As I would suggest to those wishing to pursue cross-racial research where every moment with a participant is a moment of vulnerability, where trust is possible or doubtful, every moment of reading the pages of this book is also a chance for me to gain or betray your trust as a reader in this regard.

Appendix B

Participants Quoted in the Book

Table 8.

Pseudonym	Chapters Where Quoted	HBCU or PWI for Undergraduate Degree	First-Generation Status	Decade of Undergraduate Degree	Highest Degree Completed (at Time of Study)
Acra	chap. 5, 6	HBCU, PWI graduate degree	No	2000s	PhD
Alianna	chap. 3	PWI	No	2000s	MBA
Amanda	part 3, chap. 5, 6, 7	HBCU, PWI graduate degree	No	2010s	master's
Ayana	chaps. 3, 7	PWI	N/A	1990s	DVM
Brie	chap. 7	HBCU, PWI graduate degree	No	2000s	PhD
Brynn	chaps. 5, 6, 7	HBCU, PWI graduate degree	No	2000s	master's
Cassie	chap. 4	PWI	No	2000s	master's
Charlie	chaps. 3, 4	PWI	Yes	1990s	master's
Colle	chap. 3	PWI	Yes	2000s	master's
Crystal	chaps. 4	PWI	Yes	1990s	master's
Dana	chaps. 3, 4	PWI	Yes	2000s	master's
Denise	chap. 3	PWI	No	1990s	master's
Diane	chaps. 3, 4	PWI	No	1990s	master's (though pursuing PhD at time of study)
Dianna	chap. 3	PWI	Yes	1990s	EdS
Elaine	chap. 6	HBCU	No	1990s	master's

Elle	chap. 6	HBCU		Yes	2000s	bachelor's
Erin Goseer Mitchell*	chaps. 5, 6	HBCU, PWI graduate degree		No	1950s	master's
Faygen	chap. 8	PWI		No	2010s	bachelor's
Freedom	chap. 8	PWI		Yes	2000s	bachelor's
Gen	chap. 8	PWI		Yes	1990s	master's
Janelle	chaps. 3, 4, 6, 8	PWI		Yes	1970s	DBA (doctorate in business administration)
Jasmine	chap. 4	PWI		Yes	2000s	EdS
Jordan	chap. 6	HBCU		No	2000s	bachelor's
Josephine	chaps. 3, 4	PWI		No	2000s	master's
Karen	chap. 5	HBCU, PWI graduate degree		Yes	1970s	master's
Keisha	chap. 4	PWI		Yes	2000s	JD
Keys	chap. 3	PWI		Yes	2000s	master's
Lark	chap. 4	PWI		No	2000s	master's
Leah	chaps. 4, 5	PWI		Yes	N/A	bachelor's
Lisa	chaps. 5, 7	HBCU		No	2000s	master's
Maciel	chap. 7	PWI, HBCU graduate degree		No	2010s	master's
Marwa	chaps. 5, 6, 7	HBCU		No	1970s	PhD
Michelle	chap. 4	PWI		N/A	1990s	JD
Mimi	chap. 5	HBCU		No	1960s	MSW

continued on next page

Table 8. Continued.

Pseudonym	Chapters Where Quoted	HBCU or PWI for Undergraduate Degree	First-Generation Status	Decade of Undergraduate Degree	Highest Degree Completed (at Time of Study)
Nadia	chaps. 5, 7	HBCU, PWI graduate degree	No	2000s	master's (though pursuing PhD at time of study)
Nicole	chaps. 6, 7	HBCU, PWI graduate degree	No	2000s	PhD
Nina	chap. 5	HBCU, PWI graduate degree	No	1980s	PhD
Nosipha	chap. 4	PWI	Yes	1990s	PhD
Nzinga	chap. 6	HBCU, PWI graduate degree	No	2000s	master's
Olivia	chap. 4	PWI	Yes	2000s	master's (pursuing PhD at time of study)
Patrice	chap. 2	PWI	No	1960s	master's
Princess	chaps. 3, 4	PWI	No	1990s	PhD
Ramycia	chap. 3	PWI	Yes	2000s	master's (though pursuing PhD at time of study)
Rita Mae	part 1	PWI	Yes	1960s	EdD
Samantha	chap. 3	PWI	Yes	2000s	bachelor's (though pursuing master's at time of study)
Shayla	chap. 4	PWI	Yes	2000s	PhD

Sonya	chaps. 3, 8	PWI		No	2000s	PhD
Sunshine	chap. 6	HBCU, PWI graduate degree		No	2000s	master's
Theresa	chap. 5	HBCU		Yes	1980s & 1990s	bachelor's
Tiffany A.	chaps. 5, 6	HBCU, PWI graduate degree		Yes	2000s	PhD
Tiffany T. (also called Tiff)	chaps. 3, 4, 8	PWI		No	1990s	master's
Tweedy	chaps. 3, 6	PWI		Yes	1960s	JD
Valencia	chap. 5	HBCU		No	1980s	bachelor's
Vivian	chaps. 3, 4, 8	PWI		No	2000s	bachelor's
Viviane	chap. 8	PWI		Yes	2000s	master's
Zeta	chap. 4	PWI		N/A	1990s	bachelor's

*This is not a pseudonym.

Appendix C

Reading List of Other Publications from the Project

Reavis, T., Winkle-Wagner, R., Kelly, B., Luedke, C., & McCallum, C. (2022). Letters to my Sisters: Advice from Black women alumnae about how to thrive and survive in college. *Teachers College Record, 124*(4), 180–204. DOI: Available online first at https://doi.org/10.1177/01614681221096798

Winkle-Wagner, R., Kelly, B. T., Luedke, C. L., & Reavis, T. B. (2018). Authentically me: Examining expectations that are placed upon Black women in college. *American Educational Research Journal.* Online first at http://journals.sagepub.com/doi/abs/10.3102/0002831218798326

Winkle-Wagner, R., Luedke, C., McCallum, C., & Ota-Malloy, B. (2019). Instrumental of meaningful friendships: Black alumnae perspectives on peer relationships during college. *Journal of Women and Gender in Higher Education,* 1–16. DOI: https://doi.org/10.1080/19407882.2019.1593201

Winkle-Wagner, R., Luedke, C. L., McCallum, C. M. (2017). Black women's advice on the role of confidence in the pursuit of a college degree: Believe you will achieve. In L. D. Patton & N. N. Croom (Eds.), *Critical perspectives on Black women and college success* (pp. 44–56). Routledge.

Winkle-Wagner, R., Reavis, T. B., Forbes, J., & Rogers, S. (2019). A culture of (HBCU) success: Black alumnae discussions of how Spelman College creates greatness. *Journal of Higher Education.* DOI:10.1080/00221546.2019.16549 65 online first at https://doi.org/10.1080/00221546.2019.1654965

Notes

Foreword by Diana Slaughter Kotzin

1. Female (or its binary counterpoint reference, male) refers to a particular biological sex at birth in this case. It is used here as a quotation and shows how gender and sex identifiers shift and change over time.

Part I: Black Women's Self-Determination in Education from Here to Eternity

1. Consistent with the oral histories in this book, I use Black and African American interchangeably to be as inclusive as possible to both the way that people self-identify and to include all those who have African, Caribbean, and Latin American heritage and identify with Pan-African ideas of Blackness. As with all racial signifiers, I recognize that these descriptors are ever-changing and that there may be a time when the descriptors I used here are less common or accepted, but at the time of writing this book, these racial identifiers were common.

2. I use the term "woman" or "women" to refer to all woman-identifying people in the study, mirroring the way they referred to their own gender identity and gender expression. Like racial identifiers, gender identifications are in a continual state of change; the people in the study commonly rereferred to themselves as "women."

3. While race is socially constructed, I choose to capitalize racial identifiers "Black" and "White" throughout the book to connote the important ways that race has been institutionalized and connected to social structures such that these color-coded racial descriptors are given power in society to structure people's lives, to categorize, and often to grant or deny advantage. At the time of writing this book, some authors were starting to only capitalize Black in an effort to disempower Whiteness. Yet in the oral histories here, Whiteness continues to emerge as

a form of structural power in people's lives and the capitalization of the term is one way to show the structured way that being White was often treated in people's lives. Like racial identifiers, the choice to capitalize racialized terms will continue to shift and change and I therefore choose to frame these terms in the way they emerged across the oral histories in the study—as signifiers of racialized social and structural experiences, levels of advantage and levels of power.

Chapter 1: The Collective History of Black Women's Ways of Knowing

1. Epistemology is how one comes to know about the world and social experiences, how one knows what one knows (Crotty, 1998).

2. For example, if one comes to know about the world and social experience through the senses, objectivist epistemology (Crotty, 1998), the types of questions might relate to this sensory way of knowing leading to observations, measurement, trends, and trying to understand one set of experiences (e.g., Black women) in comparison to others (e.g., often White women). Or, if one believes that knowledge is constructed out of experience and communication with others, constructivist epistemology (Crotty, 1998), research process would necessitate interpersonal engagement with participants such as interviews.

3. In his analysis of how epistemology and theory inform research designs, Crotty (1998) defined theory as a philosophical perspective that informs research methodology and thinking about a particular topic.

4. Theories make some suppositions, hypotheses, predictions, descriptions, or theories can aspire toward a better world as is often the case with critical theory, which attempts to identify social inequalities and work toward ameliorating those problems (Adams & Searle, 1986; Bronner & Kellner, 1989). Critical approaches are primarily considered critical theories. Phil Francis Carspecken's (2014/1996) use of critical theory in methodology attempted to consider a critical epistemology, a way of knowing that centered the uncovering of inequality and paths toward social action. Critical theory, often rooted in Marxist theory, which was historically more interested in class conflicts than in theorizing racial inequality, has an interest in the idea of liberation across social categories such as race, class, or gender (Adams & Searle, 1986; Bronner & Kellner, 1989; Crotty, 1998; Habermas, 1984, 1987). There are many authors writing at the same time as those who were deemed to be "critical theorists," many of whom centered racial inequality and racial justice in their theories (e.g., Cooper, 1988/1892; Du Bois, 1903).

5. There are clearly many others who deserve credit for advancing critical theoretical perspectives that went far beyond a class-based analysis such as Fanon (2008/1952), Césaire (2001/1955), Wynter (1995) or critical race theorists (Bell,

1992/2018; McCoy & Rodericks, 2015). W. E. B. Du Bois's (1903) analysis of racial oppression perpetrated on Black people in the United States was a critical theory that emphasized a racial justice frame (Morris, 2015). Anna Julia Cooper, authoring her *A Voice from the South* (1892) a decade earlier than Du Bois's book, centered race and gender analysis.

6. Jürgen Habermas (1984, 1987), a German philosopher and the leader of the second generation of the Frankfurt School, aimed his project of critical theory toward emancipation. Habermas initiated a project of deconstruction of theory, and then, through dialogue and dialectical reasoning (through the process of considering the thesis and antithesis, the idea that something is "not that, not that" in order to find what it is (see Hegel, 1807/1952/1977), a process of reconstruction of theory that was aimed at emancipation. Habermas adapted the idea of the whole-and-the-parts that initiated by Hegel (1807/1952/1977) and adapted by social theorists like Marx, Durkheim, and Weber. Habermas (1987) would argue that action is part of social critique. Habermas argued for a moral emphasis within critical theory or the idea that one should view critique of social systems as an ethically driven endeavor that leads to social change and emancipation.

7. The emphasis on dialogue as a way of knowing is also emphasized in Habermas's (1984, 1987) critical theory. Habermas (1984, 1987) argued for a communication-centered, dialogic approach where meaning, progress, and emancipation linked to communicative action instead of goal-oriented or instrumental action. Habermas maintained that through mutual understanding, people could be liberated from social oppression. Collectivity for Habermas stems from understanding one another through and position-taking through communicative acts. Language and communication (verbal and nonverbal) can help to disseminate, reinforce, and recreate cultural knowledge through mutual understanding.

8. Ladson-Billings's (1994) three-year ethnography with women who taught African American children is an example of how dialogue can be part of the research process (some data came from collaborative group meetings where dialogue was centered as a teaching practice) and part of the findings (data were presented in dialogic ways throughout the book). The book led to Ladson-Billings's culturally relevant pedagogy, which reshaped how teachers were trained, and how many students were able to learn in schooling (see also Ladson-Billings, 2001).

9. Other critical theorists, such as Paulo Freire (1970/2018) also described dialogue as connected to care, which he referred to as an act of love.

10. Some White scholars have pointed to the necessity of care in theory (Noddings, 2013), in analysis of data (Korth, 2003), and in relationships within research processes (Carspecken, 2014/1996).

11. Habermas (1984, 1987) also implied personal responsibility in the idea of shifting critical theory toward a model theory of social action, although it was admittedly lacking gender or racial analysis.

12. The idea of asserting Black women as agents of knowledge is crucially important for this analysis and it is absent from other critical theoretical approaches such as those of Habermas or Freire.

Chapter 2: From the Unchosen Me to the Chosen We

1. There were five researchers on the team conducting interviews, including me, three of whom are Black women, and one who is multiracial. The team has and continues to publish together on other parts of the data (Winkle-Wagner et al., 2018). See appendix C for a reading list of other publications from the project.

2. Immaculate Heart College closed in 1981 because of financial problems and became Immaculate Heart College Center, which also closed by 2000 (Wirpsa, 1997).

3. For more on the Immaculate Heart Community and its history as it relates to Immaculate Heart College, see: http://www.immaculateheartcommunity.org/rootshistory.html.

4. Eunice Kennedy was a sister to John F. Kennedy and Robert F. Kennedy, both civil rights leaders. She married Sargent Shriver, a US ambassador to France and a Democratic vice presidential candidate in 1972. The family was very liberal and major supporters of the civil rights movement and other progressive movements.

5. Pronounced "boosh-ee," this is a reference to the bourgeoisie or two-class structure in Marxist economic theory where there are the upper-class landowners who structure how the proletariat, or lower classes, will work.

6. For details on the full list of questions asked on birth certificates, see http://www.cdc.gov/nchs/data/dvs/birth11-03final-ACC.pdf.

7. For more information on the 2003 report on live birth certificate revisions, see http://www.cdc.gov/nchs/data/dvs/panelreport_acc.pdf.

8. The *Me* is the objectified part of self, according to Mead (1934). Another part of identity for Mead was the *I*—or pure subjectivity—is a reflective part of self that one can never fully grasp or objectify (e.g., a little voice in one's head, the part of self that surprises oneself). While the *I* can be a point of resistance in that it is the part of self where one reflects on the *Me* and realizes one is "not-that, not-this" (one is never fully explained by an objectified "identity"), the *I* is almost impossible to study because, as Mead (1934) would suggest, as soon as it is objectified, it is no longer an *I*—it becomes a *Me*.

9. One of Gutmann's (2009) hallmarks is the specification of how immigration functions within group identities, and she separates voluntary group identities as is the case with some immigrants who choose to migrate for a better life, or involuntary group identities as was the case with enslaved peoples who were forced to come to the United States. In so doing, she is able to identify the

very different ways in which collective identity might emerge, such that these identities can influence political participation.

10. In this way, the *Chosen We* is an ontological question.

11. Some groups did not initially have a way to speak of themselves as individuals, in their native language (Winkle-Wagner, 2006).

12. Georg Wilhelm Friedrich Hegel, living between 1770 and 1831, a German idealist continental philosopher considered to be one of the most formative philosophers whose thinking influenced subsequent philosophy for the better part of two centuries. One of the main parts of Hegel's (1807/1952/1977) theorizing was an attempt to explore the possibility of concepts that were universal (see also Knapp, 1985, 1986).

13. I want to clearly point out that Heidegger's ideology of anti-Semitism, his Nazi membership, and some of his philosophical diaries, in his so-called "Black notebooks" (Fried, 2014; Zielinski, 2016) are objectionable, deplorable, and undeniably wrongheaded. Heidegger's idea of being-with relates to some of the ways that the *We* emerged here.

14. Hegel (1807/1952/1977), in his description of the way that the individual connects with those around her, initiated a discussion about the accordion-like relationship between the whole-and-the-parts, interested in uncovering connections between the universal and the particular. Hegel maintained that the only way to possibly garner a glimpse (which he referred to as a "trace") into the universal was to study the particulars or parts of it (p. 16).

15. For Hegel (1807/1952/1977) the interaction between self and others is at the root of all awareness and understanding. This interaction between self and others, between the whole and its parts, is the epicenter of all things, including human struggles. Hegel initiated considerations of the unbreakable connection between the whole and its parts, arguing that the Truth is the whole. For Hegel, the *whole* is related to universal truth and universality more generally—almost like a universal "spirit" that connects all things.

16. Behaviorism, a theory of human and animal behavior that relied on conditioning as a central tool of understanding, predominated ways of approaching thought about the study of human development, particularly during the time Mead (1934) was writing. Behaviorism is often divorced from emotion and tries to present a value-neutral or so-called "objective" stance toward observation.

17. In Mead's (1934) theory of self, there are multiple *Me* parts of identities that are often related to the roles one accepts in a particular social context. There can be as many *Me* identities as there are roles to take. Then there is an *I* part of self that is the location of pure subjectivity, a reflective part of self that cannot be objectified and is therefore very difficult to empirically study.

18. Sheldon Stryker (1980) empirically studied the *Me* by relating it to the roles one takes, the commitment one has to particular roles, and the resulting salience of that role in a particular social setting.

19. Mead's (1934) generalized other came from his observations of children where he differentiated between "play" (mimicking behaviors) and "game" (where a child can anticipate reactions to her actions).

20. Mead (1934) goes so far as to say that the generalized other becomes a way that the "community exercises control over the conduct of its individual members" (p. 155). The "generalized other" serves a self-constraining function in this way, according to Mead.

21. Hegel's (1807/1952/1977) idea of recognition desires pinpoints humans' desires to be fully understood while also being unique and beyond understanding. That is, humans desire to feel understood but they still want to feel as if they could surprise others, as if there is a part of humanity that is beyond understanding. He considered the master-slave dialectic as a way to understand the interdependence of people and humans' desires to be recognized. Hegel maintained that the enslaved person must know both her own consciousness and desires and those of the "master." Yet the master only knows his own consciousness and desires and therefore can never be fully recognized. Hegel (1807/1952/1977) argued that the sense of being fully recognized would mean that humans are so interconnected that if one human is in bondage, the "lord" or person who holds the other person in bondage will eventually be limited. Importantly, by oppressing others, one would oppress oneself.

22. As Stryker (2008) put it, "Mead's concept of 'generalized other' erases distinctions among social structures within societies, despite variations consequential for social interaction. That is, collectivities are all (at least potentially) generalized others, all serving equivalently as representatives of society in an internal *I-Me* dialogue that is the self" (p. 15).

23. The *Chosen We*, as I am specifying it here, has some similarities to Habermas's (1984/1987) idea of a limit case (the inherent goal even if never fully reached) of the ideal speech situation where people are in egalitarian, mutually respectful relationships with the motivation toward understanding one another. The *Chosen We* must include choice, agency, and an equal opportunity to voluntarily recognize and accept this form of identity for it to exist.

24. The *Chosen We* connects with Gutmann's (2009) notion of a "voluntary identity," giving specificity to one type of voluntary identity where an individual can simultaneously assert a sense of individuality while also connecting deeply with a collective identity. The *Chosen We* must be voluntary in that one must feel a sense of agency to *choose* the collective identity. One must be able to choose *not* to assert the collective identity at the same time that she is choosing it.

25. *Chosen We* communities may come into being out of a process of reflection and consciousness raising, similar to the Freirean notion of conscientization (Freire, 1970/2018).

26. An individual's various *Me* identities may relate to a single generalized other or multiple generalized other(s) (or the accumulation of possible actions in that location). Mead (1934) maintained a singular generalized other, whereby an individual takes into oneself the norms and possible actions of a collective social

group. But Mead did not account for the pluralism that exists in contemporary times (Winkle-Wagner, 2009a). I argue that as an individual becomes embedded in multiple social groups at one time, that person may encounter multiple generalized others.

27. There could be multiple generalized other(s) embedded in one's *Chosen We* communities.

28. The *We* may be influenced by generalized other(s), or the aggregate of attitudes of a group, but it is not initiated from generalized others per se. Where I part ways with the generalized other(s) is that the generalized other is likely more representative of the majority, while the *Chosen We* could be the location of chosen communal identities of those who are *not* majoritized or made to be dominant in a particular social context.

Part II: From Individualism to Transformative Community at Predominantly White Institutions

1. For instance, in Louisiana when the state funding for higher education was cut, the PWI experienced a massive 25 percent cut while the HBCUs in the same state were cut by 35–46 percent (there were three institutions that experienced difference cuts) (Boland & Gasman, 2014).

2. For instance, 37.8 percent of all Black students are enrolled at public, four-year institutions. *Chronicle* analysis of US Department of Education data for 2018–2019, available online at https://www.chronicle.com/specialreport/The-Almanac-of-Higher/214.

Chapter 3: Creating an Oasis Out of Isolation

1. White supremacist, heteronormative patriarchy is a way to describe the social structural inequalities that work to privilege Whiteness, heterosexuality, and maleness over all other identities or ways of being (e.g., Blackness, homosexuality or queerness, female, etc.).

2. To read more about the federal program of McNair, see https://www2.ed.gov/programs/triomcnair/index.html.

3. *Leviathan* is a book written by Thomas Hobbes in his social contract theory, a moral and political philosophy. For a summary of the book, see https://plato.stanford.edu/entries/hobbes-moral/.

Chapter 4: Unapologetically Embracing Blackness

1. See the following website for a longer history of Black Thursday including interviews with some of the 94 African American students who were expelled and forcibly removed from campus: http://www.blackthursday.uwosh.edu/index.html

2. Reverend Floyd Flake was a senior pastor at the Great Allen African Methodist Episcopal Cathedral in Queens, New York. He was a representative to the US House of Representatives for 10 years from 1987 to 1997 (Flake & Williams, 2000). In 1990, Flake and his wife were charged with fraud and embezzlement of church money, although they were later acquitted (Farber, 1991). For more on the Greater Allen A.M.E. Cathedral, see: http://allencathedral.org/about-us/allen-ame-floyd-flake/.

3. Mackenzie's family helped to finish the book for Angus because he died before she could finish the final production.

4. See this website for more information: http://apply.emory.edu/discover/fastfacts.php

5. Management Leadership for Tomorrow, https://mlt.org.

6. For more information on NPHC sororities and fraternities, see: http://www.nphchq.org/mission/.

7. Unless alumnae mention the sorority name specifically, I chose to leave the groups unnamed so as not to elevate one organization over another and to protect anonymity of the participants.

8. There were only a handful of African American or Black students at this institution and so I chose a pseudonym for the institution to protect Diane's confidentiality.

9. For more information on the Nation of Islam, see: https://www.noi.org/.

10. For the list of hate groups from the Southern Poverty Law Center and for explanation of the rationale for listing the Nation of Islam as a hate group, see: https://www.splcenter.org/fighting-hate/extremist-files/group/nation-islam.

11. Nelson Mandela was one of the major leaders of the African National Congress (ANC) who pushed against apartheid in South Africa; the ANC was eventually banned in the country in an attempt to continue the apartheid rule (Benson, 1994). For more information on Mandela, see: https://www.nelson mandela.org/content/page/biography.

12. The enforcement of Jim Crow laws were part of the reason for the massive Black migration from the South to the North from 1915 to 1970, where millions of Black Americans moved out of Southern states to attempt to have better lives free from racial terror and legal segregation (Wilkerson, 2010). Some scholars have argued that there are ways in which the Jim Crow era never ceased because racial segregation and terror has continued in the form of mass incarceration or killing of Black people by the police (Alexander, 2012).

13. The NAACP is an organization that works for "political, educational, social, and economic equality of rights of all persons and to eliminate race-based discrimination." See: https://www.naacp.org/about-us/.

Part III: From a Collective Legacy of Racial Uplift to Empowered Individual Identity at Historically Black Colleges and Universities

1. The Colored Conventions website (http://coloredconventions.org) offers pathbreaking digital resources of the minutes, transcripts, and documents from the 60 years of meetings among free Black people in the United States and is created by P. Gabrielle Forman, a scholar in African American studies and nineteenth-century literary history and culture.

2. Spelman College in Atlanta, Georgia, Clark Atlanta University (which was a merger of Clark College and Atlanta University), and Xavier University in New Orleans, Louisiana, all have racial uplift in their missions. See the following for more details: http://www.spelman.edu/about-us, http://www.cau.edu/gen_info/opar/opar_fb_purp.pdf, http://www.xula.edu/about-xavier/.

3. For current lists of HBCUs nationally, see https://nces.ed.gov/fastfacts/display.asp?id=667.

4. There were 25 separate references to those words.

Chapter 5: Blackness-as-Greatness

1. For more on the life and career of Nikki Giovanni, see http://www.nikki-giovanni.com/biography.

2. For more information on the history of Clark College and Atlanta University within the Atlanta University Consortium of HBCUs, see https://aucenter.edu/.

Chapter 6: HBCUs as Home and Family

1. For more on the life of Mary McLeod Bethune, see https://www.biography.com/people/mary-mcleod-bethune-9211266 and https://aaregistry.org/story/civil-rights-pioneer-mary-mcleod-bethune/.

2. For more information on Bethune-Cookman College/University, see https://www.cookman.edu/about_BCU/history/index.html.

3. To learn more about the Spelman College orientation program, see http://www.spelman.edu/admissions/admissions-events.

Chapter 7: From "Unity" to "Isolation

1. For more information, see https://www.collegefactual.com/colleges/georgia-state-university/student-life/diversity/#secOverall.

Chapter 8: In Sickness and Health on Campus

1. Typically, the idea of fugitive spaces is connected to Afropessimist theorizing. See Grant et al., 2020, for more details.

References

Abrams, J. A., Maxwell, M., Pope, M., & Belgrave, F. Z. (2014). Carrying the world with the grace of a lady and the grit of a warrior: Deepening our understanding of the "strong Black woman" schema. *Psychology of Women Quarterly, 38*(4), 503–518.

Adams, C. J. (2014). Posses keep students on academic track: Posse program puts social motivation to good use. *Education Week, 33*(34), 10–12.

Adams, H., & Searle, L. (Eds.) (1986). *Critical theory since 1965.* University Press of Florida.

Ahmad, A. S. (2020, July 6). A survival guide for Black, Indigenous, and other Women of Color in academe. *Chronicle of Higher Education.* https://chronicle.com/article/a-survival-guide-for-black-indigenous-and-other-women-of-color-in-academe

Akom, A. A. (2003). Reexamining resistance as oppositional behavior: The Nation of Islam and the creation of a Black achievement ideology. *Sociology of Education,* 305–325.

Albritton, T. J. (2012). Educating our own: The historical legacy of HBCUs and their relevance for educating a new generation of leaders. *Urban Review, 44*(3), 311–331.

Alexander, M. (2012). *The new Jim Crow: Mass incarceration in the age of colorblindness.* New Press.

Allen, T., & Heald, S. (2004) HIV/AIDS policy in Africa: What has worked in Uganda and what has failed in Botswana? *Journal of International Development, 16,* 1141–1154.

Allen, W. (1992). The color of success: African-American college student outcomes at predominantly White and historically Black public colleges and universities. *Harvard Educational Review, 62*(1), 26–45.

Allen, W. R., Epps, E. G., & Haniff, N. Z. (1991). College in Black and White: African American students in predominantly White and in Historically Black public universities. State University of New York Press.

Allen, W. R., Jewell, J. O., Griffin, K. A., & Wolf, D. S. S. (2007). Historically Black colleges and universities: Honoring the past, engaging the present, touching the future. *Journal of Negro Education*, 263–280.

Anderson, J. D. (1988). *The education of Blacks in the South, 1860–1935*. University of North Carolina Press.

Antonio, A. L. (2001). Diversity and the influence of friendship groups in college. *Review of Higher Education*, *25*(1), 63–89.

Anzaldúa, G. (1987). *Borderlands: la frontera* (vol. 3). Aunt Lute.

Appiah, K. A. (1992). *In my father's house*. Oxford University Press.

Arroyo, A. T., & Gasman, M. (2014). An HBCU-based educational approach for Black college student success: Toward a framework with implications for all institutions. *American Journal of Education*, *121*(1), 57–85.

Ashmore, R. D., Deaux, K., & McLaughlin-Volpe, T. (2004). An organizing framework for collective identity: Articulation and significance of multidimensionality. *Psychological Bulletin*, *130*(1), 80.

Atkinson, R. (1998). *The life story interview*. Sage.

Banks, J. A. (2014). Diversity, group identity, and citizenship education in a global age. *Journal of Education*, *194*(3), 1–12.

Beauboeuf-Lafontant, T. (2007). You have to show strength: An exploration of gender, race, and depression. *Gender & Society*, *21*(1), 28–51.

Bell, D. (1992/2018). *Faces at the bottom of the well: The permanence of racism*. Hachette UK.

Bell, D. A., Jr. (1980). *Brown v. Board of Education* and the interest-convergence dilemma. *Harvard Law Review*, 518–533.

Bell, R. H. (2002). Understanding African philosophy: A cross-cultural approach to classical and contemporary issues. Routledge.

Benson, M. (1994). *Nelson Mandela: The man and the movement*. Penguin.

Benton, A. V. (2020). *I am doing more than coding: A qualitative study of Black women HBCU undergraduates' persistence in computing*. Michigan State University.

Bettez, S. C., & Suggs, V. L. (2012). Centering the educational and social significance of HBCUs: A focus on the educational journeys and thoughts of African American scholars. *Urban Review*, *44*(3), 303–310.

Billingsley, A., & Caldwell, C. H. (1991). The church, the family, and the school in the African American community. *Journal of Negro Education*, *60*(3), 427–440.

Blackmon, Douglas. A. (2009). *Slavery by another name: The re-enslavement of black Americans from the Civil War to World War II*. Anchor.

Blackshear, T., & Hollis, L. P. (2021). Despite the place, can't escape gender and race: Black women's faculty experiences at PWIs and HBCUs. *Taboo: The Journal of Culture and Education*, *20*(1), 3.

Bloom, J., & Martin, W. E. (2013). *Black against empire: The history and politics of the Black Panther Party*. University of California Press.

Boland, W., & Gasman, M. (2014). *America's public HBCUs: A four state comparison of institutional capacity and state funding priorities*. Report of the Center for MSIs at the University of Pennsylvania. https://cmsi.gse.upenn.edu/sites/default/files/four_state_comparison.pdf

Boncana, M., McKayle, C. A., Engerman, K., & Askew, K. (2021). "What is going on here"? Exploring why HBCU presidents are successful in producing STEM graduates. *Journal of Negro Education*, *90*(3), 277–287.

Bond, P. (2014). *Elite transition: From apartheid to neoliberalism in South Africa*. Pluto Press.

Bonilla-Silva, E. (2006). *Racism without racists: Color-blind racism and the persistence of racial inequality in the United States*. Rowman & Littlefield.

Bonner, F. B. (2001). Addressing gender issues in the historically Black college and university community: A challenge and call to action. *Journal of Negro Education*, 176–191.

Boren, M. E. (2013). *Student resistance: A history of the unruly subject*. Routledge.

Borr, T. G. (2019). The strategic pursuit of Black homophily on a predominantly White campus. *Journal of Higher Education*, *90*(2), 322–346.

Bowean, Lolly. (2018, October 11). Michelle Obama's goal: Girls' educations. *Chicago Tribune*. https://digitaledition.chicagotribune.com/tribune/article_popover.aspx?guid=a7b369c3-a3e3-4221-b680-84ef1799566f

Brazzell, J. C. (1992). Bricks without straw: Missionary-sponsored Black higher education in the post-emancipation era. *Journal of Higher Education*, *63*(1), 26–49.

Brewer, M. B., & Gardner, W. (1996). Who this "We"? Levels of collective identity and self-representations. *Journal of Personality and Social Psychology*, *71*(1), 83.

Brewer, R. M. (2016). Theorizing race, class, and gender: The new scholarship of Black feminist intellectuals and Black women's labor. In *Race, gender and class* (pp. 58–64). Routledge.

Brodkin, K. (1998). *How Jews became white folks and what that says about race in America*. Rutgers University Press.

Bronner, E., & Kellner, M. (1989). *Critical theory and society: A reader*. Routledge.

Brooms, D. R. (2019). Not in this alone: Black men's bonding, learning, and sense of belonging in Black male initiative programs. *Urban Review*, 1–20.

Brown v. Board of Education of Topeka, 347 US 483 (1954).

Brown, E. B. (1989). African American women's quilting: A framework for conceptualizing and teaching African American women's history. *Signs*, *14*(4), 921–929.

Brown, T. B. (2013). No more 'Negro' for Census Bureau forms and surveys. *NPR*. https://www.npr.org/sections/thetwo-way/2013/02/25/172885551/no-more-negro-for-census-bureau-forms-and-surveys

Brown, T. L., Parks, G. S., & Phillips, C. M. (Eds.). (2012). *African American fraternities and sororities: The legacy and the vision.* University Press of Kentucky.

Cannella, G. S., Pérez, M. S., & Pasque, P. A. (2016). The 'new materialisms': A thorn in the flesh of critical qualitative inquiry? In *Critical qualitative inquiry* (pp. 93–112). Routledge.

Carspecken, P. F. (2014/1996). *Critical ethnography in educational research: A theoretical and practical guide.* Routledge.

Caspary, A. M. (2003). *Witness to integrity: The crisis of the Immaculate Heart Community of California.* Liturgical Press.

Castillo-Montoya, M., & Torres-Guzmán, M. (2012). Thriving in our identity and in the academy: Latina epistemology as a core resource. *Harvard Educational Review, 82*(4), 540–558.

Césaire, A. (2001/1955). *Discourse on colonialism.* New York University Press.

Clabaugh, G. K. (2004). The educational legacy of Ronald Reagan. *Educational Horizons, 82*(4), 256–259.

Chen, P. D., Ingram, T. N., & Davis, L. K. (2014). Bridging student engagement and satisfaction: A comparison between historically Black colleges and universities and predominantly White institutions. *Journal of Negro Education, 83*(4), 565–579.

Cho, S., Crenshaw, K. W., & McCall, L. (2013). Toward a field of intersectionality studies: Theory, applications, and praxis. *Signs: Journal of Women in Culture and Society, 38*(4), 785–810.

Clark-Pujara, C. (2016). *Dark work: The business of slavery in Rhode Island* (vol. 12). New York University Press.

Closson, R. B., & Henry, W. J. (2008). The social adjustment of undergraduate White students in the minority on an historically Black college campus. *Journal of College Student Development, 49*(6), 517–534.

Cohen, J. S., & Miller, L. J. (2009, December 1). Interpersonal mindfulness training for well-being: A pilot study with psychology graduate students. *Teachers College Record.*

Cole, D. (2007). Do interracial interactions matter? An examination of student-faculty contact and intellectual self-concept. *Journal of Higher Education, 78*(3), 249–281.

Cole, D., & Griffin, K. A. (2013). Advancing the study of student-faculty interaction: A focus on diverse students and faculty. In *Higher education: Handbook of theory and research* (pp. 561–611). Springer, Dordrecht.

Collier-Thomas, B., & Franklin, V. P. (2000). *My soul is a witness: A chronology of the civil rights era, 1954–1965.* Macmillan.

Collier-Thomas, B., & Franklin, V. P. (Eds.). (2001). *Sisters in the struggle: African American women in the civil rights-Black Power movement.* New York University Press.

Collins, P. H. (1986). Learning from the outsider within: The sociological significance of Black feminist thought. *Social Problems, 33*(6), s14–s32.

Collins, P. H. (1989). The social construction of Black feminist thought. *Signs: Journal of Women in Culture and Society, 14*(4), 745–773.

Collins, P. H. (1998). Intersections of race, class, gender, and nation: Some implications for Black family studies. *Journal of Comparative Family Studies*, 27–36.

Collins, P. H. (2002/2009). *Black feminist thought: Knowledge, consciousness, and the politics of Empowerment*. Routledge.

Commodore, F., Baker, D. J., & Arroyo, A. T. (2018). *Black women college students: A guide to student success in higher education*. Routledge.

Conrad, C., & Gasman, M. (2015). *Educating a diverse nation*. Harvard University Press.

Cooper, A. J. (1988/1892). *A Voice from the South*. Oxford University Press.

Cooper, B. C. (2017). *Beyond respectability: The intellectual thought of race women*. University of Illinois Press.

Cottom, T. M. (2018). *Thick: And other essays*. New Press.

Coy, P. G. (Ed.). (1988). *A revolution of the heart: Essays on the Catholic worker*. Temple University Press.

Crenshaw, K. (1991). Mapping the margins: Intersectionality, identity politics, and violence against women of color. *Stanford Law Review*, 1241–1299.

Crotty, M. (1998). *The foundations of social research: Meaning and perspective in the research process*. Sage.

Dace, K. L. (Ed.). (2012). *Unlikely allies in the academy: Women of color and White women in conversation*. Routledge.

Daché, A. (2022). Bus-riding from barrio to college: A qualitative Geographic Information Systems (GIS) analysis. *Journal of Higher Education, 93*(1), 1–30.

Daché, A., Sun, J., & Krause, C. (2022). A Post-Ferguson spatial analysis of Black resistant and White fortressing geographies. *Urban Education*, 00420859221086511.

Daché-Gerbino, A. (2018). College desert and oasis: A critical geographic analysis of local college access. *Journal of Diversity in Higher Education, 11*(2), 97.

Dancy, T. E. E., & Brown, M. C. (2008). Unintended consequences: African American male educational attainment and collegiate perceptions after *Brown v. Board of Education*. *American Behavioral Scientist, 51*(7), 984–1003

Dancy, T. E., Edwards, K. T., & Earl Davis, J. (2018). Historically White universities and plantation politics: Anti-Blackness and higher education in the Black Lives Matter era. *Urban Education, 53*(2), 176–195.

Dávila, B. A. (2012). Book review: *The unchosen me: Race, gender, and identity among Black women in college*. *International Journal of Qualitative Studies in Education, 25*(8),1107–1112.

Davis, A. (1971). Reflections on the Black woman's role in the community of slaves. *Black Scholar, 3*, 4–15.

Davis, A. (1983). The approaching obsolescence of housework: A working-class perspective. *Women, Race, and Class*, 222–244.

Davis, A. (2016). *Freedom is a constant struggle: Ferguson, Palestine, and the foundations of a movement.* Haymarket Books.

Davis, M., Dias-Bowie, Y., Greenberg, K., Klukken, G., Pollio, H. R., Thomas, S. P., & Thompson, C. L. (2004). "A fly in the buttermilk": Descriptions of university life by successful Black undergraduate students at a predominately White southeastern university. *Journal of Higher Education, 75*(4), 420–445.

Dawes, R. M., Van De Kragt, A. J., & Orbell, J. M. (1988). Not me or thee but we: The importance of group identity in eliciting cooperation in dilemma situations: Experimental manipulations. *Acta Psychologica, 68*(1–3), 83–97.

Dickinson, G. H. (2005). Pledged to remember: Africa in the life and lore of Black Greek-letter organizations. In T. L. Brown, G. Parks, & C. M. Phillips (Eds.), *African American fraternities and sororities: The legacy and the vision* (pp. 11–35). University Press of Kentucky.

Dill, Bonnie. (1979). The dialectics of Black womanhood. *Signs: Journal of Women in Culture and Society, 3*: 543–545.

Dillard, C. B. (2000). The substance of things hoped for, the evidence of things not seen: Examining an endarkened feminist epistemology in educational research and leadership. *International Journal of Qualitative Studies in Education, 13*(6), 661–681.

Domina, T., Penner, A., & Penner, E. (2017). Categorical inequality: Schools as sorting machines. *Annual Review of Sociology, 43*, 311–330.

Donovan, R. A., & West, L. M. (2015). Stress and mental health: Moderating role of the strong Black woman stereotype. *Journal of Black Psychology, 41*(4), 384–396.

Dortch, D. (2016). The strength from within: A phenomenological study examining the academic self-efficacy of African American women in doctoral studies. *Journal of Negro Education, 85*(3), 350–364.

Dovidio, J. F., & Gaertner, S. L. (2000). Aversive racism and selection decisions: 1989 and 1999. *Psychological Science, 11*(4), 315–319.

Dovidio, J. F., Gaertner, S. L., & Kawakami, K. (2003). Intergroup contact: The past, present, and the future. *Group Processes & Intergroup Relations, 6*(1), 5–21.

Dovidio, J. F., Gaertner, S. L., & Saguy, T. (2008). Another view of "we": Majority and minority group perspectives on a common ingroup identity. *European Review of Social Psychology, 18*(1), 296–330.

Dovidio, J. F., Gaertner, S. L., Ufkes, E. G., Saguy, T., & Pearson, A. R. (2016). Included but invisible? Subtle bias, common identity, and the darker side of "we." *Social Issues and Policy Review, 10*(1), 6–46.

Du Bois, W. E. B. (1903). *Souls of black folk.* Routledge.

Dumas, M. J. (2016). Against the dark: Antiblackness in education policy and discourse. *Theory into Practice, 55*(1), 11–19.

Duran, A. (2019). Queer and of color: A systematic literature review on queer students of color in higher education scholarship. *Journal of Diversity in Higher Education, 12*(4), 390.

Duran, A., Garcia, C. E., & Reyes, H. L. (2022). Sorority and fraternity life professionals' perspectives on challenges faced by culturally based sororities and fraternities. *Oracle: The Research Journal of the Association of Fraternity/Sorority Advisors, 17*(2), 35–50.

Durkheim, E. (1893/1984). *The division of labor in society* (W. D. Halls, Trans.). Free Press.

Durkheim, E. (1895/1964). *The rules of the sociological method* (S. A. Solovay & J. H. Mueller, Trans., G. E. G. Catlin, Ed.). Free Press.

Durkheim, E. (1897/1951). *Suicide: A study in sociology* (J. A. Spaulding & G. Simpson, Trans.). Free Press.

Dyson, M. E. (1996). *Making Malcolm: The myth and meaning of Malcolm X.* Oxford University Press on Demand.

Eltoukhi, H. M., Modi, M. N., Weston, M., Armstrong, A. Y., & Stewart, E. A. (2014). The health disparities of uterine fibroid tumors for African American women: A public health issue. *American Journal of Obstetrics and Gynecology, 210*(3), 194–199.

Espino, M. M., Muñoz, S. M., & Marquez Kiyama, J. (2010). Transitioning from doctoral study to the academy: Theorizing trenzas of identity for Latina sister scholars. *Qualitative Inquiry, 16*(10), 804–818.

Evans, S. Y. (2008). *Black women in the ivory tower, 1850–1954: An intellectual history.* University Press of Florida.

Evans, N. J., & Reason, R. D. (2001). Guiding principles: A review and analysis of student affairs philosophical statements. *Journal of College Student Development, 42*(4), 359.

Fairchild, H. H. (1995). Unmasking pseudoscience: Comments on "How Skewed Is the Bell Curve?" *Journal of Black Psychology, 21*(3), 297–299.

Fanon, F. (2008). *Black skin, White masks.* Grove Press.

Farber, M. A. (1991, April 5). Demise of Flake case: Choice of tactic at issue. *New York Times.* http://www.nytimes.com/1991/04/05/nyregion/demise-of-flake-case-choice-of-tactic-at-issue.html

Feagin, J. R., & Barnett, B. M. (2004). Success and failure: How systemic racism trumped the *Brown v. Board of Education* decision. *University of Illinois Law Review,* 1099.

Feagin, J. R., & Sikes, M. P. (1994). *Living with racism: The Black middle-class experience.* Beacon Press.

Feagin, J. R., Vera, H., & Imani, N. (2014/1996). *The agony of education: Black students at a White university* (2nd ed.). Routledge.

Feagin, J. R., Vera, H., & Imani, N. (2014, 2nd Ed.). *The agony of education: Black students at a White university.* Routledge.

Few, A. L. (2007). Integrating Black consciousness and critical race feminism into family studies research. *Journal of Family Issues, 28*(4), 452–473.

Few, A. L., Stephens, D. P., & Rouse-Arnett, M. (2003). Sister-to-sister talk: Transcending boundaries and challenges in qualitative research with Black women. *Family Relations, 52*(3), 205–215.

Flake, F. H., & Williams, D. M. (2000). *The way of the bootstrapper: Nine action steps for achieving your dreams.* Harper Collins.

Fleming, J. (1978). Fear of success, achievement-related motives and behavior in Black college women 1. *Journal of Personality, 46*(4), 694–716.

Fleming, J. (1985). *Blacks in college: A comparative study of students' success in Black and in White institutions.* Jossey-Bass.

Flores, S. M., & Park, T. J. (2013). Race, ethnicity, and college success: Examining the continued significance of the minority-serving institution. *Educational Researcher, 42*(3), 115–128.

Fordham, S. (1993). "Those loud Black girls": (Black) women, silence, and gender "passing" in the academy. *Anthropology & Education Quarterly, 24*(1), 3–32.

Fordham, S. (1996). *Blacked out: Dilemmas of race, identity, and success at Capital High.* University of Chicago Press.

Fordham, S. (2008). Beyond capital high: On dual citizenship and the strange career of "acting White." *Anthropology & Education Quarterly, 39*(3), 227–246.

Frankenberg, R. (1993). *The social construction of Whiteness: White women, race matters.* Routledge.

Franklin, J. H. (1969). *From slavery to freedom: A history of Negro Americans* (3rd ed.). Random House.

Franklin, J. H. (1994). *Reconstruction after the Civil War.* University of Chicago Press.

Franklin, J. H. (2002). *The militant South, 1800–1861.* University of Illinois Press.

Franklin, J. H. (2005). *Mirror to America: The autobiography of John Hope Franklin* (vol. 1). Macmillan.

Freeman, K. (2002). Black colleges and college choice: Characteristics of students who choose HBCUs. *Review of Higher Education, 25*(3), 349–358.

Fredrickson, George M. (2015). *Racism: A short history.* Princeton University Press.

Freire, P. (1970/2018). *Pedagogy of the oppressed.* Bloomsbury.

Fried, G. (2014, November–December). What Heidegger was hiding: Unearthing the philosopher's anti-Semitism. *Foreign Affairs.* https://www.foreignaffairs.com/reviews/review-essay/what-heidegger-was-hiding

Fries-Britt, S. (1998). Moving beyond Black achiever isolation: Experiences of gifted Black collegians. *Journal of Higher Education, 69*(5), 556–576.

Fries-Britt, S., & Kelly, B. T. (2005). Retaining each other: Narratives of two African American women in the academy. *Urban Review, 37*(3), 221–242.

Fries-Britt, S. L., & Turner, B. (2001). Facing stereotypes: A case study of Black students on a White campus. *Journal of College Student Development*, *42*(5), 420–429.

Gardner, S. K. (2008). Fitting the mold of graduate school: A qualitative study of socialization in doctoral education. *Innovative Higher Education*, *33*(2), 125–138.

Gardner, S. K., & Holley, K. A. (2011). "Those invisible barriers are real": The progression of first-generation students through doctoral education. *Equity & Excellence in Education*, *44*(1), 77–92.

Gasman, M. (2007a). *Envisioning black colleges: A history of the United Negro College Fund*. Johns Hopkins University Press.

Gasman, M. (2007b). Swept under the rug? A historiography of gender and Black colleges. *American Educational Research Journal*, *44*(4), 760–805.

Gasman, M. (2011). Passive activism: African American fraternities and sororities and the push for civil rights. In M.W. Hughey, & G. S. Park (Eds.), *Black Greek-letter organizations* (pp. 27–46). University Press of Mississippi.

Gasman, M., & Arroyo, A. (2019). Black college student success: A landscape. In *Examining student retention and engagement strategies at historically Black colleges and universities* (pp. 1–15). IGI Global.

Gasman, M., Nguyen, T. H., & Conrad, C. F. (2015). Lives intertwined: A primer on the history and emergence of minority-serving institutions. *Journal of Diversity in Higher Education*, *8*(2), 120.

Geronimus, A. T., Hicken, M. T., Pearson, J. A., Seashols, S. J., Brown, K. L., & Cruz, T. D. (2010). Do US Black women experience stress-related accelerated biological aging? *Human Nature*, *21*(1), 19–38.

Giddings, P. J. (1996/1984). *From when and where I enter: The impact of Black women on race and sex in America*. Harper Collins Perennial.

Giddings, P. J. (2009). *In search of sisterhood*. HarperCollins.

Giddings, P. J. (2014). *When and where I enter*. HarperCollins.

Goldberg, R. A. (2008). *Enemies within: The culture of conspiracy in modern America*. Yale University Press.

Golde, C. M. (2005). The role of the department and discipline in doctoral student attrition: Lessons from four departments. *Journal of Higher Education*, *76*(6), 669–700.

Goldstein, E. L. (2006). *The price of Whiteness: Jews, race, and American identity*. Princeton University Press.

Good, C., Aronson, J., & Harder, J. A. (2008). Problems in the pipeline: Stereotype threat and women's achievement in high-level math courses. *Journal of Applied Developmental Psychology*, *29*(1), 17–28.

Goode-Cross, D. T., & Grim, K. A. (2016). "An unspoken level of comfort": Black therapists' experiences working with Black clients. *Journal of Black Psychology*, *42*(1), 29–53.

Goosby, B. J., & Heidbrink, C. (2013). The transgenerational consequences of discrimination on African American health outcomes. *Sociology Compass*, *7*(8), 630–643.

Goosby, B. J., Malone, S., Richardson, E. A., Cheadle, J. E., & Williams, D. T. (2015). Perceived discrimination and markers of cardiovascular risk among low-income African American youth. *American Journal of Human Biology*, *27*(4), 546–552.

Goosby, B. J., & Walsemann, K. M. (2012). School racial composition and race/ethnic differences in early adulthood health. *Health & Place*, *18*(2), 296–304.

Graham, L. O. (2000). *Our kind of people: Inside America's Black upper class*. Harper Collins.

Grant, C. A., Woodson, A. N., & Dumas, M. J. (Eds.). (2020). *The future is Black: Afropessimism, fugitivity, and radical hope in education*. Routledge.

Grant-Vallone, E. J., & Ensher, E. A. (2000). Effects of peer mentoring on types of mentor support, program satisfaction and graduate student stress. *Journal of College Student Development*, *41*(6), 637–642.

Graves, J. L., Jr., & Graves, J. L. (2001). *The emperor's new clothes: Biological theories of race at the millennium*. Rutgers University Press.

Graves, J. L., Jr., & Johnson, A. (1995). The pseudoscience of psychometry and the bell curve. *Journal of Negro Education*, *64*(3), 277–294.

Gregory, S. T. (2001). Black faculty women in the academy: History, status, and future. *Journal of Negro Education*, *70*(3), 124–138.

Greyerbiehl, L., & Mitchell, D., Jr. (2014). An intersectional social capital analysis of the influence of historically Black sororities on African American women's college experiences at a predominantly White institution. *Journal of Diversity in Higher Education*, *7*(4), 282.

Griffin, K. A. (2012a). Black professors managing mentorship: Implications of applying social exchange frameworks to our understanding of the influence of student interaction on scholarly productivity. *Teachers College Record*, *114*(5), 1–37.

Griffin, K. A. (2012b). Learning to mentor: A mixed methods study of the nature and influence of Black professors' socialization into their roles as mentors. *Journal of the Professoriate*, *6*(2), 27–58.

Griffin, K. A. (2013). Voices of the "Othermothers": Reconsidering Black professors' relationships with Black students as a form of social exchange. *Journal of Negro Education*, *82*(2), 169–183.

Griffin, K. A., Bennett, J. C., & Harris, J. (2013). Marginalizing merit? Gender differences in Black faculty D/discourses on tenure, advancement, and professional success. *Review of Higher Education*, *36*(4), 489–512.

Griffin, K., Del Pilar, W., McIntosh, K., & Griffin, A. (2012). "Oh, of course I'm going to go to college": Understanding how habitus shapes the college choice process of Black immigrant students. *Journal of Diversity in Higher Education*, *5*(2), 96.

Griffin, K. A., & Reddick, R. J. (2011). Surveillance and sacrifice: Gender differences in the mentoring patterns of Black professors at predominantly White research universities. *American Educational Research Journal, 48*(5), 1032–1057.

Griffin, R. A. (2012). I am an angry Black woman: Black feminist autoethnography, voice, and resistance. *Women's Studies in Communication, 35*(2), 138–157.

Guiffrida, D. A. (2003). African American student organization as agents of social integration. *Journal of College Student Development, 44*(3), 304–319. DOI:10.1353/csd.2003.0024

Gullatt, Y., & Jan, W. (2003). How do pre-collegiate academic outreach programs impact college-going among underrepresented students. Pathways to College Network Clearinghouse.

Gutmann, A. (2009). *Identity in democracy.* Princeton University Press.

Guy-Sheftall, B. (1982). Black women and higher education: Spelman and Bennett Colleges revisited. *Journal of Negro Education, 51*(3), 278–287.

Guy-Sheftall, B. (Ed.). (1995). *Words of fire: An anthology of African American feminist thought.* New Press.

Habermas, J. (1984). *The theory of communicative action, volume one: Reason and the rationalization of society.* Beacon Press.

Habermas, J. (1987). *The theory of communicative action, volume two: Lifeworld and System: A Critique of Functionalist Reason.* Beacon Press.

Hall, B., & Closson, R. B. (2005). When the majority is the minority: White graduate students' social adjustment at a historically Black university. *Journal of College Student Development, 46*(1), 28–42.

Hansberry, L. (1959). *A raisin in the sun: A drama in three acts.* Random House.

Hardy, P. M., Kaganda, E. J., & Aruguete, M. S. (2019). Below the surface: HBCU performance, social mobility, and college ranking. *Journal of Black Studies, 50*(5), 468–483.

Harper, S. R. (2015). Black male college achievers and resistant responses to racist stereotypes at predominantly White colleges and universities. *Harvard Educational Review, 85*(4), 646–674.

Harper, S. R., Carini, R. M., Bridges, B. K., & Hayek, J. C. (2004). Gender differences in student engagement among African American undergraduates at historically Black colleges and universities. *Journal of College Student Development, 45*(3), 271–284.

Harrington, E. F., Crowther, J. H., & Shipherd, J. C. (2010). Trauma, binge eating, and the "strong Black woman." *Journal of Consulting and Clinical Psychology, 78*(4), 469.

Harris, A. P. (2008). From color line to color chart: Racism and colorism in the new century. *Berkeley Journal of African American Law & Policy, 10*, 52.

Harris, K. (2019). *The truths we hold: An American journey.* Penguin Press.

Harris-Lacewell, M. (2001). No place to rest: African American political attitudes and the myth of Black women's strength. *Women & Politics, 23*(3), 1–33.

Harris-Perry, M. V. (2011). *Sister citizen: Shame, stereotypes, and Black women in America*. Yale University Press.

Hart, G. P. (2002). *Disabling globalization: Places of power in post-apartheid South Africa* (vol. 10). University of California Press.

Hartman, C. W. (2006). *There is no such thing as a natural disaster: Race, class, and Hurricane Katrina*. Taylor & Francis.

Heckman, J. J. (1995). Lessons from the bell curve. *Journal of Political Economy*, *103*(5), 1091–1120.

Heidegger, M. (1953/1927). *Being and time* (J. Stambaugh, Trans.). State University of New York Press.

Hegel, G. W. F. (1807/1952/1977). *Hegel's phenomenology of spirit* (A. V. Miller, Trans.). Oxford University Press.

Henrich, J., Heine, S. J., & Norenzayan, A. (2010). *Behavioral brain science*. DOI:10.1017/S0140525X0999152X.

Hernandez, E. (2010). Book review: *The unchosen me: Race, gender, and identity among Black women in college. Journal of College Student Development*, *51*(6), 732–734.

Hernández, E. (2016). Utilizing critical race theory to examine race/ethnicity, racism, and power in student development theory and research. *Journal of College Student Development*, *57*(2), 168–180.

Higginbotham, E. B. (1992). African American women's history and the meta-language of race. *Signs*, *17*(2), 251–274.

Hikido, A., & Murray, S. B. (2016). Whitened rainbows: How White college students protect Whiteness through diversity discourses. *Race Ethnicity and Education*, *19*(2), 389–411.

Hill, L. M. (2016). Hidden names and complex fate: Black students who integrated the University of Iowa. In L. M. Hill & M. D. Hill (Eds.), *Invisible Hawkeyes: African Americans at the University of Iowa during the long civil rights era* (pp. 1–16). University of Iowa Press.

Hill, M. D. (2016). An invisible legacy: Iowa and the conscience of democracy. In L. M. Hill & M. D. Hill (Eds.), *Invisible Hawkeyes: African Americans at the University of Iowa during the long civil rights era* (pp. 175–186). University of Iowa Press.

Hoffman, C. M. (1996). *Historically Black colleges and universities, 1976–1994*. US Department of Education, National Center for Education Statistics.

Hogg, M. A., Terry, D. J., & White, K. M. (1995). A tale of two theories: A critical comparison of identity theory with social identity theory. *Social Psychology Quarterly*, *58*(4), 255–269.

Honey, M. K. (2002). *Black workers remember: An oral history of segregation, unionism, and the freedom struggle*. University of California Press.

hooks, b. (1989). *Talking back: Thinking feminist, thinking black* (vol. 10). South End Press.

hooks, b. (1990). *Yearning: Race, gender, and cultural politics*. South End Press.

hooks, b. (2000). *Feminist theory: From margin to center*. Pluto Press.

hooks, b. (2003a). *Communion: The female search for love*. Perennial.

hooks, b. (2003b). *Teaching community: A pedagogy of hope* (vol. 36). Psychology Press.

hooks, b. (2014). *Ain't I a woman: Black women and feminism*. Routledge Press.

Howard-Hamilton, M. F. (2003). Theoretical frameworks for African American women. *New Directions for Student Services, 104*, 19–27.

Howard-Hamilton, M. F., Hinton, K. G., & Hughes, R. L. (2010). Critical borders: Student development theoretical perspectives applied to culture centers. In L. D. Patton, *Culture centers in higher education: Perspectives on identity, theory, & practice*. Stylus Publishing, LLC, 105–118.

Huddleston-Mattai, B. (1995). The Black female academician and the "superwoman syndrome." *Race, Gender & Class, 3*(1), 49–64.

Hughes, L. (2001). *The collected works of Langston Hughes: Essays on art, race, politics, and world affairs* (vol. 9). University of Missouri Press.

Hughey, M. W. (2008). Brotherhood or brothers in the "hood"? Debunking the "educated gang" thesis as Black fraternity and sorority slander. *Race Ethnicity and Education, 11*(4), 443–463. DOI:10.1080/13613320802479026

Hull, G. T., Scott, P. B., & Smith, B. (1982). *All the women are White, all the Blacks are men, but some of us are brave*. Feminist Press, City University of New York.

Hunter, M. L. (2002). "If you're light you're alright": Light skin color as social capital for women of color. *Gender & Society, 16*(2), 175–193.

Hurston, Z. N. (1984). *Dust tracks on a road: An autobiography*. University of Illinois Press.

Hypolite, L. I. (2020a). People, place, and connections: Black cultural center staff as facilitators of social capital. *Journal of Black Studies, 51*(1), 37–59.

Hypolite, L. I. (2020b). "We're drawn to this place": Black graduate students' engagement with a Black cultural center. *Journal of Diversity in Higher Education, 15*(1), 86–96.

Hyun, J., Quinn, B., Madon, T., & Lustig, S. (2007). Mental health need, awareness, and use of counseling services among international graduate students. *Journal of American College Health, 56*(2), 109–118.

Imbo, S. (1998). *An introduction to African philosophy*. Rowman & Littlefield.

Ingraham, C. (1994). The heterosexual imaginary: Feminist sociology and theories of gender. *Sociological Theory, 12*(2), 203–203.

Jean-Marie, G. (2006). Welcoming the unwelcomed: A social justice imperative of African American female leaders at historically Black colleges and universities. *Educational Foundations, 20*(1–2), 85–104.

Johnson, J. M. (2017). Social norms, gender ratio imbalance, perceptions of risk, and the sexual behaviors of African American women at historically Black colleges and universities. *Journal of African American Studies, 21*(2), 203–215.

Johnson, J. M., Scott, S., Phillips, T., & Rush, A. (2022). Ivy issues: An exploration of Black students' racialized interactions on Ivy League campuses. *Journal of Diversity in Higher Education.* Advance online publication. https://doi.org/10.1037/dhe0000406

Jones, C. (1949/1995). An end to the neglect of the problems of the Negro woman! In B. Guy-Sheftall (Ed.), *Words of fire: An anthology of African American feminist thought* (pp. 108–124). New Press.

Jones, C., & Shorter-Gooden, K. (2004). *Shifting: The double lives of Black women in America.* Perennial.

Jones, J. (1992). *Soldiers of light and love: Northern teachers and Georgia Blacks, 1865–1873.* University of Georgia Press.

Jones, J. (2009). *Labor of love, labor of sorrow: Black women, work, and the family from slavery to the present.* Basic Books.

Jordan, J. (1981). *Civil wars.* Beacon Press.

Jordan, J. (1985). *On call.* South End Press.

Jordan, J. (2015/1992). A new politics of sexuality. In *Transformations: Feminist pathways to global change* (p. 133–135). Routledge.

Joseph, G. (1988). Black feminist pedagogy and schooling in capitalist White America. In M. Cole (Ed.), *Bowles and Gintis revisited: Correspondence and contradiction in educational theory* (pp. 13–26). Falmer Press.

Katz, W. L. (Ed.). (1969). *History of schools for the colored population.* Arno Press.

Kelly, B., & Winkle-Wagner, R. (2017). Finding a voice in predominantly White institutions: A longitudinal study of Black women faculty members' journeys toward tenure. *Teachers College Record, 119*(6), 1–36. http://www.tcrecord.org/library/abstract.asp?contentid=21771

Kelly, B. T., Raines, A., Brown, R., French, A., & Stone, J. (2019). Critical validation: Black women's retention at predominantly White institutions. *Journal of College Student Retention: Research, Theory & Practice, 23*(2). https://doi.org/10.1177/1521025119841030

Kendi, Ibram X. (2016). *Stamped from the beginning: The definitive history of racist ideas in America.* Nation Books.

Kennedy, S., & Winkle-Wagner, R. (2014). Earning autonomy while maintaining family ties: Black women's reflections on the transition into college. *NASPA Journal about Women in Higher Education, 74*(2), 133–151.

Kerr, A. E. (2005). The paper bag principle: Of the myth and the motion of colorism. *Journal of American Folklore, 118*(469), 271–289.

Keyssar, A. (2009). *The right to vote: The contested history of democracy in the United States.* Basic Books.

Kim, M. M., & Conrad, C. F. (2006). The impact of historically Black colleges and universities on the academic success of African American students. *Research in Higher Education, 47*(4), 399–427.

Kimbrough, W. M. (1995). Self-assessment, participation, and value of leadership skills, activities, and experiences for Black students relative to their membership in historically Black fraternities and sororities. *Journal of Negro Education, 64*(1), 63–74.

Kimbrough, W. M. (2003). *Black Greek 101: The culture, customs, and challenges of Black fraternities and sororities.* Fairleigh Dickinson University Press.

King, D. K. (1988). Multiple jeopardy, multiple consciousness: The context of a Black feminist ideology. *Signs: Journal of Women in Culture and Society, 14*(1), 42–72.

Kluger, R. (2011). *Simple justice: The history of* Brown v. Board of Education *and Black America's struggle for equality.* Vintage.

Knapp, P. (1985). The question of Hegel's influence on Durkheim. *Sociological Inquiry, 55*(1), 1–15.

Knapp, P. (1986, September). Hegel's universal in Marx, Durkheim and Weber: The role of Hegelian ideas in the origin of sociology. *Sociological Forum, 1*(4), 586–609.

Knight, M. G., Norton, N. E., Bentley, C. C., & Dixon, I. R. (2004). The power of Black and Latina/o counterstories: Urban families and college-going processes. *Anthropology & Education Quarterly, 35*(1), 99–120.

Kochman, T. (1981). *Black and White styles in conflict.* University of Chicago Press.

Koonce, J. B. (2012). "Oh, those loud Black girls!" A phenomenological study of Black girls talking with an attitude. *Journal of Language and Literacy Education, 8*(2), 26–46.

Korth, B. (2003). A critical reconstruction of care-in-action. *Qualitative Report, 8*(3), 487–512.

Kugelmann, R. (2005). An encounter between psychology and religion: Humanistic psychology and the Immaculate Heart of Mary nuns. *Journal of the History of the Behavioral Sciences, 41*(4), 347–365.

Ladner, J. (1986). Black women face the twenty-first century: Major issues and problems. *Black Scholar, 17*(5), 12–19.

Ladner, J. A. (1989). Black women as do-ers: The social responsibility of Black women. *Sage, 6*(1), 87.

Ladson-Billings, G. (1994). *The dreamkeepers: Successful teachers of African American students.* Jossey-Bass.

Ladson-Billings, G. (2001). Crossing over to Canaan: The journey of new teachers in diverse classrooms. Jossey-Bass.

Ladson-Billings, G. (2009). *The dreamkeepers: Successful teachers of African American children.* John Wiley & Sons.

Lamb, C. M. (2005). *Housing segregation in suburban America since 1960: Presidential and judicial politics.* Cambridge University Press.

Lauritsen, J., & Thorstad, D. (1974). *The early homosexual rights movement (1864–1935).* Times Change Press.

Leath, S., Jones, M. K., & Butler-Barnes, S. (2022). An examination of ACEs, the internalization of the Superwoman Schema, and mental health outcomes among Black adult women. *Journal of Trauma & Dissociation, 23*(3), 307–323.

Leath, S., Quiles, T., Samuel, M., Chima, U., & Chavous, T. (2022). "Our community is so small": Considering intraracial peer networks in Black student adjustment and belonging at PWIs. *American Educational Research Journal*, *59*(4), 752–787.

Lee, P. (2011). The curious life of in loco parentis at American universities. *Higher Education in Review*, *8*(Spring), 65–90. https://ssrn.com/abstract=1967912

Lee, V. (1996). *Granny midwives and Black women writers: Double-dutched readings*. Psychology Press.

Lee-Johnson, J. L. (2021). Authentically leading: Supporting undergraduate Black women leaders at HBCUs to authentically be themselves. *About Campus*, *26*(3), 29–33.

Lefever, H. G. (2005). *Undaunted by the fight: Spelman College and the civil rights movement, 1957/1967*. Mercer University Press.

Lemley, C. K. (2017). *Practicing critical oral history: Connecting school and community*. Routledge.

Lengermann, P. M., & Niebrugge, G. (2006). *The women founders: Sociology and social theory 1830–1930, a text/reader*. Waveland Press.

Leonardo, Z. (2013). *Race frameworks: A multidimensional theory of racism and education*. Teachers College Press.

Lewis, A. E., & Diamond, J. B. (2015). *Despite the best intentions: How racial inequality thrives in good schools*. Oxford University Press.

Lewis, K. S., & McKissic, S. C. (2009). Drawing sustenance at the source: African American students' participation in the Black campus community as an act of resistance. *Journal of Black Studies*. DOI:10.1177/0021934709338043

Lieberson, S. (1980). *A piece of the pie: Blacks and white immigrants since 1880*. University of California Press.

Locks, A. M., Hurtado, S., Bowman, N. A., & Oseguera, L. (2008). Extending notions of campus climate and diversity to students' transition to college. *Review of Higher Education*, *31*(3), 257–285.

Loo, C. M., & Rollison, G. (1986). Alienation of ethnic minority students at a predominantly White university. *Journal of Higher Education*, *57*(1), 58–77.

Lorde, A. (1988). *A burst of light: Essays*. Firebrand Books.

Lorde, A. (2012). *Sister outsider: Essays and speeches*. Crossing Press.

Lovett, B. L. (2015). *America's historically black colleges and universities: A narrative history, 1837–2009*. Mercer University Press.

Luedke, C. L. (2017). Person first, student second: Staff and administrators of color supporting students of color authentically in higher education. *Journal of College Student Development*, *58*(1), 37–52.

Luedke, C. L. (2020). Lifting while we climb: Undergraduate students of color communal uplift and promotion of college-going within their communities. *Review of Higher Education*, *43*(4), 1167–1192.

Luker, K. (2009). *Salsa dancing into the social sciences*. Harvard University Press.

Lundy-Wagner, V., & Gasman, M. (2011). When gender issues are not just about women: Reconsidering male students at historically Black colleges and universities. *Teachers College Record, 113*(5), 934–968.

Mack, K. W. (2012). Civil rights history: The old and the new. *Harvard Law Review, 126*, 258.

Mackenzie, A. (1999). *Secrets: the CIA's war at home.* University of California Press.

MacLeod, J. (1987/2008). *Ain't no makin' it: Aspirations and attainment in a low-income neighborhood.* Routledge.

Mandela, N. (2011). *Conversations with myself.* Anchor Canada.

Martinez Alemán, A. M. (2010). College women's female friendships: A longitudinal view. *Journal of Higher Education, 81*(5), 553–582.

Marx, K., & Engels, F. (1848/1967). *The communist manifesto* (S. Moore, Trans.). Penguin.

May, V. M. (2012). *Anna Julia Cooper, visionary black feminist: A critical introduction.* Routledge.

McCabe, J. (2009). Racial and gender microaggressions on a predominantly White campus: Experiences of Black, Latina/o and White undergraduates. *Race, Gender & Class, 16*, 133–151

McCabe, J. (2011). Doing multiculturalism: An interactionist analysis of the practices of a multicultural sorority. *Journal of Contemporary Ethnography, 40*(5), 521–549. DOI:10.1177/0891241611403588

McCabe, J. M. (2016). *Connecting in college: How friendship networks matter for academic and social success.* University of Chicago Press.

McCall, L. (2005). The complexity of intersectionality. *Signs: Journal of Women in Culture and Society, 30*(3), 1771–1800.

McCallum, C. (2017). Giving back to the community: How African Americans envision utilizing their PhD. *Journal of Negro Education, 86*(2), 138–153.

McClusky, A. T., & Smith, E. M. (Eds). (2001). *Mary McLeod Bethune: Build a better world—Essays and selected documents.* Indiana University Press.

McCormick, R. P. (1990). *The Black student protest movement at Rutgers.* Rutgers University Press.

McCoy, D. L., Luedke, C. L., & Winkle-Wagner, R. (2017). Encouraged or "weeded out" in the STEM disciplines: Students' perspectives on faculty interactions within a predominantly White and a historically Black institution. *Journal of College Student Development, 58*(5), 657–673.

McCoy, D. L., & Rodricks, D. J. (2015). *Critical race theory in higher education: 20 years of theoretical and research innovations.* ASHE Higher Education Report, Volume 41, Number 3. John Wiley & Sons.

McCoy, D. L., & Winkle-Wagner, R. (2015.). Bridging the divide: Developing a scholarly habitus for aspiring graduate students through summer bridge program participation. *Journal of College Student Development, 56*(5), 423–439.

McCoy, D. L., Winkle-Wagner, R., & Luedke, C. L. (2015). Colorblind mentoring? Exploring white faculty mentoring of students of color. *Journal of Diversity in Higher Education, 8*(4), 225.

McGee, E. O. (2016). Devalued Black and Latino racial identities: A by-product of STEM college culture? *American Educational Research Journal, 53*(6), 1626–1662.

McGee, E. O., & Martin, D. B. (2011). "You would not believe what I have to go through to prove my intellectual value!" Stereotype management among academically successful Black mathematics and engineering students. *American Educational Research Journal, 48*(6), 1347–1389.

McRae, E. G. (2018). *Mothers of massive resistance: White women and the politics of White supremacy.* Oxford University Press.

McVeigh, R. (2009). *The rise of the Ku Klux Klan: Right-wing movements and national politics* (vol. 32). University of Minnesota Press.

Mead, G. H. (1934). *Mind, self, and society.* Chicago: University of Chicago Press.

Meer, F. (1988). *Higher than hope: The authorized biography of Nelson Mandela.* Harper Collins.

Menkiti, I. (1984). Persons and community in African traditional thought. In R. A. Wright (Ed.), *African philosophy: An introduction,* 3rd ed. University Press of America.

Mignolo, W. D. (2012). *Local histories/global designs: Coloniality, subaltern knowledges, and border thinking.* Princeton University Press.

Minor, J. T. (2008). Segregation residual in higher education: A tale of two states. *American Educational Research Journal, 45*(A), 861–885.

Mitchell, E. G. (2005). *Born colored: Life before Bloody Sunday.* Ampersand.

Mitchell, E. G. (2006). *Born colored: Life before Bloody Sunday.* Ampersand.

Mitchell, E. G. (2017). *From colored to Black: A bittersweet journey.* Ampersand.

Mitchell, H. H., & Lewter, N. C. (1986). *Soul theology: The heart of American Black culture.* Harper & Row.

Mobley, S. D., Jr. (2017). Seeking sanctuary: (Re)claiming the power of historically Black colleges and universities as places of Black refuge. *International Journal of Qualitative Studies in Education, 30*(10), 1036–1041.

Mobley, S. D., Jr., & Johnson, J. M. (2015). The role of HBCUs in addressing the unique needs of LGBT students. *New Directions for Higher Education, 170,* 79–89.

Mobley, S. D., Jr., Johnson, J. M., & Drezner, N. D. (2022). "Why aren't all the White kids sitting together in the cafeteria?" An exploration of White student experiences at a public HBCU. *Journal of Diversity in Higher Education, 15*(3), 300.

Moraga, C., & Anzaldúa, G. (Eds.). (2015). *This bridge called my back: Writings by radical women of color.* State University of New York Press.

Morris, A. (2015). *The scholar denied: W. E. B. Du Bois and the birth of modern sociology.* University of California Press.

Moses, Y. T. (1989). *Black women in academe: Issue and strategies.* Project on the Status and Education of Women. American Association of American Colleges.

Murray, M. J. (1994). *Revolution deferred: The painful birth of post-apartheid South Africa.* Verso Books.

Murray, P. (1970). The Negro woman's stake in the Equal Rights Amendment. *Harvard Civil Rights, Civil Liberties Law Review, 6,* 253.

Murray, P. (1970/1995). The liberation of Black women. In B. Guy-Sheftall (Ed.), *Words of fire: An anthology of African American feminist thought* (pp. 186–197). New Press.

Murray, P. (1987). *Pauli Murray: The autobiography of a Black activist, feminist, lawyer, priest, and poet.* University of Tennessee Press.

Mycoff, J. D., Wagner, M. W., & Wilson, D. C. (2009). The empirical effects of voter-ID laws: Present or absent? *PS: Political Science & Politics, 42*(1), 121–126.

Nash, J. C. (2008). Re-thinking intersectionality. *Feminist Review, 89*(1), 1–15.

Nasir, N. S., & McKinney de Royston, M. (2013). Power, identity, and mathematical practices outside and inside school. *Journal for Research in Mathematics Education, 44*(1), 264–287.

Nasir, N. S., McKinney de Royston, M., O'Connor, K., & Wischnia, S. (2017). Knowing about racial stereotypes versus believing them. *Urban Education, 52*(4), 491–524.

Nelson, A. (2011). *Body and soul: The Black Panther Party and the fight against medical discrimination.* University of Minnesota Press.

Nettles, M. T., & Millett, C. M. (2006). *Three magic letters: Getting to PhD.* Johns Hopkins University Press.

Nguyen, T. H., Boland, W. C., & Gasman, M. (2019). Historically Black colleges and universities, STEM education, and the pursuit for legitimacy? *British Journal of Sociology of Education, 40*(8), 1055–1071.

Njoku, N. R., & Patton, L. D. (2017). Explorations of respectability and resistance in construction of Black womanhood at HBCUs. In L. D. Patton & N. N. Croom (Eds.), *Critical perspectives on Black women and college success* (pp. 143–158). Routledge.

Noddings, N. (2013). *Caring: A relational approach to ethics and moral education.* University of California Press.

Noguera, P. A. (2003). The trouble with Black boys: The role and influence of environmental and cultural factors on the academic performance of African American males. *Urban Education, 38*(4), 431–459.

Nxumalo, F., & Ross, K. M. (2019). Envisioning Black space in environmental education for young children. *Race Ethnicity and Education, 22*(4), 502–524.

Omi, M., & Winant, H. (2014/1986). *Racial formation in the United States.* Routledge.

Orfield, G., Bachmeier, M. D., James, D. R., & Eitle, T. (1997). Deepening segregation in American public schools: A special report from the Harvard Project on School Desegregation. *Equity and Excellence in Education, 30*(2), 5–24.

Orfield, G., Marin, P., & Horn, C. L. (2005). *Higher education and the color line: College access, racial equity, and social change.* Harvard Education Press.

Palmer, R. T., Davis, R. J., & Maramba, D. C. (2010). Role of an HBCU in supporting academic success for underprepared Black males. *Negro Educational Review, 61,* 85–106.

Palmer, R. T., Davis, R. J., & Thompson, T. (2010). Theory meets practice: HBCU initiatives that promote academic success among African Americans in STEM. *Journal of College Student Development, 51*(4), 440–443.

Palmer, R. T., Maramba, D. C., & Dancy, T. E. (2013). The magnificent "MILE": Impacting Black male retention and persistence at an HBCU. *Journal of College Student Retention, 15*(1), 65–72.

Palmer, R., & Gasman, M. (2008). It takes a village to raise a child: The role of social capital in promoting academic success for African American men at a Black college. *Journal of College Student Development, 49*(1), 52–70.

Park, J. J. (2009). Are we satisfied? A look at student satisfaction with diversity at traditionally white institutions. *Review of Higher Education, 32*(3), 291–320.

Parks, G. S., Jones, S. E., Ray, R., & Hughey, M. W. (2015). White boys drink, Black girls yell: A racialized and gendered analysis of violent hazing and the law. *Journal of Gender, Race & Justice, 18,* 93.

Pascoe, P. (1996). Miscegenation law, court cases, and ideologies of "race" in twentieth-century America. *Journal of American History, 83*(1), 44–69.

Pattillo, M. (2013). *Black picket fences: Privilege and peril among the Black middle class.* University of Chicago Press.

Patton, L. D. (2006a). The voice of reason: A qualitative examination of Black student perceptions of Black culture centers. *Journal of College Student Development, 47*(6), 628–646.

Patton, L. D. (2006b). Black culture centers: Still central to student learning. *About Campus, 11*(2), 2–8.

Patton, L. D. (2009). My sister's keeper: A qualitative examination of mentoring experiences among African American women in graduate and professional schools. *Journal of Higher Education, 80*(5), 510–537. http://works.bepress.com/loripattondavis/12

Patton, L. D. (2010). *Culture centers in higher education: Perspectives on identity, theory, and practice.* Stylus.

Patton, L. D., Blockett, R. A., & McGowan, B. L. (2020). Complexities and contradictions: Black lesbian, gay, bisexual, and queer students' lived realities across three urban HBCU contexts. *Urban Education,* DOI:10.1177/0042085920959128

Patton, L. D., & Croom, N. N. (Eds.). (2017). *Critical perspectives on Black women and college success.* Taylor & Francis.

Patton, L. D., & Haynes, C. (2018). Hidden in plain sight: The Black women's blueprint for institutional transformation in higher education. *Teachers College Record, 120*(14), 1–18.

Patton, L. D., & Winkle-Wagner, R. (2012). Race at first sight: The funding of racial scripts between Black and White women. In K. Dace (Ed.), *Unlikely allies in the academy: Women of color and White women in conversation* (pp. 181–191). Routledge.

Perna, L., Lundy-Wagner, V., Drezner, N. D., Gasman, M., Yoon, S., Bose, E., & Gary, S. (2009). The contribution of HBCUs to the preparation of African American women for STEM careers: A case study. *Research in Higher Education, 50*(1), 1–23.

Perna, L. W., & Thomas, S. L. (2008). Theoretical perspectives on student success: Understanding the contributions of the disciplines. *ASHE Higher Education Report, 34*(1), 1–87.

Pettigrew, T. F. (2004). Justice deferred a half century after *Brown v. Board of Education*. *American Psychologist, 59*(6), 521.

Plessy v. Ferguson, 163 US 537 (1896).

Polletta, F., & Jasper, J. M. (2001). Collective identity and social movements. *Annual Review of Sociology, 27*(1), 283–305.

Porter, C. J., & Byrd, J. A. (2021). Juxtaposing #BlackGirlMagic as "empowering and problematic": Composite narratives of Black women in college. *Journal of Diversity in Higher Education*. Advance online publication. https://doi.org/10.1037/dhe0000338

Porter, C. J., & Dean, L. A. (2015). Making meaning: Identity development of Black undergraduate women. *NASPA Journal about Women in Higher Education, 8*(2), 125–139.

Posey-Maddox, L. (2013). Professionalizing the PTO: Race, class, and shifting norms of parental engagement in a city public school. *American Journal of Education, 119*(2), 235–260.

Posey-Maddox, L., Kimelberg, S. M., & Cucchiara, M. (2016). Seeking a "critical mass": Middle-class parents' collective engagement in city public schooling. *British Journal of Sociology of Education, 37*(7), 905–927.

Price, R. M. (1991). *The apartheid state in crisis: Political transformation in South Africa, 1975–1990*. Oxford University Press on Demand.

Rafalko, F. (2011). *MH/CHAOS: The CIA's campaign against the radical New Left and the Black Panthers*. Naval Institute Press.

Ray, R. (2013). Fraternity life at predominantly White universities in the US: The saliency of race. *Ethnic and Racial Studies, 36*(2), 320–336. DOI:10.1080/01419870.2012.676201

Reavis, T., Winkle-Wagner, R., Kelly, B., Luedke, C., & McCallum, C. (2022). Letters to my sisters: Advice from Black women alumnae about how to thrive and survive in college. *Teachers College Record, 124*(4). https://doi.org/10.1177/01614681221096798

Reeder, M. C., & Schmitt, N. (2013). Motivational and judgment predictors of African American academic achievement at PWIs and HBCUs. *Journal of College Student Development, 54*(1), 29–42.

Rendòn, L. I. (1994). Validating culturally diverse students: Toward a new model of learning and student development. *Innovative Higher Education, 19*(1), 33–51.

Reynolds-Dobbs, W., Thomas, K. M., & Harrison, M. S. (2008). From mammy to superwoman: Images that hinder Black women's career development. *Journal of Career Development, 35*(2), 129–150.

Richardson, M. (1987). *Maria W. Stewart, America's first Black woman political writer: Essays and speeches.* Indiana University Press.

Rhodes, J. (2017). *Framing the Black Panthers: The spectacular rise of a Black Power icon.* New Press.

Ricard, R. B., & Brown, M.C., II. (2008). *Ebony towers in higher education: The evolution, mission, and presidency of historically Black colleges and universities.* Stylus.

Ringer, F. (1969). *The decline of the German Mandarins.* Harvard University Press.

Robinson, C. J. (2000). *Black Marxism: The making of the Black radical tradition.* University of North Carolina Press.

Robinson, K. J., & Roksa, J. (2016). Counselors, information, and high school college-going culture: Inequalities in the college application process. *Research in Higher Education, 57*(7), 845–868.

Robnett, B. (2000). *How long? How long? African American women in the struggle for civil rights.* Oxford University Press.

Roebuck, J. B., & Murty, K. S. (1993). Historically Black colleges and universities: Their place in American higher education. Praeger.

Rogers, I. (2009). Remembering the Black campus movement: An oral history interview with James P. Garrett. *Journal of Pan-African Studies, 2*(10), 30.

Rogers, I. (2012). *The Black campus movement: Black students and the racial reconstitution of higher education, 1965–1972.* Palgrave Macmillan.

Rooks, N. T. (1996). *Hair raising: Beauty, culture, and African American women.* Rutgers University Press.

Root, M. P. (2001). *Love's revolution: Interracial marriage.* Temple University Press.

Ross, L. C. (2001). *The divine nine: The history of African American fraternities and sororities.*

Rutledge, N. M. (2021, January 20). Weary but undaunted: Black women made the Joe Biden-Kamala Harris inauguration happen. *USA Today.*

Sabia, D. R., Jr. (1988). Rationality, collective action, and Karl Marx. *American Journal of Political Science,* 50–71.

Schlesinger, P. (1991). *Media, state, and nation: Political violence and collective identities* (vol. 4). Sage.

Senghor, L. S. (1998). Negritude and African socialism. *African philosophy reader,* 438–448.

Sidran, B. (1971). *Black talk.* Da Capo Press.

Sims, G. A. (2008). Irrelation as a social construct for African American college women on a predominantly White campus. *College Student Journal, 42*(2), 691–709.

Shavers, M. C., & Moore, J. L. (2019). The perpetual outsider: Voices of Black women pursuing doctoral degrees at predominantly White institutions. *Journal of Multicultural Counseling and Development, 47*(4), 210–226.

Sherrard, C. (2017). *Vixen.* Autumn House Press.

Shohat, E., & Stam, R. (2014). *Unthinking Eurocentrism: Multiculturalism and the media.* Routledge.

Simon, B., & Klandermans, B. (2001). Politicized collective identity: A social psychological analysis. *American Psychologist, 56*(4), 319.

Simons, R. L., Lei, M. K., Beach, S. R., Philibert, R. A., Cutrona, C. E., Gibbons, F. X., & Barr, A. (2016). Economic hardship and biological weathering: The epigenetics of aging in a US sample of Black women. *Social Science & Medicine, 150,* 192–200.

Skocpol, T. (2011). Foreword. In M. W. Hughey & G. S. Parks (Eds.), *Black Greek-letter organizations 2.0: New directions in the study of African American fraternities and sororities* (pp. xiii–x). University Press of Mississippi.

Slaughter, D. T. (1972, February). Becoming an Afro-American woman. *School Review, 80*(2), 299–318. https://www.jstor.org/stable/1084402

Smith, A. (2010). Queer theory and native studies: The heteronormativity of settler colonialism. *GLQ: A Journal of Lesbian and Gay Studies, 16*(1–2), 41–68.

Smith, C. M. (2016). *Reparation and reconciliation: The rise and fall of integrated higher education.* University of North Carolina Press.

Smith, T. W. (1992). Changing racial labels: From "colored" to "negro" to "Black" to "African American." *Public Opinion Quarterly, 56*(4), 496–514.

Smith, W. A. (2014). *Racial battle fatigue in higher education: Exposing the myth of post-racial America.* Rowman & Littlefield.

Smith, W. A., Allen, W. R., & Danley, L. L. (2007). "Assume the position . . . you fit the description": Psychosocial experiences and racial battle fatigue among African American male college students. *American Behavioral Scientist, 51*(4), 551–578.

Smith, W. A., Yosso, T. J., & Solórzano, D. G. (2007). Racial primes and Black misandry on historically White campuses: Toward critical race accountability in educational administration. *Educational Administration Quarterly, 43*(5), 559–585.

Smitherman, G. (1977). *Talkin and testifyin: The language of Black America.* Houghton Mifflin.

Solomon, B. M. (1985). *In the company of educated women: A history of women and higher education in America.* Yale University Press.

Solórzano, D., Ceja, M., & Yosso, T. (2000). Critical race theory, racial microaggressions and campus racial climate: The experiences of African American college students. *Journal of Negro Education, 69*(1/2), 60–73. http://www.journalnegroed.org/

Solórzano, D. G., & Yosso, T. J. (2002a). A critical race counterstory of race, racism, and affirmative action. *Equity & Excellence in Education, 35*(2), 155–168. DOI: 10.1080/713845284

Solórzano, D. G., & Yosso, T. J. (2002b). Critical race methodology: Counter-storytelling as an analytical framework for education research. *Qualitative Inquiry, 8*(1), 23–44. DOI: 10.1177/107780040200800103

Spencer, S. J., Steele, C. M., & Quinn, D. M. (1999). Stereotype threat and women's math performance. *Journal of Experimental Social Psychology, 35*(1), 4–28.

Stanley, M. (2022). 1900–2000: Changes in life expectancy in the United States. SeniorLiving.org. https://www.seniorliving.org/history/1900-2000-changes-life-expectancy-united-states

Steele, C. M. (1997). A threat in the air: How stereotypes shape intellectual identity and performance. *American Psychologist, 52*(6), 613.

Steele, C. M., & Aronson, J. (1995). Stereotype threat and the intellectual test performance of African Americans. *Journal of Personality and Social Psychology, 69*(5), 797–811.

Stets, J. E., & Burke, P. J. (2000). Identity theory and social identity theory. *Social Psychology Quarterly, 63*(3), 224–237.

Stewart, D. L. (2008). Being all of me: Black students negotiating multiple identities. *Journal of Higher Education, 79*(2), 183–207.

Stewart, E. A., Nicholson, W. K., Bradley, L., & Borah, B. J. (2013). The burden of uterine fibroids for African American women: Results of a national survey. *Journal of Women's Health, 22*(10), 807–816.

Stewart, M. M. (1831/1995). Religion and the purse principles of morality, the sure foundation on which we must build. In B. Guy-Sheftall (Ed.), *Words of fire: An anthology of African American feminist thought* (pp. 25–34). New Press.

Stewart, M. W. (1832/1987). *Maria W. Stewart: America's First Black Woman Political Writer* (Marilyn Richardson, Ed.). Indiana University Press.

Stryker, S. (1980). *Symbolic interactionism: A social structural version.* Benjamin-Cummings.

Stryker, S. (2008). From Mead to a structural symbolic interactionism and beyond. *Annual Review of Sociology, 34*, 15–31.

Stryker, S., & Burke, P. J. (2000). The past, present, and future of an identity theory. *Social Psychology Quarterly, 63*(4), 284–297.

Sule, V. T., Winkle-Wagner, R., & Maramba, D. (2017). Who deserves a seat? Popular opinion of college access policy. *Equity, Excellence & Education, 50*(2), 196–208. DOI:10.1080/10665684.2017.1301836

Tajfel, H. (1974). Social identity and intergroup behaviour. *Information (International Social Science Council)*, *13*(2), 65–93.

Tatum, B. D. (2003). *Why are all the Black kids sitting together in the cafeteria? And other conversations about race*. Basic Books.

Tatum, B. D. (2017). *Why are all the Black kids sitting together in the cafeteria? And other conversations about race*. Basic Books.

Taylor, K-Y. (2016). *From #BlackLivesMatter to Black liberation*. Haymarket.

Terhune, C. P. (2008). Coping in isolation: The experiences of Black women in White communities. *Journal of Black Studies*, *38*(4), 547–564.

Terrill, R. E. (2007). *Malcolm X: Inventing racial judgment*. Michigan State University Press.

Theiss-Morse, E. (2009). *Who counts as an American? The boundaries of national identity*. Cambridge University Press.

Thelamour, B., Mwangi, C. G., & Ezeofor, I. (2019). "We need to stick together for survival": Black college students' racial identity, same-ethnic friendships, and campus connectedness. *Journal of Diversity in Higher Education*, *12*(3), 266–279.

Thelin, J. R. (2011). *A history of American higher education* (2nd ed.). Johns Hopkins University Press.

Thomas, B. (1997). *Plessy v. Ferguson: A brief history with documents*. Macmillan.

Thomas, A. J., Witherspoon, K. M., & Speight, S. L. (2008). Gendered racism, psychological distress, and coping styles of African American women. *Cultural Diversity and Ethnic Minority Psychology*, *14*(4), 307.

Tichavakunda, A. A. (2020). Studying black student life on campus: Toward a theory of black placemaking in higher education. *Urban Education*. https://doi.org/10.1177/0042085920971354.

Tichavakunda, A. A. (2021). Black joy on White campuses: Exploring Black students' recreation and celebration at a historically White institution. *Review of Higher Education*, *44*(3), 297–324.

Tienda, M. (2013). Diversity ≠ inclusion: Promoting integration in higher education. *Educational Researcher*, *42*(9), 467–475.

Tischauser, L. V. (2012). *Jim Crow laws*. Greenwood.

Tobolowsky, B. F., Outcalt, C. L., & McDonough, P. M. (2005). The role of HBCUs in the college choice process of African Americans in California. *Journal of Negro Education*, 63–75.

Tucker, R. K. (1991). *The dragon and the cross: The rise and fall of the Ku Klux Klan in middle America*. Archon Books.

Tyson, W. (2010). Book review: *The unchosen me: Race, gender, and identity among Black women in college*. *American Journal of Sociology*, *116*(3), 1035–1037.

Valandra Fields, L., Sebree, W., & Sober, W. (2022). Navigating an anti-Black campus climate: # black@ pwi. *Race Ethnicity and Education*, 1–18. DOI:1 0.1080/13613324.2022.2088720

Van Deburg, W. L. (1992). *New day in Babylon: The Black Power movement and American culture, 1965–1975*. University of Chicago Press.

Walker, V. S. (1996). *Their highest potential: An African American school community in the segregated South*. University of North Carolina Press.

Walker, V. S. (2000). Valued segregated schools for African American children in the South, 1935–1969: A review of common themes and characteristics. *Review of Educational Research, 70*(3), 253–285.

Walker, V. S. (2001). African American teaching in the South: 1940–1960. *American Educational Research Journal, 38*(4), 751–779.

Wallace, M. (1990). *Black macho and the myth of the Superwoman* (vol. 26). Verso.

Wallenstein, P. (2008a). Black southerners and nonblack universities: The process of desegregating southern higher education, 1935–1965. In P. Wallenstein (Ed.), *Higher education and the civil rights movement: White supremacy, Black southerners, and college campuses* (pp. 1–17). University Press of Florida.

Wallenstein, P. (Ed.). (2008b). *Higher education and the civil rights movement: White supremacy, Black southerners, and college campuses*. University Press of Florida.

Walley-Jean, J. C. (2009). Debunking the myth of the "angry Black woman": An exploration of anger in young African American women. *Black Women, Gender & Families, 3*(2), 68–86.

Ware, V. (2015). *Beyond the pale: White women, racism, and history*. Verso Books.

Warikoo, N., Sinclair, S., Fei, J., & Jacoby-Senghor, D. (2016). Examining racial bias in education: A new approach. *Educational Researcher, 45*(9), 508–514.

Watkins, W. H. (2001). *The White architects of Black education: Ideology and power in America, 1865–1954*. Teachers College Press.

Watson, N. N., & Hunter, C. D. (2015). Anxiety and depression among African American women: The costs of strength and negative attitudes toward psychological help-seeking. *Cultural Diversity and Ethnic Minority Psychology, 21*(4), 604–612.

Watt, S. K. (2006). Racial identity attitudes, womanist identity attitudes, and self-esteem in African American college women attending historically Black single-sex and coeducational institutions. *Journal of College Student Development, 47*(3), 319–334.

Waxman, O. B. (2021, November 10). Stacy Abrams and other Georgia organizers are part of a long—but often overlooked—tradition of Black women working for the vote. *Time*.

Weber, M. (1922/1978). *Economy and society*. University of California Press.

Weiss, N. J. (2014). *Whitney M. Young, Jr., and the struggle for civil rights*. Princeton University Press.

West, C. (2010). *The Black Panther Party: service to the people programs*. UNM Press.

West, L. M., Donovan, R. A., & Daniel, A. R. (2016). The price of strength: Black college women's perspectives on the strong Black woman stereotype. *Women & Therapy, 39*(3–4), 390–412.

White, D. G. (1999a). *Ain't I a woman? Female slaves in the plantation South.* W.W. Norton.

White, D. G. (1999b). *Too heavy a load: Black women in defense of themselves, 1894–1994.* W. W. Norton.

White, S., & White, G. J. (2005). *The sounds of slavery: Discovering African American history through songs, sermons, and speech* (vol. 2). Beacon Press.

Wilder, C. S. (2014). *Ebony and ivy: Race, slavery, and the troubled history of America's universities.* Bloomsbury USA.

Wilder, J. (2010). Revisiting "color names and color notions": A contemporary examination of the language and attitudes of skin color among young Black women. *Journal of Black Studies, 41*(1), 184–206.

Wilder, J. (2015). *Color stories: Black women and colorism in the 21st century.* ABC-CLIO.

Wilkerson, I. (2010). *The warmth of other suns: The epic story of America's great migration.* Vintage.

Williams, C. C. (2018). Critical oral history: Reflections on method and medium. *Qualitative Social Work, 18*(5), 787–799.

Williams, J. (2007). *Self-taught: African American education in slavery and freedom.* University of North Carolina Press. http://dx.doi.org/10.5149/uncp/9780807858219

Williams, K. L., Burt, B. A., Clay, K. L., & Bridges, B. K. (2018). Stories untold: Counternarratives to anti-Blackness and deficit-oriented discourse concerning HBCUs. *American Educational Research Journal, 56*(2). https://doi.org/10.3102/0002831218802776.

Williams, K. L., Mobley, S. D., Campbell, E., & Jowers, R. (2022). Meeting at the margins: culturally affirming practices at HBCUs for underserved populations. *Higher Education, 84*(5), 1067–1087.

Williams, M. S., & Johnson, J. M. (2018). Predicting the quality of Black women collegians' relationships with faculty at a public historically Black university. *Journal of Diversity in Higher Education, 12*(2), 115–125.

Williamson, J. A. (1999). In defense of themselves: The Black student struggle for success and recognition at predominantly White colleges and universities. *Journal of Negro Education, 68*(1), 92–105.

Williamson, J. A. (2003). *Black power on campus: The University of Illinois, 1965–75.* University of Illinois Press.

Williamson, J. A. (2008). Black colleges and civil rights: Organizing and mobilizing in Jackson, Mississippi. In P. Wallenstein (Ed.), *Higher education and the civil rights movement: White supremacy, Black southerners, and college campuses* (pp. 117–136). University Press of Florida.

Willie, S. S. (2003). *Acting Black: College, identity and the performance of race.* Routledge.

Willis, P. (2017). *Learning to labour: How working-class kids get working-class jobs.* Routledge.

Wilson, D. C., Brewer, P. R., & Rosenbluth, P. T. (2014). Racial imagery and support for voter ID laws. *Race and Social Problems, 6*(4), 365–371.

Winkle-Wagner, R. (2006). An endless desert walk: Perspectives of education from the San in Botswana. *International Journal of Educational Development, 26*(1), 88–97.

Winkle-Wagner, R. (2008). Not "feminist" but "strong": African American women's reflections of race and gender in college. *Negro Educational Review, 59*(3–4), 181–196.

Winkle-Wagner, R. (2009a). *The unchosen me: Race, gender, and identity among Black women in college.* Johns Hopkins University Press.

Winkle-Wagner, R. (2009b). The perpetual homelessness of college experiences: The tensions between home and campus for African American women. *Review of Higher Education, 33*(1), 1–36.

Winkle-Wagner, R. (2009c). Get real: The process of validating research across racial lines. In R. Winkle-Wagner, C. A. Hunter, & D. H. Ortloff (Eds.), *Bridging the gap between theory and practice in educational research: Methods at the margins* (pp. 127–140). Palgrave.

Winkle-Wagner, R. (2010a). An asset or an obstacle? The power of peers in African American women's college transitions. In V. B. Bush, C. R. Chamber, & M. Walpole (Eds.), *From diplomas to doctorates: The success of Black women in higher education and its implications for equal educational opportunities for all* (pp. 55–72). Stylus.

Winkle-Wagner, R. (2010b). Choosing college as a life-or-death decision: First-generation African American women's reflections on college choice. In T. L. Strayhorn & M. C. Terrell (Eds.), *The evolving challenges of Black college students: New insights for policy, practice, and research* (pp. 26–48). Stylus.

Winkle-Wagner, R. (2012). Self, college experiences, and society: Rethinking student development theory from a sociological perspective. *College Student Affairs Journal, 30*(2), 45–60.

Winkle-Wagner, R. (2015). Lives not narrowed down: The state of African American women's experiences in higher education. *Review of Educational Research, 85(2),* 171–204. http://rer.sagepub.com/content/early/2014/09/24/00346543 14551065?papetoc

Winkle-Wagner, R., Kelly, B. T., Luedke, C. L., & Reavis, T. B. (2018). Authentically me: Examining expectations that are placed upon Black women in college. *American Educational Research Journal.* http://journals.sagepub.com/doi/abs/10.3102/0002831218798326

Winkle-Wagner, R., & Locks, A. M. (2020). *Diversity and inclusion on campus: Supporting students of color in higher education.* Routledge.

Winkle-Wagner, R., Luedke, C., McCallum, C., & Ota-Malloy, B. (2019). Instrumental of meaningful friendships: Black alumnae perspectives on peer relationships during college. *Journal of Women and Gender in Higher Education,* 1–16. DOI:https://doi.org/10.1080/19407882.2019.1593201

Winkle-Wagner, R., & McCoy, D. (2016). Feeling like an "alien" or "family"? Comparing students and faculty experiences of diversity in STEM disciplines at an HBCU and a PWI. *Race Ethnicity and Education.* DOI:10.108 0/13613324.2016.1248835

Winkle-Wagner, R., McCoy, D., & Lee-Johnson, J. L. (2019). Creating porous ivory towers: Two-way socialization processes that embrace Black students' identities in academia. In J. Weidman & L. DeAngelo (Eds.), *Socialization in higher education and the early career: Theory, research and application.* Springer International.

Winkle-Wagner, R., Reavis, T. B., Forbes, J., & Rogers, S. (2019). A culture of (HBCU) success: Black alumnae discussions of how Spelman College creates greatness. *Journal of Higher Education.* DOI:10.1080/00221546.2019.1654 965

Winkle-Wagner, R., Sulè, V. T., & Maramba, D. C. (2012). When race disappears: Merit in the college admissions policy decision-making process in the state of Texas. *Educational Policy, 28*(4), 516–545. DOI:10.1177/0895904812465114. Also available at http://epx.sagepub.com/cgi/reprint/28/4/516.pdf?ijkey=PEcc WLW8kzf9av6&keytype=ref

Wiredu, K. (1996). *Cultural universals and particulars: An African perspective.* Indiana University Press.

Wirpsa, L. (1997, December 12). Feminist spirituality core of unique MA—Immaculate Heart College Center of Los Angeles offers the only master's program on women's spirituality. *National Catholic Reporter.*

Woods-Giscombé, C. L. (2010). Superwoman schema: African American women's views on stress, strength, and health. *Qualitative Health Research, 20*(5), 668–683.

Woodson, J. (2014). *Brown girl dreaming.* Penguin.

Woodward, C. V. (1955/2002). *The strange career of Jim Crow.* Oxford University Press.

Wynter, S. (1995). 1492: A new world view. In V. L. Hyatt & R. Nettleford (Eds.), *Race, discourse, and the origin of the Americas: A new world view* (pp. 5–57). Smithsonian Institution.

Yancy, G. A. (2003). *Who is White? Latinos, Asians, and the new Black/Nonblack divide.* Lynne Rienner.

Yancy, G. (2016). *Black bodies, White gazes: The continuing significance of race in America.* Rowman & Littlefield.

Yancy, G. (2017). *On race: 34 conversations in a time of crisis.* Oxford University Press.

Zielinski, L. (2016). In his own words. *Paris Review.* https://www.theparisreview. org/blog/2016/10/18/in-his-own-words/

Zinn, H. (1960). Finishing school for pickets. *Nation, 6,* 71–73.

Zinn, H. (1980/2016). *A people's history of the United States.* Harper.

Zinn, M. B. (1989). Family, race, and poverty in the eighties. *Signs, 14*(4), 856–874.

Zuberi, T. (2004). W. E. B. Du Bois's sociology: The Philadelphia Negro and social science. *Annals of the American Academy of Political and Social Science*, *595*(1), 146–156.

Index

.

Milton Keynes UK
Ingram Content Group UK Ltd.
UKHW012244180624
444315UK00005B/587